D0220137

UNDERSTANDING
CENTRAL AMERICA

SEVENTH EDITION

UNDERSTANDING CENTRAL AMERICA

Global Forces and Political Change

John A. Booth
UNIVERSITY OF NORTH TEXAS

Christine J. Wade
WASHINGTON COLLEGE

Thomas W. Walker
OHIO UNIVERSITY

Routledge
Taylor & Francis Group

NEW YORK AND LONDON

Seventh edition published 2020
by Routledge

52 Vanderbilt Avenue, New York, NY 10017
and by Routledge
2 Park Square, Milton Park, Abingdon, Oxon, OX14 4RN

Routledge is an imprint of the Taylor & Francis Group, an informa business

© 2020 Taylor & Francis

First edition published by Westview Press 1989
Sixth edition published by Westview Press 2015

Library of Congress Cataloging-in-Publication Data
A catalog record has been requested for this book

ISBN: 978-0-367-36168-6 (hbk)
ISBN: 978-0-367-36170-9 (pbk)
ISBN: 978-0-429-34428-2 (ebk)

Typeset in Adobe Garamond Pro
by Swales & Willis, Exeter, Devon, UK

In memory of Laura Caroline Booth, 1977–2019

CONTENTS

Tables, Maps, and Figures

TABLES

MAP

FIGURES

PREFACE TO THE SEVENTH EDITION

FOR THIS, THE 30TH ANNIVERSARY OF *Understanding Central America*'s first edition in 1989, we have once again extensively updated coverage, data, and narrative. This edition follows the same organization as the fourth through sixth but updates country chapters to 2019 including recent elections. Chapter 9, on political participation and attitudes, integrates new survey data on the region from 2014, and, where possible, traces trends since the 1990s. Revised tables and figures draw upon new data on trends in politics, economics, social conditions, and election outcomes through August 2019.

ACKNOWLEDGMENTS

WE OWE MANY PEOPLE AND INSTITUTIONS IN CENTRAL AMERICA and the United States our sincerest thanks for their time, support, and encouragement. For fieldwork support over the decades while our book was written and repeatedly updated, we thank the Latin American Studies Association; the Advisory Council on Church and Society of the United Presbyterian Church, USA; the Inter-American Dialogue; the International Human Rights Law Group; the Washington Office on Latin America; Hemispheric Initiatives; the late Alice McGrath; the University of North Texas; the Heinz Foundation, University of Pittsburgh; Ohio University; Washington College and the Louis L. Goldstein Program in Public Affairs; and the Carter Center. For collaboration in Central America we gratefully acknowledge the assistance of the Facultad Latinoamericana de Ciencias Sociales and the Centro Superior Universitaria Centroamericana in Costa Rica, the Asociación de Investigación y Estúdios Sociales in Guatemala, and the Confederación Nacional de Profesionales Héroes y Mártires in Nicaragua. We thank the United Presbyterian Church, USA, for granting the right to reuse some material Thomas Walker originally wrote for a Presbyterian Church publication (incorporated into Chapters 1 through 3 and 10). We acknowledge the cooperation of the US Agency for International Development, the Latin American Public Opinion Project (LAPOP), and Professor Mitch A. Seligson, of Vanderbilt University, for access to various surveys employed in Chapter 9, and most recently the 2014 AmericasBarometer surveys. For the underwriting acquisition of the 2008 AmericasBarometer surveys we thank Professor T. David Mason, the Elizabeth Rhodes Peace Research Fund, and the Johnie Christian Family Peace Professor Endowment of the University of North Texas.

Dozens of kind Central Americans have granted us interviews and helped us collect data on their countries. Without them this book would have been impossible to write. E. Bradford Burns, Richard E. Clinton Jr., Sung Ho Kim, Harold Molineu, Mitch Seligson, and several anonymous reviewers read portions of the manuscript at different stages in its evolution through all six editions and made valuable suggestions. Our thanks to Cece Hannah for typing the first-edition manuscript, and for research assistance over the years to Steve Lohse, Mehmet Gurses, Nikolai Petrovsky, Brittany Weaver, and Ryan Salzman. Over time several editors encouraged and directed us at Westview Press: Miriam Gilbert, Barbara Ellington, Karl Yambert, Jennifer Chen, Steve Catalano, Kay Mariea, Sandra Beris, Kelli Fillingim, and at Routledge: Charles Baker, Natalja Mortensen, and Elizabeth Riley with this edition.

John A. Booth
Christine J. Wade
Thomas W. Walker

Acronyms

Abbreviations of countries:
CR = Costa Rica; ES = El Salvador; G = Guatemala; H = Honduras; N = Nicaragua

ACC	Civil Society Association (Asociación de la Sociedad Civil) (G)
AL	Liberal Alliance (Alianza Liberal) (N)
ALBA	Bolivarian Alliance for the Americas (Alianaza Bolivariana para las Américas)
ALIPO	Popular Liberal Alliance (Alianza Liberal Popular) (H)
ALN	Nicaraguan Liberal Alliance (Alianza Liberal Nicaragüense)
AMNLAE	Luisa Amanda Espinosa Nicaraguan Women's Association (Asociación de Mujeres Nicaragüenses Luisa Amanda Espinosa)
AMPRONAC	Association of Women Confronting the National Problem (Asociación de Mujeres Frente a la Problemática Nacional) (N)
ANEP	National Association of Private Enterprises (Asociación Nacional de Empresas Privadas) (ES)
APH	Honduran Patriotic Alliance (Alianza Patriótica Hondureña)
APRE	Alliance for the Republic (Alianza para la República) (N)
ARDE	Revolutionary Democratic Alliance (Alianza Revolucionaria Democrática) (Costa Rican-based Contra forces)
ARENA	Nationalist Republican Alliance Party (Alianza Republicana Nacionalista) (ES)
ASC	Assembly of Civil Society (Asamblea de la Sociedad Civil) (G)
ATC	Rural Workers' Association (Asociación de Trabajadores del Campo) (N)

BCR	Bank of Costa Rica (Banco de Costa Rica)
BPR	Revolutionary Popular Bloc (Bloque Popular Revolucionario) (ES)
CACM	Central American Common Market
CAFTA	Central American Free Trade Agreement
CARSI	Central America Regional Security Initiative
CBI	Caribbean Basin Initiative
CC	Court of Constitutionality (Corte de Constitucionalidad) (G)
CD	Democratic Convergence (Convergencia Democrática) (ES)
CD	Democratic Change (Cambio Democrático) (ES)
CDC	Civil Defense Committee (Comité de Defensa Civil) (N and H)
CDS	Sandinista Defense Committee (Comité de Defensa Sandinista) (N)
CDU	United Democratic Center (Centro Democrático Unido) (ES)
CEB	Christian base communities (comunidades eclesiales de base)
CEH	Historical Clarification Commission (Comisión de Esclarificación Histórica) (G)
CENIDH	Nicaraguan Center for Human Rights (Centro Nicaragüense de Derechos Humanos) (N)
CGUP	Guatemalan Committee of Patriotic Unity (Comité Guatemalteco de Unidad Patriótica)
CIA	Central Intelligence Agency
CICIG	International Commission Against Impunity in Guatemala (Comisión Internacional contra la Impunidad en Guatemala)
CN	National Conciliation (Conciliación Nacional) (ES)
CODEH	Human Rights Committee of Honduras (Comité de Derechos Humanos de Honduras)
CONABUSQUEDA	National Commission on the Search for Adult Persons Disappeared in the Context of the Armed Conflict of El Salvador (Comisión Nacional de Búsqueda de Personas Adultas Desaparecidas en el Contexto del Conflicto Armado de El Salvador)

COPIHN	Council of Popular and Indigenous Organizations of Honduras (Consejo Cívico de Organizaciones Populares e Indígenas de Honduras) (H)
COSEP	Superior Council of Private Enterprise (Consejo Superior de la Empresa Privada) (N)
COSIP	Superior Council of Private Initiative (Consejo Superior de la Iniciativa Privada) (N)
CPC	Citizens' Power Councils (Consejos del Poder Ciudadano) (N)
CPI	Consumer Price Index
CREO	Commitment, Renewal and Order party (Compromiso, Renovación y Orden) (G)
CRIES	Regional Coordinating Body for Economic and Social Research (Coordinadora Regional de Investigaciones Económicas y Sociales) (N)
CRM	Revolutionary Coordinator of the Masses (Coordinadora Revolucionaria de Masas) (ES)
CSE	Supreme Electoral Council (Consejo Supremo Electoral) (N)
CSJ	Supreme Court of Justice (Corte Supremo de Justicia) (G and N)
CST	Sandinista Workers' Federation (Central Sandinista de Trabajadores) (N)
CUC	Peasant Unity Committee (Comité de Unidad Campesina) (G)
DC	Christian Democratic Party (Partido Demócrata Cristiano) (G)
DINADECO	National Community Development Directorate (Dirección Nacional de Desarrollo de la Comunidad) (CR)
DNC	Joint National Directorate (Dirección Nacional Conjunta) (N)
DNU	National Directorate of Unity (Dirección Nacional de Unidad) (H)
ECLAC	Economic Commission for Latin America and the Caribbean (Comisión Económica para América Latina y el Caribe)
EG	Encounter for Guatemala (Encuentro por Guatemala)
EGP	Guerrilla Army of the Poor (Ejército Guerrillero de los Pobres) (G)
EPS	Sandinista People's Army (Ejército Popular Sandinista) (N)
ERP	Revolutionary Army of the People (Ejército Revolucionario del Pueblo) (ES)
ERP27	Army of Patriotic Resistance (Ejército de Resistencia Patriótica) (H)
ESAF	Enhanced Structural Adjustment Facility

EXA	export agriculture
FAL	Armed Forces of Liberation (Fuerzas Armadas de Liberación) (ES)
FAO	Broad Opposition Front (Frente Amplio Opositor) (N)
FAPU	United Popular Action Front (Frente de Acción Popular Unida) (ES)
FAR	Revolutionary Armed Forces (Fuerzas Armadas Revolucionarias) (G)
FARC	Revolutionary Armed Forces of Colombia (Fuerzas Armadas Revolucionarias de Colombia)
FARN	Armed Forces of National Resistance (Fuerzas Armadas de Resistencia Nacional) (ES)
FCN	National Convergence Front (Frente de Convergencia Nacional) (G)
FDCR	Democratic Front Against Repression (Frente Democrático Contra la Represión) (G)
FDN	Nicaraguan Democratic Force (Fuerzas Democráticas Nicaragüenses)
FDNG	New Guatemala Democratic Front (Frente Democrático Nueva Guatemala)
FDR	Revolutionary Democratic Front (Frente Democrático Revolucionario) (ES)
FGEI	Edgar Ibarra Guerrilla Front (Frente Guerrillero Edgar Ibarra) (G)
FMLH	Morazán Front for the Liberation of Honduras (Frente Morazanista para la Liberación de Honduras)
FMLN	Farabundo Martí National Liberation Front (Frente Farabundo Martí de Liberación Nacional) (ES)
FNT	National Workers' Front (Frente Nacional de Trabajadores) (N)
FOL	Forward Operating Location
FOSALUD	Fund for Health Solidarity (Fondo Solidario para la Salud) (ES)
FP13	January 13th Popular Front (Frente Popular 13 de Enero) (G)
FPL	Popular Forces of Liberation (Fuerzas Populares de Liberación) (ES)
FPN	National Patriotic Front (Frente Patriótico Nacional) (N)
FPR	Lorenzo Zelaya Popular Revolutionary Forces (Fuerzas Populares Revolucionarias "Lorenzo Zelaya") (H)
FRG	Republican Front of Guatemala (Frente Republicano de Guatemala)
FRNP	National Popular Resistance Front (Frente Nacional de Resistencia Popular) (H)

FSLN	Sandinista National Liberation Front (Frente Sandinista de Liberación Nacional) (N)
FUR	United Front of the Revolution (Frente Unido de la Revolución) (G)
FUSEP	Public Security Forces (Fuerzas de Seguridad Pública) (H)
GANA	Grand National Alliance (Gran Alianza Nacional) (G)
GANA	Grand Alliance for National Unity (Gran Alianza por la Unidad Nacional) (ES)
GDP	gross domestic product
GIEI	Interdisciplinary Group of Independent Experts (Grupo Interdiscipinario de Expertos Independientes) (N)
HIPC	(World Bank's) Heavily Indebted Poor Countries
IACHR	Inter-American Commission on Human Rights
IAD	Inter-American Development Bank
ICE	Costa Rican Electrical Institute (Instituto Costarricense de Electricidad)
ICJ	International Court of Justice
IIRIRA	Illegal Immigration Reform and Immigrant Responsibility Act
IMF	International Monetary Fund
INE	National Statistical Institute (Instituto Nacional de Estadística) (G)
LAPOP	Latin American Public Opinion Project
LGBTQ	Lesbian, Gay, Bisexual, Transgender, and Queer
LIBRE	Liberty and Refoundation Party (Partido Libertad y Refundación) (H)
LIDER	Renewed Democratic Liberation Party (Libertad Democrática Renovada) (G)
LP28	28th of February Popular Leagues (Ligas Populares 28 de Febrero) (ES)
MACCHI	Mission to Support the Fight against Corruption and Impunity in Honduras (Misión de Apoyo contra la Corrupción y la Impunidad en Honduras) (H)
MAS	Solidarity Action Movement (Movimiento de Acción Solidaria) (G)
MINUGUA	United Nations Mission in Guatemala (Misión de las Naciones Unidas en Guatemala)
MLN	National Liberation Movement (Movimiento de Liberación Nacional) (G)

MLP   Popular Liberation Movement (Movimiento de Liberación
              Popular) (ES)
MLP   Movement for the Liberation of Peoples (Movimiento para la
              Liberación de los Pueblos) (G)
MNR   National Revolutionary Movement (Movimiento Nacional
              Revolucionario) (ES)
MPL   Popular Movement for Liberation (Movimiento Popular de
              Liberación) (H)
MPU   United People's Movement (Movimiento Pueblo Unido) (N)
MR13   13th of November Revolutionary Movement (Movimiento
              Revolucionario del 13 de Noviembre) (G)
MRP-Ixim   People's Revolutionary Movement Ixim (Movimiento
              Revolucionario del Pueblo Ixim) (G)
MRS   Sandinista Renovation Movement (Movimiento de
              Renovación Sandinista) (N)
MUCA   Unified Peasant Movement (Movimiento Unificado
              Campesino del Aguán) (H)
NAFTA   North American Free Trade Agreement
OAS   Organization of American States
OHCHR   Office of the High Commissioner on Human Rights
OPEC   Organization of Petroleum Exporting Countries
ORDEN   Nationalist Democratic Organization (Organización
              Democrática Nacionalista) (ES)
ORPA   Organization of the People in Arms (Organización del
              Pueblo en Armas) (G)
PAC   Anti-Corruption Party (Partido Anti-Corrupción) (H)
PAC   Citizen Action Party (Partido de Acción Ciudadana) (CR)
PAC   Civil Self-Defense Patrols (Patrullas de Autodefensa Civil) (G)
PAN   National Advancement Party (Partido de Avance
              Nacional) (G)
PARLACEN   Central American Parliament (Parlamento Centroamericano)
PASE   Accessibility without Exclusion Party (Partido Accesibilidad
              sin Exclusión) (CR)
PC   Citizen Prosperity (Prosperidad Ciudadana party) (G)
PCH   Honduran Communist Party (Partido Comunista de
              Honduras)
PCN   National Conciliation Party (Partido de Conciliación
              Nacional) (ES)

PCN	Nicaraguan Conservative Party (Partido Conservador Nicaragüense)
PCS	Communist Party of El Salvador (Partido Comunista de El Salvador)
PDC	Christian Democratic Party (Partido Demócrata Cristiano) (ES)
PDCG	Christian Democratic Party of Guatemala (Partido Demócrata Cristiano de Guatemala)
PDCH	Christian Democratic Party of Honduras (Partido Demócrata Cristiano de Honduras)
PES	Party of Hope (Partido de la Esperanza) (ES)
PGT	Guatemalan Labor Party (Partido Guatemalteco del Trabajo)
PID	Institutional Democratic Party (Partido Institucional Democrático) (G)
PINU	Innovation and Unity Party (Partido de Inovación y Unidad) (H)
PLC	Liberal Constitutionalist Party (Partido Liberal Constitucionalista) (N)
PLH	Honduran Liberal Party (Partido Liberal de Honduras)
PLN	Liberal Nationalist Party (Partido Liberal Nacionalista) (N)
PLN	National Liberation Party (Partido de Liberación Nacional) (CR)
PML	Libertarian Movement Party (Partido Movimiento Libertario) (CR)
PMOP	Military and Public Order Police (Policía Militar y de Orden Público) (H)
PN	The National Party (Partido Nacional) (H)
PNC	National Civil Police (Policía Nacional Civil) (ES)
PNDH	National Plan for Human Development (Plan Nacional para el Desarrollo Humano) (N)
POLSEPAZ	Policy for Integral and Sustainable Citizen Security and Promotion for Peace (Política Integral y Sostenible de Seguridad Ciudadana y Promoción de la Paz Social para Costa Rica) (CR)
PP	Patriot Party (Partido Patriota) (G)
PR	Revolutionary Party (Partido Revolucionario) (G)
PRN	National Restoration Party (Partido de Restauración Nacional) (CR)
PRTC	Revolutionary Party of Central American Workers (Partido Revolucionario de Trabajadores Centroamericanos) (CR)

xxvi   *Acronyms*

PRTCH	Revolutionary Party of Central American Workers of Honduras (Partido Revolucionario de Trabajadores Centroamericanos de Honduras)
PRTCS	Revolutionary Party of Central American Workers (Partido Revolucionario de Trabajadores Centroamericanos) (ES)
PRUD	Revolutionary Party of Democratic Unification (Partido Revolucionario de Unificación Democrática) (ES)
PSD	Social Democratic Party (Partido Social Demócrata) (ES)
PSD	Democratic Socialist Party (Partido Socialista Demócrata) (G)
PTS	Political Terror Scale
PU	Unionist Party (Partido Unionista) (G)
PUSC	Social Christian Unity Party (Partido de Unidad Social Cristiano) (CR)
RACCN	Autonomous Region of the North Caribbean Coast (Región Autónoma de la Costa Caribe Norte) (N)
RACCS	Autonomous Region of the South Caribbean Coast (Región Autónoma de la Costa Caribe Sur) (N)
RN	Nicaraguan Resistance (Resistencia Nicaragüense)
SAA	structural adjustment agreements
TPS	temporary protected status
TSE	Supreme Electoral Tribunal (Tribunal Supremo Electoral) (CR, ES, G)
UCA	Universidad Centroamericana José Simeón Cañas (Central American University) (ES)
UCN	Union of the National Center (Unión del Centro Nacional) (G)
UCN	National Union of Change (Unión del Cambio Nacionalista) (G)
UD	Democratic Unification party (Unificación Democrática) (H)
UDEL	Democratic Liberation Union (Unión Democrática de Liberación) (N)
UDN	Democratic National Union (Unión Democrática Nacionalista) (ES)
UFCO	United Fruit Company
UN	United Nations
UNAG	National Union of Farmers and Ranchers (Unión Nacional de Agricultores y Ganaderos) (N)
UNAN	National Autonomous University of Nicaragua (Universidad Nacional Autónoma de Nicaragua) (N)
UNDP	United Nations Development Program

UNE	Nicaraguan Unity for Hope alliance (Unidad Nicaragüense por la Esperanza) (N)
UNE	National Unity of Hope (Unidad Nacional de la Esperanza) (G)
UNIDAD	Unity Movement (Movimiento Unidad) (ES)
UNO	National Opposition Union (Unión Nacional Opositora) (N, ES)
UPOLI	Nicaraguan Polytechnic University (Universidad Politécnica de Nicaragua) (N)
URNG	Guatemalan National Revolutionary Union (Unidad Revolucionaria Nacional Guatemalteca, sometimes on ballot as URNG-MAIZ) (G)
USAID	United States Agency for International Development
USDEA	United States Drug Enforcement Agency
USSR	Union of Soviet Socialist Republics
Vamos	Let's Go with Eduardo (Vamos con Eduardo [Montealegre]) (G)
VIVA	Vision with Values party (Visión con Valores) (G)
YATAMA	Sons of Mother Earth party (Yapti Tasba Masraka Nanih Aslatakanka) (N)
ZEDE	Employment and Economic Development Zones (Zonas de Empleo y Desarrollo Económico) (H)

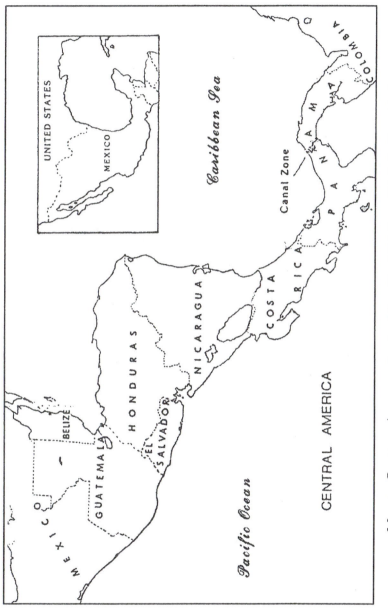

MAP OF CENTRAL AMERICA Reprinted from Harold Molineu, *U.S. Policy Toward Latin America: From Regionalism to Globalism*, 2nd ed. (Boulder, CO: Westview Press, 1990), p. 4. Copyright © Westview Press, 1990.

1

CRISIS AND TRANSFORMATION

CENTRAL AMERICAN COUNTRIES OCCUPY SMALL SPACES IN A big, challenging world. The region lies so close to the United States that from Miami or Houston one can fly to Managua or Guatemala City more quickly than to Chicago or Boston. Amid its rugged scenery, beautiful beaches, and Mayan ruins, however, political and economic turmoil have tormented much of the region most of two centuries.

For two decades after World War II, the area's mostly poor and despotic regimes remained friendly to US interests. In the 1960s the isthmus developed a regionally planned common market that sought to insulate governments from political challengers by promoting rapid economic growth. Yet in the 1960s governments' missteps spawned pushback from workers, civil society, and opposition parties. Rebel groups appeared, imitating Cuba's revolutionaries. Within a decade the region's five countries and roughly 20 million citizens experienced a tsunami of political and economic turmoil. Central America captured worldwide headlines as some regimes, aided by the United States, cracked down hard on multiplying opposition. The intensifying repression brought ever more demands for change. By 1980 revolutionary insurrection, counterrevolution, state terror, and external meddling engulfed the region. These forces eventually took more than 300,000 lives, turned millions into refugees, and devastated economies and infrastructures.

Regional and global actors struggled in the 1990s to manage this turmoil. By the first decade of the twenty-first century the area temporarily appeared to calm after Central American countries all adopted constitutional, elected civilian governments. US policymakers' geopolitical concerns turned elsewhere, and political news from the region ebbed in the US media. But poor economic performance still plagued several countries. Many Central Americans evaluated their new governments poorly, and new political freedoms and increased participation rates pointed toward new political instability. In 2009 the region had its first democratic breakdown of the new century when the Honduran military and Congress overthrew President Manuel Zelaya. Nicaragua under Daniel Ortega began sliding back into authoritarianism. Since then a panoply of other problems has risen—corruption, criminal violence by gangs, and international drug smuggling. Waves of emigrants, including many children, have fled Honduras, Guatemala, and El Salvador seeking refuge in the United States.

The first two editions of *Understanding Central America* focused on political violence during the 1970s and 1980s and why revolutionary movements emerged in three Central American countries while two others remained relatively stable.[1] We argued that grievances arose from region-wide economic problems and from the political repression of demands for reform. When Nicaragua's, Guatemala's, and El Salvador's regimes violently resisted these demands, their opponents coalesced and radicalized into revolutionary opposition. Nicaragua's victorious insurrection brought 11 years of social revolution under the Sandinistas. El Salvador's and Guatemala's civil wars led to protracted stalemates eventually followed by negotiated peace and significant political changes. Meanwhile Honduras and Costa Rica undertook modest economic and political reforms and kept repression at moderate levels. They remained stable while rebellion and war raged nearby.

External actors, especially the United States, struggled to shape these events by providing resources to some political actors and denying them to others. Fearing leftist revolutionaries, the United States expended enormous diplomatic and political energy and several billion dollars to determine winners and losers. This outside manipulation mostly intensified and prolonged Central America's conflicts, but eventually also affected institutions and policies. By the late 1990s each Central American nation, from different starting points and by divergent paths, had adopted a common regime type—minimalist electoral democracy. Global pressures had encouraged local elites to adopt this regime type rather than revert to the region's traditional military or personalistic authoritarianism. The Cold War had waned and with it fears of Communist expansion in the hemisphere. This allowed grudging tolerance among local elites and the United States of leftist parties' openly participating in governance. Human rights performance improved over previous decades.

Subsequent editions of *Understanding Central America* have increasingly focused on how global forces continue to shape the region in the new century. *Neoliberalism*, a new strategy of economic development pushed by the United States, has exposed Central America to the world economy more openly than ever. It reduced barriers to trade and foreign investment and shrank the size and role of governments. With more democratic politics, liberalized economies, and the anti-Communist geopolitical imperative receding, unexpected global forces exerted severe new pressures on wobbly new Central American regimes. The international narcotics trade, destined to the voracious demand in the United States, prompted strong US and Mexican anti-narcotics efforts. International smugglers shifted transshipment routes from Mexico into Central America. Independently, gang violence appeared and escalated to horrific levels in Honduras and El Salvador because the United States deported thousands of Central American-origin gang members to the region. Local gangs spread organized crime and violent territorial competition. On the local level, fractious Honduran elites mounted the coup that shocked regional and hemispheric governments. Nicaragua and El Salvador elected leftist presidents. Corruption scandals roiled several countries. Democratization had clearly not solved Central America's problems.

This seventh revised and updated edition tracks how such evolving global forces continue affecting Central America. Powerful political and economic pressures from abroad assail Central America's small countries, but their political institutions and scant resources cannot always cope. Crisis has gripped the region's so-called Northern Triangle countries—Guatemala, El Salvador, and Honduras—as criminal violence has surged and governments have failed to provide citizen security or political stability. Costa Rica has fared better, but Nicaragua has both controlled crime and reverted to pre-revolutionary strongman traditions.

WHY STUDY CENTRAL AMERICA?

Central American countries interact with the evolving forces from the larger economic and political world. Despite their proximity and many similarities, their differences have produced intriguing variations in social and economic outcomes. Why, for example, have Costa Rica and Nicaragua had such divergent political, economic, and social conditions despite being poor neighbors similarly situated in the world economy? Why, when operating in the same world economy, has Costa Rica's output grown seven times faster than Nicaragua's since 1960, and two to three times faster than the other three economies? What events, leadership, public policy, political culture, and international factors pushed some nations forward and left others behind? Why, despite international encouragement, has democracy prospered in Costa Rica yet failed to gain sure footing in the other nations?

The region merits our attention because it remains mostly poor despite patchy economic and human progress. An estimate for 2017 put the number of direly poor Central Americans (as defined by their governments) at around 20.1 million of the region's then 42 million people.[2] Despite some improvement of the region's economies since 2000, millions remain in grinding poverty. Older sources of poverty persist, and new ones have developed as Central America's economies opened to the world and as climate change occurs.

Another reason to examine Central America is its population growth and migration. The region's combined population had risen above 43 million by 2019, with half its citizens facing limited economic opportunity and many plagued by violent crime. Many Central Americans have fled the region, seeking economic opportunity as migrant workers or as residents of Mexico and Costa Rica. Indeed, the 2010 US Census revealed that approximately 4 million Central Americans lived in the United States.[3] Since then hundreds of thousands of Central Americans, especially youths, from the Northern Triangle countries have emigrated toward or to the United States. They have become a hotly contested issue in US national politics.

Central America warrants careful examination of how big forces act upon small countries. *Globalization* refers to compelling systemic forces that penetrate local affairs from beyond the nation-state. What are these global forces? World-scale economic forces generate markets, price cycles, and crises that shape domestic economies and subpopulations. Changes in the structure of the global economy, licit and illicit trade, and class systems realign domestic economic organizations and reshape classes. New ways of organizing the world economic and political arenas produce new ideologies and operating policies for institutions. These constrain local actors by favoring some, weakening others, and reshaping institutions to fit global needs and preferences. We believe Central America's revolutions, regime changes, economic development strategies, evolving classes, social problems, persistent poverty, and migration flows reveal the impact of the global upon the local.

The "Central America" upon which we focus in this book consists of Guatemala, El Salvador, Honduras, Nicaragua, and Costa Rica.[4] We do not address

Belize and Panama individually. Although Belize is geographically Central American, that English-speaking microstate only became independent from Great Britain in 1981; its history is distinct from the region's other countries. Panama lies outside Central America historically. Its pre-Columbian indigenous cultures were South American. From 1821 until 1903, Panama formed part of the South American republic of Colombia. "The five" share a common political heritage from the colonial period, during which Spain administered them as a unit. During the national period (1823 to 1838) they formed a single state called the United Provinces of Central America. In the late nineteenth century, several attempts to reunify failed. In the 1960s the five formed a common market, and more recent unification efforts include a common regional parliament and shared trade agreements with the United States. Out of this history comes a sense of Central American national identity.

As defined above, Central America's small combined land mass of 431,812 square kilometers is barely larger than that of California (404,975 square kilometers). Its estimated total 2019 estimated population of around 43 million was 10 percent larger than California's. The country with the smallest surface area, El Salvador, is smaller than Maryland. The largest, Nicaragua, is barely larger than Iowa. In 2019 population, the five varied between Costa Rica's low of 5 million (similar to the population of South Carolina) and Guatemala's high of 16.9 million (similar to New York).[5] Central America's population has more than doubled since the 1970s, but the rates of population growth have slowed in recent decades due to rapid urban growth and out-migration (see Appendix, Table A.2).

Central America's natural resources are modest. However, had different political systems and economic models prevailed across Central America during the nineteenth and twentieth centuries, there certainly would have been enough arable land to provide adequate sustenance for the population and some primary products for export. Yet responses to international market demands by the region's elites led to land-ownership concentration, an over-emphasis on exports, and inadequate production of consumer food staples. Instead of growing beans, corn, rice, plantain, and cassava for local consumption, big landholders normally concentrated on lucrative exports such as coffee, cotton, sugar, and beef.

Central America has varied but scant mineral resources. Guatemala has modest nickel and oil reserves. Nicaragua has long been viewed as a promising site for a future trans-isthmian waterway, but a recent Chinese-led project has foundered. Three nations now rely heavily on imported oil for electricity generation. Costa Rica produces over 90 percent of its electricity with a combination of hydroelectric, wind, and solar power, while Nicaragua generates over half of its electricity through renewables. In Guatemala, Honduras, and Nicaragua mining and other extractive activities, including hydroelectric projects, have caused conflict with local populations. Climate change has increasingly adversely affected the region. A "dry corridor" emerged in El Salvador, Guatemala, Honduras, and Nicaragua in the early 2000s, threatening crops, food supplies, and water resources. Central Americans from that zone, particularly the western highlands of Guatemala where malnutrition was already acute, have increasingly cited climate change as the reason for their migration.[6]

Central America's population is diverse. While majorities in El Salvador, Honduras, and Nicaragua are mestizo, meaning of mixed Amerindian and European descent, about half of Guatemala's population is indigenous, including 24 mostly Mayan ethnic groups.[7] Afro-origin Central American populations exist in all countries, the largest in Costa Rica and Nicaragua, which also have smaller Asian communities, predominantly from China. Indigenous and other minority communities are poorer than the general population and more likely to be impacted by violence at the intersection of land rights and development projects. More than 120 environmental activists have been killed in Honduras since 2010, while nearly 200 rights activists were murdered in Guatemala between 2000 and 2016; 26 indigenous leaders were killed in Guatemala in 2018 alone.[8]

Despite their similarities of geography and juxtaposition to the world outside the isthmus, there are some sharp differences among the Central American nations (see Table 1.1). For example, in economic development, Costa Rica in 2017 had a gross domestic product (GDP) per capita—a comparative measure of overall economic activity per citizen—of $9,809 measured in constant 2010 US dollars. For comparison, US GDP per capita in 2014 was over five times greater than Costa Rica's. Table 1.1 shows that Costa Rica's 2017 GDP per capita was over $6,400 greater than that of its nearest regional rival, El Salvador. With over four times more output per person than Honduras and Nicaragua, the Costa Rican economy in 2017 strongly outperformed its poorer neighbors.

Are such stark economic differences inevitable in the region? Not at all. In 1950, the countries of Central America had much more similar levels of economic activity than today; the richest (then El Salvador) had only 1.8 times the GDP per capita of the poorest (Nicaragua). But as Table 1.1 reveals, overall economic growth from 1960 to 2017 differed enormously. Costa Rica's GDP per capita rose 238 percent over this period and Guatemala's 114 percent,

TABLE 1.1 Basic Socioeconomic Data on Central American Countries

	Costa Rica	El Salvador	Guatemala	Honduras	Nicaragua
Population 2019 (estimated, in millions)[a]	5.04	6.20	16.87	9.33	6.14
GDP per capita 1990 (in constant 2010 US$)[b]	4,922	2,158	2,147	1,561	1,134
GDP per capita 2017 (in constant 2010 US$)[b]	9,809	3,464	3,124	2,211	2,016
Percent change in GDP per capita from 1990 to 2017 (in constant 2010 US$)[b]	99	61	46	42	78
Percent change in GDP per capita from 1960 to 2017 (in constant 2010 US$)[b]	238	81	114	102	34
Percent growth rate of GDP per capita 2017[b]	3.3	2.3	2.8	4.8	4.9
Percent of self-reported Afro-origin population in 2014[c]	3	2	0	3	7
Percent of self-reported indigenous population in 2014[c]	2	5	51	6	7
Percent literate of population aged 15 and older (2015)[a]	98	88	82	89	83
Percent literate of population aged 15 and older (1970)[a]	88	58	45	51	54
Percent internet users within previous year as of 2014[c]	69	50	44	39	32
Life expectancy at birth (2018)	79	75	72	71	74
Infant mortality per 1,000 live births (2018)[a]	8	16	23	17	18
Infant mortality 1990–1995 per 1,000 live births	15	40	55	43	48

(continues)

TABLE 1.1 *(continued)*

	Costa Rica	El Salvador	Guatemala	Honduras	Nicaragua
Change in infant mortality from 1990–1995 to 2018 per 1,000 live births	-7	-24	-33	-26	-30
Mean annual percentage growth in population 2000–2013	1.8	.03[d]	2.2	1.5	1.8
Percent urban population 2018[a]	79	72	51	57	59
Intentional homicides per 100,000 (2017)[e]	12.1	60	26.1	42.8	7

[a] Authors' projection based on Central Intelligence Agency, *The World Factbook*, www.cia.gov/library/publications/the-world-factbook/geos/nu.html, accessed January 29, 2019.
[b] Authors' estimate from World Bank Group, https://data.worldbank.org/indicator/NY.GDP.MKTP.KD?locations=NI&view=chart, accessed January 30, 2019.
[c] Drawn from the 2014 AmericasBarometer surveys of each country by the Latin American Public Opinion Project (LAPOP), www.LapopSurveys.org.
SOURCES: World Bank, https://data.worldbank.org/indicator/NY.GDP.MKTP.KD?view=chart; United Nations Economic Commission for Latin America and the Caribbean (ECLAC), *Statistical Yearbook for Latin America and the Caribbean 2007*, http://websie.eclac.cl/anuario_estadistico/anuario_2008, accessed July 29, 2008; United Nations Economic Commission for Latin America and the Caribbean (ECLAC), http://interwp.cepal.org/sisgen/ConsultaIntegrada.asp?idIndicador=2206&idioma, accessed February 24, 2016; Central Intelligence Agency *The World Factbook*, www.cia.gov/library/publications/the-world-factbook/geos/nu.html, accessed January 29, 2019.
[d] Emigration kept El Salvador's population rise from 5.96 million to 6.33 million from 2000 to 2013. An estimated 2 million Salvadorans have emigrated since 1979, reducing population growth.
[e] Tristan Clavel, "2017 Homicide Rate in Latin America and the Caribbean," *InSight Crime*, January 19, 2018, www.insightcrime.org/news/analysis/2017-homicide-round-up/, accessed February 6, 2019.

but Nicaragua's grew only 34 percent. Masked by the data's six-decade span is something that makes this startling fact even worse: Nicaragua's GDP per capita doubled from 1950 to the early 1970s but reversed to pre-1950 levels because of war, revolution, a US-imposed economic embargo, and capital flight. Over this period Costa Rica's politically stable democratic government pursued development by investing more than other isthmian countries in its citizens' education and health. Costa Ricans thus weathered intervening economic turmoil in better shape than their neighbors. They now enjoy much more prosperity, literacy, and better health than their neighbors. Recent economic growth rates somewhat mirror the five-decade history of economic development, with more prosperous Costa Rica growing fastest.

These comparisons of economic change argue against the inevitability of extreme poverty, at least within Central America. Starting out poor and with scarce resources, Costa Rica's development strategy and democratic government succeeded. The next chapter explains that by spending almost double on social programs and education as the other countries, Costa Rica achieved much higher GDP per capita, literacy, internet access, life expectancy, improved water systems, and the lowest outmigration and infant mortality rates (Table 1.1). In comparison, Guatemalan leaders' choices over five decades have left only 82 percent of its population over the age of 15 literate, infant mortality the highest in the region, and over a quarter of children aged 10 to 14 working (see Table 2.1). These developments have occurred despite a 114 percent increase in Guatemala's GDP per capita between 1960 and 2017. Contrasting Costa Rica's performance with any of its neighbors reveals how much decisions by political and economic elites shape development and welfare outcomes.

Even well-intentioned Central American elites, however, now face tough domestic and global obstacles. Table 1.1 highlights other characteristics of the populations of some Central American countries that pose problems. Guatemala struggles with how to integrate its 50 percent indigenous population, much of which speaks little or no Spanish. El Salvador continues to confront an enormous social headache posed by the country's high population density (approximately 306 persons per square kilometer in 2019—six times more concentrated than Nicaragua, and nine times more than the United States).[9]

By the late twentieth century, powerful economic policy guidelines known as neoliberalism confronted Central America's governments. Under pressure from foreign lenders in the 1980s and 1990s, all isthmian nations adopted constrictive neoliberal development strategies. To get needed loans from the international banking system, they had to adopt an austere capitalist development model that discouraged public social spending and human-capital investment. Thus by 2000, no isthmian country could fully embrace even the social-democratic development model that Costa Rica followed from 1950 to 1985, much less a revolutionary development model like Nicaragua's of the early 1980s. For example, when concerns about a loss of domestic control over social spending in Costa Rica held up ratification of the Central America Free Trade Agreement from 2004 to 2007, the United States pushed hard to secure ratification. One countervailing external force helped Nicaragua and

Honduras offset neoliberal pressure—Venezuela for several years supplied oil at favorable prices and donated funds for social welfare programs. Moreover, remittances, funds sent from emigrants abroad, increasingly buoyed households throughout the region.

In sum, Central America remains small in area and population, relatively resource poor, and beset by problems. Poverty reduction remains quite difficult for isthmian governments, even assuming national leaders should wish to move in that direction. Nevertheless, progress has been made in literacy, life expectancy, and infant mortality in recent decades (Table 1.1). Poverty in Central America has not always been inevitable. Early in the twenty-first century, these problems mostly affect the region's own people, although emigration, elevated levels of violence, and an increase in drug trafficking have spilled over into Latin American neighbors and the United States.

US interests and involvement in the isthmus have fluctuated widely over the past century. Protracted US inattention to Central America after World War II contrasted with intense US concern in the late 1970s when Nicaraguans rebelled against the Somoza regime. Although the Carter and Reagan administrations lavished attention on Central America, they described and treated the region so differently as to bewilder many observers, especially Central Americans. The first Bush administration remained powerfully involved in Central America but gave the region much less noisy public attention than had its predecessors.[10] With the Cold War clearly over and problems looming in the Balkans and Middle East, the Clinton and second Bush administrations paid less attention to Central America, nevertheless laboring to keep neoliberal economic policies on track and block leftist parties from power. Despite these efforts leftists won presidencies anyway—Nicaragua's Daniel Ortega Saavedra in 2006, and El Salvador's Mauricio Funes Cartagena in March 2009 and Salvador Sánchez Cerén in 2014. The Obama and Trump administrations encountered high levels of corruption, worsening narcotics trafficking, deteriorated democratic performance in several countries, and the wave of Central American immigrants into the United States.

The waning of frontline US attention as geopolitical winds changed did not eliminate Central America's endemic poverty, its problems with development strategies, political order, and elite culture, its adverse climate change, its constant need to adjust to evolving global forces, or pressures from the United States. In our effort to help the reader understand Central America, we examine these issues and consider the interwoven effects of evolving domestic and external influences on the region.

Notes

1. John A. Booth and Thomas W. Walker, *Understanding Central America*, 1st and 2nd eds. (Boulder, CO: Westview Press, 1989 and 1993).

2. Calculated by the authors from World Bank Group, Indicators, poverty, accessed September 6, 2019, https://data.worldbank.org/indicator/SI.POV.NAHC?locations=CR-NI&view=chart.

3. See Chapter 10 for details.

4. See Presbyterian Church USA, *Adventure and Hope: Christians and the Crisis in Central America: Report to the 195th General Assembly of the Presbyterian Church* (Atlanta, 1983), pp. 57–91, 97–101. The authors thank the Presbyterian Church for its permission to draw upon this material in previous editions (which Walker wrote in 1982 while he was part of the United Presbyterian Church USA Task Force on Central America).

5. Population estimates for Central America for 2019 from Table 1.1; World Population Review, US states' populations from "U.S. States Ranked by Population," http://worldpopulationreview.com/states/, accessed February 8, 2019.

6. Jonathan Blitzer, "How Climate Change is Fueling the U.S. Border Crisis," *The New Yorker*, April 3, 2019, www.newyorker.com/news/dispatch/how-climate-change-is-fuelling-the-us-border-crisis.

7. While the official 2010 Guatemalan census says that 41 percent of the country's population is indigenous, AmericasBarometer surveys from 2008 to 2014 indicate that between 38 and 51 percent of the population classify themselves as indigenous, AmericasBarometer surveys, the AmericasBarometer by the Latin American Public Opinion Project (LAPOP), www.LapopSurveys.org.

8. Simon Granovsky-Larsen, "Terror in Guatemala." *NACLA*, June 21, 2018, https://nacla.org/news/2018/06/21/terror-guatemala.

9. World Population Review, "Total Population by Country 2019," http://worldpopulationreview.com/countries/, accessed February 6, 2019.

10. Although lying just outside our region, the United States invaded Panama in 1989 to oust its dictator and install in power the true victors of the 1989 election. The US government's focus on our five nations was less overtly public and confrontational than under President Reagan.

Recommended Readings and Resources

Sánchez-Ancochea, Diego and Salvador Martí I Puig, eds. 2014. *Handbook of Central American Governance*. London: Routledge.

2

GLOBAL FORCES AND SYSTEM CHANGE IN CENTRAL AMERICA

COMMON FORCES LINK CENTRAL AMERICA'S GREATEST PAST and future problems of political and economic system change. Despite certain differences, Central American states share marked commonalities of history, global context, and political and economic development. These reveal that much that affects the region is part of a larger world dynamic. Common forces have led to Central America's rebellions and have shaped regime changes, new economic development strategies, and emergent problems with crime and emigration.

Our theory about system change in Central America comes from simple premises. First, much of what occurs in the political world stems from economic forces, and political decisions affect economic outcomes. Second, nations exist within an evolving global environment. Local problems can quickly become global problems and cycle back to the local. For example, political unrest in an oil-producing country (a local problem) can elevate oil prices and cause problems for consumers around the globe. Third, inequality exists within and between societies and outcomes usually follow advantage and power. Societies have hierarchies of elites (minorities who control resources and institutions) and majorities of ordinary citizens (poorer and less powerful). Among nations, there are hierarchies of more powerful and weaker states. Elites from different societies often cooperate across national boundaries for mutual benefit, while non-elites find this more difficult. Elites acting as individuals or through organizations, governments, and multilateral institutions cooperate with each other to promote their personal, corporate, and national interests. Small nations' elites sometimes promote small-nation cooperation, but rarely achieve as much of what they desire as elites from powerful nations. Small nations' elites more often benefit most by cooperating with external elites representing powerful governmental or private interests. Increasingly since World War II, global economic elites operating above the level of the nation-state have forged a world economy that favors global capital above the interests of even powerful nation-states.

Nations as small as those of Central America tend to be sensitive to powerful global forces and actors. This sensitivity stems from their limited resources, populations, and military power. Central Americans depend heavily on what their countries export (commodities) and import (manufactured goods and energy). They also have large, powerful, and often pushy neighbors. In this globalized world, problems cross borders quickly. Powerful actors—bigger states, international organizations, or even global non-state elites including criminals—can often compel the compliance or cooperation of others.

After World War II, Central American economies faced economic stagnation and deep poverty. The region's leaders feared possible leftist revolutions, so their governments collaborated on a regional economic integration scheme to promote capitalist economic growth and to preserve their regimes. Although successful for a while, that system crashed in world economic and domestic political crises during the 1970s and 1980s. After several decades recovery has been incomplete and uneven, and new economic and political challenges have arisen. We seek to understand the region's persistent poverty, how governments have perpetuated or ameliorated it, and how the region's economies fit into the world economy. We begin by examining Central America's poverty and its causes, with special attention to the economic situation of Central Americans from 1970 onward. We then offer a theory to explain how this has affected political regimes over time.

POVERTY AND ITS CAUSES

Common-sense explanations of political turmoil in Central America often stress serious, ongoing poverty. Even relatively prosperous Costa Rica has always had many poor people. Common sense betrays us, however, if we blame poverty alone for Central America's 1970s and 1980s rebellions, or for Nicaragua's more recent unrest. Many of the world's people are very poor, yet they rarely rebel. Indeed, if poverty sufficed to cause rebellions, poor Hondurans should have exploded with fury long before Nicaraguans or Salvadorans. We thus encounter the paradox that from the 1960s to the 1980s, Central America's poorest and richest nations (Honduras and Costa Rica, respectively; see Table A.1) were the region's most stable. Meanwhile, the three countries that industrialized and grew fastest in the 1960s and 1970s became the most unsettled. More recently, Nicaragua's political protests of 2018 broke out among more advantaged economic sectors, not the very poor.

We do not argue, however, that poverty did not contribute to Central America's rebellions. Indeed, there is an important link between *becoming* impoverished (experiencing loss) and popular unrest. Large segments of Central America's poor and middle classes *became* worse off during the 1970s and early 1980s. It was not grinding, persistent deprivation, but this change—impoverishment—that motivated unrest. This section examines how Central America's longstanding deprivation shaped recent economic and political history. Following country chapters explain how impoverishment has driven popular unrest and rebellion.

Poverty Measured

The human condition in Latin America generally stands between the extreme deprivation of parts of Africa and the relative prosperity of North America, Europe, and Japan. Within Latin America, most Central American economic indicators fall below the regional medians. Latin American and Caribbean countries in 2017 had a gross domestic product (GDP) per capita (in current 2010 US dollars) of roughly $9,400. Only relatively wealthy Costa Rica, with a GDP per capita of $9,809, exceeded that figure. The other four ranged from El Salvador's $3,464 per capita downward to Nicaragua's $2,016.[1]

GDP per capita figures require some explanation and context. First, for comparison, consider that per person economic activity in the United States in 2017 (GDP per capita in 2010 constant US dollars), at $53,129, was nearly 15 times that of Central America's average ($3,554).[2] Second, consider that the "average" indicated in GDP data distorts reality. GDP divides the annual total value of goods and services produced in a country by its population. In Central America, where small minorities control most resources and earn most of the income, averaging the economic activity of the wealthy and the rest of the population overstates the real condition of most people. Indeed, the real annual income per capita of the poorer half of the population in most of Central America probably runs between $750 and $1,500. Finally, while "average" Salvadorans thus struggled to get by on roughly one-fifteenth of what the average US citizen had to work with in 2017, they and other Central Americans faced consumer prices akin to those in the United States. Funds remitted by family members living abroad provide a vital supplement to many household incomes, in 2018 amounting to one fifth of GDP in El Salvador and Honduras (see Table A.1).

Survey data from 2014 provide more evidence on within-nation inequality by ethnicity/race and gender. Using a measure of artifacts owned by one's family to assess living standards, whites and mestizos were better off than the indigenous or blacks and mulattos. In Guatemala the living standards among the mestizo/white population was 62 percent higher than among the indigenous. The differences were 28 and 20 percent respectively in Nicaragua and Honduras. In El Salvador and Nicaragua, respectively, whites/mestizos had 16 and 30 percent higher living standards than black/mulattos. For educational attainment by ethnic group, similar patterns prevailed. The largest difference occurred in Guatemala, where mestizos/whites had completed 56 percent more years of schooling than the indigenous, reflecting centuries of neglectful education policy. Men averaged 17 percent more schooling than women in Guatemala and El Salvador; differentials were much lower in the other three countries.[3] In short, indigenous, black/mulatto and female populations around the region suffer from less education and lower living standards; Guatemala's indigenous fared worst of all.

Table 2.1 and Table A.1 present further insight into poverty's dynamics. Comparatively low income and poor living standards have long afflicted many Central Americans. The income ratios of the wealthiest 10 percent of the people to the poorest 10 percent in 2014 reveal extreme inequality. A regional wealthy-to-poor income ratio ranges from a low of 14.6 among Salvadorans to a high of 32.0 among Hondurans. (El Salvador's owes its relatively lower income inequality to the flow of monetary remittances from Salvadorans abroad to their families back home, and to social policies enacted under two successive leftist governments.) Putting inequality more concretely, if we estimate that the poorest tenth of Hondurans lived on $750 per year around in 2017, the wealthiest 10 percent would have enjoyed a comfortable $24,000 each. Another measure is the Gini index of income inequality, in which lower scores indicate lower inequality (range 0–100). In 2014 El Salvador's Gini index of 38 was the region's lowest. The other four countries' indexes ranged between 47 and 53 (highest in Guatemala). Interestingly, income inequality declined in El Salvador, Honduras, and Nicaragua from 1990 to 2014, but increased in Costa Rica. This shows that increasing overall economic output may not improve equality—the incomes of wealthier Costa Ricans have risen faster than those of their poorer brethren.

TABLE 2.1 Dynamics of Poverty in Central America

	Costa Rica	El Salvador	Guatemala	Honduras	Nicaragua
EDUCATIONAL INEQUALITY					
Mean years of education by national education quintiles in 2014 (20% of population in least-to-most order of education)[a]					
Quintile					
1	2.7	1.3	0.6	1.6	0.7
2	6.0	5.7	3.7	4.5	3.7
3	8.3	9.0	6.0	6.3	6.7
4	10.8	11.7	9.1	9.6	10.3
5	14.4	15.5	12.9	13.0	14.5
Mean years of schooling (population over 25)					
in 1960[b]	3.9	1.7	1.4	1.7	2.1
in 2014[a]	8.4	7.9	5.7	6.9	6.4
Percent of population over 25 with no schooling, c. 2000					
c. 2000[b]	9.4	35.0	47.1	25.9	18.0
in 2014[a]	2.7	9.5	17.4	8.3	13.3
Gini index of education inequality,[a] among population ages 25–65, c. 2000[b]					
	29.7	47.3	61.8	47.7	48.3
INCOME, WEALTH, AND SERVICE INEQUALITY					
Percent below poverty line					
c. 1990	26.2	54.0	64.6	80.5	73.6
c. 2014	21.7	31.8	53.7	62.8	29.6
change 1990–2014	-4.5	-22.2	-10.9	-17.7	-44.0
Percent of families with female heads of household, 2004 (% change since 1990)					
	27.6(+8.7)	32.2(+5.5)	19.3(+2.4)	25.7(+4.3)	32.2(+4.1)
Percent of children ages 7–14 who work					
	2.5	6.4(est.)	19.2	9.2	9.2(est.)
Percent affected by under-nourishment[d]					
c. 1991	5.2	16.2	14.9	23.0	54.4
c. 2015	<5.0	12.4	15.6	12.2	16.6
Income ratio of wealthiest 10% to poorest 10% of population, 2014[c]					
	24.6	14.7	24.0	32.0	26.17
Percent of homes with improved water 2015[d]					
	97.8	93.8	92.8	91.2	87

(continues)

TABLE 2.1 *(continued)*

	Costa Rica	El Salvador	Guatemala	Honduras	Nicaragua
Percent of homes with improved sanitation facility access 2015[e]					
	94.5	75	63.9	82.6	67.9
Gini index of income inequality[f]					
c. 1990	43.8	50.7	58.2	61.5	58.2
c. 2014	48.5	38.0	53.0	47.1	47.1
change 1990–2014	+4.7	-12.7	-5.2	-17.4	-11.1

[a] Data drawn from 2014 national sample AmericasBarometer surveys of each country by the Latin American Public Opinion Project (LAPOP), www.LapopSurveys.org.
[b] Other sources: World Bank, Data: Poverty, www.worldbank/indicator, accessed March 15, 2016; United Nations Economic Commission for Latin America and the Caribbean (ECLAC), *Statistical Yearbook for Latin America and the Caribbean 2007*, http://websie.eclac.cl/anuario_estadistico/anuario_2008, accessed July 29, 2008; ECLAC, http://estadisticas.cepal.org/cepalstat/WEB_CEPALSTAT/estadisticasIndicadores.asp?idioma=i; accessed August 28, 2013; David E. de Ferranti, et al., *Inequality in Latin America: Breaking with History?*, Washington DC., The World Bank 2004, www-wds.worldbank.org/external/default/WDSContentServer/WDSP/IB/2004/06/22/000160016_20040622141728/Rendered/PDF/28989.pdf, accessed July 29, 2008; Matthew Hammill, "Growth Poverty and Inequality in Central America," Serie Subregional de la CEPAL en México, United Nations, Economic Commission for Latin America, Social Development Unit, Mexico, DF, 2007.
[c] Data drawn from 2012 national sample AmericasBarometer surveys of each country by the Latin American Public Opinion Project (LAPOP), www.LapopSurveys.org.
[d] *Quinto Informe: Estado de la región en desarrollo sostenible*, San José, Costa Rica, Programa Estado de la Nación-Región, 2016, Cuadro 3.16, p. 149.
[e] The Gini index is a measure of inequality that ranges from zero (perfect equality) to 100 (perfect inequality); the higher the index score, the greater the inequality within a population; data source for 1990 T.H. Gindling and Juan Diego Trejos, "The Distribution of Income in Central America," Discussion Paper Series No. 7236, Institute for the Study of Labor (Bonn, Germany), February 2013, table 1, p. 22; for 2014 Central Intelligence Agency, *World Factbook 2019*, www.cia.gov/library/publications/the-world-factbook/, accessed February 10, 2019.
[f] Central Intelligence Agency, *World Factbook 2019*, www.cia.gov/library/publications/the-world-factbook/, accessed February 10, 2019.

Table 2.1 data on the share of citizens below the regional poverty line from the early 1990s and 2014 reveal relative economic improvement: 26 percent of Costa Ricans had incomes below the regional poverty line around 1990, but that share declined to 21.7 percent in 2014. Elsewhere in the region, the populations in poverty in those countries also shrank, and by greater percentages than in Costa Rica, but that still left large portions of the people in poverty. The share of children aged 7 to 14 who work ranged from 2.5 percent

(Costa Rica) to 19.2 percent (Guatemala). The proportion of undernourished Central Americans ranged from 5 percent in Costa Rica in 2015 to 16.6 percent in Nicaragua.

Two poverty- and health-related measures of household living standards appear in Table 2.1. In 2015, households with improved drinking water were the norm region-wide, but clean drinking water was unequally distributed among nations. While nearly 98 percent of Costa Rican homes had access to improved drinking water, only 87 percent of Nicaraguans did. Regarding sanitation (sewerage) facilities, nearly 95 percent of Costa Rican households had improved sanitation, but only 64 percent of Guatemalans and 68 percent of Nicaraguan households did.

Education can provide one way out of poverty. Data reveal both the difficulties Central Americans confront and the progress they have made in recent decades. Literacy among those 15 years and older in 2015 ran from a high of 98 percent in Costa Rica to a low of 82 percent in Guatemala (see Table 1.1). Outside of regional leader Costa Rica, literacy rates progressed 29 or more percentage points from 1970 to 2015. Elite-dominated systems had long neglected public education, especially secondary schooling in rural areas. However, Table 2.1 provides evidence that many more Central Americans now attend school than once did, likely facilitated by the region's increasing urbanization. The population over age 25 with no schooling at all in 2014 ranged from a low of 2.7 percent in Costa Rica to between 8.3 and 17.4 percent in the other four countries, an improvement from 2000 (Table 2.1). Another positive sign is the rise in education among the population over 25 between 1960 and 2014. Costa Rica's average more than doubled from 3.9 to 8.4 years of schooling over this 54-year span, while the other four countries more than tripled their averages to between 6.2 and 6.8 years of schooling. While improved, these national averages showing only primary-school educational attainment among adults in four countries indicate a continuing drag on individual and national development potential. These disadvantages are worse for the indigenous and for females.

To explore educational inequality in 2014, Table 2.1 divides the populations aged 18 or older into quintiles (fifths) by country according to levels of education attained as of 2012. For each quintile the table reports the mean years of education, allowing us to compare education inequalities. Costa Ricans once led considerably in education equality and attainment, but by 2014 El Salvadorans were approaching or exceeding Costa Rican averages among the third to fifth quintiles. Guatemalans, Hondurans, and

Nicaraguans lagged one to two years behind Costa Ricans and Salvadorans in every quintile of education achieved.

Food security provides one measure of poverty. Many Central Americans still eat little animal protein; they derive their essential amino acids, instead, from corn and beans. But even these foods are expensive because they are costly imports that replace dwindling domestic production resulting from both shifts in the economies and climate change. Based on combined affordability, availability, and quality/safety, Nicaragua in 2013 had the worst food security score in the region at 46, based on a scale of zero to 100, but Honduras, El Salvador, and Guatemala scored between 47 and 50 (Costa Rica scored 66). In 2015 Nicaragua and Guatemala had the largest percentages of undernourished citizens (16.6 and 15.6 percent, respectively), particularly among indigenous children. By comparison Costa Rica had less than 5 percent.[4] Even after improvements, much privation persisted in four countries.

Recent trends in public health reveal progress. Especially since World War II, improved weapons against communicable diseases have allowed Central American governments and international health organizations to curtail several killer diseases. Death rates have declined and life expectancies risen. Life expectancy in 2018 ranged from around 73 years for four countries to 79 in Costa Rica (see Table 1.1). Costa Rica, whose governments have for decades provided decent, low-cost health care to much of the populace, widely bested its neighbors in reducing infant mortality. Costa Rica for 2018 experienced eight infant deaths per 1,000 live births (similar to advanced industrial countries). All four other countries also dramatically lowered their infant deaths per 1,000 live births to between 16 and 23 by 2018. Urbanization likely helped lower infant mortality by bringing more Central Americans nearer to doctors and hospitals.

Improved preventive medicine has extended Central Americans' lives, but many still faced serious health problems in the early twenty-first century. Except for Costa Rica, the curative medical system was inadequate for the rural population. Expensive private medical care remained beyond the reach of citizens outside the upper and urban middle classes. As a result, good health remained largely a matter of privilege and geography. That said, Table 1.1 reveals that national efforts to improve health services and population shifts had brought health benefits.

Widespread poverty and low urbanization contribute to high fertility and population growth. High natural population growth rates exacerbate poverty by adding people faster than economies can grow. Urban women receive more schooling and use birth control more than rural women. Although poverty persists, much of Central America has significantly urbanized in recent decades (see Table A.1). After prior decades with much faster population growth, urbanization, education, and emigration have reduced Central America's population growth rates to an estimated 1 percent per year in each country by 2018. Modern contraception use among Central American women aged 15 to 49 was higher in 2016 than the world mean of 56 percent everywhere but in Guatemala (49 percent). It was highest in Costa Rica and Nicaragua (75 and 79 percent, respectively). Central American nations have very restrictive abortion access, including complete bans in some countries. Even at this new lower growth rate, Central America's population could reach 59 million by 2040—an increase of 44 percent.[5]

Population continues to grow for several reasons. First, public health advances have reduced death rates. Second, the median age in four of five countries is between 23 and 28 (compared to 32 in Costa Rica and 38 in the United States). Thus, much of the female population is of childbearing age.[6] Third, many very young women become pregnant. Although down by half since 1960, a weighted regional average of 71 of 1,000 women aged 15 to 19 became pregnant as of 2017, well above the world mean of 44 and US mean of 19.[7]

For the region as a whole, therefore, despite some recent progress in education, health conditions, and income (mainly in urban areas), many Central Americans still have low incomes, uncertain employment prospects, poor housing, poor basic services, and inadequate publicly financed health care (social security), public schools, and cultural opportunities. It will take decades of continued investment in education and economic development to lift Guatemala, Honduras, and Nicaragua to the living standards of El Salvador today, much less to catch up with Costa Rica. While continuing population growth makes reducing social inequities and improving living conditions harder, progress has nevertheless occurred in recent decades.

The Causes of Poverty

Poverty in Central America is neither completely natural nor inevitable. Foreigners once argued that Central Americans were poor because they were racially inferior. For instance, one geography text used widely in US primary schools in the 1920s claimed that

> except where white men have established plantations, the resources [of Central America] are poorly developed. Most of the Indians, mestizos, and negroes are poor and ignorant ... few care to work hard. More white men are needed to start plantations and to fight tropical diseases.[8]

Today we recognize such statements, once found in prominent encyclopedias, to be racist nonsense. Likewise, one cannot maintain that the region lacks sufficient resources to support its human population. El Salvador *is* overpopulated. But as a whole Central America has enough good land to produce some primary products for export and foreign exchange and also to grow sufficient staples to feed its people. And though not exceptionally blessed in natural resources, the region also has some minerals, hydroelectric, and wind energy resources, and possibly unexploited potential in oil.

In fact, much of Central America's poverty is a human artifact—produced by exploitation of the many by the region's powerful upper classes as they operate within the world economic system. Influential foreign interests often joined and supported Central America's local elites in this exploitation. Evidence that that human volition caused much of the region's poverty leaps out of some of the data in Tables 1.1 and 2.1. There, one repeatedly finds that Costa Rica has done better than its neighbors in economic growth, economic equality, poverty reduction, education, and promoting its citizens' health. Moreover, Costa Rica accomplished these things while exporting agricultural commodities and having only modest resources. It did so despite starting the second half of the twentieth century ranked with roughly the same per capita income as Guatemala, El Salvador, and Nicaragua.[9] How did Costa Rica do so much better by its citizens than its four northern neighbors since 1950? The answer, we contend, stems from the political will of Costa Rican leaders. Even though they shared the same disadvantageous economic context of the rest of Central America, Costa Rica's leaders adopted and kept democracy, abolished the military, ameliorated economic inequality, and invested in education and health over the long haul. The leaders of the other nations did not make these choices, at least not consistently enough to do the job. Costa Rica's democratic stability while strife roiled other nations also made investing there more attractive.

Dependency. What developed over time and accounts for much of the Central American economic system was *dependency.*[10] Though some disagree on specifics, most experts view dependency as a complex political, economic, and social system that retards the human development of the majority in certain privilege-dominated countries with heavily externally oriented economies. In such countries, even during periods of rapid economic growth, the benefits of growth normally do not meaningfully "trickle down" to the majority. Dependency theorists argue that dependent countries' social stagnation derives from the combination of an income-concentrating, externally oriented, externally conditioned form of capitalism with political systems controlled by privileged minorities who benefit from poorly distributed growth.

We emphasize that for the *dependency syndrome* to exist, a country needs *both* an externally oriented economy (specializing in commodity exporting) *and* a socially irresponsible political elite. External economic orientation, though essential, is not sufficient to cause the socially regressive dependency. Korea and Japan are both heavily externally oriented, but their elites have demonstrated a greater sense of social responsibility than Latin America's and have allowed growth to promote generally improved living standards. Cuba from 1959 to the collapse of the Socialist bloc and Soviet Union in 1989 provides another example of dependence without the poverty-generating dependency syndrome. Cuba's critics argue that its revolutionary government simply replaced dependence on the United States with dependence on the Socialist bloc. Quite so, but Cuba's political elite distributed the income from its externally dependent economy so as to significantly improve general levels of public health, education, and nutrition. Thus, while long dependent on the Soviet bloc for aid, Cuba for a time avoided the dependency syndrome per se.

Capitalist development in dependent Central America differs sharply from what occurred in the industrialized countries. In the Western industrial nations, common citizens became crucial to the economy as consumers. In the United States for much of the twentieth century, for instance, domestic consumers absorbed much of the industrial production. Thus it was not in the US ruling class' interest to so exploit ordinary citizens that they could no longer consume. In an internally oriented economic system like that of the United States, income redistribution through the graduated income tax, social-welfare programs, and a free labor movement served the interest of the moneyed elite as well as that of the common citizen. However, in dependent developing countries, the tiny upper and middle classes that control the political systems derive most of their income from commodity exports or from the products manufactured by multinational corporations that the upper and middle classes—but not the masses—consume. In this system the common citizen becomes important not as a consumer but as a vulnerable source of cheap labor.

Under this type of system, average citizens have little opportunity to lift themselves by the bootstraps because they lack either the means of production or the riches that flow therefrom. By its nature, elite-run dependency produces an inexorable concentration of property and income. In rural areas, stimulated by the lure of high profits through export, the rich and the powerful simply buy out or drive poor peasants from the land. Basic food production illustrates how this works. Land in the region is very inequitably distributed. The rich and powerful control the best land and on it grow export products rather than food staples. In a capitalist economy, this makes good sense to landowners because export products earn greater profits than domestically marketed staples. But over time this process has allowed export producers to progressively buy up and concentrate land in fewer hands, and so countries have produced fewer staple goods in relation to population. Meanwhile, the prices of these ever scarcer items rose with population growth and thus forced ordinary citizens to make do on less and cheaper food. Recently, this problem has been compounded by climate change. Floods and droughts have resulted in crop loss and increasing emigration of Central Americans seeking work abroad.

In the cities, local elites and foreign enterprises dominate the usually modest industrial production. Foreign firms enjoy advantages in technology and brand recognition that retards the formation of locally based industry. Nevertheless, the local elites benefit from contracts, services, and employment for the educated few, as well as occasional payoffs and bribes. Meanwhile, only limited advantages accrue to a host country from the foreign firms that export both profits and earnings from licenses, patents, and materials sold at inflated prices by parent companies. They tend to use capital-intensive rather than labor-intensive technology, thus draining foreign exchange for the purchase of costly industrial equipment and providing limited "trickle-down" in the form of wages. And finally, by obtaining much of their capital locally, they dry up domestic capital that might otherwise be available to native entrepreneurs.

This system privileges a local elite and its foreign associates while ignoring the interests of the vast majority. Powerful economic disincentives discourage elites from improving the miserable condition of the masses. Adopting a more socially responsible, mixed economic system could involve economic dislocation and personal sacrifice that many among Central America's dominant elites would resist. Indeed, the two main Central America experiments with such a more socially responsible, state-led development model only arose at least in part from violent political conflicts—the Costa Rican civil war of 1948 and the Nicaragua revolution of 1979.

Here one might reasonably ask why the dependency system developed in Central America while a consumer-driven economy arose in North America. And why have the great bulk of the Central American people proven unable to alter a system so contrary to their interests? Much of the answer to the first question lies in the distinct ways in which North America and Central America were colonized. European nonconformists originally settled North America seeking a new life and greater freedom. These people tamed the land with their own labor and eventually developed into a large class of freeholders.

North America developed an aristocracy of sorts around slavery but it never completely dominated the common citizen.

In Central America, the conquistadores sought quick riches. They superimposed their administration over that of the indigenous peoples and immediately began exacting tribute in gold and slaves. Within decades, the Spaniards plundered the region's gold and decimated much of its native population by slavery and contagion with European diseases. The Spanish steadily drained resources from the region. Subjugated masses of indigenous *peones*, mestizos, and black slaves and mulattoes supplied most of the labor. Only in Costa Rica, with scant easily exploitable resources and few native peoples, did many Spaniards come to till the soil. Costa Rican economic and political elites, absent a coercible indigenous workforce, learned to coopt and cajole their working classes.

Small wonder, then, that over five centuries later, the four northern countries of Central America had severe mass poverty and class disparities, whereas Costa Rica had developed a relatively more democratic and socially just system. Evidence that elite decisions underlie these within-region differences stands out in certain facts: after 1950 Costa Rica's governments collected more tax revenue while spending more on health, education, and welfare than other Central American governments. Costa Rica did this partly because, after 1949, it no longer had armed forces to support. The Costa Rican government's overall expenditure and social spending as a percent of GDP were nearly always greater than those in other isthmian countries (see Table 2.2 and Table A.5). Guatemala's relative social expenditures in 2012 consistently lagged well behind the other countries. On its stronger economic base, we estimate that Costa Rica in 2015 spent an estimated four to nine times more per citizen on health and education than the other four countries (Table 2.2).

This also helps explain why ordinary citizens' lives improved so little for so long in several countries. Rather than docilely accept their imposed and sorry lot, numerous groups did rebel when things got rapidly worse. Indigenous peoples resisted the conquistadores. Peasants revolted against land concentration caused by the late-nineteenth-century Liberal reforms and the spread of coffee cultivation. Peasants and workers, united under Nicaraguan nationalist Augusto C. Sandino, resisted US occupation from 1927 to 1933. Workers led by El Salvador's home-grown Communist Agustín Farabundo Martí revolted in 1932. Nicaraguans successfully rebelled against the Somoza regime in 1978–1979. Mass-based insurrections took place in El Salvador and Guatemala beginning in the late 1970s.

TABLE 2.2 Recent Economic Data on Central American Governments

	Costa Rica	El Salvador	Guatemala	Honduras	Nicaragua
General government consumption as percent of GDP					
1965	12.6	8.7	7.4	10.0	8.0
1980	18.2	14.0	8.0	12.5	19.7
2000	13.8	13.1	7.0	13.4	8.7
2017	17.3	15.8	9.7	13.8	15.3
Government social spending as percent of GDP					
c. 2000	17	13	8	8	9
c. 2012	23	15	9	12	13
Estimated per person government spending on education and health, 2015 (current US$)[a]					
	1,492	334	174	241	194
External debt as percent of GDP in selected years, 1982–2017					
1982	110.3	42.0	17.6	69.4	121.5
1991	73.0	36.7	29.8	118.9	649.1
2007	13.8	24.5	11.1	41.7	93.8
2017	46.0	62.5	30.3	37.5	81.9

[a] Authors' estimate based on data from World Bank Group, Indicators, https://data.worldbank.org/indicator/SH.XPD.GHED.CH.ZS?locations=, accessed March 15, 2019.
Sources: Economic Commission for Latin America and the Caribbean, CEPALSTAT/Databases and Statistical Publications, http://estadisticas.cepal.org/cepalstat/WEB_CEPALSTAT/perfilesNacionales.asp?idioma=e, accessed December 5, 2013; Interamerican Development Bank, www.iadb.org/gl/, accessed January 25, 2009; Interamerican Development Bank, *Economic and Social Progress in Latin America, 1983 Report* (Washington, DC, 1983), country profiles; Interamerican Development Bank, *Economic and Social Progress in Latin America, 1992 Report* (Washington, DC, 1992), country profiles; Economic Commission for Latin America and the Caribbean, Statistics and Indicators, http://interwp.cepal.org/sisgen/ConsultaIntegradaFlashProc_HTML.asp, accessed February 11, 2019; *Summary: Fifth State of the Region Report on Sustainable Human Development, 2016*, Programa Estado de la Nación (San José, Costa Rica 2016), Graph 1.7, p. 35; US Central Intelligence Agency, *World Factbook*, www.cia.gov/library/publications/the-world-factbook/fields/209.html#NU, accessed March 12, 2019; World Bank Group, Indicators, https://data.worldbank.org/indicator/SH.XPD.GHED.CH.ZS?locations=, accessed March 15, 2019.

Such struggles between popularly based movements and those in power have usually been very unequal. Entrenched elites typically enjoyed huge military, economic, and propaganda advantages. The elites usually also counted on foreign support—from Spain in the colonial period and the United States in the twentieth century. During the Cold War, Central America's ruling classes learned that by labeling their opposition "Communist" they would usually win US economic and military aid and sometimes direct armed intervention. From 1946 through 1992 the United States provided $1.8 billion in military assistance to the region (98 percent of it to Guatemala, El Salvador, Honduras, and pre-revolutionary Nicaragua) to shore up authoritarian regimes against challenges from the left (see Table A.3).

During the 1960s the United States assisted Central American governments with the Alliance for Progress. From 1962 through 1972 it provided $617 million (see Table A.3) to help build Central America's roads, ports, schools, and service infrastructures. This complemented the five-nation Central American Common Market's (CACM) effort to establish a common state-directed, import-substitution industrialization program and customs union. Intended to advance economic development and security objectives, the CACM stimulated rapid economic growth, but national elites mismanaged the distribution of its benefits. Rejecting the strategy of Costa Rican leaders, the regimes of Guatemala, El Salvador, and Nicaragua resisted sharing the benefits of growth with most citizens.

Afflicted by rising oil prices and falling commodity prices in the mid-1970s, the Common Market development model failed spectacularly. For every isthmian country this crisis elevated inflation, unemployment, and foreign debt while sharply lowering productivity and real wages. Worsening circumstances mobilized many citizens in protest, and some to violence, destabilizing several governments. Despite $5.6 billion in economic aid from 1977 to 1988 (see Table A.3) and assistance from other nations, turmoil blocked Central America's economic recovery. Eventually the United States and the major world multilateral lending organizations pressured all five countries into adopting a new economic model known as *neoliberalism* and enacting *structural adjustment* economic reforms mandated by foreign lenders.

Neoliberalism complemented regional and international political efforts to end the civil wars and promote electoral democracy. That outside elites and Central American leaders pushed together for peace, democratization, and neoliberal economic reform is no accident. Robinson summarizes:

> As the transnational ruling bloc emerged in the 1980s and 1990s it carried out a "revolution from above," involving modifications in global social and economic structures through the agency of [transnational system]

apparatuses aimed at promoting the most propitious conditions around the world for ... the new global capitalist production system. This global restructuring, the so-called "Washington consensus," [or] neo-liberalism, is a doctrine ... [that calls for] worldwide market liberalization, ... the internal restructuring and global integration of each national economy ... [and] an explicitly political component ... [that] revolved around the promotion of "democracy."[11]

Those pushing neoliberalism for Central America included the US Agency for International Development (USAID), the International Monetary Fund (IMF), and Inter-American Development Bank. Together they exacted political and economic "reforms" from debt-strapped Central American nations in exchange for loans critical to keep their economies functioning.

Promoted by international lenders, the United States and Europe, this neoliberal development model advocated (1) downsizing government by laying off public employees; (2) balancing public budgets by cutting programs and subsidies to food, transport, and public services; (3) privatization of state-owned enterprises; (4) deregulation of private enterprise; (5) currency devaluations to discourage imports and encourage investment; and (6) reduction of tariff barriers. Advocates argued such measures would eliminate inflation, increase productivity, stimulate international trade (especially exports), and lay a foundation for future economic growth. Although many citizens would be dislocated and suffer in the short run, long-term economic growth would in theory eventually trickle down to everyone.

For Central Americans with a sense of history, neoliberalism portended mixed blessings. Peace, democracy, and neoliberalism's monetary and price stability brought parts of the region economic recovery through improved growth, investment, and trade. Operating under the new economic austerity rules, Central American governments by 2007 reduced their large foreign debts (see Table 2.2). On the one hand, economic growth from 1960 to 2017 varied from an average of 4 percent per year in Costa Rica down to around 1 percent annually elsewhere (see Table 1.1). On the other hand, debt repayment, government layoffs, and program cutbacks reduced governments' capacities to protect and assist their citizens. They also increased disparities between the rich and poor and hurt the small middle class. Ironically, then, after achieving hard-fought political reforms, Central Americans found their governments still pursuing (or in Costa Rica's case, newly pursuing) economic policies that might worsen inequality—one of the central problems that drove the violence of the 1970s and 1980s.

The Great Recession of 2008–2009 left major nations and international lending institutions divided over neoliberal vs. Keynesian stimulative recovery policies. This argument relieved external pressure on Central American governments as their economies experienced renewed aggregate economic growth. Regional governments responded differently to the recession, recovery, and external lenders' divided policy preferences. Between 2007 and 2017, Costa Rica and Guatemala trebled their ratios of external debt to GDP, with El Salvador not far behind. Four of five countries increased their social spending from 2000 to 2012 (see Table 2.2), but consistently conservative Guatemala changed little over this period. Meanwhile external loan forgiveness programs lowered Nicaragua's and Honduras' international debts sharply by 2007.

Whether the newly democratic institutions born of the struggles of the 1970s and 1980s would allow Central American nations to curtail poverty remains to be seen. Four countries increased social spending, but a long-prevailing regional pattern persisted—Costa Rica invested relatively and absolutely more resources to its citizens' well-being compared to the other four. This left two major questions: would, or could, the other nations' elites attempt to balance growth with equity, as Costa Rica had for six decades? And would foreign lenders continue to allow relaxation of neoliberal strictures to accommodate greater social equity? The quality of life of the poor majority of the region's people depends on the answer to these questions.

REGIME CHANGE IN CENTRAL AMERICA

We turn now to the transformations of Central America's political regimes since the 1970s. We believe regional political transformations and the economic processes just discussed are related and largely driven by common forces.

Regimes are coherent systems of rule over mass publics established among a coalition of a nation's dominant political actors. A system's coherence refers to persistent, identifiable political rules determining access to power and decision making.[12] Political regimes thus stand distinct from the particular governments or administrations that operate under the same rules. For instance, Costa Rica has had a single civilian democratic regime since the 1950s—a series of constitutionally elected presidential administrations. Likewise, Guatemala in the 1970s had a military authoritarian regime, subdivided into governments headed by various president-generals.

A new regime arises when change occurs in *both the fundamental rules of politics and its ruling coalition.* We identify nine basic regime types in Central America between 1970 and 2019:

1. *Military-authoritarian*, dominated by a corporate military establishment in coalition with a narrow range of civilian sectors.
2. *Personalistic-military*, the only case of which was Nicaragua under the Somozas and their family-controlled military, in coalition with segments of the Liberal and Conservative parties and key financial interests.
3. *Military-transitional*, dominated by reformist military elements and willing to liberalize or democratize the political system.
4. *Civilian-autocratic*, dominated by a single person or narrow coalition (supported by a dominant political party and security institutions subservient to the ruler), limited to no checks or balances to executive power, and uncompetitive elections.
5. *Civilian-transitional*, with elected civilian rulers backed by a strong military and mainly incorporating center and rightist parties.
6. *Civilian-democratic*, with freely and fairly elected, civilian, constitutionally restrained governments, broad ruling coalitions, and political competition open from left to right.
7. *Revolutionary*, dominated by a weakly restrained revolutionary party with a center-left coalition.
8. *Revolutionary-transitional*, civilian-dominated and moving toward accommodating the revolutionary party and toward constitutional restraints in preparation for becoming civilian-democratic.
9. *Semi-democracy*, defined by Peter Smith as a regime in which "elections are free but not fair, ... [or] elections are free and fair, but effective power does not go to the winner ... [but] resides outside the realm of elective offices."[13] To this we add one additional characteristic—serious deviations from constitutional rule.

Table 2.3 locates Central America's political regimes since 1970 within this scheme. Since 1970 only Costa Rica remained politically stable. Among the other four countries we count 16 regime shifts (changes between categories).[14] Nicaragua's 1978–1979 insurrection culminated in a four-and-a-half-year period of revolutionary rule until internationally observed elections took place in 1984. With new members in the ruling coalition and National Assembly and top public officials separated from the revolutionary armed forces, the new revolutionary transitional regime's National Assembly drafted a new constitution. Its promulgation in 1987 instituted constitutional civilian democracy. Following constitutional and election-system changes and the collapse of

TABLE 2.3 Central American Regime Types, 1970–2019

Costa Rica	El Salvador	Guatemala	Honduras	Nicaragua
CD[a]	MA	MA	MA	MA
	MT (1979)	MT (1982)	MT (1980)	Rev (1979)
	CT (1984)	CT (1985)	CT (1982)	RevT (1984)
	CD (1992)	CD (1996)	CD (1996)	CD (1987)
			SD (2009)	SD (c. 2006)
			CA (2017)	CA (2016)

[a] Uninterrupted from 1949 to the present.
Note: CA = civilian-autocratic, CD = civilian-democratic, CT = civilian-transitional,
M = military-authoritarian, PM = personalistic-military, MT = military-transitional,
Rev = revolutionary, RevT = revolutionary-transitional, SD = semi-democracy. See text for
fuller explanation. Date of inception of new regimes is in parentheses.

the Liberal family of opposition parties in the mid-2000s, Nicaragua became
a semi-democracy under President Daniel Ortega and the dominance of the
Sandinista National Liberation Front (FSLN) around 2006, and then became
a civilian autocracy by 2016.

El Salvador and Guatemala traversed similar stages after military authoritarian rule: in each, a military-led transitional regime during civil war engineered changes that led to a civilian transitional regime. Each war's settlement
established a more inclusive civilian democratic government. Honduras' military regime, anxiously eyeing neighboring Nicaragua's turmoil at the end of the
1970s, moved quickly toward transitional civilian democratic rule. The military
retained veto authority for a long time—full civilian democracy came only in
1996. Hopes for consolidation of full civilian democracy proved vain with the
2009 coup. In mid-2009 Honduras became a semi-democracy when the Congress, Supreme Court, and armed forces ousted President Manuel Zelaya from
office. Despite the late 2009 election that put an elected president in office,
Honduras clearly had a new regime in which effective power "resides outside the
realm of elective offices."[15] Both Nicaragua and Honduras since these changes
have also deviated further from constitutional rule (see Chapters 5 and 8).

How and why did these regime shifts occur? We examine both what caused
them and the mechanisms or processes of change.

Causes of Regime Change

Several interacting factors drove most regime change: rapid economic growth in the 1960s, followed by severe reversals in the 1970s, impoverished many and generated widespread mobilization and demands for political and economic reform. Economic crisis bred mass unrest and helped undermine authoritarian coalitions. Violent repression of those demanding reform by several governments drove opposition unification, radicalization, and revolutionary insurrection. Fear of a revolution like Nicaragua's prompted the militaries of other nations, some with US aid, to initiate gradual political changes toward transitional civilian regimes with liberalized rules. The failure of the armed forces to defeat insurgencies added weight to calls from neighboring Latin American states, Europe, and the Catholic Church to accept negotiated regime change. Finally, the Cold War's end convinced the United States in the early 1990s that it could safely accept or promote rather than resist the negotiated settlements all Central American regimes had agreed to in principle in 1987.

In the twenty-first century, new factors arose to affect Central America. First, US influence over Latin America declined. Larger, more prosperous, and resource-rich countries like Brazil, Mexico, Argentina, Venezuela, and Chile gained economic and political influence in the hemisphere. Hugo Chávez's election to Venezuela's presidency in 1999 escalated expressions of anti-imperialist views and brought about new regional organizations to promote regional cooperation outside US influence, including the Union of South American Nations and the Bank of the South. The Bolivarian Alliance for the Americas (ALBA by its Spanish acronym) distributed economic assistance to poorer nations and counterbalanced US aid. Venezuela aligned with and provided assistance to left-leaning and populist governments in Cuba, Bolivia, and Ecuador, along with Honduras and Nicaragua until around 2016.

Second, the United States turned much of its attention away from Latin America after the terrorist attacks of September 11, 2001. The G.W. Bush, Obama, and Trump administrations paid much less mind to the region, concentrating on counter-narcotics operations and placing less emphasis on democracy promotion. The United States especially lost credibility as a promoter of democracy in the region when US officials endorsed the failed coup against President Chávez in early 2002.

Finally, shifting political alignments and elite attitudes within some countries weakened electoral democracy. Key elites in Honduras and Nicaragua had not embraced constitutional democratic rules of the political game. Deviation from these norms to their narrow advantage cost democracy greatly. And in Nicaragua, the several parties within the Liberal movement dissolved into a bitter factionalism that allowed the FSLN's Daniel Ortega to recapture the presidency in 2006. He consolidated power over state institutions and won re-election in 2011 and 2016.

Processes of Regime Change

If these were the likely causes of regime transformation, how did the changes occur? A widely based mass insurrection initiated the revolutionary regime in Nicaragua by defeating the authoritarian Somoza regime in 1979. The Nicaraguan revolutionary government enacted party and electoral laws similar to those of Western Europe and Costa Rica in 1983 and won internationally observed elections in 1984. In the ensuing revolutionary-transitional period, the National Assembly wrote a new constitution that took effect in 1987, ushering in the civilian democratic regime.

The overthrow of Somoza and beginning of the Nicaraguan revolution in 1979 were political earthquakes that motivated regime change elsewhere in the isthmus. Military coups d'état ushered in transitional military regimes in El Salvador, Guatemala, and Honduras. The new Salvadoran and Guatemalan military regimes at first kept repression high. Their critics doubted that meaningful changes in political rules had occurred, but military transitional leaders eventually produced new constitutions (some exculpating the military for their crimes while in power). They then allowed elections that brought civilians to nominal power while permitting some formerly excluded centrist and center-left civilian groups back into the political arena. The region's transitional regimes eventually allowed full civilian electoral democracy to operate. But these regimes failed to fully consolidate. After operating for a while, the post-2000 vacuum of US attention to the region contributed to democratic backsliding by some countries. Honduras and Nicaragua first became semi-democratic, and then civilian-autocratic.

Isthmian nations have much of their history, global contexts, and political and economic development in common. As noted, these common attributes demonstrate that Central America exists within a larger world dynamic that similarly constrains its component states. Just as common forces caused Central America's three great national revolts in the 1970s, the same forces influenced the process of regime change leading from authoritarianism toward electoral democracy. In fact, the revolutionary movements were key steps in regime change toward formal democratization. Declining external pressure for continued democracy has allowed domestic elites to undermine civilian constitutional rule in two countries, with more democratic break-downs possible.

THREE LITERATURES ON REGIME CHANGE

Our explanation for Central America's multiple regime transformations employs the theories just discussed. We first briefly review the political science literatures on regime change, revolution, and democratization to identify how they overlap and inform each other. Their common features lead us toward a general explanation of the remarkable alterations of Central American politics since the 1970s.

Causes, Processes, and Outcomes of Regime Change

Students of regime change examine their causes, processes, and outcomes. Barrington Moore explored how the traits of several established regimes interacted with social class structure to shape emerging new regimes.[16] Guill-ermo O'Donnell examined how military–middle class coalitions shaped new bureaucratic-authoritarian governments in Argentina and Brazil.[17] Con-tributors to Guillermo O'Donnell et al.'s *The Transitions from Authoritarian Rule* examined the causes and processes of the breakdowns of authoritarian governments of southern Europe and Latin America.[18] Mark Gasiorowski quantitatively analyzed factors that contributed to regime change.[19] Dietrich Rueschemeyer and Evelyne and John Stephens' *Capitalist Development and Democracy* contended that regimes shift toward democracy when organized working- or middle-class groups obtain sufficient power to undermine the wealth of entrenched elites.[20] Carles Boix argued that democratic regimes arise when pressured by masses if key elites have mobile rather than fixed assets capital (industrial or financial assets rather than extensive landholdings or minerals). Capital mobility, he believes, makes elites more willing to negotiate concessions.[21]

Differences among these theories aside, the regime-change literature clearly views regimes as systems of rule over mass publics established among a coali-tion of a nation's dominant political actors. Regime coalition members ben-efit from inclusion in the regime. Social and especially economic change can mobilize political actors who seek inclusion into the ruling coalition and its benefits. They may or may not be admitted by those within the regime (details of why concessions occur are disputed). Contented, indifferent, unorganized, or effectively repressed populations and groups seldom seek inclusion in the regime, nor do they violently rebel. Strong, flexible regimes with satisfied allies rarely collapse or wage war against their populations.

Charles Anderson's classic work explains that Latin American regimes have tended to admit new actors to the regime coalition only when they prove themselves capable, if excluded, of destabilizing the regime. Regime transformations therefore have often involved conflict because excluded forces must fight for inclusion.[22] This view accounts for the well-documented case of Costa Rica's last regime shift. The narrowly based coffee grower-dominated semi-democracy of the 1930s was disrupted first by emergent Communist-led unions, who made a pact with the reformist president to win social protections in the early 1940s. In 1948, middle-class actors and elements of the coffee elite rebelled in a brief but violent civil war. Their victory led to the new democratic regime.[23]

Political Violence, Revolution, and Regime Change

The second relevant literature concerns political violence and revolution, part of which concerns regime change. We have extensively reviewed this literature in earlier editions, so we merely highlight key portions here.[24] First, a rebellion requires a fundamental basis of conflict defining groups or categories of affected persons that provide "recruiting grounds for organizations."[25] What bases of conflict would most likely lead citizens to widespread rebellion, a phenomenon that John Walton usefully designates the *national revolt*?[26] Walton, Theda Skocpol, Jeffrey Paige, Mancur Olson, David Mason, and others argue that rapid economic change and evolving class relations typically drive the mobilization required for a violent challenge to a regime.[27] For agrarian societies, inclusion into the world capitalist economy through a shift to heavy reliance upon export agriculture may harm huge sectors of the peasantry, urban poor, and middle class and thus provide large numbers of aggrieved citizens.

Once motivated, groups must organize and focus their struggle for change upon some target, most likely the regime in power. Rod Aya and Charles Tilly have shown that effective organization for opposition requires the mobilization of resources. They emphasize the key role of the state in shaping rebellion. The state is not only the rebels' target, but it also reciprocally affects the revolt as it represses rebels and promotes change.[28] Walton, Skocpol, Jack Goldstone, and Ted Gurr concur that once a contest over sovereignty begins, political factors such as organization and resource mobilization by both sides eventually determine the outcome.[29] Goldstone, James DeFronzo, and Bill Robinson particularly emphasize the contribution to successful revolutionary movements of both external actors and inter-elite competition, elite alienation, and other factors that weaken the state's capacity to act.[30] Perhaps the most satisfactory explanation is that offered by Timothy Wickham-Crowley.[31] Rejecting single-factor theories, he argues from recent Latin American history that successful insurrection requires a combination of four factors: the right social conditions in the countryside; an intelligent and flexible guerrilla movement; a despicable target regime ("mafiacracy"); and the right international conditions. The last of these can include economic forces (e.g., falling international commodity prices that impoverish and mobilize local actors) and political ones (e.g., a hegemonic actor distracted from its normal clients, new international power configurations, or overt decisions not to assist a challenged regime).

Democratization, Democratic Breakdown, and Regime Change

The third literature concerns democratization and de-democratization— moving from an authoritarian to a democratic regime and vice versa. A first consideration involves the quality of democracy. As we argue in Table 2.3, democratic regimes vary in how well they meet ideal but changeable conditions of citizen participation, free political competition, information freedom, and the rule of law.[32] Central America's post-conflict political regimes, according to William Robinson, exemplify "polyarchy," a minimalist variant of formal electoral democracy. In these, global economic and political forces and institutions impose weak democratic rules (and openness to international markets with domestic austerity) on local elites.[33] Critics have presciently described the region's new democracies as "illiberal" and at risk of slipping into authoritarianism.

Turning first to democratization, the main explanations focus on political culture, political processes, social structures and forces (both domestic and external), and elites. The cultural approach argues that a preference for political democracy can develop within a society or spread among nations by cultural diffusion among elite and mass political actors.[34] Mass—and especially elite—preferences for democracy promote its adoption and help sustain it.

Process approaches to democratization examine the mechanics of and paths toward democratic transition.[35] Structural theories emphasize how shifts in the distribution of material and organizational resources among political actors can create conditions that favor democracy and undermine authoritarianism.[36] Democratic regimes emerge when the distribution of political and economic resources and the mobilization of actors permit excluded actors to disrupt the extant authoritarian coalition. Another structural approach examines the imposition of democracy by external actors (e.g., the 1989 US invasion of Panama to depose the Noriega dictatorship with electoral democracy).[37] The fourth approach examines the roles of key societal elites who must engineer specific democratic arrangements (elite settlements) and then abide by them. The broader the coalition, the more stable and consolidated a democratic regime will be.[38]

Explaining regime change away from democracy to some extent involves the inverse of those just cited for change toward it. De-democratization or democratic breakdown has a cultural component. The longer democracies exist, the more likely they are to survive because key political elites tend to gradually absorb democratic norms. Newer democratic regimes are more fragile. Structural factors, especially economic stressors, can undermine the legitimacy of democratic regimes and thus facilitate anti-democratic actors. Anti-democratic elites may undermine democratic rules by weakening the integrity and neutrality of courts and elections for example. Political polarization, especially partisan, ethnic, or religious differences, may contribute to antagonisms, disruptive behaviors, and political unrest.

Further, foreign governments, international institutions, and other nations can act as players in domestic economics and politics. They can support a prevailing regime, oppose it, or withhold support. External resources can enhance or reduce domestic actors' capabilities. Key external actors can pressure domestic actors to alter policies or regime rules using the inducements of money, trade, arms, and political cooperation. The international context can also constrain a nation's regime type by demonstration effect—having mostly democratic neighbors makes it easier to adopt or retain a democratic regime.[39]

These three literatures have much in common. All concern regime change, whether toward or away from democracy. Elements of each envision polities with many actors, whose makeup and roles can evolve. All treat political regimes as coalitions that survive by successful mobilization of resources in and around the state. All recognize that regimes can experience such crises, challenges from without, deterioration from within, or erosion of state capacity. All have causal explanations for change, although the approaches disagree somewhat over the importance of psychology, political culture, leaders and elites, masses, and social structures.

A THEORY OF REGIME CHANGE IN CENTRAL AMERICA

From these elements we draw our theory of regime change: political systems are nation-states with defined populations and territorial boundaries. They exist within an international context of diverse actors: nation-states, alliances among nations, corporations, the world political economy, international organizations, and political and ideological groupings. A *political regime* consists of a coherent system of rule over a mass public established by a coalition of the nation's dominant political actors. Political actors include individuals, organized groups, factions, ideological groupings, parties, interest sectors, or institutions. Each pursues objectives within the political system and each has resources to bring to bear. Actors may stand inside or outside the regime coalition, the group of actors who dominate and benefit most from the state, its resources, and its policies.

Political regimes persist based upon two things: they must manage the state and economy well enough to retain coalition members' loyalty. And they must keep actual and potential outside-the-regime actors (both domestic and external) content or indifferent. Failing that, they must distract, disorganize, or effectively repress them. Many factors can potentially destabilize a regime. International or domestic economic forces may disrupt the political economy or the security of regime coalition members or other actors. Such forces may include rapid economic growth followed by a sharp downturn, or a sharp recessive episode by itself. Powerful external actors may withdraw support and resources from a regime or shift from tacit support to active opposition and thus create a permissive external environment for opponents. Ideologies or different real-world examples may suggest alternative rules (e.g., socialism instead of capitalism, or civilian democracy instead of military authoritarianism) to actors within or outside the regime coalition.

A *regime crisis* occurs when such forces (1) undermine the loyalty and cooperation of some or all of the coalition members, (2) undermine the resource base and capacity of the regime to respond to challengers, or (3) mobilize external actors against the regime. Crises can vary according to the severity of the challenge and distribution of resources among actors. In response, the regime coalition may renegotiate the political rules and benefits and deny significant adjustments to outside actors. Alternatively they may adjust rules or policies to mollify aggrieved outside actors. Reforming extant political rules and payoffs and incorporating new coalition members can quell a disruptive challenge. Outside-the-regime actors may violently challenge the regime's sovereignty by coup d'état, insurrection, or even invasion. Inside-the-regime actors may employ a coup to displace incumbents or initiate a new regime. Leaders may voluntarily institute regime change on their own terms, even absent a regime crisis, although likely in response to anticipated challenges. Whatever the motivation, we consider this combination of alterations—change in the coalition membership plus an adjustment of the rules—to constitute a *regime change*.

The outcome of a regime crisis will depend upon the ability of the contenders to mobilize and deploy resources. The closer they are to resource parity and the stronger they are, the longer and more violently they will struggle. A powerful actor such as the military, confronted with a significant but potentially growing opposition, might initiate a regime change by incorporating new actors to minimize expected damage to its interests. (The "military transitional" regime type discussed above provides an example.) Other things equal, a strong, flexible, resource-rich regime will likely reform, or successfully repress its opponents and thus survive. A weak regime confronting a strong opposition coalition may fail and be replaced. A resulting revolutionary regime would likely then exclude some of the old regime's coalition members. A protracted crisis, especially a lengthy civil war, eventually increases the prospects for a negotiated settlement with new political and economic rules and redistributed benefits. The resulting new regime will include former challengers and old-regime actors.

The settlement upon a new regime will derive from the resolution of forces among the various actors, and may, in turn, depend heavily upon external actors. A single regime shift may not bring enough change to permit political stability. Military reformism (a transitional military regime), for instance, although intended to pacify a polity by including certain new actors and by enacting policy reforms, may not assuage violent, ideologically antagonistic opponents. Despite establishing a new coalition, new rules, and new policies, a revolutionary regime may quickly attract direct or indirect external opposition. If important actors (internal or external) remain unsatisfied or unsuccessfully repressed, the new regime may be unstable. Protracted instability for a newly constituted regime, we believe, increases the likelihood of its failure and further regime shifts.

EXPLAINING REGIME CHANGE IN CENTRAL AMERICA

Based on the framework elaborated above we offer the following account of regime change in Central America since the 1970s. We discuss two phases of regime change. In the first, the evolving world economic and geopolitical context interact with domestic forces from the 1970s until 2000. The interplay of domestic and external forces and their respective resources shaped the ultimate outcomes in electoral democracy. In the second phase, since 2001, domestic actors in several countries have taken advantage of domestic conditions and an evolved external environment to degrade democracy.

Phase I: 1970–2000

The Evolving US Viewpoint. The geopolitics of the Cold War set the context for Central American geopolitics in the 1970s. US policymakers focused on perceived threats from the Soviet Union and Cuba to expand US influence in the Western Hemisphere. The United States regarded most of the region's political and economic reformists and opponents of Central America's US-friendly, anti-Communist, authoritarian regimes as unacceptable potential allies of Communist subversion. Civilian democracy, though an ideological preference of the United States, remained secondary to security concerns in this tense world environment. US policymakers viewed promoting civilian democracy as risky because it might encourage leftists.

Central America's authoritarian regimes thus usually enjoyed political, military, and economic support from the United States. US military personnel trained Latin American officers during the Cold War, even explicitly advocating illegal detention, torture, and murder (state-sponsored terror) against a groups opposed to pro-US regimes.[40] This behavior created a profound contradiction between the proclaimed values of the United States and its actual policy in the region. It also caused some Central Americans in the center and on the left to doubt the potential virtues of formal electoral democracy as practiced against a backdrop of state terror under pro-US regimes.

US views of the ideological geopolitics of Central America evolved from the 1970s through the early 2000s. In the latter half of the 1970s, Congress and the Carter administration came to view the inhumane anti-Communist authoritarian regimes of Nicaragua, Guatemala, and El Salvador as unacceptable. This policy change encouraged Central America's reformists and revolutionaries and briefly opened the international environment toward regime change. After the Sandinistas' victory in 1979, however, US human rights policy in Central America was "put on the back burner,"[41] and Washington again encouraged Central American regimes to clamp down on "subversives." That posture encountered congressional opposition early in the Reagan administration, which led US diplomats again to favor elections in pro-US countries, even as some engaged in repression and state terror. This policy persisted until the Cold War ended in 1989. After that Washington's second-order preference for civilian democracy resurfaced as US support for peace negotiations and cleaner, more inclusive elections in El Salvador and Guatemala.

Evolving Central American Viewpoints. Prior to 1979 many leftists in Central America mistrusted electoral "democracy" as practiced by the US-sponsored regimes that excluded them from elections and otherwise repressed them. However, from the time of their victory in 1979, many Sandinistas viewed electoral democracy as compatible with the economic/participatory democracy it sought to construct in Nicaragua. The FSLN (Frente Sandinista de Liberación Nacional, or Sandinista National Liberation Front) also believed promoting electoral democracy would enhance their revolution's acceptability to the openly hostile United States and skeptical regional neighbors. Thus in 1983–1984 they implemented a well-designed electoral system to replace their revolutionary government.

However they initially envisioned their ideal post-victory government, the insurgents in El Salvador (by 1982) and Guatemala (by 1986) had decided not to seek military victory but a negotiated settlement including demilitarization and civilian rule open to their participation. As the Cold War waned, the armed forces of each nation—exhausted by the long civil wars—decided to accept electoral rules of the game, with the leftists included, in exchange for peace and institutional survival.

Certain capitalist sectors sympathetic to trade liberalization, involved in non-traditional exporting and linked to transnational capital, emerged to challenge traditional economic elites for control of private-sector organizations and rightist parties. These groups also embraced electoral democracy as a key to peace, neoliberal economic reforms, and revitalized economies. Operating through business-dominated organizations and political parties and supported by powerful external actors like USAID and the IMF, these groups eventually helped negotiate peace and run transitional and post-settlement governments. As powerful coalition members across the region, they heavily influenced economic policy.

Other Actors' Views. European nations, other Latin American countries, and such international organizations as the United Nations and Organization of American States once largely deferred to US influence in Central America. However, during the 1980s they increasingly feared that isthmian civil wars and US intervention could escalate. These actors therefore embraced and promoted electoral democracy as the best path toward peace in Central America. The preference for formal democratization at first put Europe at odds with the strenuous US military and diplomatic efforts to contain Central American leftist movements. With the Cold War's passing, the major industrial powers' shared desire for a healthy global capitalist environment contributed to the emergence of the *Washington Consensus* favoring formal democracy and neoliberal economics.

Liberation theology influenced the Catholic Church in the isthmus during the 1960s and 1970s. This encouraged mobilization for social justice, which in some cases contributed to insurrection. By the 1980s, however, the institutional Church reined in liberation theology and emphasized formal democracy and improved human rights as the appropriate path toward social justice. Catholic hierarchs on balance became more politically conservative. Some local variation in practice and policy performance could be observed among Church human rights offices in the region. With the main exception of Nicaragua in the 1970s, evangelical Protestants (growing rapidly in number since the 1960s) tended to either eschew politics or identify during elections with conservative and sometimes anti-democratic forces.

The 1970s Regimes. In the early 1970s only Costa Rica among the region's nations had a broadly inclusive, constitutional, civilian-led democratic regime. It had evolved from that country's 1948 civil war and 1948–1949 revolution.

The other four nations had military-dominated authoritarian regimes: Nicaragua's was a personalistic military regime dominated by the Somoza dynasty, a narrow coalition of business interests and parts of the two major parties. Guatemala and El Salvador had corporately run military authoritarian regimes, allied with some businesses, large-scale agricultural interests, and weak political parties. Honduras' military authoritarian regime incorporated one of the two strong traditional political parties and tolerated a strong but anti-Communist labor sector.

Causes of Regime Crises. A wave of economic problems afflicted all regional countries in the late 1970s and early 1980s. Rapidly escalating oil prices and resultant inflation, the deterioration of the Central American Common Market (in the mid- and late 1970s), and natural or economic catastrophes (e.g., the 1972 Managua earthquake, 1978–1979 Common Market trade disruptions) greatly reduced real income and employment among working-class and some white-collar sectors.

The grievances caused by increasing inequalities, declining income, economic/natural catastrophes, and the political dissatisfactions of would-be competing elites led in the mid- and late 1970s to various events: the development of opposition parties; the rapid growth of agrarian, labor, neighborhood, and community self-help organization; and reformist demands upon the state and protests of public policy. Regime coalitions experienced defections, and the economic resources of all five regimes eroded.

Regime Responses to Crisis. Central American regimes reacted very differently to demands for change, mobilization, and unrest. Where regimes responded with policies to ameliorate poverty and restore eroded wages, political reform, and low or modest repression, protests typically failed to escalate further or subsided.

Costa Rica's regime did not change. Honduras' military authoritarian regime voluntarily returned nominal control to civilians as the armed forces gradually reduced military tutelage of national politics. In contrast, regimes in Nicaragua, El Salvador, and Guatemala in the short run rejected ameliorative policies. With US assistance they sharply escalated repression by public security forces. Waves of protest ensued, and oppositions stepped up organization and resource mobilization. In the longer run, the regimes that responded with violent repression and refusal to ameliorate the effects of economic crisis faced violent, broadly based insurrections. They struggled to mobilize their economic and political resources to resist the revolts, including by seeking more aid from the United States. They eventually made extensive policy changes in their struggles to manage, repress, divide, and isolate their challengers. Nicaragua under Somoza was the least flexible. Military authoritarian regimes in El Salvador and Guatemala were overthrown from within by military reformers. The resulting military transitional regimes gradually adopted policy reforms and, unable to crush their armed opponents, eventually moved toward civilian transitional regimes.

Outcomes. The outcomes of Central America's regime crises depended upon the relative success of each regime in mobilizing and maintaining domestic and external material support and organization. Failure to placate or repress enough outside-the-regime actors eventually brought regime shifts.

In Nicaragua, dictator Anastasio Somoza Debayle lost direct US and regional support and vital economic resources, which helped the Sandinistas oust him and establish the revolutionary regime. The Somoza wing of the old Liberal Party was discredited. Somoza's National Guard was defeated and disbanded. The Sandinistas formed a center-left coalition and governed by revolutionary rules for several years. Top FSLN leaders dominated the executive branch and the Sandinista armed forces replaced all security forces. Center and right-wing political forces grew increasingly unhappy with the regime. The FSLN itself contained less-democratic "vanguardists" as well as more genuine democrats. Likely because the revolutionary regime found itself in the world media spotlight and needed to retain as much international support as possible, the more democratic faction prevailed. Somocista Liberals and an increasing number of other disaffected economic and political elements formed various outside-the-regime forces, including the US-backed Contra rebels. The revolutionary regime's response to this challenge and the counter-revolutionary war included nearly continuous economic and political reform, including adopting democratic electoral rules, holding the 1984 election, and writing a new constitution. We consider the adoption of the constitution in early 1987 the beginning of civilian democratic rule in Nicaragua because it formalized the rules of the political game along traditional liberal-democratic lines, with clear division of powers and checks on executive authority.[42]

The Honduran military regime, in 1979 facing turmoil at home and the Nicaraguan revolution next door, pre-emptively initiated transition to civilian democracy. The traditional Liberal and National parties dominated the transitional civilian regime. Meanwhile the armed forces—flush with political, economic, and military resources earned by cooperating with US efforts to defeat revolutionaries in Nicaragua and El Salvador—retained great power and influence. This delayed transition to civilian democracy until after the military's power was eventually trimmed again in the mid-1990s.

A 1979 coup d'état in El Salvador and another in Guatemala in 1982 instituted ostensibly transformation-oriented military regimes (early on their reformist intentions appeared questionable). These governments at first repressed moderates and centrists who remained outside the regime coalitions while attempting to defeat leftist rebel coalitions. The failure of this strategy and pressure from the United States (a major resource supplier to the Salvadoran regime), led the transitional military regimes to complete the transfer of nominal power to civilian transitional governments. These transitional civilian regimes, although weak, broadened coalitions and liberalized rules. This tactic won over some of the political center in each country, deprived the rebel coalitions of important allies and resources, and contributed to the stagnation of both civil wars. The Central American Peace Accord of 1987 provided a mechanism for eventual negotiations between the stalemated combatants. Military exhaustion, US exasperation with the Central American quagmires, the rise of new domestic transnational elites, and the Cold War's end moved all actors' positions. The United States, other outside actors, national militaries, the civilian reformist regimes, and the rebels eventually embraced more inclusive civilian democracy and some economic reforms, position changes that helped settle both wars.

Phase II: 2001–2019

Evolving US Policy and Behavior. After Al Qaeda attacked the United States in 2001, US policy veered toward enhancing national security and pursuing two wars in the Middle East. This undermined President George W. Bush's wish to improve relations with Latin America and reform immigration policy. US deportations of Central Americans with criminal records pushed US urban gang members into several isthmian countries. US democracy promotion in Latin America stumbled in 2002 when the White House applauded the unsuccessful attempted coup against constitutionally elected

Venezuelan president, Hugo Chávez. The United States also interfered in elections in Brazil, Bolivia, El Salvador, and Nicaragua by telling voters there that electing leftist candidates could bring US sanctions. As of 2017 the Trump administration aggressively sought to restrain immigration to the United States from Latin America, particularly from northern Central America. Some measures taken appeared counterproductive to this end, including curtailing US democracy promotion and economic development assistance. Ironically, by 2019 beefed-up immigration controls at the US border seemingly encouraged rather than dissuaded ever more Central Americans to emigrate in hopes of winning refuge before anti-immigration policies stiffened further.

Other Actors' Views. European powers joined the United States in the Iraq and Afghanistan wars and counterterrorism efforts, and thus provided less of a counterbalance for US policy in Central America than during the 1980s. The Hugo Chávez-inspired rise of Latin American international cooperative organizations, combined with Venezuelan economic assistance, encouraged Central America's leftist and populist governments. Venezuela's economy under President Nicolás Maduro deteriorated rapidly after 2015, aggravated by US sanctions imposed by Congress and the Obama and Trump administrations. This sharply curtailed Venezuelan economic aid to Cuba, Nicaragua, and Honduras. China also increased its interest in the region, particularly in growing trade and building a new canal across Nicaragua.[43] The canal project, however, collapsed.

Evolving Central American Viewpoints. The main change within the region in this phase involved key elites in Honduras and Nicaragua demonstrating weak commitment to democratic rule as US and European pressure for democracy waned during a lull in US attention. Venezuela provided material support to partially offset US influence and boost populist leaders, including Nicaragua's Daniel Ortega and Honduras' Manuel Zelaya before his ouster. As noted, this Venezuelan assistance, especially by importing Nicaraguan goods, diminished sharply after 2015.

Nicaragua's slide to autocracy demonstrated its elites' weak allegiance to democratic rules of the game. First came FSLN leader Daniel Ortega and former Liberal president Arnoldo Alemán, who cooperated on legislation that degraded election quality and undermined small parties. Sandinistas in the Supreme Court later invalidated a constitutional provision against re-election of former office-holders, allowing Ortega and many FSLN mayors to return to office. Meanwhile the FSLN purged reformists and Ortega opponents, leaving the "Danielistas" dominant. An unresolved split among the multiple Liberal parties divided the electoral opposition to the FSLN. These actions permitted FSLN nominee

Ortega to regain the presidency in 2006. Irregularities marred the 2008 municipal elections. The Liberals remained split in 2011, effectively collapsing, and President Ortega comfortably won renewed terms in 2011 and 2016, when we judge the semi-democracy to have become a civilian autocracy. Reforms to retirement laws in 2018 prompted widespread protests. When the government repressed them, violence erupted. Over 300 Nicaraguans died in rioting and the regime jailed hundreds. Ortega rebuffed opposition demands for early elections and the situation remained stalemated as we wrote this. In Honduras, President Zelaya attempted to hold a referendum on whether to amend the constitution, a move the courts blocked as unconstitutional and leaders of both major parties rejected. Opposing elites acted anti-democratically when the Congress, Supreme Court, and military collaborated to oust Zelaya from office and unconstitutionally exiled him. The ensuing crisis lasted months as the de facto government resisted international mediation seeking to restore Zelaya to office. After the Obama administration imposed sanctions on Honduras the de facto government conducted regularly scheduled elections in late 2009. Ironically, Honduras' Constitutional Chamber cleared the way for President Juan Orlando Hernández to run for re-election in 2017, although a second term was unconstitutional. Hernández's "re-election" had US support, despite irregularities that prompted the Organization for American States (OAS) to call for new elections.

The 2009 Honduran coup and Nicaraguan turmoil of 2018–2019 demonstrate that, just as elites can embrace democracy when useful, they can reject it when domestic or external constraints weaken.

DISCUSSION

What has regime change actually meant? Many observers have expressed doubts about the quality of the new regimes that developed in Central America in the 1990s. Some derided them as "democracy light" or "low-intensity democracy"—civilian electoral regimes dominated by elites unresponsive to mass publics despite the rupture with open authoritarianism. Recent events in the region further justify such skepticism.

We share many of these misgivings but disagree with the implication that regime change toward or away from democracy means little for the ordinary citizen. The most recent backsliding toward authoritarianism demonstrates how much even modest changes in democratic performance matter. The authors have personally witnessed how much democracy, however flawed, makes life safer from state violence. More democratic governments after 2000 allowed citizens to participate in politics more openly and safely than their undemocratic predecessors, as demonstrated by Figures 2.1 and 2.2. Evaluations by outside observers summarized in Figure 2.1 show evolving democracy levels since the early 1970s. The line for each country represents a composite democracy measure ranging from 0 (the lowest) to 10 (the highest possible score) in 1973–1974 through 2016–2017.[44] Several patterns stand out. Starting at the highest possible democracy evaluation assigned in the early 1970s, Costa Rica's score changed negligibly over the 43 years. In contrast, the other four countries moved from well in the nondemocratic range (below 5) to scores above 7 (in the democratic range) by the early 2000s. Among them only El Salvador retained its new level while the other three lost ground.

What about security and human rights? Figure 2.2 presents the Political Terror Scale (PTS), a measure ranging from 1 (very low violence and few human rights abuses) to 5 (generalized violence and severe human rights abuses). Costa Rica's scores remained low across the four decades. In contrast, violence and

FIGURE 2.1 Change in Democracy Levels, 1973–2017

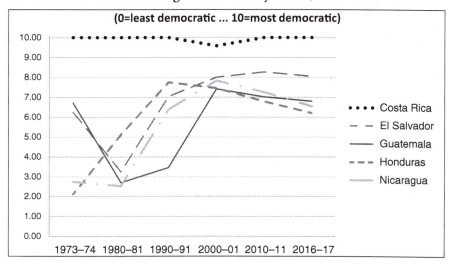

Source: Freedom House, Freedom in the World, www.freedomhouse.org/report-types/ freedom-world, accessed September 10, 2013 and March 23, 2019; and Monty G. Marshall, Center for Systemic Peace, Polity IV Individual Country Regime Trends, 1946–2013, www.systemicpeace.org/polity/polity4x.htm, accessed March 23, 2019.
Note: Values are the mean of the two systems' democracy scores, standardized to a zero to 10 range by the authors.

FIGURE 2.2 Evolution of Political Violence and
Repression over Time, 1976–2017

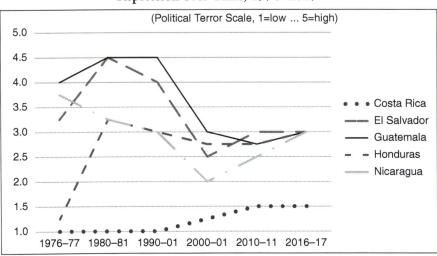

Source: Gibney, Mark, Linda Cornett, Reed Wood, Peter Haschke, and Daniel Arnon.
2017. The Political Terror Scale 1976–2017, www.politicalterrorscale.org/; accessed
March 23, 2019.
Note: Values are means for each period for the Political Terror Scale.

repression rose sharply in Guatemala, El Salvador, and Honduras from the mid-
1970s to 1980–1981 and beyond. The end of the civil wars in Guatemala and
El Salvador sharply reduced political violence by 2000–2001. Political violence
in Nicaragua, horrific in the late 1970s, declined gradually over the next three
decades. Finally, four countries had PTS scores of 3 in 2016–2017 after their
democracy performance worsened. This testifies to their governments' failure to
manage criminal behavior (gangs, narcotics trafficking) rooted in social pathologies (extreme poverty, gang members deported from the United States, homeless
children in urban areas). Moreover, police have often responded heavy-handedly
to crime and problems—or failed to respond at all in many areas.

These dry statistics have real meaning for Central Americans. The repression
and violence index represents political murders and rights abuses by government, and the democracy scores reflect freedom to exercise rights and liberties
that once improved but have begun to wane. Lower violence scores have meant
fewer people murdered and repressed, although many flaws remain in these
performances. Even Costa Rica could do better on violence levels (Figure 2.2).

The other four nations have considerable room to improve and some have regressed on both democratic performance and citizen security since 2001. But regime change even to civilian transitional rule or semi-democracy left the glass of political freedom at least partly filled, if not to the brim. The glass may of course empty again, as the Honduran coup of 2009 and the turmoil in Nicaragua in 2018 vividly demonstrated.

Since the 1970s, Central American polities have changed dramatically: rapid, inequitable economic development drove mass mobilization and protest that shattered several seemingly stable, US-backed authoritarian regimes. These authoritarian breakdowns occurred variously through military-led transformation, violent insurrection, and revolutionary transition. From such disparate processes, however, a new and coherent pattern emerged in the late 1980s and 1990s—all of Central America's governments became civilian electoral democracies. That change improved the security and freedoms of citizens of four of the region's five countries, opportunities for further progress notwithstanding. Democratic regimes can also deteriorate into non-democratic regimes and lose ground on the security of their citizens, as Honduras and Nicaragua demonstrate. Chapters 4 through 8 discuss these changes in detail by country.

NOTES

1. Latin American and Caribbean GDP per capita in constant 2010 US dollars for 2017 drawn from the World Bank Group, https://data.worldbank.org/indicator/, accessed February 10, 2019.

2. Ibid., authors' estimates.

3. The AmericasBarometer by the Latin American Public Opinion Project (LAPOP), www.LapopSurveys.org, authors' analysis, 2014 data. Survey respondents defined their own ethnic-racial identities.

4. The Economist Intelligence Unit, *Food Security in Focus, Central and South America 2014* (London, 2014), www.foodinsecurityindex.eiu.com, accessed March 24, 2016; Food and Agricultural Organization of the United Nations, *The State of Food Insecurity in the World: Meeting the 2015 International Hunger Targets: Taking Stock of Uneven Progress* (Rome: Food and Agricultural Organization of the United Nations, 2015), www.fao.org/3/a-i4646e.pdf, accessed March 24, 2016.

5. Authors' calculations from Table 1.1 2016 population estimates and growth rates from Central Intelligence Agency's *World Factbook*, www.cia.gov/library/publications/resources/the-world-factbook/, accessed March 25, 2019; contraception use estimate is the authors' based on World Bank Group, Indicators, accessed September 7, 2019, https://data.worldbank.org/indicator/SP.DYN.CONM.ZS?locations=NI-GT-HN-SV

6. Median-age data drawn from CIA *World Factbook*, see note 5.

7. Regional estimate is the authors' based on World Bank Group, Indicators, accessed September 7, 2019, https://data.worldbank.org/indicator/SP.ADO. TFRT?locations=HN-CR-1W-US.

8. Wallace W. Atwood and Helen Goss Thomas, *The Americas* (Boston, MA: Ginn and Co., 1929), p. 45.

9. Author's calculations, from Robert C. Feenstra, Robert Inklaar, and Marcel P. Timmer, "The Next Generation of the Penn World Table," *American Economic Review* 105, No. 10 (2015), pp. 3150–3182, accessed April 15, 2019, www.rug.nl/ggdc/productivity/pwt/.

10. For an overview see Ronald H. Chilcote and Joel C. Edelstein, *Latin America: Capitalist and Socialist Perspectives of Development and Underdevelopment* (Boulder, CO: Westview Press, 1986).

11. William I. Robinson, *Transitional Conflicts: Central America, Social Change, and Globalization* (London: Verso, 2003), pp. 50–53.

12. The political regimes concept draws upon Charles W. Anderson, "The Latin American Political System," in Charles W. Anderson, *Politics and Economic Change in Latin America: The Governing of Restless Nations* (New York: Van Nostrand Reinhold, 1967); John Higley and Michael Burton, "The Elite Variable in Democratic Transitions and Breakdowns," *American Sociological Review* 54, No. 1 (1989), pp. 17–32; and Gary Wynia's *Politics of Latin American Development* (Cambridge: Cambridge University Press, 1990), pp. 24–45.

13. Peter H. Smith, *Democracy in Latin America: Political Change in Comparative Perspective* (Oxford: Oxford University Press, 2005), pp. 10–11.

14. Any such categorization of regimes is somewhat arbitrary, but we attempt it here to illustrate the extent and frequency of regime changes in Central America. The authors discussed and to some extent disagreed about labeling the regime types and dates of change, especially for Nicaragua, without straying from the regime change criterion (new rules and new coalition) laid out above.

15. Smith, *Democracy in Latin America*, p. 11.

16. Barrington Moore, *Social Origins of Dictatorship and Democracy* (Boston, MA: Beacon Press, 1966).

17. Guillermo O'Donnell, *Modernization and Bureaucratic Authoritarianism: Studies in South American Politics* (Berkeley and Los Angeles: University of California Press, 1973).

18. Guillermo O'Donnell, Philippe C. Schmitter, and Laurence Whitehead, eds., *Transitions from Authoritarian Rule* (Baltimore, MD: Johns Hopkins University Press, 1986).

19. Mark J. Gasiorowski, "Economic Crisis and Regime Change: An Event History Analysis," *American Political Science Review* 89 (1995), pp. 882–897; Mark

J. Gasiorowski, "An Overview of the Political Regime Dataset," *Comparative Political Studies* 21 (1996), pp. 469–483.

20. Dietrich Rueschemeyer, Evelyne Huber Stephens, and John D. Stephens, *Capitalist Development and Democracy* (Chicago, IL: University of Chicago Press, 1992).

21. Carles Boix, *Democracy and Redistribution* (Cambridge: Cambridge University Press, 2003).

22. Charles W. Anderson, "Toward a Theory of Latin American Politics," in Howard J. Wiarda, ed., *Politics and Social Change in Latin America: Still a Distinct Tradition?* (Boulder, CO: Westview Press, 1992), pp. 239–254.

23. See John Peeler, *Latin American Democracies* (Chapel Hill, NC: University of North Carolina Press, 1985); Deborah J. Yashar, *Demanding Democracy: Reform and Reaction in Costa Rica and Guatemala, 1870s–1950s* (Stanford, CA: Stanford University Press, 1997); John A. Booth, *Costa Rica: Quest for Democracy* (Boulder, CO: Westview Press, 1998); Iván Molina Jiménez, *Demoperfectocracia: La democracia pre-reformada en Costa Rica (1885–1948)* (Heredia, Costa Rica: Editorial Universidad Nacional, 2005), Ch. 8–10; and John A. Booth, "Democratic Development in Costa Rica," *Democratization* 15, No. 4 (August 2008), pp. 714–732.

24. John A. Booth and Thomas W. Walker, *Understanding Central America*, 2nd ed. (Boulder, CO: Westview Press, 1993), Ch. 5. For an excellent integrated overview of why and how revolutions occur, see T. David Mason, *Caught in the Crossfire: Revolutions, Repression, and the Rational Peasant* (Lanham, MD: Rowman & Littlefield, 2004).

25. Louis Kriesberg, *Social Conflicts*, 2nd ed. (Englewood Cliffs, NJ: Prentice-Hall, 1982), p. 29.

26. John Walton, *Reluctant Rebels: Comparative Studies in Revolution and Underdevelopment* (New York: Columbia University Press, 1984), p. 13.

27. Ibid. See also Theda Skocpol, *States and Social Revolutions* (Cambridge: Cambridge University Press, 1979); Mancur Olson, "Rapid Growth as a Destabilizing Force," *Journal of Economic History* 23, No. 4 (1963), pp. 529–552; and Jeffrey M. Paige, *Agrarian Revolution: Social Movements and Export Agriculture in the Underdeveloped World* (New York: Free Press, 1975). For specific applications to Central America, see Charles Brockett, *Land, Power, and Poverty: Agrarian Transformation and Political Conflict in Central America* (Boston, MA: Unwin Hyman, 1988); Timothy P. Wickham-Crowley, *Guerrillas and Revolution in Latin America* (Princeton, NJ: Princeton University Press, 1992); Robert Williams, *Export Agriculture and the Crisis in Central America* (Chapel Hill, NC: University of North Carolina Press, 1986); John A. Booth, "Socioeconomic and Political Roots of National Revolts in Central America," *Latin American Research Review* 26, No. 1 (1991), pp. 33–73; Edelberto Torres Rivas, *Crisis del poder in Centroamérica* (San José, Costa Rica: Editorial Universitaria Centroamericana, 1981); and Mason, *Caught in the Crossfire*.

28. Kriesberg, *Social Conflicts*, pp. 66–106; Charles Tilly, *From Mobilization to Revolution* (Reading, MA: Addison-Wesley, 1978); Rod Aya, "Theories of Revolution Reconsidered: Contrasting Models of Collective Violence," *Theory and Society* 8 (June–December 1979), pp. 39–100; Mason, *Caught in the Crossfire*.

29. Jack A. Goldstone, "An Analytical Framework," in Jack A. Goldstone, Ted Robert Gurr, and Farrokh Moshiri, eds., *Revolutions of the Late Twentieth Century* (Boulder, CO: Westview Press, 1991), pp. 37–51; Ted Robert Gurr, *Why Men Rebel* (Princeton, NJ: Princeton University Press, 1970); Walton, *Reluctant Rebels*; Skocpol, *States and Social Revolutions*.

30. Goldstone, "An Analytical Framework"; James DeFronzo, *Revolutions and Revolutionary Movements* (Boulder, CO: Westview Press, 1991), pp. 7–25; Robinson, *Promoting Polyarchy* and *Transitional Conflicts*.

31. Timothy P. Wickham-Crowley, *Guerrillas and Revolution*.

32. Several entities grade democracies on such standards, including Freedom House, the Polity IV Project, and the Economist Intelligence Unit.

33. Robinson, *Promoting Polyarchy and Transitional Conflicts*. Robinson's interpretation is similar to Boix's but examines the added dimension of international capital's influence on domestic economic elites.

34. Ronald Inglehart, "The Renaissance of Political Culture," *American Political Science Review* 82 (November 1988), pp. 1203–1230; Mitchell A. Seligson and John A. Booth, "Political Culture and Regime Type: Evidence from Nicaragua and Costa Rica," *Journal of Politics* 55 (August 1993), pp. 777–792; Edward N. Muller and Mitchell A. Seligson, "Civic Culture and Democracy: The Question of Causal Relationships," *American Political Science Review* 88 (September 1994), pp. 645–652; Larry Diamond, "Introduction: Political Culture and Democracy," and "Causes and Effects," both in Larry Diamond, ed., *Political Culture and Democracy in Developing Countries* (Boulder, CO: Lynne Rienner Publishers, 1994).

35. Dankwart Rustow, "Transitions to Democracy: Toward a Dynamic Model," *Comparative Politics* 2 (April 1970), pp. 337–363; Adam Przeworski, "Some Problems in the Study of the Transition to Democracy," in O'Donnell, Schmitter, and Laurence Whitehead, eds., *Transitions from Authoritarian Rule* (Baltimore, MD: Johns Hopkins University Press, 1986); Samuel P. Huntington, *The Third Wave: Democratization in the Late Twentieth Century* (Norman: University of Oklahoma Press, 1991); Mitchell A. Seligson and John A. Booth, eds., *Elections and Democracy in Central America, Revisited* (Chapel Hill, NC: University of North Carolina Press, 1995).

36. Seymour Martin Lipset, "Social Requisites of Democracy: Economic Development and Political Legitimacy," *American Political Science Review* 53 (March 1959), pp. 69–105; Tatu Vanhanen, *The Process of Democratization* (New York: Crane Russak, 1990); Rueschemeyer et al., *Capitalist Development and Democracy*; Robert D. Putnam, "Bowling Alone: America's Declining Social Capital," *Journal of Democracy*

7 (Summer 1996), pp. 38–52; Boix, *Democracy and Redistribution*; and Robert D. Putnam, *Making Democracy Work: Civic Traditions in Modern Italy* (Princeton, NJ: Princeton University Press, 1993).

37. Laurence Whitehead, "The Imposition of Democracy," in Abraham F. Lowenthal, ed., *Exporting Democracy: The United States and Latin America* (Baltimore, MD: Johns Hopkins University Press, 1991).

38. Peeler, *Latin American Democracies*; Larry Diamond, "Introduction: Politics, Society, and Democracy in Latin America," in Larry Diamond, Juan Linz, and Seymour Martin Lipset, *Democracy in Developing Countries, Volume 4: Latin America* (Boulder, CO: Lynne Rienner Publishers, 1989); John Higley and Richard Gunther, eds., *Elites and Democratic Consolidation in Latin America and Southern Europe* (Cambridge: Cambridge University Press, 1992); and Huntington, *The Third Wave*.

39. For example, Lowenthal, ed., *Exporting Democracy*; Thomas Carothers, *In the Name of Democracy: US Policy Toward Latin America in the Reagan Years* (Berkeley, CA: University of California Press, 1991); Huntington, *The Third Wave*; Dario Moreno, "Respectable Intervention: The United States and Central American Elections," in Seligson and Booth, eds., *Elections and Democracy in Central America, Revisited*; Thomas W. Walker, "Introduction: Historical Setting and Important Issues," in Thomas W. Walker, ed., *Nicaragua Without Illusions: Regime Transition and Structural Adjustment in the 1990s* (Wilmington, DE: Scholarly Resources, 1997); Gary Prevost and Harry E. Vanden, eds, *The Undermining of the Sandinista Revolution* (New York: St. Martin's, 1997); Wickham-Crowley, *Guerrillas and Revolution*; and DeFronzo, *Revolutions and Revolutionary Movements*.

40. Seven training manuals used between 1982 and 1991 were disclosed by the Department of Defense. See US Department of Defense, "Fact Sheet Concerning Training Manuals Containing Materials Inconsistent with US Policy" (Washington, DC: September 1996). See also Dana Priest, "US Instructed Latins on Execution, Torture: Manuals Used 1982–1991, Pentagon Reveals," *Washington Post*, September 21, 1996, pp. A1, A9; Lisa Haugaard, "How the US Trained Latin America's Military: The Smoking Gun," *Envio* 16, No. 165 (October 1997), pp. 33–38.

41. Quoting US State Department official who appeared with coauthor Walker on a panel on Central America at California State University, Los Angeles, on April 20, 1979.

42. The Contra war and conflict with the United States continued during the first three years of the new civilian democratic regime and three remaining years of Daniel Ortega's first presidential term, somewhat obscuring the importance of these changes. The 1987 Central American Peace Accord eventually facilitated a negotiated end to the war. In the 1990 election Nicaragua's voters, disillusioned by a collapsing economy and the Contra war, replaced the FSLN administration with the opposition.

43. *Trade and Investments between Central America and China*, Instituto Centroamericano de Administración de Empresas—Centro Latinoamericano para la Competitividad y el Desarrollo Sostenible—CLACDS, no place of publication, August 2014.

44. The measure in Figure 2.1 combines both parts of the Freedom House 1-to-7 scale (1 = high levels, 7 = low levels of rights and liberties) into a single scale and reverses its polarity. It also takes the 21-point Polity IV scale (-10 = most authoritarian, 10 = most democratic). Each is standardized into a scale ranging from 0 (least democratic) to 10 (most democratic) and the two are averaged to provide the measure used here. These indexes provide useful comparative measures, but must be viewed with some caution because they reflect the biases and fluctuating intensity of coverage of the media from which they are drawn, and their manipulation by US foreign policymakers. Such bias appears in 1980s Freedom House scores assigned relatively rights-respectful ("enemy") Nicaragua, which were practically as poor as those for massively rights-abusive ("friends") El Salvador and Guatemala in the same period. That said, the scores illuminate change within individual countries and thus help us draw valid inferences.

RECOMMENDED READINGS AND RESOURCES

Anderson, Charles W. 1967. *Politics and Economic Change in Latin America: The Governing of Restless Nations*. New York: Van Nostrand Reinhold.

Booth, John A. 1998. *Costa Rica: Quest for Democracy*. Boulder, CO: Westview Press.

Chilcote, Ronald H. and Joel C. Edelstein. 1986. *Latin America: Capitalist and Socialist Perspectives of Development and Underdevelopment*. Boulder, CO: Westview Press.

Ferranti, David E. 2004. *Inequality in Latin America and the Caribbean: Breaking with History?* Washington, DC: International Bank for Reconstruction and Development/The World Bank.

Freedom House, *Democracy in Retreat: Freedom in the World 2019*. https://freedomhouse.org/report/freedom-world/freedom-world–2019.

Gasiorowski, Mark J. 1995. "Economic Crisis and Regime Change: An Event History Analysis." *American Political Science Review* 89: 882–897.

Haerpfer, Christian W., Patrick Bernhagen, Ronald F. Inglehart, and Christian Welzel. 2009. *Democratization*. Oxford: Oxford University Press.

Haynes, Jeffrey, ed., *Routledge Handbook of Democratization*. New York: Routledge, 2012.

Higley, John and Michael Burton. 1989. "The Elite Variable in Democratic Transitions and Breakdowns." *American Sociological Review* 54 (1): 17–32.

Linz, Juan J. and Alfred Stepan. 1978. *The Breakdown of Democratic Regimes*. Baltimore, MD: Johns Hopkins University Press.

Mason, T. David. 2004. *Caught in the Crossfire: Revolutions, Repression, and the Rational Peasant*. Lanham, MD: Rowman & Littlefield.

Moore, Barrington. 1966. *Social Origins of Dictatorship and Democracy*. Boston, MA: Beacon Press.

O'Donnell, Guillermo. 1973. *Modernization and Bureaucratic Authoritarianism: Studies in South American Politics*. Los Angeles: University of California Press.

O'Donnell, Guillermo, Philippe C. Schmitter, and Laurence Whitehead. 1986. *Transitions from Authoritarian Rule*. Baltimore, MD: Johns Hopkins University Press.

Peeler, John. 1985. *Latin American Democracies*. Chapel Hill, NC: University of North Carolina Press.

Robinson, William I. 1996. *Promoting Polyarchy: Globalization, US Intervention, and Hegemony*. Cambridge: Cambridge University Press.

Robinson, William I. 2003. *Transnational Conflicts: Central America, Social Change and Globalization*. London: Verso.

Sánchez-Ancochea, Diego, and Salvdor Martí i Puig, eds., *Handbook of Central American Governance*. New York: Routledge, 2014.

Yashar, Deborah J. 1997. *Demanding Democracy: Reform and Reaction in Costa Rica and Guatemala, 1870s–1950s*. Stanford, CA: Stanford University Press.

3

THE COMMON HISTORY

ONE TRUTH ABOUT CENTRAL AMERICA IS THAT WHILE MANY similarities exist among the five countries, there are also significant differences. Both arose largely from the early history of Spanish conquest, colonization, independence, union with Mexico, and 15 years of shared identity as part of the United Provinces of Central America.[1] The global economy and political system have shaped them in similar ways.

PRECONQUEST

The first humans of Mesoamerica originated from ancestors who crossed to North America around 11000 BCE. These hunter-gatherers quickly spread south as far as remote South America, establishing myriad diverse populations eventually encountered by European explorers/conquerors after AD 1500. In what is now modern Central America and southern Mexico, these paleo-indigenous groups diverged into hundreds of cultural and language groupings. By 5000 BCE some had become sedentary and developed agriculture in temperate areas. By 1500 BCE tribal structures began evolving into what became complex civilizations. Over the next three millennia these cultures developed mathematics, astronomy and calendarization, writing, hydrological and architectural engineering, urbanization, and complex religious and political organization. These complex cultures allowed population growth that likely peaked in the region at tens of millions of individuals prior to European contact.

At the northern end of Mesoamerica first came the Olmecs (1200–400 BCE), followed by the Teotihuacans, then diverse Mayan city states which went into decline after AD 900, and the Aztecs (AD 1300–1521). At the southern end of the region, early hunter-gathers evolved into sedentary farmers, but did not develop complex urban societies. Their political culture developed from tribal structures into larger chiefdoms prior to European contact. From north to south (modern Mexico/Guatemala/Honduras to Costa Rica, respectively) great cultural and linguistic diversity developed, but trading systems and cultural diffusion linked these distinct communities.

CONQUEST TO 1838

Spanish conquest profoundly affected the present-day Central America. Spain took the territories that are today Nicaragua, Honduras, El Salvador, and Guatemala over two decades following the first Spanish penetration in 1522. It imposed its rule upon those indigenous peoples who survived the tremendous depopulation of the region by ecological disruption, enslavement, and exposure to European diseases. Costa Rica's experience soon set it apart from the other countries. Spaniards did not settle there until the 1560s because, unlike the other areas, it offered no easily exploitable resources in either gold or natives, who resisted European encroachment. Ultimately the Spanish neither pacified nor conquered Costa Rica's original inhabitants, but either exterminated them or pushed them into remote areas. Thus the population of the Central Valley of Costa Rica became heavily Iberian and a racially distinct, exploited underclass never developed there. New elements slowly increased Costa Rica's population diversity.[2]

In the rest of Central America, however, Spaniards imposed their dominion despite active and passive native resistance. Although this annihilated many, some of the original millions survived in the four northernmost countries of Central America. By coopting and controlling native *caciques* (chiefs), the Spanish adeptly extracted local riches in the form of gold and native slaves. In addition, the conquistadores unwittingly brought several diseases to which Old World populations had become partially immune or resistant. Lacking natural immunity, the native people perished in large numbers.

In western Nicaragua alone, a population of over one million soon declined to a few tens of thousands. It is unlikely that the Spaniards killed very many Nicaraguan natives outright. Records indicate that the Spanish exported as many as half a million indigenous enslaved Nicaraguans to Panama and Peru. Most died either in passage or in slavery within a year or two. Much of the rest of the populace succumbed to disease.[3] Only in Guatemala did large numbers of indigenous survive, perhaps partly because the conquistadores found it harder to completely subjugate the relatively more advanced societies they encountered there. Perhaps, too, the cooler climates of the mountainous parts of Guatemala presented a less congenial environment for the spread of disease.

The population collapse was only one change wrought by the Spanish. Prior to the conquest, labor-intensive agriculture predominated. People grew corn, beans, peppers, and squash on land consigned to them by their caciques. Although obliged to provide part of the crop to the chief as tribute, the rest they controlled for home consumption, barter, or sale in local markets. By the end of the conquest, depopulation had converted most of the indigenous farmlands back to jungle. The economy then became externally oriented as Spaniards seized human and natural resources to produce articles for trade among the colonies and with Spain. The remaining indigenous population (still outnumbering white colonists) supplied the forced labor that produced the gold, silver, timber, and cattle products (hides, tallow, and dried beef) for export. Most of the wealth produced went to the white elite. The culture and process of dependent underdevelopment had begun.

Social culture changed quickly as the conquistadores sought to impose their religion, language, and ways on the conquered. Of course, nowhere was native culture *completely* obliterated. In Guatemala, hispanicization was least effective. Indigenous peoples retained their languages (over 20 survive today) and hid many aspects of their religions under a patina of Catholicism. Even in El Salvador, Honduras, Nicaragua, and Costa Rica, where the native populations were the most decimated, some indigenous traits remained. For instance, to this day corn and beans (native staples) constitute the heart of local cuisines everywhere. Many indigenous place names remain, as do the names of hundreds of common objects, from peppers and turkeys to grindstones. Yet, by and large, Central America was hispanicized. Spanish became the lingua franca except in rural Guatemala and certain remote regions elsewhere. A mystical, elite-supporting, pre-Reformation version of Catholicism became the nearly universal religion. Cities, often built on or next to the sites of pre-Columbian centers, eventually took on Spanish characteristics, with the typical Iberian arrangement of plazas, cathedrals, and public buildings.

The conquest established new class patterns. The larger pre-Columbian societies of Central America were ordered hierarchically, with priestly elites or chiefs dominating the masses. That likely facilitated the Spaniards superimposing themselves on the system. But what changed most after the conquest was a new racial configuration of class. With the exception of Costa Rica, there emerged a highly unequal, two-class society, with people of Spanish birth or descent constituting the ruling upper class and everyone else a downtrodden lower class. Within the lower class, there evolved a subsystem of stratification as the biological union between Spaniards and native women produced mestizos, who, though never considered equals by the Spaniards, held higher status than persons of pure indigenous origin or enslaved Africans.

From the late sixteenth century to 1821, the Viceroyalty of New Spain (Mexico) nominally ruled over the Kingdom of Guatemala, which included the territory of today's five modern countries of Central America (plus Chiapas in present-day Mexico). In fact, the viceroyalty exercised little control over the kingdom, which in practice was administered directly by Spain. In turn, the nominal capital, Guatemala, only loosely controlled the other isthmian provinces. Underpopulated, geographically isolated, and economically insignificant, the tiny Costa Rican colony became a neglected backwater and began its distinctive evolution. Elsewhere, resentment grew between the provinces and the central administration in Guatemala as the newly emerging system of dependency inevitably brought the greatest development there. Within individual provinces regional differences and rivalries developed and festered. Despite much common experience, seeds of division germinated among Central Americans.

Other economic and social patterns that emerged during the conquest persisted into the colonial era. Costa Rica's relative isolation led to a more self-contained economy. A persistent labor shortage, relatively equal land distribution, access to unclaimed crown lands for poor farmers, and the lack of an easily exploitable indigenous population produced a large class of free farmers unused to subjugation by leading families. Though such factors can be overvalued, they likely set Costa Rica on its distinctive developmental path toward democracy by the mid-twentieth century—decades before its neighbors.

Elsewhere, in contrast, an externally oriented, elite-controlled, dependent pattern of economic activity became more entrenched. The Spanish first exploited the region's human and material resources to produce and export cacao, silver, gold, timber, and cattle. Later, export production expanded to include indigo and cochineal for blue and red dyes coveted by a growing European textile industry. As in present-day Central America, fluctuating external demand produced booms and busts in the local dependent economies. New groups joined the population. Producers imported enslaved Africans to replace some of the labor supply lost with the decimated indigenous population, which further diversified racial, ethnic, and cultural milieus.

The social and economic gap between the European and criollo elite and the non-European majority remained wide.[4] Spaniards occupied the top of the social hierarchy and controlled colonial government and the Catholic Church. Many enriched themselves as land grantees. Criollos, descendants of Spaniards born in the colonies, held directly gifted (crown land grants) or inherited wealth and social standing but limited political power. The top two groups enforced an unequal and coercive economic system on other social groups with military force. Lowest in the status system and with the fewest rights and worst conditions resided enslaved Afro-origin people who were effectively chattel. Central America's criollo economic elites imported enslaved Africans by the many thousands to replace the rapidly shrinking indigenous population. After the genocides wrought by conquest, geographic dislocations, and imported diseases, the remaining indigenous—many confined to reserves—were not enslaved but many were bound to tribute payments (taxes or as uncompensated labor). In the middle of the status hierarchy were rapidly growing mixed-race populations (mestizos, "Ladinos" in Guatemala, originating from unions of Spanish and indigenous and sometimes blacks). Mestizos usually spoke Spanish and worked as free peasants or artisans, but were predominantly poor. With the premium placed on export and maximizing profits for the elites, mestizo, indigenous, and enslaved persons consumed at or near a subsistence level, while Spanish bureaucrats, clergy, and criollos absorbed the surpluses generated by the haciendas, slavery, taxes, and tributes.

This system functioned with considerable continuity for three centuries, although Spaniards exited the system with independence, leaving the squabbling but wealthy criollo elites in charge of very weak states. Slavery was legally abolished soon after independence. Those freed became another poor population whose numbers increased with the arrival of Afro-origin, Anglophone contract workers and formerly enslaved peoples shipwrecked on the Caribbean coasts. Mestizos eventually grew into a majority everywhere but Guatemala. They evolved occupationally and economically into a diverse peasantry, urban artisans and laborers, and merchants. The four republics of northern Central America to this day manifest wide social and economic disparities generated by centuries of control by socially irresponsible economic elites.

Central America passed from colonial rule to independence with little violence. When Mexico broke from Spain in mid-1821, Central America also

declared its independence. In January 1822, it joined the Mexican empire of
Agustín de Iturbide. El Salvador resisted union with Mexico but was incorporated by force. However, by mid-1823, soon after Iturbide's abdication,
Central America declared independence from Mexico. Only Chiapas chose
to remain a part of the larger country to the north. From then until 1838,
the isthmus was fused—legally, at least—into a federation called the United
Provinces of Central America, or the Central American Republic.

At first Central Americans believed this union made good sense. Clearly,
a federated republic could be stronger politically and economically than five
tiny independent nations. Yet from the start, several factors undermined the
United Provinces. First was the outlying provinces' resentment of Guatemala.
As the largest province, Guatemala received 18 of the 41 seats in the congress
(by proportional representation) and therefore dominated policymaking. Second, although the constitution of 1824 declared the states to be "free and
independent" in their internal affairs, it also contained nationalist and centrist
features that undermined the provinces' autonomy. Finally, rivalries developed
between emerging Liberal and Conservative factions of the ruling elites that
generated conflict within and across provincial boundaries. Meddling in their
neighbors' affairs became common among Central American leaders. These
problems provoked constant tension and recurrent civil war. The experiment
finally collapsed in 1838. Despite reunification efforts later in the nineteenth
century, the bitter rivalries that destroyed the United Provinces blocked its
resurrection.

1838 TO THE PRESENT

Continuing hardship for most of the region's people has prevailed since the
disintegration of the federation. The patterns of dependency and elite rule
that took firm root in each of the republics except Costa Rica during the colonial period continued through the nineteenth century and into the twentieth
century. Costa Rica, too, eventually developed debilitating external economic
dependencies as it integrated into the world economy in the nineteenth century. Overall, despite bringing occasional surges of development, dependency
and elite rule seldom benefited the majority of Central Americans.

After independence, Central America's tiny, privileged elites—heirs to
economic power and social standing—continued using their control of government to repress popular demands. They perpetuated for their own benefit an essentially unregulated, externally oriented, "liberal" economic system.
Except in Costa Rica, ongoing Liberal–Conservative factionalism, relatively

large indigenous communities for forced labor, and the emergent hacienda system strengthened the military's political role. Armies (at first belonging to individual caudillos) fought civil wars, subdued peasants forcibly deprived of their land, and implemented forced labor laws against these new "vagrants." Heavy military involvement in national life retarded the civil political institutions and spawned both military rule and political violence. Central American nations spent most of the period from 1838 until 1945 under civilian or military dictatorships. Even Costa Rica showed little democratic promise. Although less turbulent than its neighbors, it experienced elite rule, militarism, dictatorship, and political instability into the mid-twentieth century.

Politics

In the nineteenth century, basic intra-elite conflict occurred between Conservatives and Liberals. Before independence and for decades afterward, Conservatives advocated authoritarian, centralized government (sometimes even monarchy), greater economic regulation, and special privileges for the Catholic Church. Liberals espoused limited representative democracy, decentralized government, free trade, reduced economic regulation, and Church–state separation. Conservatives tended to come from large-scale landholders who had benefited from crown licenses and export monopolies. Liberals tended to include disgruntled large landowners who lacked crown export licenses and urban commercial elites.

Conservatives generally remained wedded to more traditional economic practices, but Liberals—who by the late nineteenth century had come to dominate all five countries—advocated "modernization" within an externally oriented, laissez-faire economic framework. Specifically, Liberals championed new export products—such as coffee and bananas—and new government institutions and material infrastructure (highways, railroads, and ports) to facilitate growth in exports. Liberals sought to reduce the role of the Catholic Church in some countries. To promote exports, they enacted legislation stripping most indigenous communities of lands once reserved for them by the Spanish crown. Despite such early contrasts and after considerable warfare between them, by the late nineteenth century Liberal–Conservative ideology and policy differences largely vanished. In power, Liberals ruled as authoritarians and eventually accommodated the Church, thus eliminating a longstanding argument. Conservatives eventually supported laissez-faire economics and expanded coffee production.

The Liberal and Conservative movements eventually degenerated into ideologically indistinguishable clan-based political factions. Conservatives generally ruled in the mid-nineteenth century but Liberal regimes eventually supplanted them. Liberal hegemony in Central America thereafter lasted well into the twentieth century. As it died, it spawned an extreme right-wing form of militarism that plagued Guatemala, El Salvador, and Honduras until the 1990s. One should not confuse the Central American meaning of "Liberal" with the vernacular meaning of that word in the United States. Central American Liberals were exponents of classical Liberal economic policies (capitalism) and republican government. They held elitist attitudes, advocated essentially unregulated free enterprise, and generally believed that the "government is best which governs least." Indeed, in today's US political system, modern conservatives would likely sympathize with the economic policies of nineteenth-century Central American Liberals (possibly excepting President Trump's advocacy of tariffs). The modernization liberalism brought accelerated concentration of wealth and income among elites and increased the external economic dependency.

Central American liberalism eventually drew fire from more popularly oriented political movements motivated by the Great Depression and World War II's economic dislocations. In Costa Rica, challenges to Liberal dominance and political reforms began in the late nineteenth century; a labor movement developed early in the twentieth. In the mid-1940s, the government of Rafael Calderón Guardia allied with Communist-dominated labor unions and the Catholic Church to enact labor and social security legislation. In 1948 and 1949, a social-democratic revolution broke with the unions, yet retained Calderón's reforms, abolished the army, and gave the state regulatory and planning roles. In El Salvador during the 1930s, Liberals responded to depression-driven labor and peasant discontent by ruling through the military. An abortive labor and leftist uprising in 1932 prompted the army and landowners to massacre 30,000 peasants. The military controlled the presidency for the next five decades, and by the 1970s sometimes acted independently on economic policy and ignored the wishes of its former Liberal masters.

In Guatemala in 1944, social democrats overthrew a "modernizing" dictator, Jorge Ubico, and began a mild democratic revolution that accommodated indigenous groups and organized labor. A successful US Central Intelligence Agency (CIA)-sponsored counterrevolution took place in 1954. Soon the military took power and ruled the country into the 1980s. In Nicaragua, US armed intervention favored Conservatives between 1909 and 1927. The United States then switched sides and helped reinstate Liberal Party rule, which in turn created the Somoza family dictatorship. The Somozas ruled Nicaragua from 1936 until 1979, when a mass-based insurrection brought to power the social-revolutionary Sandinista National Liberation Front (Frente Sandinista de Liberación Nacional, FSLN). Many Nicaraguan Liberals exiled themselves in the United States and waited for the revolution to end in 1990 before returning to national politics. The 16-year interlude between the FSLN's exit from the presidency and its return saw the Liberal movement's leaders squabble and bargain so inefficaciously with Daniel Ortega that they lost their power to compete. Upon returning to power, Ortega steadily concentrated power and changed rules, and thus ended Nicaragua's too brief period of democracy.

In Honduras, Liberals (the Honduran Liberal Party, PLH) and Conservatives (the National Party, PN) traded the presidency under the watchful eye of the military from the 1980s into the 1990s. It was only in the mid-1990s that Honduras' civilian leaders came to effective power. But after only three presidential terms Liberal Party infighting contributed to the coup that not only ended democracy but shattered the PLH itself. Under the PN's subsequent control, manipulation of courts, police corruption, election manipulation, brutal repression, and Washington looking away, Honduras also became an autocratic regime.

Interestingly, the "neoliberalism" that would come to dominate the region in the late twentieth and early twenty-first centuries would, in many ways, recall the crude Liberalism prevalent at the turn of and into the twentieth century. Like its forerunner, neoliberalism promoted free trade, largely unregulated capitalism, and government limited mainly to "housekeeping" activities and trade promotion. And, like nineteenth-century Liberalism, it tended to accentuate inequitable distribution of income and property even as it achieved sometimes impressive economic growth.

Burgeoning crime and corruption have become as important as neoliberalism to the region's economic systems and politics. Drug traffickers have staggering amounts of funds to use to buy the cooperation of police, military, courts, legislators, and presidents across the region. Civilian politicians— democrats and the newly autocratic—have stolen and embezzled astonishing amounts of public funds. The illicit enrichment of the few contributes to inequality and denies citizens services they need. It undermines the legitimacy of government, weakens democratic norms, and increases the likelihood of future instability.

External Involvement

Spain experienced two centuries of competition with northern European powers in the western Caribbean from the early 1600s. Britain especially pursued economic, political, and security interests on the eastern Mesoamerican isthmus. It encouraged piracy against Spanish merchant vessels, logged forests, established trading outposts, and engaged with indigenous peoples resisting Spain. Britain established protectorates with the Miskito indigenous along Nicaragua's eastern coast (1630s–1850s) to keep the Spanish and Nicaraguan governments at bay. It also entrenched itself in eastern Guatemala among Mayans and Garífunas and eventually established the colony of British Honduras in 1862.

International pressures crescendoed after 1850 as the United States entered competition with other powers, partly motivated by California's gold rush. British sway peaked in the mid-nineteenth century; thereafter US influence increasingly supplanted that of Britain. Intensifying foreign intervention exacerbated the Central American nations' penchant for interfering in each others' affairs, caused international disputes within the region, and brought military and political intervention by outsiders. Tennessean William Walker undertook the most flagrant (but not the only) intervention into Nicaragua. Contracted by business partners of Cornelius Vanderbilt to hijack Vanderbilt's transit route across the isthmus, Walker brought mercenaries to Nicaragua in 1855. In league with out-of-power Liberals, his forces toppled the Conservative government. The United States quickly recognized Walker's fledgling Liberal government, which announced his intentions to reinstitute slavery (banned in 1823), make English the official language, and seek US statehood.

Conservative governments in the other four Central American nations reacted by sending troops to oust Walker. War ensued in 1856, with Conservative forces partly financed by the British and by Vanderbilt. Walker capitulated in 1857 and fled Nicaragua under US protection. He soon attempted another filibuster, but Honduras captured and executed him in 1860. This 1856–1857 National War against Walker's takeover of Nicaragua briefly rekindled interest in reunifying Central America, reinforced Conservative political hegemony in Nicaragua for decades, and contributed to anti-US nationalism among Central Americans.[5]

The United States, by 1900 the dominant outside power in the isthmus, energetically promoted its economic and security interests. US diplomats served US banks by peddling loans to the region's governments. US customs agents seized Central American customs houses to repay the loans, and US marines intervened in domestic politics in Honduras, Nicaragua, and Panama. Transit across the narrow isthmus via a ship canal especially motivated Washington. When President Theodore Roosevelt could not win Colombian or Nicaraguan assent to a proposed canal lease, he dispatched US troops in 1903 to ensure that local and foreign insurgents could "liberate" Colombia's province of Panama. This intervention secured for the United States the right to build a canal through what then became the Republic of Panama. When Nicaragua's President José Santos Zelaya contemplated a canal deal with Germany in 1909, the United States fomented a Conservative rebellion against him and landed US troops to back the rebels. Zelaya resigned, and the new government gave the United States a canal-rights treaty that effectively guaranteed that Nicaragua would likely never have a canal. US marines returned to Nicaragua in 1912 and remained there most of the period until 1933.

The United States under Franklin Roosevelt flirted with good neighborliness toward Central America during the 1930s. During World War II, security interests led to heavy US assistance to train and modernize Central America's armies. During the Cold War after 1945, the United States promoted containment of communism by backing anti-Communist regimes. It enlisted other Central American governments to help oust the reformist civilian government of Guatemala in 1954, and again to reinforce the Somoza regime after Managua's catastrophic earthquake of 1972.

The Cuban revolution in 1959 reinforced the US tendency to concentrate upon containment of communism in Central America. US economic and military assistance strengthened the region's armies, pursued counterinsurgency against leftist rebels, promoted regional economic integration and development, and worked to divide organized labor and undermine leftist and centrist political reformers. The Carter administration's novel emphasis on human rights (1977 to 1979) led to aid cut-offs for abusive military governments in Guatemala and El Salvador and to reduced US support for Nicaragua's Somoza regime.

When the FSLN-led popular rebellion toppled Anastasio Somoza Debayle from power in 1979, however, US policy in Central America shifted sharply back toward containment. Washington lifted its military aid ban for El Salvador and deepened its efforts to block the growing rebellion there. The US tactic of allying with military despots was modified under the Reagan and subsequent administrations, which found it useful, in dealing with a reticent Congress, to appear to promote electoral democracy as the best model for the isthmus. US policy had two prongs: it encouraged elections and nominal transition to civilian rule. It also promoted and financed a large counterrevolutionary force to fight Nicaragua's Sandinista government; devoted massive economic, military, and political aid to bolster nominally civilian governments (under military tutelage) in El Salvador and Honduras; and invaded Panama to overthrow its military government in 1989. Even after the Cold War ended in 1989, the Sandinistas lost power, and the Salvadoran and Guatemalan insurgents signed peace accords, the United States retained certain habitual Cold War attitudes in Central America.[6] US officials repeatedly interfered in Central American elections to discourage voting for leftist parties. The practice continued into the 2000s. US democracy promotion began to flag in the aftermath of the massive 2001 terrorist attack on the World Trade Center. Meanwhile, US attention to the region shifted heavily toward curtailing drug transshipment and, later, stemming the flow of immigrants to the US.

Economic and Social Change

Central America has specialized in exporting agricultural commodities since 1838. After 1850 coffee gradually became a major export throughout the region. During the twentieth century, other commodity export production developed (bananas, cacao, cotton, sugar, and beef). Like coffee, each was subject to great world market price swings. Cyclical recessions and depressions in the international economy hit Central America hard. Industrialization was slow, the inequalities in the class systems intensified, and dependency upon imported food and manufactures grew.

Coffee production wrought major socioeconomic changes in the late nineteenth century: It concentrated landownership in the hands of major coffee growers, millers, and exporters, who in several countries constituted new national economic elites who advanced their interests by controlling (or sharing control of) the state.[7] Other export crops had regional importance with similar effects on the distribution of wealth and political power. Agro-export elites eventually enlisted the national armed forces to suppress popular discontent. Together they opposed socioeconomic reform so tenaciously that their rule has been labeled "reactionary despotism."[8] Writing about the 1970s and 1980s, Baloyra described the reactionary coalitions of Central America as:

> bent on the preservation of privilege [and their] monopoly of public roles and of the entrepreneurial function ... The dominant actors of the reactionary coalitions of Central America do not believe in suffrage, do not believe in paying taxes, and do not believe in acting through responsible institutions. Their basic ideological premise is that the government exists to protect them from other social groups in order to continue to accumulate capital without the restraints created by labor unions, competition, and government regulation.[9]

During the 1950s and 1960s Central American investors began extensively cultivating grains for the regional market and cotton for export. Except for

Honduras,[10] each Central American nation by the mid-1970s had reduced its smallholding- and subsistence-agricultural sector (small-scale farmers) and had expanded migrant wage-labor forces. A rural labor surplus developed, urban migration by unemployable campesinos swelled, domestic food production shrank, and land ownership and agricultural production became ever more concentrated. National dependency upon imported foodstuffs rose throughout the region, as did the number of citizens directly affected by imported inflation.

Following the 1959 overthrow of Fulgencio Batista in Cuba,[11] Central American governments despaired of the region's slow growth rates. In 1960 they formed the Central American Common Market (CACM) to spur regional economic integration, foreign investment, intraregional trade, and industrialization. A stated rationale was to diversify and increase production so that wealth might "trickle down" to the poor and undercut the potential appeal of socialism. The CACM's objectives converged in 1961 with those of the US Alliance for Progress, which wished to bolster capitalist development. The Alliance sought to undercut the left by increasing public development aid to Central America and thus encouraging private investment. During the 1960s, to varying degrees in each nation, the CACM and Alliance stimulated considerable domestic and foreign investment in the capital-intensive production of consumer goods, manufactured mainly with imported raw materials and fuel. Gross domestic products (GDP) overall and per capita grew rapidly into the early 1970s because of increasing industrial production, while input prices remained stable.[12]

However, this industrialization failed to absorb the expanding labor supply and in some nations shifted wealth and income away from working-class groups. Industrialization and economic diversification expanded factory and middle-class jobs until the early 1970s, but rural and urban unemployment simultaneously rose throughout the region. The CACM's development model began to exhaust its growth potential in the 1970s. Imported industrial raw materials prices rose 150 percent from 1968 to 1976. Higher costs eroded investment, productivity, output growth, and the competitiveness of regional products.[13] In Nicaragua, El Salvador, and Guatemala, the industrial sector's share of exports declined about 6 percent from the 1970–1974 to the 1975–1979 period. Balance-of-payments pressures afflicted all the Central American economies in the 1970s because of declining terms of trade (the relative costs of imports versus exports), a recession in the world economy, and higher foreign interest rates. According to Weeks, "each government in effect decided to pursue a separate strategy to weather the crisis, rather than a collective one."[14]

By the late 1970s the CACM accord began to erode, and in the 1980s the breakdown became complete.

Socioeconomic change accelerated after World War II (see Tables A.1 and A.2). Population almost doubled between 1960 and 1980 and high growth rates persisted. Expanding commercial agriculture and the increasing land concentration forced peasants off the land, swelling agricultural labor migration and urbanization. Enhanced educational programs increased school attendance, literacy, and participation in higher education throughout the isthmus. Ownership of radio and television receivers spread and broadcasters multiplied. Improved roads and transportation systems developed. With easier and faster communication, public awareness of national problems grew. Economic activity shifted away from agriculture and toward manufacturing and services. Overall economic activity (measured as GDP per capita) increased 156 percent between 1960 and 1980. However, this growth was unevenly distributed internally, and as noted, a sharp recession reduced production region-wide in the late 1970s and the 1980s.

Wrenching economic strains in the 1970s caused cascading political and economic difficulties, as detailed in the country chapters. At the macro-social level, Central American nations tried to borrow their way through recession and political crisis. All multiplied their foreign debt several-fold while their economies eroded. The resulting interest payments undermined economic recovery, increased government dependency on foreign lenders, and eventually forced them to undergo neoliberal structural adjustment programs in the late 1980s and 1990s. By 2000, under neoliberal policies, Costa Rica and El Salvador had found new sources of growth in assembly plant production, non-traditional exports, and tourism so that their economic growth resumed and their foreign debt shrank. During the 1990s, El Salvador and Costa Rica recovered and surpassed their 1980 levels of GDP per capita, and some analysts believed trade liberalization had effectively promoted growth and development in the region.[15] The benefits were uneven, however. Between 1980 and 2010 neither Guatemala, Honduras, nor Nicaragua had experienced real net economic growth. Tragically, Nicaragua's 2010 per capita GDP was only half that of 1970 (see Table A.1) Reeling from a decade of externally financed civil war and economic destabilization, Nicaragua experienced one of the hemisphere's most dramatic economic collapses.

Another great consequence was political turmoil, which exacerbated economic crisis throughout the 1980s by disrupting production and frightening away capital. At the microsocial level, living conditions among rural and urban working-class citizens deteriorated while they witnessed the rapid enrichment of economic elites. This impoverishment and growing inequality stimulated region-wide mobilization of protest, opposition, and demands for economic and political reform. Some governments violently repressed such mobilization, which brought revolution to Nicaragua and civil wars in El Salvador and Guatemala. These combined with deepening economic crisis and escalating foreign intervention to spark multiple regime changes in the region's governments between 1979 and 1996. Only Costa Rica—the region's sole democracy in the 1970s—escaped regime change.

In summary, rapid but inequitable economic growth of the 1960s and 1970s caused economic policies and class conflict that transformed Central America both politically and economically in the 1980s and 1990s. Political change was generally toward electoral democracy and less repression and violence, but economic results varied widely. All countries suffered in the crises of the 1970s and 1980s, and all eventually adopted the neoliberal economic model as their best hope for development. It worked best in Costa Rica, whose economy recovered and began to grow again. But the other four nations either remained stagnant or lost ground in comparison to developed economies.[16]

Between 2000 and 2017 most of Central America experienced real economic growth that somewhat alleviated poverty. Guatemala's performance was the weakest, with only 13 percent GDP per capita growth over 17 years. Already the region's wealthiest country, Costa Rica's GDP per capita grew 57 percent for this period. Nicaragua grew second fastest from 2000 to 2017 (a 54 percent GDP per capita increase). Honduras and El Salvador fell in between the best and worst performers, each registering around 2 percent per year GDP per capita increase.[17] The countries that have sent the most migrants north toward the United States in recent years are also those that have had the least economic growth per capita since 2010—El Salvador, Guatemala, and Honduras. This is not the only source of emigration, of course, but it is an important driver.

Finally, we must mention the contemporary status of women and of the lesbian, gay, bisexual, and transgendered (LGBT) populations of the region. Issues of their rights and safety have entered political discourse in recent decades in the region. Latin America, infamous for its *machismo*, has longstanding cultural norms that assign women inferior social status and legal rights to those of men. Females, gays, and non-cisgendered populations often become targets of discrimination and horrific violence. Movements seeking redress have emerged and made some progress, as later chapters reveal. Legislation has provided women improved legal standing and representation in public office. Some countries have adopted policies to reduce discrimination based on sexual orientation. But resistance to such reform remains strong among influential elites, including both Catholic and evangelical churches and, ironically, criminal enterprises that coerce or traffic women and girls for sex. Laws generally provide little right to reproductive freedom. Public opinion on rights for women and homosexuals vary, but opposition to gay rights predominates.

As we write this in 2019, Central America still has more democracy overall than in the 1970s. However, democracy's breakdown in Nicaragua since 2006 and in Honduras since the 2009 coup d'état, and the eroding democratic performance of Guatemala, reveal weak elite commitment to democratic rules of the game. These changes undermine the hope that democracy had consolidated in the isthmus. Nicaraguans are also still on average poorer than five decades ago, but Costa Rica's peace, stability, and human capital investments have left its citizens better off over the same period. New threats to social stability have also emerged in the last decade. El Salvador, Guatemala, and Honduras struggle with levels of violence among the highest in the world, another force driving emigration toward the United States.

Notes

1. Good histories are Ralph Lee Woodward, Jr., *Central America: A Nation Divided*, 2nd ed. (New York: Oxford University Press, 1985); Hector Pérez Brignoli, *A Brief History of Central America* (Berkeley, CA: University of California Press, 1989); James Dunkerley, *Power in the Isthmus: A Political History of Modern Central America* (London: Verso, 1988); Fabrice LeHoucq, *The Politics of Modern Central America: Civil War, Democratization, and Underdevelopment* (Cambridge: Cambridge University Press, 2012).

2. African slaves were brought in during the colonial era. Anglophone blacks from Jamaica came to the Atlantic coast during the nineteenth century. Meanwhile the annexation of Guanacaste from Nicaragua in 1824 added indigenous Chorotegas and eventually mestizos to the demographic mix.

3. See David Richard Radell, "An Historical Geography of Western Nicaragua: The Spheres of Leon, Granada, and Managua, 1519–1965," Ph.D dissertation (Berkeley, CA: University of California, 1969), pp. 66–80.

4. Criollos (creoles) were of European origin born in the colonies. Descendants of the conquerors and land grantees, many had wealth but no political or administrative power.

5. Karl Bermann, *Under the Big Stick: Nicaragua and the United States since 1848* (Boston, MA: South End Press, 1986).

6. For an inside perspective on US intervention in Nicaragua and El Salvador during the 1980s and 1990s, see Todd Greentree, *Crossroads of Intervention: Insurgency and Counterinsurgency Lessons from Central America* (Westport, CT: Praeger Security International, 2008).

7. Honduras never really developed a landowning aristocracy; economic and political power remained in the hands of regional hacendados and newer urban industrial-commercial-financial entrepreneurs.

8. Enrique A. Baloyra, "Reactionary Despotism in Central America," *Journal of Latin American Studies* 15 (November 1983), pp. 295–319.

9. Ibid., pp. 309–310.

10. In Honduras, agrarian colonization and expanding employment in the modern capitalist sector of agriculture continued to absorb much of the growth of the rural labor force.

11. Victor Bulmer-Thomas, *The Political Economy of Central America since 1920* (Cambridge: Cambridge University Press, 1987), pp. 177–180.

12. See Tables A.1 and A.2 of John A. Booth and Thomas W. Walker, *Understanding Central America*, 3rd ed. (Boulder, CO: Westview Press, 1999).

13. John Weeks, "The Industrial Sector," in Thomas W. Walker, ed., *Nicaragua: The First Five Years* (New York: Praeger, 1985), pp. 281–296; John Weeks, *The Economies of Central America* (New York: Holmes and Meier, 1985), pp. 101–151.

14. Weeks, *The Economies of Central America*, p. 284.

15. Guillermo Perry, Daniel Lederman, and Rodrigo Suescún, "Trade Structure and Policy," in Robert Rennhack and Erik Offerdal, eds., *The Macroeconomy of Central America* (New York: Palgrave-Macmillan, 2004).

16. Ana Corbacho and Hamid R. Davoodi, "Public Expenditure and Governance," in Robert Rennhack and Erik Offerdal, eds., *The Macroeconomy of Central America*. See also Trevor Evans, "The Fruits of Interest: Financial Liberalization and Banking in Central America," in Anders Danielson and A. Geske Dijkstra, eds., *Towards Sustainable Development in Central America and the Caribbean* (New York: Palgrave-Macmillan, 2001).

17. Values are calculated for GDP per capita in 2010 constant dollars, as reported by the World Bank Group, Indicators, https://data.worldbank.org/indicator/NY.GDP.PCAP.KD?locations=CR-SV-GT-HN-NI, accessed April 24, 2019.

RECOMMENDED READINGS AND RESOURCES

Brignoli, Hector Pérez. 1989. *A Brief History of Central America*. Berkeley, CA: University of California Press.

Bulmer-Thomas, Victor. 1987. *The Political Economy of Central America since 1920*. Cambridge: Cambridge University Press.

Danielson, Anders and A. Geske Dijkstra, eds. 2001. *Towards Sustainable Development in Central America and the Caribbean*. New York: Palgrave-Macmillan.

Dunkerley, James. 1988. *Power in the Isthmus: A Political History of Modern Central America*. London: Verso.

Fabrice, LeHoucq. 2012. *The Politics of Modern Central America: Civil War, Democratization, and Underdevelopment*. Cambridge: Cambridge University Press.

Rennhack, Robert and Erik Offerdal, eds. 2004. *The Macroeconomy of Central America*. New York: Palgrave-Macmillan.

Weeks, John. 1985. *The Economies of Central America*. New York: Holmes and Meier.

Woodward, Ralph Lee, Jr. 1985. *Central America: A Nation Divided*, 2nd ed. New York: Oxford University Press.

4

COSTA RICA

A POPULAR T-SHIRT FOR TOURISTS IN COSTA RICA PROCLAIMS
"*¡Costa Rica es diferente!*" (Costa Rica is different). The slogan evokes the country's stable democracy, high levels of social development, and myth of Costa
Rican exceptionalism. Schools, the media, and popular tradition tell Costa
Ricans their country stands apart from the rest of Central America's record of
dictatorship, political violence, and underdevelopment.[1] Costa Rica's is indeed
distinctive, yet in the twenty-first century there is less to the myth than meets
the eye. For most of the nineteenth and twentieth centuries, Costa Rica's economy experienced the same commodity price swings and dependent development as its neighbors. From the 1950s on, however, Costa Rica's governments
managed these economic problems better, easing their impact and masking
underlying similarities to neighbors.

But as the twentieth century ended, Costa Rica's neighbors had also adopted
electoral democracy and improved their human rights performance. Meanwhile in the economic arena, forced like its neighbors to embrace neoliberal
policies, Costa Rica opened up to the world economy and changed domestic
welfare policies. It temporarily retreated from its post-civil war development
strategy that had improved its people's well-being for decades. Some observers
feared neoliberalism would push Costa Rica toward the human development

levels of other Central American nations.[2] But by 2019 Costa Rican exceptionalism had reasserted itself. Economic growth outpaced its neighbors, while deteriorating democratic performance elsewhere (see Figures 2.1 and 2.2) again highlighted the country's distinctiveness.

Costa Rica's evolution through the common contextual forces pressuring the region has thus differentiated it variably over time. This emphasizes that one should pay attention to the similarities in pressures driving change, and to how human agency can produce varying political and economic outcomes.

HISTORICAL BACKGROUND

Costa Rica deviated from certain patterns in the rest of Central America during the colonial period. Isolated from the rest of Central America by long distances and rugged terrain, Costa Rica remained more racially and economically homogeneous than its neighbors. This does not mean that it lacked social disparities or that it remained economically self-contained. Rather, its social inequities never allowed one class or race to wholly dominate others to the detriment of the majority, as elsewhere in the isthmus. Despite embracing export agriculture, Costa Rica never fully developed the dependency system prevalent elsewhere in the isthmus, with its tremendous human costs.

The roots of Costa Rican democracy were planted in the nineteenth century, although true democratic rule would not materialize until the 1950s. From 1824 to 1899, one Costa Rican government in five ended by coup d'état. The military held power 44 percent of the time.[3] Moneyed rural families governed the country. The elections that occurred were indirect, confined to a tiny, literate elite, and often rigged. However, certain economic trends and political reforms prevented a total domination of Costa Rican national politics by a landed oligarchy. The first dictator president, Braulio Carrillo (1835 to 1842), for instance, increased the already fairly large number of small farmers by distributing municipal lands to the inhabitants. He also promoted coffee cultivation and included small-scale farmers, in contrast to elsewhere in Central America. This helped form a class of smallholding yeoman farmers that continuously renewed itself by expanding the agricultural frontiers.

The incipient landed elite continued to rule until it lost control to the military, which greatly expanded after the 1857 Central American war. The military's leader, Liberal dictator Tomás Guardia (1870–1882), took power, confiscating some of the properties of the wealthy and exiling some of their leaders. Guardia contracted foreigners to construct new roads and railways to move coffee to market. A late nineteenth century labor shortage kept rural wages high as coffee production spread. By then market forces in the rapidly growing coffee industry had begun to concentrate land ownership and had pushed many smallholders off the land. In order to secure the labor essential to the nation's wealth, large coffee farmers had to pay decent wages and the government had to pass reformist public policies. Costa Rican peasants and workers therefore generally experienced less exploitation and repression than common elsewhere in Central America.

Despite the militarization of politics during the Guardia dictatorship, precursors of democracy developed in the second half of the nineteenth century. Elections, though indirect, elite-dominated, and often rigged, became important by the 1840s. The growth of commerce, government, transport, immigration, and urban centers swelled the number of people available for political activity. The modernizing Liberals (Guardia and his civilian successors) greatly increased education spending and thus literacy by 1900. Because literacy was a key criterion for voter eligibility, its increase expanded suffrage.[4]

By 1889 an economic slowdown and the Liberals' anti-clericalism generated support for an opposition Catholic Union Party and its presidential candidate José J. Rodríguez. Backed by the Catholic Church, Rodríguez won the vote among the electors, but the army tried to block him from taking office. Incited by the Church, angry citizens took to the streets and forced the army to relent. Often incorrectly cited as the birth of Costa Rican democracy, this election nevertheless forced the military to respect an opposition victory and mobilized ordinary citizens to defend an election. After Rodríguez, however, authoritarian elite rulers and election fraud returned.[5]

From 1905 to 1914, presidents Cleto González Víquez and Ricardo Jiménez Oreamuno further broadened suffrage, established direct popular election of public officials, and permitted free and open opposition campaigns. A military regime led by brothers Federico and José Tinoco seized power in 1917 during the recession caused by World War I. In 1919 popular protest and an invasion by exiled elites toppled the Tinoco regime, Costa Rica's last military government. Civilian rule continued thereafter, and the Costa Rican electorate expanded continuously.

The Atlantic railroad's completion in 1990 eventually added bananas to Costa Rica's export crops. The foreign-owned banana industry, concentrated in the sparsely populated Atlantic coastal lowlands, had little effect on Costa Rican politics in the early twentieth century. But as hard times developed later, Communist labor organizers unionized the banana plantations. Union influence and political power grew. By the 1940s, the Great Depression and World War II had caused severe social dislocations. Factions of the political-economic elite, working classes, and unions, and an emerging middle class struggled for political influence. In the early 1940s, President Rafael Calderón Guardia, a physician and reformist coffee aristocrat, broke with the rest of the coffee growers. Bidding to dominate the government, he allied with the Communist unions and the Catholic Church. Assisted by Communist legislators, Calderón enacted and began implementing Costa Rica's first labor and social security laws.

Calderón's alliance with the Communists and, in 1948, electoral fraud and legislative tampering with the presidential election results provided pretexts for a brief but violent civil war. A coalition of elite politicos angry at Calderón and middle-class elements, dominated by a junta of social democrats led by José "Pepe" Figueres Ferrer, rebelled and defeated the government within a few months. From that time to the 1990s, the country's social democrats—the National Liberation Party (Partido de Liberación Nacional, PLN), led for three decades by Figueres—set the tone of Costa Rican political life. In keeping with a well-established tradition of political accommodation, the victorious National Liberation junta retained Calderón's social reforms for workers. The junta went even further by nationalizing the banking and insurance industries. A constituent assembly rewrote the constitution in 1949, enfranchising women and blacks and abolishing the army. The latter act ensured future political stability. In late 1949, the junta turned the presidency over to the rightful winner of the 1948 election, Otilio Ulate, who was not a part of the National Liberation movement.

When the PLN and Figueres first won the presidency in 1954, they expanded the social legislation initiated under Calderón by increasing the scope of health and social security coverage. Even the conservative coalition governments that periodically replaced the PLN in power preserved and expanded these social benefits. After 1949, successive governments held regular and clean elections administered by the powerful and independent Supreme Electoral Tribunal. When defeated at the polls, the PLN willingly relinquished control of the presidency and Legislative Assembly to opposition coalitions. The PLN won the presidency nine times and the opposition won it seven times between 1949 and 2010. Opinion surveys showed strong citizen support for democratic civil liberties and competing party alternation in power.

In sum, Costa Rica's center-left social democratic PLN governments took power and consolidated a new political and economic regime in the 1950s, despite countervailing trends elsewhere in the isthmus. Similar post-World War II movements favoring democracy appeared in Guatemala, Honduras, Nicaragua, and El Salvador, but all failed. Instrumental in this failure of democracy elsewhere were US anti-Communist policies that aided and encouraged national armed forces and rightist elites to block the left's struggle for reform. In contrast, Costa Rica's pro-democracy reformers had defeated the Communists in the 1948 civil war and thereafter contained their influence. This put Costa Rica's new regime on the good side of the United States and helped it survive where others nearby would not.

Despite developing and consolidating a constitutional electoral democracy, Costa Rica would face challenges. From the 1970s forward great-power geopolitics, civil wars nearby, and commodity price shifts repeatedly tested Costa Rica's institutions and citizens' confidence in them, and forced frequent adjustment to changing realities.

WEATHERING GLOBAL FORCES

Costa Rica experienced similar global economic forces to its neighbors during the 1970s and 1980s. This generated some unrest but not the violent strife and regime change that afflicted much of the isthmus. This relative stability was no accident—political elites acted to correct eroding popular living standards and to avoid political repression. These decisions stemmed from distinctive historical factors. Late nineteenth century rulers and landowners had accommodated peasants to secure a labor supply, and mid-twentieth century leaders placated mobilized working and middle classes with political and economic reforms. This tradition of elites accommodating mobilized lower sectors, we believe, provided Costa Rica's leaders with tactics that preserved stable electoral democracy despite grave challenges in the 1970s–1980s.

The government's task proved difficult. Costa Rica's post-civil war social democratic development model relied on state-led development projects and Central American Common Market (CACM)-coordinated import-substitution industrialization that enlarged the government's payroll and economic role. Costa Rica's social welfare programs, ambitious for a developing country, grew during the 1950s and 1960s. Despite industrialization, the 1970s economy and budgets still depended heavily on international market prices for exported coffee, bananas, and goods sold to the CACM, and for vital imported petroleum. Problems arose, however, when oil costs skyrocketed after 1973, while export prices fell and brought inflation, layoffs, and a public revenue crunch.

Sources of Class Conflict

How did the Costa Rican variant of the Central American crisis of the 1970s arise? The CACM accelerated economic growth, especially industrialization. Costa Rican per capita gross domestic product (GDP) rose at an annual average of 3.4 percent from 1960 to 1980 (see Table A.1). Among Central American nations, Costa Rica led in workforce in manufacturing by 1983 (16 percent). By 1987, Costa Rica (at 23 percent) ranked second in the isthmus in manufacturing's contribution to domestic production. The agricultural work-force shrank from 51 percent to 29 percent between 1960 and 1980. Com-merce, services, and government expanded as the nation rapidly modernized and urbanized.

The prevailing theory about the onset of rebellion in Central America in the 1970s contends that severe declines in real working-class wages and living conditions mobilized many people into labor, political, and protest organiza-tion and activity.[6] Because many wage earners in Central America had little or no margin of safety, a drop in their real earnings (wages corrected for infla-tion) could impair their ability to survive. This rapid erosion of life chances provided a powerful impetus to join groups seeking to redress such problems.

Costa Rican wage workers lost ground relative to other income earners in the mid-1970s and again in 1982, but each time recovered much of their pur-chasing power and their wages remained relatively high into the late 1980s.[7] Unlike Guatemala, Nicaragua, and El Salvador, the Costa Rican government found ways to let real wages recover. Indeed, Costa Rican workers actually gained ground against inflation into the late 1990s.[8]

Income Distribution

One measure of changing income inequality during the 1970s is the share of national income paid out as employee compensation. Decreasing employee com-pensation would suggest income shifting away from salaried and wage-earning workers and toward investors and entrepreneurs. Data reveal that between 1970 and 1975, the employee-compensation share of all national income fluctuated but tended to increase as public policy redistributed income toward the mid-dle three-fifths of the populace, mainly at the expense of the richest fifth.[9] In both relative and absolute income trends, Costa Rica clearly contrasts with what the evidence will later show for Nicaragua, El Salvador, and Guatemala, where wages declined but did not recover, increasingly aggrieving those losing out.

Wealth

During the 1970s Costa Rica also avoided sharp increases in class inequal-ity observed in Nicaragua, El Salvador, and Guatemala. Although Costa Rica was in the CACM and was also hit by rapid energy-driven consumer price increases of the mid-1970s, data reveal that in Costa Rica these factors affected wealth distribution less than elsewhere in the isthmus.

Costa Rica's social democratic development model and low military expenditures allowed the country to attenuate inflation's impact on popular living conditions in the 1970s. Table A.5 reveals that Costa Rica's ratio of spending for social services versus defense was four to five times greater than that of its nearest competitor in Central America. The benefits of these policies became manifest in Costa Rica's higher literacy, greater longevity, and lower mortality rates.[10] As noted above, income distribution in Costa Rica actually became modestly more egalitarian during the 1960s and 1970s, retarding a rapid movement of wealth toward the upper classes, as observed in Nicaragua, Guatemala, and El Salvador.

In Costa Rican agriculture, concentration of land ownership grew steadily in the 1960s and early 1970s, but the availability of some land that could still be colonized and the still-growing banana industry absorbed much of the surplus agricultural work force. Moreover, from 1974 to 1978, Costa Rica aggressively distributed land to numerous peasants and thus prevented the deterioration of living standards for many.[11] Employment growth in urban services and manufacturing absorbed further surplus agricultural workers, also retarding growth of rural unemployment and poverty through the late 1980s.[12]

Popular Mobilization

The Costa Rican government carefully managed citizen mobilization among organized workers but encouraged it in others. Following the 1948 civil war, the government worked to fragment the union movement into competing, party-affiliated confederations to curtail union power.[13] In contrast, during the 1960s and early 1970s, the government promoted hundreds of communal self-help organizations. Largely uncoordinated among themselves, they worked on local improvement projects funded by legislators. This state-promoted community development movement was relatively docile and easier to coopt than leftist-led unions had been in the 1930s and 1940s.

By the 1970s union membership began to grow.[14] The oil price and inflation shocks from the global economy stirred popular mobilization, union militancy, and industrial disputes.[15] Wage disputes eventually receded in 1983 and 1984 when earnings recovered earlier purchasing power. Austerity measures imposed in the late 1980s and early 1990s (public-employee layoffs and service cuts), and inflation drove a new round of protests and strikes, but again wage and policy concessions quelled them.[16]

Costa Rica's system of political parties remained stable from the 1960s into the 1980s; the social democratic National Liberation Party (PLN) alternated in power with a coalition of moderately conservative parties under the Unity banner. The traditional Unity coalition of conservative parties reorganized themselves into the Social Christian Unity Party (Partido de Unidad Social Cristiano, PUSC) in 1985. Radical-left parties won a few seats to the Legislative Assembly during the 1970s, but they were weak outside the union movement. As living standards of most Costa Ricans declined during the 1980s, mobilization of demands by a broad array of interest groups increased and public approval of government declined. Organized labor unsuccessfully promoted a militant general confederation. Voting for leftist parties—long considered a bellwether of protest—declined in the 1982 and 1986 national elections. Costa Rica's more radical parties and labor became increasingly fractured in the early and mid-1980s. Polls revealed that even during a severe recession most citizens remained loyal to the regime.

In sum, Costa Rica experienced increased organization and protest, but no dramatic increase in anti-regime organization or coalitions from the late 1970s through the early 1990s.[17] Unlike Nicaragua, Guatemala, and El Salvador, Costa Rica experienced no significant challenge to the sovereignty of the state.

Government Response to Popular Mobilization

Central American regimes all experienced popular mobilization during the 1970s and 1980s, but responded very differently. The Salvadoran, Guatemalan, and pre-revolutionary Nicaraguan regimes reacted violently to popular organization and protest. In contrast, democratic Costa Rica and military-ruled Honduras addressed popular mobilization relatively moderately. Moderation prevented the mobilization of new opponents to the government angered by repression, and thus avoided escalating conflict.

Costa Rica's fairly elected constitutional regime provided officials who typically responded to mobilized demands by accommodating rather than resisting them. Even when demands escalated into civil disobedience, demonstrations, strikes, or riots, the government usually responded with moderate force and used study and compromise to defuse conflict. For instance, rulers met violent civil disturbances—land invasions in the early 1970s, the Limón riot of 1979, banana workers' strikes in 1980–1982, and street vendors' strikes in 1991—with moderate official force. Deaths among protesters were rare.[18] Different PLN and PUSC administrations approached demand-makers by negotiating with them, forming panels of inquiry, or making conciliatory policies.

As later chapters will show, Central America's major national revolts of the 1970s and 1980s (Nicaragua, El Salvador, Guatemala) arose from sharp increases in inequality and decreases in popular living standards during the mid-1970s. These grievances mobilized demands for redress of wages and living standards. Costa Rica experienced similar mobilization but responded to it by allowing workers' wages to recover, enacting other ameliorative policies, and by typically keeping repression low. This combination of amelioration with low repression defused popular anger, demobilized much protest, and prevented rising conflict that in three neighboring nations caused open rebellions. Thus Costa Rica's regime coped with globally driven economic uncertainty and turmoil by following the national elite's longstanding accommodative traditions. The global strains of the 1970s and 1980s nonetheless left marks on Costa Rica—not of regime change but transformations in its economic development strategy and political party system.

THE ECONOMIC DEVELOPMENT MODEL TRANSFORMED

As noted, simultaneously declining export revenues and rising energy costs pushed Costa Rica into a severe economic crisis. Rapid inflation drove down demand and real wages, which further reduced consumer demand. The governments of the mid- and late 1970s and early 1980s, rather than curtail public spending to address shrinking state revenues, kept spending and borrowed abroad to finance the growing deficit. In the short term this lightened the impact of the crisis on the public, but it disastrously affected national financial health. Foreign debt as a share of GDP rose from 12 percent in 1970 to 147 percent in 1982. Foreign interest payments consumed a third of export earnings and further weakened the public and private sectors. Similar difficulties and escalating civil wars elsewhere in Central America undermined Costa Rica's regional markets and drove away tourists and foreign capital. In 1981 the administration of Rodrigo Carazo Odio found its foreign reserve coffers empty and defaulted on Costa Rica's foreign debt. This pushed the currency (the *colón*) into a ten-year slide that eroded 90 percent of its value.[19]

When the PLN's Luis Alberto Monge became president in 1982, these predicaments forced him to seek costly international assistance. The United States wanted a southern base for its efforts to unseat Nicaragua's Sandinista revolution. The Reagan administration pressured Costa Rica, and Monge agreed to assist the Nicaraguan counterrevolutionaries and their American helpers. In exchange the United States compensated Costa Rica with over US$1.1 billion in aid during the mid-1980s, much of it in the unusual form of outright grants instead of loans. These funds delayed Costa Rica's reckoning with its sick economy, while addicting it ever more to external aid. By 1985 a second source of international help had to be invoked.

US grants for pro-Contra activities ended after Monge's successor, PLN President Oscar Arias Sánchez, in 1987 successfully promoted the Central American Peace Accord and curtailed Costa Rica's cooperation with the Contras. Although Costa Rican peace initiatives would soon win Arias the Nobel Peace Prize, the Reagan administration punished Costa Rica with sharp aid cuts that reduced economic output and increased inflation.

A second source of external aid, borrowing from intergovernmental lenders and individual nations, also came heavily conditioned. Evolving global capitalism in the late twentieth century had begun to intensify Central America's external links.[20] The previous epoch favored traditional agro-exports and import-substitution industrialization (ISI) development orientation. The preferred new development model, neoliberalism, emphasized free-market capitalism, a smaller public sector, opening markets, privatizing public-sector enterprises, and reorientation toward non-traditional exports. Its promoters included the US government, other major capitalist countries, and international lenders (the Interamerican Development Bank (IADB), International Monetary Fund (IMF), and Paris Club). These institutions, heavily influenced by the United States' great voting weight on their policy boards, pushed developing countries to adopt neoliberal economic reform.

These entities pressured Costa Rica into three structural adjustment agreements (SAAs) in 1985, 1989, and 1995, with the administrations of Luis Alberto Monge, Oscar Arias Sánchez, and José Figueres Olsen, respectively. In exchange for loans essential to restructure Costa Rica's foreign debt and keep the foreign reserve–starved state and economy afloat, the United States, Paris Club, IMF, and IADB made Costa Rica enact neoliberal economic policies that transformed its development model. Supported by conservative domestic economic interests and by the conservative PUSC (which fortuitously avoided having to sign any of the SAAs), Costa Rica trimmed its public-sector payroll, education and health programs, and infrastructure investment. It eventually privatized most of the nation's many publicly owned enterprises and banking, and at least temporarily cut subsidies to agricultural commodity producers, utility consumers, and housing. The government energetically promoted non-traditional exports and reduced trade barriers.[21] Successive governments in San José legislated and issued executive decrees in major departures from the nation's four decade-old development strategy.[22]

Economic stagnation and neoliberal policies proved a volatile mix. The successive PUSC administrations of presidents Miguel Rodríguez and Abel

Pacheco (1998–2006) pursued privatization despite legislative and popular opposition. Rodríguez won legislation allowing foreign investors to provide public services. In 2000 the Legislative Assembly approved privatizing the Costa Rican Electrical Institute (ICE). Following perhaps the largest demonstrations in the country's history, the Constitutional Tribunal overturned the measure.[23] Public-sector employees increasingly challenged economic policy. In 1999, 15,000 teachers walked out to protest wages and education budget cuts.[24] Teachers and energy and telecommunications workers continued strikes throughout the Pacheco administration as measures indicated growing poverty caused by increased food prices.[25] Pacheco had pledged to address poverty during his campaign, but instead deepened spending cuts. His administration suffered not only public protests but legislative stagnation, internal divisions, and very low public approval.[26]

A debate over free trade dominated the 2006 election. PLN candidate Oscar Arias, like most candidates, supported the Central American Free Trade Agreement (CAFTA). Ottón Solís of the Citizen Action Party (Partido de Acción Ciudadana, PAC) advocated renegotiating CAFTA's terms and a dialogue with civil society. The major candidates offered different proposals to ameliorate poverty and inequality. Arias defeated Solís by the slimmest victory in the country's history (40.5 to 40.3 percent—see Table A.6) amid very low voter turnout.

The CAFTA brouhaha continued after the 2006 election. The Supreme Electoral Tribunal (TSE) recommended submitting the agreement to a popular referendum. The Assembly concurred, making Costa Rica the only country to put the measure to a popular vote. Although the treaty's constitutionality was challenged before the referendum, the Supreme Court upheld it.[27] Support for CAFTA slipped to only 39 percent in 2007 during the referendum campaign, but urged on by President Arias and business leaders, Costa Ricans approved the treaty by 51.6 percent. The passage of required enabling laws delayed final implementation until January 2009. Arias promised fiscal reform and energetic poverty reduction and succeeded on both, assisted by economic recovery.

The give and take over neoliberal economic policy brought Costa Rica many political signs of economic discontent. Besides protests, voters ousted the governing party in successive elections in 1990, 1994, and 1998. Turnout dropped from the usual level above 80 percent to only 73 percent in 1998, and then to 59 percent in 2002. Voter turnout recovered slightly in the next two elections but meanwhile the two-party system in place since the rise of the PUSC began to change rapidly.[28]

In contrast to these political discontents, the new development model's short- and middle-run economic successes made Costa Rica a poster child for neoliberalism, despite its leaders having evaded or worked around many budget constraints. Growing non-traditional exports, economic liberalization, the settlement of the region's civil conflicts in the 1990s, and Costa Rica's human capital advantages stimulated a period of rapid economic growth, helping attenuate losses in wages. During the 1990s Costa Rica's combined rate of investment between government and private sector sources was high for the region. Government spending on social services still far exceeded any other country in the area. GDP per capita grew by nearly 25 percent between 1990 and the early 2000s, driven by a tourism boom, domestic and foreign investment, new computer assembly and online-services industries, and expanded textile manufacturing.[29]

In the 2000s, the effects of the new Costa Rican development model were still unfolding. Deregulation had allowed a new private banking system dominated by international capital, which deepened integration into the world economy. Investment in traditional agriculture and agricultural extension services declined along with domestically consumed agricultural production, pushing underemployed rural populations toward urban areas. Investment in industry lost ground relative to investment in the commercial and service sectors. The informal sectors (petty commerce and services—often street vendors, unlicensed taxis, etc.) grew rapidly for a time, drawing in those unable to find formal-sector employment. Female workforce participation rose sharply without a proportionate accompanying public investment in family social services and childcare. Many Nicaraguan immigrants flooded Costa Rica to assume lower-paying jobs in non-traditional agriculture, construction, and domestic service. Immigrant workers experienced harassment by police and exploitation by employers. Their presence also depressed wages and undermined Costa Rican workers' organizations and mobilization.[30]

Statistics on income, inequality, and poverty lag social change, so we cannot at this writing fully assess which of these trends would continue in Costa Rica. The evidence is conflicting. Inequality worsened measurably in the 1990s and early 2000s, diminished slightly around 2008 but worsened again by 2014.[31] Alternatively, the share of people living in poverty in the early 1990s was 26.2 percent, a level reduced to 21.7 percent in 2014 (see Table 2.1). Costa Rica's GDP per capita as of 1990 doubled by 2017 (see Table 1.1), the best performance in the region.

Beginning after 2005, Costa Rica became less fiscally austere than in the previous two decades. Under neoliberal SAAs, public spending shrank and net public spending (revenue minus expenses) had oscillated between small deficits (-1.6 percent of GDP in 1995) and small surpluses (+0.2 percent of GDP in 2000). In 2010, however, deficits began rising and reached -5.2 percent of GDP in 2015.[32] External debt climbed from 16 percent of GDP in 2000 to 46 percent by 2017 (see Table A.1). The government thus had begun spending more and financing deficits by borrowing. Costa Rica began slipping away from the neoliberal development model and apparently back toward its social democratic traditions of investing in its population.

In sum, external forces used the debt crisis of the 1980s to force Costa Rica to adopt a neoliberal development model. Even when coerced into distributively stingy policies, Costa Rican governments managed to cushion some of the economic blows to citizens, produced a short-term macroeconomic turnaround, and found new industries to bolster economic output over the longer run. As of 2017, Costa Rica was growing government spending and deficits. This seemed to be raising macroeconomic output while keeping most inequality measures lower than in other countries, though inequality had risen. Throughout this difficult period, the overarching framework of the constitutional democratic regime established in early 1950s remained in place, but national politics began to change.

CHANGES IN POLITICS AND PARTIES

Despite the long life of Costa Rica's political regime, the country's economy affected the political party system.[33] Scholars believe globalization and neoliberalism affected Latin American parties in two main ways: at the macro level, neoliberalism's constraints undermined ruling social democratic parties by undercutting their preferred redistributive and protectionist policies. This alienated their working- and middle-class supporters and boosted competitors friendlier toward neoliberal reforms. At the micro level, social democratic parties divided ideologically and sent confusing messages as they lost traditional campaign themes that ran against neoliberal doctrine. This forced them to embrace personalistic appeals designed to distract voters from unpalatable economic options.[34] Costa Rica experienced both these changes, which harmed the long-dominant social democratic PLN and temporarily benefited the newer PUSC. (Tables A.6 and A.7 present selected presidential and legislative election results.)

The PLN

Neoliberalism harmed the social democratic National Liberation Party because its presidents had to sign and implement all three structural adjustments accords. As Costa Rica's leftist parties declined in the 1970s and early 1980s, popular-sector interests within the PLN lost influence relative to the party's emerging advocates of neoliberalism. The neoliberal imperative divided traditional social democrats from neoliberal reformers, and the party's neoliberal technocrats holding office from aspiring presidential candidates.[35] Other factors also divided the party and reduced its discipline and appeal. Technocrats gained control over policymaking while the party was in power, displacing long-term party loyalists and activists. The PLN adopted presidential primary elections open to non-PLN members. Presidential campaign organizations rose to dominate the traditional party apparatus. Finally, a rapid shift to retail campaigning via television in the 1980s combined with the presidential primary nominating election to collapse the PLN's tradition of face-to-face, grassroots organization.

By the late 1980s the PLN's messages became muddled as its actions in power betrayed traditional Liberación ideology and policies. The PLN lost its perennial control of the Legislative Assembly from 1990 on (see Table A.7). It won the presidency only once during the 1990s and only twice in five elections since 2000. Its presidential vote share shrank from 40 percent and above to only 18.6 percent in 2018. The struggling party in 1994 nominated for president José Maria Figueres Olsen, son of PLN founder and two-time president José Figueres Ferrer. This helped win the presidency in 1994. Figueres Olsen had to implement the unpopular 1995 SAA, and his administration experienced several scandals. Turnout in the 1997 PLN presidential primary election fell sharply because of "the negative weight of an unpopular Liberación administration, ... [and] a very fragmented party."[36]

By 2002 the PLN split and many voters and top leaders defected to the new Citizen Action Party (Partido de Acción Ciudadana, PAC). Liberación recovered somewhat in 2006 with 41 percent of the presidential vote, although much of its success that year owed to the candidacy of former president Oscar Arias. In 2010 PLN nominee Laura Chinchilla did well by taking 47 percent of the presidential vote. Following several scandals in her administration, however, the party lost the presidency to Acción Ciudadana in 2014 and 2018. The PLN won only 30 percent of the Assembly seats in 2018.

PUSC

The globalist pressures for neoliberalism that harmed the PLN favored the formation and growth of the Social Christian Unity Party. Rafael Angel Calderón

Fournier's administration (1990–1994) in principle embraced structural adjustment, which undermined the short-term economic well-being of most Costa Ricans. By good luck, however, the party escaped signing a SAA while in power and thus shifted to the PLN much of the blame for the resulting austerity. In power, the PUSC subverted austerity policies by diverting infrastructure and health and education spending into palliative social programs in housing and temporary welfare assistance.[37] In 2004, twin corruption scandals implicated former PUSC presidents Calderón and Rodríguez and their administrations in taking bribes and campaign finance violations. In 2009 Calderón was convicted of embezzlement. Rodríguez, convicted on corruption charges in April 2011, later successfully appealed his conviction. In 2006, 2010, and 2014 the PUSC's presidential vote fell to single digits in presidential elections, recuperating somewhat in 2018. The PUSC's share of Assembly seats has not exceeded 9 of 57 since 2006 (see Tables A.6 and A.7).

PAC

The PAC arose in 2000 from a schism in the PNL. By emphasizing citizen participation, transparency, and anti-neoliberalism, it capitalized on growing disenchantment with the status quo. The party reached out to popular organizations and promised to allocate half of its legislative seats to women, 10 percent more than required by the 1996 quota law.[38] For a new party the PAC did very well; in 2002 its presidential candidate Ottón Solís captured 26 percent of the vote, while the party captured 14 of 57 seats in the Assembly. By 2006, the PAC had displaced the PUSC as the second party in Costa Rica's duopoly. Arias narrowly defeated Solís, but the PAC won 17 Assembly seats. PAC's Luis Guillermo Solís won the presidency in 2014, as did Carlos Alvarado in 2018. Acción Ciudadana held the second-largest Assembly delegations from 2006 on, but it lost ground to ten deputies in 2018.

Other Parties

As the traditionally dominant PLN and PUSC declined, other parties multiplied (see Tables A.6 and A.7). Seven parties/coalitions fielded presidential candidates in 1994, rising to 15 in 2018. Fifteen parties sought Assembly seats in 1994 (four succeeded), while 25 competed in 2018 (nine won seats). Meanwhile, older parties of the left shrank and lost representation in the Legislative Assembly. The Broad Front (Frente Amplio) leftist coalition won nine deputy seats in 2014 but slipped to only one in 2018. Several small regional parties occasionally captured a single seat until 1994, but have faded since.[39] The Libertarian Movement Party of Costa Rica (Partido Movimiento Libertario de Costa Rica, PML) had some success channeling discontent in Assembly elections and won several seats in each Assembly from 2002 to 2014. Their best election came in 2010 (9 of 57 seats), but in 2018 voters shut them out completely.

Party System Legitimacy

Costa Rica's party system, in sum, became unstable and changed rapidly beginning in the 1990s. Older dominant parties declined or split, and many new ones jousted for influence in the disorganized space. The obvious short-term winner has been the PAC, victor in the last two presidential elections, but as of 2018 unable to control the Assembly and losing ground there. Could this party system turmoil threaten the legitimacy of Costa Rica's democratic regime, or is it a sign of citizens' dissatisfaction? Surveys conducted after 1990 found citizens expressing declining support for parties and other national institutions, and a waning interest in politics. Public trust in parties declined in the 1990s, registering as the lowest in Central American in a 2008 survey, but rising to 20 percent in 2016—in the middle for the region.[40]

CONTEMPORARY COSTA RICAN POLITICS

The PLN, having won so narrowly in 2006, dominated the 2010 elections. The PLN's Laura Chinchilla, vice president and minister of justice under Oscar Arias, won 47 percent of the vote and easily defeated newer party candidates Ottón Solís (PAC) and Otto Guevara of the Libertarian Movement Party. The PUSC continued its dramatic decline, winning less than 4 percent of the vote. The PLN captured 24 of 57 seats in the Legislative Assembly. It was a momentous year for women, as Chinchilla became Costa Rica's first woman president and women won 39 percent of the seats in the Legislative Assembly.

Despite her decisive victory, President Chinchilla's administration began and continued in crisis. She inherited a public deficit of almost $1 billion, a growing public security problem, and a border dispute with Nicaragua over the San Juan River. The growing presence of Mexican drug cartels and public perceptions of insecurity necessitated a swift response to crime, so Chinchilla quickly authorized the training of 1,000 new police officers. In 2011, she unveiled a ten-year crime plan to improve law enforcement training, institutional coordination, and crime prevention. Critics attacked it for offering few specific solutions and not identifying a source of funding.[41] Although low for the region, Costa Rica's homicide rates fluctuated, rising in 2013 because of increased drug trafficking.[42]

Dissatisfaction with President Chinchilla arose early in her administration. In April 2011, the Legislative Assembly elected the PAC's Juan Carlos Mendoza as the body's president, the first time in over four decades the key position went to someone outside the ruling party.[43] Corruption scandals bloomed. During Chinchilla's first two years in office, 13 cabinet ministers resigned. Several top administration officials were implicated in corruption scandals, including the finance minister, education minister, a presidential advisor, and one of the two vice presidents. Although the attorney general's ethics office found that Vice President Luis Liberman and Education Minister Leonardo Garnier had breached ethics rules, Chinchilla rejected the Assembly's calls to dismiss them, an overwhelmingly unpopular decision. The scandals and resignations complicated her relationship with the Legislative Assembly, which refused to pass any bills until the end of July 2012.[44]

Minister of Public Works Francisco Jiménez resigned in May 2012 amid allegations of corruption on a road project along the San Juan River. Scandal embroiled Chinchilla herself in 2013 when she traveled to Peru and Venezuela on a jet linked to drug traffickers. This caused several more resignations, including vice-minister of the presidency (also head of the Office of Intelligence and Security and the anti-drug commissioner), the communications minister, and a presidential aide. This calamitous record undermined public confidence in her administration and her ability to govern. By July 2013, only 9 percent of Costa Ricans approved of her performance, the worst presidential approval rating in two decades.[45] A 2012 LAPOP survey revealed that Costa Rican support for the political system and democracy had declined under Chinchilla.[46]

2014 Elections

By 2014, incumbent Chinchilla had one of the lowest presidential approval ratings in the entire hemisphere. Corruption scandals, tensions with Nicaragua, rising crime, and a growing deficit had taken their toll on voters heading into the 2014 elections. Two notable developments marked the 2014 elections: a new quota system required that half of party candidate lists be women, and Costa Ricans living abroad could now vote in the elections.

Thirteen candidates entered the presidential race's first round. Luis Guillermo Solís of Acción Ciudadana (PAC) won 30.6 percent of the vote, followed by Liberación's Johnny Araya with 29.7 percent. In mid-campaign of the presidential runoff, Araya suddenly abandoned his campaign. Solís, a former university professor, was elected with 78 percent of the vote. Araya was subsequently suspended from the PLN.

In elections for the Legislative Assembly, the PLN won 18 seats, followed by PAC (13), Frente Amplio (9), and PUSC (8). Five smaller parties divided the remaining nine seats. Although holding the most seats, the PLN had lost six from the previous session. For the sixth time since 1994, the 2014 election left Costa Rica without a majority party in the Assembly. Like his predecessors, President Solís and the Assembly faced the problem of rising public deficit, which reached nearly 7 percent of GDP in 2016. Solís encountered legislative gridlock when trying to address public spending and revenue, but enjoyed greater success on other fronts. The president was vocal in his support for the rights of the LGBT community, raising the rainbow diversity flag at the presidential palace in observance of the International Day Against Homophobia and Transphobia. In May 2014, the Assembly passed a law extending medical benefits to same-sex couples. That said, the Assembly also stalled on passing legislation to support a 2015 court ruling granting common-law marital status to same-sex couples. In June 2015, the Assembly gave important recognition to Costa Rica's often overlooked minorities by passing a constitutional amendment declaring Costa Rica to be multiethnic and plurinational.

2018 Elections

The 2018 election cycle was overshadowed first by a massive government scandal and then by an international court opinion. Months before the election, President Solís was implicated in an influence peddling scandal involving Chinese cement exports to Costa Rica. The case involved more than $30 million in questionable loans made by the Bank of Costa Rica (BCR) to businessman Juan Carlos Bolaños to import Chinese cement. The scandal, or *Cementazo*, ensnared many officials. Solís was at first cleared, but the vice minister of finance, attorney general, president of the Supreme Court, a Supreme Court magistrate, legislators, and the BCR chair were forced to resign. The scandal overshadowed the 2018 elections and fed an anti-establishment mood. In September 2019 the Assembly urged the Attorney General to reinvestigate Solís.

In January 2018, the Inter-American Court of Human Rights (IACHR) issued an advisory opinion that Latin American countries, including Costa Rica, must legalize same-sex marriage. In the February 4 elections, no candidate secured the required 40 percent of the vote to avoid a runoff. Fabricio Alvarado Muñoz of the conservative National Restoration Party (PRN) won nearly 25 percent of the vote, followed by PAC's Carlos Alvarado Quesada, novelist and former labor minister with almost 22 percent. Alvarado Muñoz, an evangelical singer and pastor, had trailed in the pre-election polls, but moved to the front of the pack following the IACHR opinion on same-sex marriage.[47] Alvarado Muñoz campaigned vigorously against gay marriage, which won support among conservative Costa Ricans. In the Assembly elections, the PLN won 17 seats, followed by the PRN with 14 seats and PAC with 10 seats. The PUSC filled nine seats while the remaining seven were divided among three smaller parties. Women won 46 percent of seats in the newly elected Legislative Assembly. Though polls had suggested a tight race for April's runoff election, PAC's Alvarado Quesada easily defeated Alvarado Muñoz by nearly 20 points. His running mate Epsy Campbell Barr became the first Afro-Costa Rican woman to serve as vice president. Again, for the seventh session in a row, no party held a majority of seats in the Assembly.

In August 2018, the Supreme Court ruled that the prohibition of same-sex marriage was unconstitutional and gave the Assembly 18 months to legalize same-sex marriage or the ruling would simply take effect by May 2020. In December 2018, President Alvarado signed several decrees granting rights to the LGBT community, including requiring residency cards to recognize transgender people's preferred identity and covering hormone treatments for transgender people in the public health system.

The new government faced several policy challenges. In 2017 Costa Rica's homicide rate reached a record of 12.1 per 100,000. While much lower than in El Salvador, Guatemala, or Honduras, this was nearly double Nicaragua's homicide rate. The country had long been a transshipment route for cocaine, but a local market had developed. In August, President Alvarado Quesada announced a new security plan to improve collaboration between national and local authorities and develop prevention efforts.[48] Costa Rica was also facing an influx of Nicaraguan refugees fleeing political violence there. The United Nations High Commissioner on Refugees (UNHCR) estimated that by March 2019, that more than 55,000 Nicaraguans had fled to Costa Rica and nearly 30,000 had filed asylum applications.[49] In August 2018, hundreds of Costa Ricans accusing Nicaraguans of being criminals and straining public resources marched in an anti-Nicaraguan rally San José.[50] In December 2018, the Assembly passed the Law on Strengthening Public Finances that replaced the old sales tax system with a new 13 percent value added-tax (VAT) on good and services, created new taxes on capital gains and losses, and other reforms designed to increase state revenue to tackle the public debt. The reforms passed during the middle of a three-month teacher's strike, the longest in the country's history. Striking workers, who originally included those from other trade unions, objected to the proposed VAT, which workers said placed burdens on the working class. The teacher's strike closed many public schools for a month. It was eventually ruled legal after an initial adverse labor court ruling.[51]

CONCLUSIONS

During the 1970s, Costa Rica somewhat ameliorated the growing difficulties of working-class victims of rapid economic change and carried this off with low repression. Working-class wages recovered or retained purchasing power. Policy changes shifted some wealth and income to certain lower-class groups. This combination of low repression and some accommodation of working-class interests contrasted with the opposite in Somoza's Nicaragua, Guatemala, and El Salvador, and kept Costa Rica relatively politically stable.

Costa Rica's consolidated democracy weathered several decades intact, but the country nevertheless experienced two major middle-term effects from its shifting role in the international political economy. External structural and political pressures forced Costa Rica to curtail its longstanding social democratic economic model and embrace neoliberalism. This transformation shattered the longstanding party duopoly. It undermined the National Liberation Party's position as the system's dominant party. Though resurgent in the presidency from 2006 to 2014, the PLN has since faded to capture only a fifth of the vote in the 2018 presidential election and fewer than a third of the Assembly seats. The Social Christian Unity Party, once a formidable competitor, suffered multiple scandals and collapsed into third or fourth place in influence and Assembly seats from 2006 on. The main beneficiary of these changes was ultimately the Citizen Action Party, which has now won the presidency twice. The old duopoly party system is gone, with PAC as the most successful player remaining, though it still lags the PLN in Assembly delegates. The PRN in 2018 appeared as a relatively new conservative challenger, doing well in the Assembly election. The PLN, Libertarians, PUSC, and PRN compete with variable success in the now highly divided Legislative Assembly.

Costa Rica's erstwhile social democratic development model has apparently partly survived, despite neoliberalism. The economy is more open to foreign investment, and government has curtailed some equality-enhancing economic and human development policies. However, the government appears to have abandoned austerity and have begun borrowing to finance growing deficits. Historically previous Costa Rican governments survived for some time on deficit spending—an approach that eventually led to crippling debt. These programs and their effects had once distinguished Costa Rica from its Central American neighbors and for decades validated the country's exceptionalist myth. Recent advances in rights and recognitions of minority populations combine with the stability of its democracy to continue to distinguish Costa Rica from its neighbors.

NOTES

1. On the negative side, critics argue that Costa Rican exceptionalism has xenophobic and racist elements, especially vis-à-vis Nicaraguans. Carlos Sandoval-Garcia in *Threatening Others: Nicaraguans and the Formation of National Identities in Costa Rica* (Athens, OH: Ohio University Press, 2004).

2. Bruce M. Wilson, *Costa Rica: Politics, Economics, and Democracy* (Boulder, CO: Lynne Rienner Publishers, 1998); John A. Booth, *Costa Rica: Quest for Democracy* (Boulder, CO: Westview Press, 1998); William I. Robinson, *Transnational Conflicts: Central America, Social Change, and Globalization* (London: Verso, 2003).

3. John A. Booth, "Representative Constitutional Democracy in Costa Rica: Adaptation to Crisis in the Turbulent 1980s," in Steve Ropp and James Morris, eds., *Central America: Crisis and Adaptation* (Albuquerque, NM: University of New Mexico Press, 1984), Table 5.1; Mitchell A. Seligson and Miguel Gómez, "Ordinary Elections in Extraordinary Times: The Political Economy of Voting in Costa Rica," in John A. Booth and Mitchell A. Seligson, eds., *Elections and Democracy in Central America* (Chapel Hill, NC: University of North Carolina Press, 1989); John A. Booth, "Costa Rica: The Roots of Democratic Stability," in Larry Diamond, Juan J. Linz, and Seymour Martin Lipset, eds., *Democracy in Developing Countries, Volume 4: Latin America* (Boulder, CO: Lynne Rienner Publishers, 1989), pp. 387–422; Lowell Gudmundson, *Costa Rica Before Coffee* (Baton Rouge, LA: Louisiana State University Press, 1986); Booth, *Costa Rica: Quest for Democracy*, Ch. 3.

4. Astrid Fischel, *Consenso y represión: Una interpretación sociopolítica de la educación costarricense* (San José: Editorial Costa Rica, 1987), and Booth, *Costa Rica: Quest for Democracy*, pp. 40–42.

5. Booth, *Costa Rica: Quest for Democracy*, p. 42; and Fabrice E. Lehoucq and Ivan Molina, *Stuffing the Ballot Box: Fraud, Electoral Reform, and Democratization in Costa Rica* (Cambridge: Cambridge University Press, 2002), Ch. 1.

6. See Chapter 2.

7. Booth and Walker, *Understanding Central America*, 3rd ed., Appendix, Table A.6.

8. See also Victor Bulmer-Thomas, *The Political Economy of Central America Since 1920* (New York: Cambridge University Press, 1987), Table 10.7, p. 219; Víctor Hugo Céspedes, Alberto di Mare, and Ronulfo Jiménez, *Costa Rica: La economía en 1985* (San José, Costa Rica: Academia de Centroamérica, 1986), Cuadro 19, p. 71.

9. Víctor Hugo Céspedes, *Evolución de la distribución del ingreso en Costa Rica* (San José, Costa Rica: Instituto de Investigación en Ciencias Económicas, Universidad de Costa Rica, 1979), Cuadro 6; and Céspedes et al., *Costa Rica: La economía en 1985*, Cuadro 20, p. 73; David Felix, "Income Distribution and the Quality of Life in Latin America: Patterns, Trends, and Policy Implications," *Latin American Research Review* 18, No. 2 (1983), pp. 3–34.

10. For further data, see John A. Booth, "Representative Constitutional Democracy in Costa Rica: Adaptation to Crisis in the Turbulent 1980s," in S. Ropp and J. Morris, eds., *Central America: Crisis and Adaptation* (Albuquerque, NM: University of New Mexico Press, 1984), p. 171. On the operation and impact of the Costa Rican development model, see John A. Booth, *Costa Rica: Quest for Democracy* (Boulder, CO: Westview Press, 1998), Ch. 3 and 8.

11. Mitchell A. Seligson, *Peasants of Costa Rica and the Development of Agrarian Capitalism* (Madison, WI: University of Wisconsin Press, 1980), pp. 122–170; see also Francisco Barahona Riera, *Reforma agraria y poder político* (San José: Editorial Universidad de Costa Rica, 1980), pp. 221–422; and Donaldo Castillo Rivas, "Modelos de acumulación, agricultura, y agroindustria en Centroamérica," in D. CastilloRivas, ed., *Centroamérica: Más allá de la crisis* (México: Ediciones SIAP, 1983), pp. 210–213.

12. Booth and Walker, *Understanding Central America*, 3rd ed., Appendix, Table A.8.

13. E. Lederman et al., "Trabajo y empleo," in Chester Zelaya, ed., *Costa Rica contemporánea, Tomo II* (San José: Editorial Costa Rica, 1979); James Backer, *La Iglesia y el sindicalismo en Costa Rica* (San José: Editorial Costa Rica, 1978), pp. 135–207; Gustavo Blanco and Orlando Navarro, *El solidarismo: Pensamiento y dinámica social de un movimiento obrero patronal* (San José: Editorial Costa Rica, 1984).

14. Rodrigo Fernández Vásquez, "Costa Rica: Interpretación histórica sobre reforma social y acción eclesiástica: 1940–1982," *Estudios Sociales Centroamericanos* 33 (September–December 1982), pp. 221–248.

15. This material is from John A. Booth, "Costa Rica: The Roots of Democratic Stability," in Larry Jay Diamond, Seymour Martin Lipset, and Juan J. Linz, eds., *Democracy in Developing Countries, Volume 4: Latin America* (Boulder, CO: Lynne Rienner Publishers, 1989); and Booth, "Representative Constitutional Democracy."

16. Booth and Walker, *Understanding Central America*, 3rd ed., Appendix, Tables A.5 and A.6; "Costa Rica," *Mesoamérica* (April 1990), pp. 11–12; "Costa Rica," *Mesoamérica* (July 1990), pp. 7–8; "Costa Rica," *Mesoamérica* (October 1990), p. 9; "Costa Rica," *Mesoamérica* (November 1990), pp. 9–10; "Costa Rica," *Mesoamérica* (December 1990), p. 11; "Costa Rica," *Mesoamérica* (January 1991), pp. 4–7; "Costa Rica," *Mesoamérica* (February 1991), pp. 4–5; "Costa Rica," *Mesoamérica* (April 1991), pp. 1–2.

17. John A. Booth, "Political Parties in Costa Rica: Sustaining Democratic Stability in a Latin American Context," in Paul Webb and Stephen White, eds., *Political Parties in New Democracies* (Oxford: Oxford University Press, 2007); Mitchell A. Seligson and Edward Muller, "Democracy, Stability, and Economic Crisis: Costa Rica, 1978–1983," *International Studies Quarterly* 31 (September 1987), pp. 301–326; and Booth, "Costa Rican Democracy."

18. Booth, "Representative Constitutional Democracy," pp. 173–176; Booth, "Costa Rican Democracy," pp. 39–40; Seligson, *Peasants,* pp. 105–114; US Department of State, *Country Reports on Human Rights Practices* (Washington, DC: US Government Printing Office, February 2, 1981), pp. 241–244. See also Booth, *Costa Rica: Quest for Democracy,* pp. 114–121.

19. This section draws heavily on Booth, "Political Parties in Costa Rica." Data are drawn from Mary A. Clark, "Nontraditional Export Promotion in Costa Rica: Sustaining Export-Led Growth," *Journal of Interamerican Studies and World Affairs* 37, No. 2 (1995), pp. 181–223; Wilson, *Costa Rica: Politics, Economics, and Democracy,* pp. 113–150; Booth, *Costa Rica: Quest for Democracy,* Ch. 8; and Booth and Walker, *Understanding Central America,* 3rd ed., Appendix, Tables A.1, A.4, and A.5.

20. Robinson, *Transnational Conflicts,* pp. 64–65.

21. Booth, *Costa Rica: Quest for Democracy,* Ch. 8.

22. Ibid.

23. "Protests Put Privatization on Hold," *Central America Report* (April 7, 2000), p. 6; "Telecom Privatization Ruled Unconstitutional," *Central America Report* (May 12, 2000), p. 6.

24. *Central America Report* (May 1999), p. 7.

25. "Poverty Increases," *Central America Report* (January 7, 2005).

26. *Central America Report* (September 2003).

27. Latin American Database, "Constitutional Way Cleared for Cafta in Costa Rica; Referendum Is Next," *NotiCen* (July 12, 2007).

28. International Institute for Democracy and Electoral Assistance, Voter Turnout: Voter turnout data for Costa Rica, www.idea.int/vt/countryview.cf?id=54#pres, accessed October 1, 2013.

29. Alan Heston, Robert Summers, and Bettina Aten, Penn World Table Version 6.1 (Philadelphia: Center for International Comparisons at the University of Pennsylvania [CICUP], October 2002); Interamerican Development Bank, country notes, www.iadb.org/exr/country/, accessed June 14, 2004.

30. Robinson, *Transnational Conflicts,* Ch. 4.

31. See our Table 2.1 and World Bank Group, Latin America and the Caribbean, Costa Rica: Social Spending and the Poor, http://web.worldbank.org/WBSITE/EXTERNAL/COUNTRIES/LACEXT/COSTARICAEXTN/0,contentMDK:20252791~pagePK:141137~piPK:141127~theSitePK:295413,00.html, accessed January 6, 2005.

32. Authors' calculations from World Bank Group, Indicators (revenue and expenses), accessed September 9, 2019, https://data.worldbank.org/indicator/GC.REV.XGRT.GD.ZS?locations=CR.

33. This section draws heavily on Booth, "Political Parties in Costa Rica."

34. Kenneth M. Roberts, "Rethinking Economic Alternatives: Left Parties and the Articulation of Popular Demands in Chile and Peru," and Carlos M. Vilas, "Participation, Inequality, and the Whereabouts of Democracy," both in Douglas A. Chalmers, Carlos M. Vilas, Katherine Hite, Scott B. Martin, Kerianne Piester, and Monique Segarra, eds., *The New Politics of Inequality in Latin America: Rethinking Participation and Representation* (Oxford: Oxford University Press, 1997); and William I. Robinson, *Promoting Polyarchy: Globalization, U.S. Intervention and Hegemony* (Cambridge: Cambridge University Press, 1996).

35. Regine Steichen, "Cambios en la orientación política-ideológica de los partidos políticos en la década de los '80," and Marcelo J. Prieto, "Cambios en las organizaciones políticas costarricenses," in José Manuel Villasuso, ed., *El nuevo rostro de Costa Rica* (Heredia, Costa Rica: Centro de Estudios Democráticos de América Latina, 1992); Wilson, *Costa Rica: Politics, Economics, and Democracy*; and Carlos Sojo, "En el nombre del padre: Patrimonialismo y democracia en Costa Rica," in Manuel Rojas Bolaños and Carlos Sojo, *El malestar con la política: Partidos y élites en Costa Rica* (San José, Costa Rica: Facultad Latinoamericano de Ciencias Sociales, 1995), pp. 84–86.

36. Oscar Alvarez, "Costa Rica," *Boletín Electoral Latinoamericano* 17 (January–June 1997), p. 60.

37. Ibid., and Manuel Rojas Bolaños, "Las relaciones partido gobierno," in Manuel Rojas Bolaños and Carlos Sojo, *El malestar con la política: Partidos y élites en Costa Rica* (San José, Costa Rica: Facultad Latinoamericano de Ciencias Sociales), pp. 36–50; Booth, *Costa Rica: Quest for Democracy*, Ch. 8; and Wilson, *Costa Rica: Politics, Economics, and Democracy*, p. 161.

38. Amaru Barahona, "Costa Rican Democracy on the Edge," *Envio* 250 (May 2002).

39. Tribunal Supremo de Elecciones, Costa Rica, "Elecciones 6 de febrero 2006: Escrutinio definitivo para elección de diputados," www.tse.go.cr/escrutinio_f2006/Diputados/0.htm/, accessed June 17, 2009.

40. Polling data drawn from Latin American Public Opinion surveys (see Chapter 9 for details) and Mollie J. Cohen, Noam Lupu, and Elizabeth Zechmeister, eds., *The Political Culture of Democracy in the Americas 2016/17: A Comparative Study of Democracy and Governance* (Nashville, TN: Latin American Public Opinion Project, Vanderbilt University), p. 21.

41. "Limitado aporte Polsepaz," *La Nacion* (February 17, 2011), www.nacion.com/opinion/editorial/Limitado-aporte-Polsepaz_0_1178082231.html; and Alex Sanchez, "Costa Rica: An Army-less Nation in a Problem-Prone Region," Council on Hemispheric Affairs (June 2, 2011), www.coha.org/costa-rica-an-army-less-nation-in-a-problem-prone-region/.

42. "Costa Rica's Judiciary Reports First Drop in Homicide Rate in Six Years; Minister's Goal is Eliminating Epidemic." *NotiCen*, (June 21, 2013); Corey Kane and Zac Dyer, "Drugs Drive Rising Homicide Rates in Costa Rica," *The Tico Times* (August 21, 2013), www.ticotimes.net/More-news/News-Briefs/Drugs-drive-rising-homicide-rates-in-Costa-Rica_Wednesday-August-21-2013.

43. The PLN briefly maneuvered to hold on to the presidency by holding the vote without a quorum, required by Assembly rules.

44. Esteban Oviedo, "Ministro: La gente opinó sobre una mala percepción," *La Nación* (August 4, 2012), www.nacion.com/archivo/Ministro-gente-opino-mala-percepción_0_1284871706.html; www.nacion.com/archivo/Presidenta-absuelve-Liberman-Garnier-archiva_0_1279272178.html; "Fallout From Costa Rican Tax Scandal Ceases after Congress-Government Tug of War," *NotiCen* (August 23, 2012).

45. Esteban Oviedo, "Laura Chinchilla saca peor nota de los últimos 6 gobiernos," *La Nacion* (July 8, 2013), www.nacion.com/nacional/politica/Chinchilla-saca-peor-ultimos-gobiernos_0_1352464780.html.

46. Ronald Alfaro-Redondo and Mitchell Seligson, "Cultura política de la democracia en Costa Rica, 2012: La erosión de los pilares de estabilidad política," www.vanderbilt.edu/lapop/cr/Costa_Rica_Country_Report_2012_Reduced_W.pdf.

47. Eduardo Arcos, "Costa Rica's Rollercoaster Election was About more than Gay Marriage." *World Politics Review*, February 9, 2018, www.worldpoliticsreview.com/articles/24159/costa-rica-s-rollercoaster-election-was-about-more-than-gay-marriage.

48. Bjorn Kjelstad, "What Is Behind Growing Violence in Costa Rica?" *InSight Crime*, August 16, 2018, www.insightcrime.org/news/analysis/what-is-driving-increased-violence-costa-rica/.

49. UNHCR, "One Year into Nicaraguan Crisis, More Than 60,000 Forced to Flee Their Country," April 16, 2019, www.unhcr.org/en-us/news/briefing/2019/4/5cb58bd74/year-nicaragua-crisis-60000-forced-flee-country.html.

50. Kirk Semple, "Nicaraguan Migrants Fleeing Turmoil Test Costa Rica's Good Will." *New York Times*, September 22, 2018, www.nytimes.com/2018/09/22/world/americas/nicaragua-migrants-costa-rica.html.

51. Laura Alvarado, "Labor Strike that Paralyzed Public Education for a Month in Costa Rica Deemed Illegal." *The Costa Rica Star*, October 9, 2018, https://news.co.cr/labor-strike-that-has-paralyzed-public-education-for-a-month-in-costa-rica-deemed-illegal/76585/.

RECOMMENDED READINGS AND RESOURCES

Booth, John A. 1998. *Costa Rica: Quest for Democracy*. Boulder, CO: Westview Press.

Lehoucq, Fabrice E. and Ivan Molina. 2006. *Stuffing the Ballot Box: Fraud, Electoral Reform, and Democratization in Costa Rica*. Cambridge: Cambridge University Press.

Paus, Eva. 2005. *Foreign Investment, Development, and Globalization: Can Costa Rica Become Ireland?* New York: Palgrave Macmillan.

Sandoval-Garcia, Carlos. 2004. *Threatening Others: Nicaraguans and the Formation of National Identities in Costa Rica.* Athens, OH: Ohio University Press.

Seligson, Mitchell A., 2002. "Trouble in Paradise: The Impact of the Erosion of System Support in Costa Rica." *Latin American Research Review* 37 (1): 160–185.

Seligson, Mitchell A. and Edward Muller. 1987. "Democracy, Stability, and Economic Crisis: Costa Rica, 1978–1983." *International Studies Quarterly* 31 (September): 301–326.

Wilson, Bruce. 1998. *Costa Rica: Politics, Economics and Democracy.* Boulder, CO: Lynne Rienner Publishers.

Yashar, Deborah J. 1997. *Demanding Democracy: Reform and Reaction in Costa Rica and Guatemala, 1870s–1950s.* Stanford, CA: Stanford University Press.

5

NICARAGUA

NICARAGUA HAS ABUNDANT ARABLE LAND AND WIND, hydroelectric, geothermal, timber, and mineral resources, and (possibly) petroleum reserves. It also has access to two oceans and a lake and river system that could allow an interoceanic waterway. Yet Nicaraguans today are the poorest Latin Americans. This paradox arises from extreme dependency established in the colonial period, institutionalized in the twentieth century, and deepened by war and geopolitics. Despite paroxysms of war, dictatorship, revolution, and counterrevolution, Nicaragua's perennially fractured political and economic elites continue to fail to advance the country's economic or political development. Revolution gave birth to a short-lived civilian democracy, but eventually it succumbed as caudillo-style politics brought back autocratic one-party rule and repression.

HISTORICAL BACKGROUND

Nineteenth-century Nicaragua suffered repeated civil wars and foreign interference. During the first several decades, the Liberal and Conservative elites, based in the cities of León and Granada, respectively, struggled to control the national government. At the same time, Britain and the United States—both interested in a transoceanic waterway—maneuvered to occupy the power vacuum left by Spain.

At mid-century, foreign interference and the Liberal–Conservative conflict caused a war. In the late 1840s the British and Americans almost fought over a British attempt to seize the mouth of the San Juan River. In the resulting Clayton-Bulwer Treaty (1850), the United States and Britain mutually renounced the right to any unilateral exploitation of the region. However, the California gold rush of the 1850s deepened US interest in Central America as a shortcut between the eastern and western coasts of North America. In 1855 one of two competing transit companies in Nicaragua and Panama became embroiled in Nicaragua's Liberal–Conservative clash. Liberals, seeking advantage in the business dispute, imported a small mercenary army of North Americans commanded by adventurer William Walker to help them defeat the Conservatives. The plan backfired when the Tennessean took power for himself. This left Nicaragua's Liberals so discredited by association with the interloper that, after defeating Walker, Conservatives ruled virtually unchallenged until 1893.

In the nineteenth century, globalization in the form of coffee cultivation brought profound social and economic changes. Before 1870, intra-elite turmoil and relatively low foreign economic control had helped Nicaragua develop an internal market and a numerous free peasantry. One foreign observer stated: "Peonage such as is seen in Mexico and various parts of Spanish America does not exist in Nicaragua … Any citizen whatever can set himself up on a piece of open land … to cultivate plantain and corn."[1] This pattern changed when growing international demand for coffee brought its cultivation to Nicaragua. Coffee required new land and cheap labor. By the 1870s elites began to dispossess peasant and Indian farmers in the northern highlands, using self-serving legislation, chicanery, and violence. Displaced peasants had few options except peonage on coffee plantations. When some of them rebelled in the War of the Comuneros of 1881, the government killed thousands to suppress the uprising.

Coffee production that displaced peasant smallholdings accelerated under a modernizing Liberal dictator, José Santos Zelaya (1893–1909). Zelaya also built educational and governmental infrastructure (censuses, archives, a more modern army) and defended the interests of Nicaragua and Central America against the burgeoning imperialism of the United States. After the US decision to build a trans-isthmian canal in Panama, Zelaya sought a canal deal with US rivals Germany and Japan. To protect its canal monopoly, in 1909 the United States encouraged Zelaya's Conservative opposition to rebel and then landed marines to protect the rebels. In 1909, Zelaya resigned and in 1910 the Liberals relinquished power to the Conservative Party. By 1912, however, the Conservatives performed so badly that a combined Liberal-Conservative rebellion occurred. US marines occupied Nicaragua to suppress the revolt.

From most of 1912 to 1933, the United States militarily occupied Nicaragua. US-dominated governments generally followed Washington's dictates, even when contrary to Nicaraguan interests. The Chamorro-Bryan Treaty of 1916, for example, gave the United States rights to build a canal across Nicaragua. The Americans had no intention to build a canal; they simply wanted to block competition for the US-built waterway just completed in Panama. In 1928, the United States pressured Nicaragua to cede to Colombia several Nicaraguan islands, including San Andrés, to mollify Colombia for the US role in taking Panama from Colombia in 1903.

Finally, the United States forced Nicaragua to create a modern constabulary combining army and police—the Nicaraguan National Guard (Guardia Nacional). A movement resisting US occupation sprang up in 1927, led by the charismatic guerrilla-patriot Augusto C. Sandino. US marines could not defeat Sandino's resistance, so the National Guard was enlarged to assist in the struggle. The war was a standoff, and the United States eventually withdrew its troops at the end of 1932. The National Guard then became the vehicle by which its first Nicaraguan commander, Anastasio Somoza García, created and consolidated the Somoza family dictatorship, which subsequently brutalized Nicaragua for over four decades.

As commander of the National Guard, Somoza García had Sandino assassinated in 1934 and used the Guard to capture political power in 1936. Thereafter, three Somozas dominated Nigaragua from 1936 until 1979. Somoza García was either president or the power behind puppets until his assassination in 1956. His son, Luis Somoza Debayle, ruled directly or through surrogates until 1967. Luis's younger brother, Anastasio Somoza Debayle, was "elected" to the presidency in 1967 and ruled until 1979. Throughout, the Somoza dynasty rested on two pillars of support: the United States and the National Guard. A Somoza always commanded the Guard and purposely isolated it from the people. They allowed the Guard to become thoroughly corrupt to ensure its loyalty to the Somozas. A mafia in uniform, the Guard ran prostitution, gambling, and protection rackets, took bribes, and extorted kickbacks for various legal and illegal activities.

The Somozas secured US support with personal ingratiation and political subservience. They expertly cultivated Americans. Each was educated in the United States, spoke fluent vernacular English, and knew how to be a "good old boy" among ethnocentric, often homesick North American diplomats and visitors. The Somozas always supported US policy, whether anti-Axis during

World War II or anti-Communist thereafter. They allowed Nicaragua to serve as staging grounds for the Central Intelligence Agency (CIA)-organized exile invasions of Guatemala (1954) and Cuba (1961), participated in the US occupation of the Dominican Republic (1965), and offered Nicaraguan troops for the Korea and Vietnam wars.

As a result, US support for the Somozas usually remained strong and visible. Especially after the beginning of the Alliance for Progress in 1961, the United States underwrote extensive social and economic projects (despite ample evidence that the Somozas and accomplices stole much of the aid). US ambassadors were normally unabashedly pro-Somoza. During the 1960s and 1970s, Nicaragua received far more US military support than other Central American and Latin American countries (see Table A.3).

GLOBAL FORCES AND INSURRECTION

Effects of Rapid Economic Growth. Governed by Somozas and stimulated by the Central American Common Market and Alliance for Progress, Nicaragua underwent rapid industrialization and expanded export agriculture production during the 1960s and early 1970s. Growth was impressive—per capita gross domestic product (GDP) rose an average of almost 3.9 percent each year from 1962 to 1971, and an average of 2.3 percent annually between 1972 and 1976, by far the fastest increase in the region.[2] This brought other social change. Between 1960 and 1980, Nicaragua had Central America's biggest surge in urban population and manufacturing output, and its biggest decline in the agricultural workforce (see Tables A.1 and A.2). Despite impressive growth, government policies prevented the benefits from this new economic activity from reaching poorer Nicaraguans. The regime repressed unions and kept wages—normally set by the regime—low. Consumer prices rose moderately between 1963 and 1972. But after the Organization of Petroleum Exporting Countries (OPEC) oil embargo, escalating oil prices drove inflation up to almost 11 percent a year from 1973 through 1977. Real wages (corrected for inflation) among ordinary Nicaraguans peaked in 1967 and began a long slide that by the late 1970s ate away a third of their 1967 purchasing power. Workers' share of national income increased during the 1960s but also fell sharply in 1974 and 1975.[3] Wage-earning Nicaraguans suffered a palpable drop in their ability to feed and shelter their families.

Income inequality had become very great by 1977, when the wealthiest fifth of the people earned 59.9 percent of the national income, while the poorer half was left with only 15.0 percent.[4] The devastating Managua earthquake of December 24, 1972, aggravated this income shift by putting tens of thousands of white- and blue-collar workers out of work.

Nicaragua's middle class saw living standards improve during the 1960s, then decline sharply after 1973. Middle-class employment shrank markedly after the December 1972 Managua earthquake destroyed many small businesses and commercial jobs: 9,000 manufacturing jobs (about 13 percent of the total) disappeared from 1972 to 1973, as did 15,000 service-sector jobs (over 7 percent of the total). New jobs shifted to the lesser-paying construction sector, which nearly doubled in size by 1974, and to the informal sector.[5] The government levied a stiff surtax on those still employed to finance reconstruction, but corrupt officials stole much of the proceeds. The workweek was extended by as much as 25 percent without increasing pay.[6]

During the Central American Common Market (CACM) boom, employment failed to keep up with rapid workforce growth. Unemployment rose from below 4 percent in 1970 to 13 percent by 1978, despite rapid economic growth.[7] Hardest hit were workers the earthquake left jobless and peasants forced off the land by rapidly expanding agricultural production for export. Underemployment—an inability to find full-time work, or acceptance of agricultural wage-labor because of insufficient farmland for family subsistence farming—affected five times more Nicaraguans than unemployment.

In agriculture, land ownership concentration increased from the 1950s through the 1970s, especially in the fertile and populous Pacific zone. High cotton prices permitted speculating large landholders to squeeze subsistence cultivators off the land and into the oversupplied wage-labor market.[8] "The process of agricultural development was a concentrator of both land and income."[9] In the 1950s and 1960s the government gave preferential treatment in trade, credit, financing, and material-technical support to agro-industries belonging to the Somozas and their cohorts.

During the 1960s and 1970s, Nicaragua's three major capitalist factions, which centered around the Banco de América, the Banco Nicaragüense, and the Somoza family interests, began to converge.[10] Once separated from each other by regional, clan, and political party differences, these investor factions increasingly prospered and intertwined under the CACM. Following the Managua earthquake, however, the Somoza faction became aggressively greedy, undermining other investor groups. Growing political and labor unrest caused many Nicaraguan capitalists to doubt whether the regime could sustain growth. Anastasio Somoza Debayle's upper-class support began to erode in the mid-1970s.

By both relative and absolute measures, during the 1970s poor and middle-class Nicaraguans lost some of their share of overall national income and wealth, and of their real earning power. Even some wealthy Nicaraguans lost ground in the 1970s. Such losses doubtless created strong economic grievances.

Popular Mobilization. Falling working-class wages in the late 1960s and early 1970s revitalized the nation's long-suppressed industrial labor movement,[11] which stepped up organization, work stoppages, and strikes in 1973–1975.[12] The erosion of middle-class living standards also expanded union membership and organization, and brought strikes by such public-sector workers as teachers and health personnel. Catholic social workers, missionaries, and priests began organizing unions among Pacific-zone peasant wage-laborers in the 1960s. As a tool for teaching the gospel, Catholic social promoters also organized hundreds of small Christian base communities (*comunidades eclesiales de base*, CEBs) among urban and rural poor people. CEBs, joined by Protestant-organized groups after the Managua quake, encouraged community self-help activism and demanded better urban services and housing.[13] Peasant unions increasingly pressed for wage gains, especially after 1975.[14]

With economic deterioration, Nicaraguan private-sector pressure organizations grew and more boldly criticized the government, especially after 1974. Such private-sector groups as the business leader-dominated Democratic Liberation Union (Unión Democrática de Liberación, UDEL) called for political and economic reform.

New opposition political parties (particularly, the Social Christian Party) became active in Nicaragua in the 1960s and 1970s.[15] New anti-Somoza factions of the old Conservative and Liberal parties developed during the 1970s. Conservative Party elements united with the Social Christian Party and the anti-Somoza Independent Liberal Party in the National Opposition Union (Unión Nacional Opositora, UNO) to contest the 1967 national election. Student opposition to the regime grew rapidly during the 1970s. The Sandinista National Liberation Front (Frente Sandinista de Liberación Nacional, FSLN), the only surviving rebel group of some 20 guerrilla bands that had appeared between 1959 and 1962, greatly expanded its links to and support from university student groups during the 1970s.[16]

Government Repression and Its Effect on Opposition. President Anastasio Somoza Debayle declared a state of siege and escalated repression in late December 1974 after an embarrassing FSLN hostage-taking incident. The National Guard murdered several thousand mostly innocent rural people suspected as subversives or possible FSLN sympathizers during the ensuing three-year reign of terror.[17] During a brief lifting of the state of siege because of pressure from the Carter administration, public protests rose rapidly. The government then redoubled repression in urban areas. The National Guard murdered hundreds of youths suspected of pro-Sandinista sympathies. From 1977 on, the intensifying war against the citizenry drove thousands, especially youths, into the FSLN.

Following the January 1978 assassination of Pedro Joaquín Chamorro, editor of the opposition newspaper *La Prensa*, bourgeois elements redoubled their anti-regime efforts. Key business interests such as the Superior Council of Private Initiative (Consejo Superior de la Iniciativa Privada, COSIP) joined unions and moderate parties to support general strikes, and to form the Broad Opposition Front (Frente Amplio Opositor, FAO). Backed by the United States and Nicaragua's Catholic hierarchy, the FAO strove unsuccessfully to negotiate an end to the Somoza regime lest the FSLN overthrow it.[18]

Popular uprisings spread across urban Nicaragua between August and October 1978. On August 23, 1978, a Sandinista unit seized the National Palace, capturing over 2,000 hostages, including most members of the Chamber of Deputies. They negotiated the release of 60 Sandinistas from prison, a ransom, and safe passage out of the country. Days afterward, opposition leaders called a successful general strike. In September, thousands spontaneously attacked National Guard posts and drove the regime's troops from several communities. These revolts in Masaya, Rivas, Jinotega, Matagalpa, Estelí, and Managua typically occurred without much FSLN coordination. The National Guard crushed each uprising, slaughtering civilians and damaging property and public services.

The FSLN, split for several years over tactics, eventually realized that popular outrage had rendered its internal debate sterile. The three Sandinista factions quickly reunified in 1979 under the Joint National Directorate (Dirección Nacional Conjunta, DNC) and built a network of wealthy and prominent supporters embodied by the Group of Twelve (Grupo de los Doce). When the FAO-regime negotiations collapsed in early 1979, moderate and even conservative anti-Somocistas turned to the Sandinistas as the last option to defeat the regime. In 1979 the FSLN forged the United People's Movement (Movimiento Pueblo Unido, MPU) and National Patriotic Front (Frente Patriótico Nacional, FPN) coalitions, confederations that united virtually the entire opposition in commitment to defeat the Somoza regime. In May 1979 an FSLN-led provisional government formed in San José, Costa Rica to formally embody the opposition's revolutionary claim to sovereignty.

By opening its military ranks to all regime opponents and by forging broad alliances, the FSLN garnered critical resources for a final offensive against the regime. Its military ranks ballooned from fewer than 500 troops under arms in mid-1978 to between 2,500 and 5,000 by June 1979. The revolutionary coalition in 1979 enjoyed effective control over parts of northern Nicaragua, sanctuary for bases and political operations in Costa Rica, and diplomatic support from France and various Latin American regimes. FSLN agents purchased weapons from US dealers and took delivery at a base camp in Honduras. Cuba, Venezuela, Panama, and Costa Rica provided arms shipments to the FSLN for the final offensive. Whenever FSLN forces entered a community in combat, many local residents spontaneously fought alongside them or otherwise assisted them, vastly enhancing the guerrillas' strength and capabilities.

The Outcome. The FSLN-led coalition's unity, material resources, popular support, military capacity, and external backing all grew rapidly in late 1978 and 1979. The revolutionary government in exile in 1979 took advantage of support from Costa Rica, where it enjoyed political sanctuary, popular sympathy, and secure FSLN bases. Within Nicaragua, FSLN troops enjoyed much voluntary popular support when fighting the National Guard.

The Somoza regime's strength faded in 1978 and 1979 while its opposition grew. Numerous spontaneous popular uprisings against the government took place in late 1978. The regime lost the support of most social classes and interest sectors, save portions of Somoza's Liberal Nationalist Party (Partido Liberal Nacionalista, PLN) and the National Guard. PLN and regime supporters—many corrupt and anxious to escape with their wealth—began leaving Nicaragua. The desertion of Somocistas became a flood after National Guard troops casually murdered ABC reporter Bill Stewart before the network's cameras on June 20, 1979. The tyrant's associates sensed that this act had destroyed their remaining legitimacy outside Nicaragua.

The Carter administration had announced its opposition to Somoza's continued rule, a big loss for the regime. The United States struck new aid to Nicaragua from the 1979 budget and blocked pending deliveries by some of Somoza's arms suppliers. Although the US government wanted Somoza out, it also tried ineffectually to keep the Sandinistas from power. The Organization of American States and numerous Latin American regimes had openly sided with the opposition by 1979. The National Guard fought tenaciously against the Sandinistas and Nicaraguan people but became encircled and was pushed back toward Managua during the seven-week final offensive. Having looted the national treasury, Somoza ultimately gave up and fled to Miami on July 17, 1979. When the Guard collapsed two days later, the Sandinista-led rebel coalition took power. These dramatic events mark the first great regime change we examine in Central America in the 1970s and 1980s: Nicaragua's passage from personalistic military rule to revolution. This shift started processes of transformation and violent resistance in Nicaragua, and prompted much change elsewhere in the isthmus.

The Revolution

The revolutionary government faced grievous problems. The war took 50,000 lives—almost 2 percent of the populace. (An equivalent loss to the United States today would be 6.3 million—some 110 times the US death toll in the Vietnam War.) Property losses approached $1.5 billion. Important export and domestic crops went unplanted. The new government inherited $1.6 billion in international debts from the old regime. To its chagrin, the new government realized that it would have to pay Somoza's debt to remain creditworthy in international financial circles. Grave and longstanding problems of public health, housing, education, and nutrition, all exacerbated by the war, awaited the new regime.

In power, the Sandinista-led revolutionary coalition sought to destroy the Somoza regime and its economic power base, to replace its brutality and inequities with a fairer, more humane, and less corrupt system, and to reactivate the economy. The Sandinistas wanted to move the economy toward socialism in order to improve the lot of the lower classes, to build participatory democracy under their own leadership, and to integrate all Nicaraguans into the national social and political system. Others in the coalition disagreed about much of the revolutionary program and hoped to share power with, or wrest it away from, the FSLN. Such differences quickly established new conflicts and shattered the anti-Somocista alliance.

US–Nicaraguan Relations and the Contra War. The Sandinistas feared that the United States might try to reverse the Nicaraguan revolution, as it had in Guatemala (1954), Cuba (1961), the Dominican Republic (1965), and Chile (1973). Although the Carter administration had criticized and opposed Somoza, it also worked tenaciously to deny the Sandinistas power. Even before the FSLN took over, President Carter authorized the CIA to fund segments of the press and labor movement.[19]

The Carter administration offered the new regime a nervous gesture of friendship with diplomatic recognition, emergency relief aid, and the release of suspended loans from prior years' aid packages in 1979, and a new $75 million loan commitment in 1980. In 1979–1980 the Sandinistas had decent working relations with the United States but warily regarded US links to several thousand National Guardsmen who had escaped to Honduras and the United States. First the Argentine military and then the CIA organized these ex-Somocista forces, which began to conduct terrorist attacks on Nicaragua from their Honduran refuge.[20] In 1981 the incoming Reagan administration began trying to reverse the Nicaraguan revolution and destabilize the Sandinista government. Reagan accused Nicaragua (with little evidence) of trafficking arms to El Salvador's rebels, and stopped the balance of the Carter administration's $75 million loan and wheat-purchase credits.

The United States thereafter escalated its harassment and aggression against Nicaragua. Military pressure included massive aid given to build Honduras' military, continuous "maneuvers" in Honduras, and intensive espionage activities. The United States worked continuously to isolate Nicaragua diplomatically from its Central American neighbors. These pressures, sweetened with generous US aid, persuaded both Honduras and Costa Rica to provide sanctuary to anti-Sandinista rebels. The United States blocked a possible peace agreement among Central American nations negotiated by the Contadora group (Latin American conflict-mediating nations including Mexico, Panama, Colombia, and Venezuela). Washington convinced multilateral lenders and development agencies to deny credit to Nicaragua, and in May 1985 embargoed trade with Nicaragua. US propaganda—energetic and inaccurate—denounced the revolutionary government and exalted the Sandinistas' enemies.

The Reagan administration mounted a proxy military-political effort to topple the Sandinistas. In 1981 Reagan gave the CIA $19.8 million to support and augment an exile army of anti-Sandinista counterrevolutionaries (the Contras). Their nucleus was former National Guard officers and soldiers and political allies of the former dictator. From 1982 on, attacks across the Honduran border occurred almost daily. Contra forces regularly sabotaged bridges and other economic targets, and killed almost a thousand Nicaraguan civilians and military personnel by late 1982.

By 1983 there existed four major Contra groups: the Honduras-based Nicaraguan Democratic Force (Fuerzas Democráticas Nicaragüenses, FDN), the Costa Rica-based Revolutionary Democratic Alliance (Alianza Revolucionaria Democrática, ARDE), and two Miskito Indian groups. The Reagan administration organized a Contra political directorate to present a palatable public front and facilitate continued funding by Congress. In 1983 the Contras began extensive guerrilla operations in rugged northeastern and southeastern Nicaragua. The CIA added to the destruction by blowing up Nicaraguan oil-storage tanks and pipelines, and mining harbors on both coasts. The CIA also provided the Contras with intelligence, funding, and training (including a sabotage manual for Contra soldiers and another for Contra leaders that recommended assassination of pro-Sandinista civilians).[21]

By 1985 the Contras had 15,000 troops but had achieved little success against the Nicaraguan military. They had, however, chalked up considerable economic sabotage and atrocities, killing 13,000 people. In the mid-1980s, the US Congress reacted to these developments by defunding for the Contra war and legally restraining US efforts to topple the Sandinistas. The Reagan administration responded with covert efforts to assist the Contras that included operations (some flatly illegal) by the National Security Council's Colonel Oliver North and other agencies. North brokered an illicit arms deal with Iran to provide off-the-books funds for the Contras. The United States also promoted cash gifts to the Contras from private domestic donors, compliant foreign governments, and (allegedly) even drug-smugglers.[22]

When these efforts surfaced in October 1986 they became known as the Iran-Contra scandal, which placed further US aid to the Contras in doubt. Reagan then pressed the Contras to intensify their offensive. Supported by a CIA-run military supply operation in 1987, the war escalated to its destructive peak and raised the overall death toll for the war to just under 31,000. Despite more combat operations, the Contras' military successes remained limited. After the Central American Peace Accord was signed in August 1987, the Contras eventually entered negotiations with the Sandinista government (1988), and the war wound down. The incoming Bush administration called for continued US assistance to hold the Contras together. Direct US aid to the Contras by 1989 totaled over $400 million. In the long run, they would not formally disarm and disband until mid-1990, months after the Sandinistas lost the externally manipulated election of February 1990.

The Revolutionary Government. What kind of government elicited such antagonism from three US administrations? The FSLN consolidated its political dominance over the new government by early 1980 but kept other coalition members in the junta, cabinet, and Council of State (Consejo de Estado). Though the FSLN's nine-man DNC held veto power over the government and its programs, the Sandinistas created a pluralistic system that encouraged representatives of the economic elite minority to participate. Upper-class, business, and various political party interests, although in the coalition, could not control policy and therefore became increasingly antagonistic toward the FSLN. The regime maintained a dialogue with business interests and with a coalition of opposition parties.[23]

The Sandinistas promoted their brand of democracy, emphasizing popular participation in making public policy and providing services and programs for the poor. At first scornful of elections because the Somoza regime had always manipulated them, the revolutionary government in mid-1980 announced its intention to postpone national elections until 1985. Immediately after the rebel victory, however, local elections had taken place all over Nicaragua. The Sandinistas also promoted grassroots organizations of women, workers, peasants, youth, children, and neighborhoods. Through these organizations hundreds of thousands of Nicaraguans debated and voted on issues, worked on local problems, participated in national health and literacy campaigns, petitioned their government, and met representatives of governmental bodies and national organizations. Encouraged by the regime, organized labor grew rapidly. Labor's demands for higher wages, however, soon clashed with government needs for economic austerity and the FSLN desire for dominance within the movement.

The Sandinistas argued all along that the new system must tolerate diversity of political opinion because it originated from a coalition, because they sought a mixed economy requiring the cooperation of business, and because the international climate required political pluralism to safeguard the revolution. When the junta added new pro-Sandinista groups to the Council of State in 1980, several other party groups cried foul and began voicing open opposition to the government. The climate for political opposition remained open but not completely free. Press coverage and public activities of other parties suffered under the state of emergency decreed in 1982. Pro-regime crowds (*turbas*) sometimes harassed critics of the regime, especially between 1982 and 1984.

The Council of State passed opposition-influenced election and party laws that set elections for president and National Assembly (to replace the junta and Council of State) in November 1984. The government lifted most restrictions on parties and the press for the campaign; it allowed free and uncensored access to government radio and television. A vigorous campaign ensued among seven parties. International election observers and the press[24] concurred that no fraud or intimidation by the FSLN occurred. Observers found the election marred by US pressure that contributed to one conservative coalition's decision not to participate at all and another party's presidential candidate's attempt to drop out late in the campaign. Nicaraguans elected Daniel Ortega Saavedra, DNC member and coordinator of the junta, president with 63 percent of the total vote. Opposition parties divided about one-third of the National Assembly.

The National Assembly immediately became a constituent assembly tasked to write a new constitution. Contrary to US criticism, the process was open and democratic. The resulting document provided for the rule of law, protection of human rights, checks and balances, and competitive elections to be held at six-year intervals.[25] The new election system, constitution, and government structures institutionalized the revolutionary regime. It left the Sandinistas in power, but presiding over a regime with much in common with other electoral democracies—the government accepted constitutional restraints and could be replaced in an election.

Despite external attacks and obstruction, the Sandinistas began their revolution successfully. They shaped a new governmental system, reactivated and reshaped much of the war-ravaged economy, and implemented numerous social programs. They provided expanded health services; national vaccination and health-education campaigns significantly lowered rates of polio, malaria, and infant mortality. A literacy crusade raised literacy rates from slightly under 50 percent to about 87 percent. Agrarian-reform programs promoted increased national self-sufficiency in food production, formed thousands of cooperative farms, and distributed considerable farmland to individuals and cooperatives.[26]

The growing Contra war, however, forced the government to reorganize to defend the revolution, and postponed or undermined social and economic programs. By 1987 over half of the national budget went for military expenditures; the armed forces expanded to 60,000 regulars and 100,000 militia. Social reforms, medical, health, and educational programs, and public services suffered. Medical care deteriorated, garbage pickup and water service in Managua were curtailed, schools went without supplies and repairs, buses and taxis lacked parts and repairs. From 1979 through 1983 regular visitors to Nicaragua noticed evident material progress, but after 1984 signs of decay proliferated.

The Sandinistas' human-rights performance, though not perfect, was good for a revolutionary regime and superior to that of Somoza and all other Central American governments except Costa Rica.[27] The government moved swiftly to prevent its own supporters and forces from abusing human rights in the chaos after seizing power. It established a new Sandinista Police and Sandinista Popular Army and worked to prevent abuses of authority. It humanely treated captured National Guard troops and officials, who were investigated, tried for their crimes, and sentenced. International human-rights agencies criticized the unfair procedures of the Special Tribunals used to try the 6,300 former guardsmen, but the special courts dismissed charges against or acquitted 22 percent of the prisoners. Despite the heinous crimes of some, no one was executed. By 1985 more than half of those sentenced had completed their sentences, been pardoned, or been released.[28]

Despite *La Prensa*'s receipt of CIA funding,[29] the regime allowed the opposition daily newspaper to operate for several years without censorship. During that period, however, the government briefly closed the paper several times for publishing false information in violation of the press law. Under the mounting pressure of the Contra war, the revolutionary government in 1982 decreed a state of emergency that suspended many civil guarantees. This implemented prior censorship of news content of all media, including the FSLN's own newspaper *Barricada*. Before the 1984 election, censorship eased and most civil rights were restored. Deepening war in 1985 and 1986 brought renewed rights restrictions. The government closed *La Prensa* indefinitely in June 1986 for endorsing US aid to the Contras,[30] but permitted it to reopen without prior censorship after the 1987 Central American Peace Accord was signed.

Two areas of human rights proved problematic for the revolutionary government. In 1982 the growing Contra war prompted relocation of 8,000 indigenous from their homes in the war zone along the Río Coco. The poorly handled relocation angered Miskitos. Thousands fled and many joined anti-Sandinista guerrilla groups.

> The external conflict created a context in which Miskito demands for self-determination were seen by the Sandinistas as separatist and related to US efforts to overthrow the government by arming indigenous insurgents and by attempting to turn world opinion against the Sandinistas through false accusations of "genocide."[31]

Real abuses of Miskito rights worsened tensions in the area,[32] but no credible observers concurred with US genocide charges.[33] By late 1983 the government changed course and began autonomy talks with Caribbean Coast indigenous peoples, aimed at increasing local self-determination. In 1985 it permitted the Miskitos to return to their homes. Tensions subsided and Miskito support for the Contras waned. The autonomy law passed in 1987, creating autonomous zones that gave peoples in the regions a measure of self-governance, the rights to preserve their own cultures and languages, control over resources, and made communal lands inalienable.

Religious practice remained generally free in Nicaragua under the revolution, but the government became increasingly intolerant of expressions of anti-regime political goals through religious practice or groups. The government admitted many foreign missionaries and permitted churches to take part in the literacy crusade of 1980 and 1981. Many Catholics and numerous Protestant congregations had supported the FSLN logistically during the insurrection and supported the new government. The Catholic Church hierarchy, however, increasingly opposed Sandinista rule. Church–regime conflict became overt by 1982. Certain Protestant sects' missionaries were denied entry to Nicaragua, and pro-FSLN groups on one occasion occupied properties of one sect before police evicted them.[34]

Government. Catholic Church relations nosedived with Pope John Paul II's visit to Nicaragua in 1983. Each side apparently deliberately provoked the other. Archbishop Miguel Obando y Bravo—long hostile to the Sandinistas— had become the leader of the internal opposition by 1984. Until the end of the Sandinista period, Obando (elevated to cardinal in 1985) and Catholic bishops repeatedly denounced government policy. Despite some efforts to seek dialogue with the Church, the government periodically closed Catholic Radio and deported a dozen foreign-born priests active in opposition politics. In 1986, when Bishop Pablo Antonio Vega endorsed US aid for the Contras, the government exiled him.[35] Following the signing of the Central American Peace Accord in 1987, Vega and other priests were permitted to return to Nicaragua.

In summary, assailed by increasing domestic criticism, economic woes, and the Contra war, the revolutionary government's human-rights performance deteriorated. Things improved around the 1984 election but declined again after 1985. Repression of critics and opponents remained much less violent than in Guatemala and El Salvador, but included intimidation, harassment, and illegal detention of opponents, independent union leaders, and human- rights workers; press censorship; curtailment of labor-union activity; and poor prison conditions. In 1988, however, the human-rights climate improved again with concessions to the opposition before national elections announced for early 1990.[36]

The Economy. Moderate, pragmatic economic policies diverged from those of other Marxist-led governments. The revolutionary government accepted the Somoza regime's international debt. It obtained hundreds of millions of dollars in grants and "soft" loans, mostly from Western governments and international organizations. And though it confiscated the properties of the Somozas and their cohorts, it preserved a private sector that accounted for between 50 and 60 percent of GDP. Early on, the economy recovered much of its pre-war production. Agrarian reform did not heavily promote state farming, but instead created many individual and cooperative smallholdings.[37] Though error-plagued, agrarian policy included credit and policies to encourage production by large export-oriented private farmers. US pressures to curtail Western credit to and trade with Nicaragua forced increasing reliance on the Eastern bloc for credit, other aid, and trade in the mid-1980s.[38]

Nicaraguan capitalists nevertheless felt insecure and reluctant to invest under the revolution. Contributing to their insecurity were the business sector's lack of control of politics, the Sandinista's Marxist philosophy, and new rules of the game when the government nationalized the import-export sector (providing increased control over the business environment). Moreover, industry suffered from the general decline of the Central American Common Market's import-substitution development model, a worldwide recession, and US credit and trade embargoes.[39]

The Sandinista government adopted policies to benefit the poor majority: wage increases, food subsidies, and expanded health, welfare, and education services. As economic austerity pressures grew, however, the government barred the newly expanded labor movement from striking (many strikes were nonetheless tolerated). The government borrowed abroad to cover revenue shortfalls. Security and social-welfare spending eventually outran tax and foreign-credit resources. To maintain continued critical foreign credit, the government by 1986 began serial currency devaluations and cuts in food subsidies and social programs.

The war, economic mismanagement, austerity measures, withdrawal of Soviet-bloc economic aid, and declining public and private investment drove rapid inflation of consumer prices.[40] Shortages grew between 1985 and 1989, and popular living standards and services deteriorated. "Urban wages in 1988 had fallen, according to some statistics, to only 10 percent of 1980 levels."[41] Inflation reached 1,200 percent in 1987 and then a mind-boggling 33,602 percent in 1988. Harsher austerity programs started in late 1988 curtailed 1989 inflation down to 1,690 percent.[42] These policies, however, weakened social services and benefits and left thousands of government employees jobless.

REPLACING THE REVOLUTION

The 1990 Election. By 1989 the US-orchestrated Contra war and embargo strangulation inflicted severe hardship on Nicaraguans. US policymakers knew that, in democracies, when economic conditions get bad, voters tend to vote against incumbents. Washington also knew that Nicaraguans had wearied of the war's destruction, including 30,865 people who had died by the end of 1989.[43] Thus by the late 1980s, internal conditions in Nicaragua had changed so radically that the US changed its strategy toward the 1990 elections compared to 1984.

American policy followed two tracks for Nicaragua's 1990 election. One denounced the electoral laws, procedures, and conditions in case the Nicaraguan people might re-elect the FSLN. This laid groundwork for denouncing a possible Sandinista victory as fraudulent. The second track promoted the opposition. Washington spent millions of covert and overt dollars[44] to weld a united opposition, the National Opposition Union (Unión Nacional Opositora, UNO), out of 14 squabbling microparties.[45] It then promoted Violeta Barrios de Chamorro to be the nominee. The United States thus micromanaged the FSLN's opposition while applying intense external pressure on the electorate.[46] The Contra war escalated sharply over the year before the election.[47] President Bush called President Ortega "an animal [and] a bull in a china shop,"[48] and received Violeta Chamorro at the White House. The United States promised to end the war and embargo should she win.

UNO won resoundingly on February 25, 1990. Chamorro captured 55 percent of the valid presidential votes, to Daniel Ortega's 41 percent. Of 92 seats in the National Assembly, UNO took 51 and the FSLN 39 (see Tables A.6 and A.7, for election results). On April 25, 1990, Daniel Ortega placed the presidential sash on Violeta Chamorro's shoulders.

The Chamorro Years, 1990 to 1997. The Chamorro administration challenges easy interpretation.[49] Its economic and social policies were harshly austere. Per capita GDP stagnated from 1990 through 1995, the region's worst economic performance, and real wages remained far below levels of prior decades.[50] Indeed, the UNDP's Human Development Index (based on per capita income, education levels, and life expectancy) lowered Nicaragua's rank among nations from 85th in the world when Chamorro took office to 117th when she left.[51] But her administration tamed runaway inflation and eventually restarted modest economic growth. President Chamorro labored to make peace and heal the political wounds of the Nicaraguan family. She viewed reconciliation as essential for successful governance and democratic consolidation.

The Sandinistas had already imposed harsh neoliberal structural reforms in the late 1980s in response to hyperinflation caused by Contra war spending. But the Chamorro administration embraced neoliberal economics and intensified its implementation. "The Nicaraguan government signed its first Contingency Agreement with the IMF in 1991, and then a comprehensive Enhanced Structural Adjustment Facility (ESAF) with the Fund in 1994, followed by a second ESAF in 1998."[52] Government properties were privatized, public expenditures cut, budgets balanced, and tariffs lowered. The downsizing of government, cutbacks in social services, privatization of state enterprises, and credit policy that favored export agriculture over peasant production of domestic foodstuffs exacerbated ordinary Nicaraguans' misery. For example, the US Agency for International Development (USAID) management of US-imposed "efficiency criteria" starved the peasant agricultural sector. "Deprived of credit and other state services and therefore the means to compete in the market, peasants were forced to sell their land."[53] Unemployment, underemployment, drug addiction, crime, homelessness (especially among children), and domestic violence all soared.

Other social programs changed after the Sandinistas' departure. Ideologically conservative administrators reshaped public education. They replaced carefully drafted Sandinista-era textbooks with US-approved and -financed generic texts, many of them years out of date. The demobilization of the Contras and most of the national armed forces threw tens of thousands into the economy without training or experience. The Chamorro administration failed to fulfill promises of land and resettlement benefits for ex-combatants. Sporadically throughout the 1990s rearmed Contras and ex-Sandinista soldiers renewed guerrilla activity or took up banditry in rural areas. Organized armed conflict gradually declined, but remnants persisted into the late 1990s.[54]

Despite having lost almost 3 percent of its population in the insurrection and Contra wars, Nicaragua overall progressed toward national reconciliation and democratic consolidation under Chamorro. Grassroots organizations representing the poor played a significant role. The Rural Worker's Association (Asociación de Trabajadores del Campo, ATC), the National Union of Farmers and Ranchers (Unión Nacional de Agricultores y Ganaderos, UNAG), and mixed groups of ex-combatants helped negotiate privatization of state farms and some land transfers to former workers and ex-combatants. The National Workers' Front (Frente Nacional de Trabajadores, FNT) did the same in privatizing urban state-owned properties. When the government proved unresponsive, grassroots groups protested to force government respect for their interests.

President Chamorro resisted US and domestic right-wing pressures for a vengeful "de-Sandinization" program. By allowing Sandinista General Humberto Ortega to remain head of the military, she assured that there would be no anti-Sandinista bloodbath. The FSLN accepted rapid demobilization of the army from 80,000 to 12,000 troops by 1998. The military's "senior commanders recognized that the only way to guarantee the military's survival was to sever its FSLN ties and accept increased civilian control."[55] In addition, Chamorro's government, FSLN leaders, and a wide spectrum of politicians engaged in frequent bargaining, negotiation, and pact-making. This ultimately resulted in a majority consensus in the National Assembly, which allowed promulgation of a new Military Code (1994) that unlinked the armed forces from the FSLN, some revisions of the 1987 constitution (1995), and the passage of a Property Stability Law 209 (1996) that set a framework for resolving property disputes arising from the revolution. Clean elections were held on the Caribbean Coast in 1994.

However, many problems arose. Violeta Chamorro's gestures of reconciliation toward the Sandinistas alienated parts of UNO. A nasty dispute over constitutional reforms that strengthened the National Assembly, expanded the Supreme Court, and prevented presidential self-succession paralyzed the government for much of 1994 and 1995.[56] Many former UNO leaders had become mayors in Nicaragua's cities. Nurtured with USAID funding provided exclusively to municipalities that had voted the Sandinistas out, these mayors cultivated popular support with public works. Under their leadership, the old Liberal Party—the majority party of Nicaragua until corrupted by the Somozas—resuscitated as various splinter groups and then fused into the Liberal Alliance (Alianza Liberal, AL).

A leading figure of this era was Arnoldo Alemán, a lawyer and farmer who had been a Liberal since the Somoza era. During the revolution he came to hate the Sandinistas because they had nationalized the bank he worked for, seized his farms, and put him under house arrest while his wife was dying. Elected Managua's mayor in 1990, Alemán governed the city as a neopopulist. US funds underwrote visible public works, patronage, and jobs for supporters. He courted poor constituents and blamed the Sandinistas for Nicaragua's problems. With financial and moral support from Cuban and Nicaraguan exiles in Miami, he and other Liberal mayors built the Liberal Alliance. Alemán won the AL presidential nomination for 1996.

The Sandinistas experienced difficulties during the Chamorro administration. As lame ducks in 1990, the FSLN government transferred much state property to top Sandinistas (dubbed *la piñata*). Out of power, the party's old guard discredited itself further by clinging to leadership when challenged to reform the organization in 1994. Reformist elements questioned the party's leadership, internal democracy, and trajectory.[57] A schism resulted; the breakaway Sandinista Renovation Movement (Movimiento de Renovación Sandinista, MRS) in 1995 took many talented intellectuals and leaders out of the FSLN. This left the FSLN dominated by "*Danielistas*," hard-line supporters of former president Ortega, now the party's effective caudillo.[58] Ortega easily won the FLSN presidential nomination.

The 1996 Election. Many viewed the 1996 election as problematic. In the polarized pre-election atmosphere, the right wing had insisted on a series of last-minute changes in the electoral law and personnel of the Supreme Electoral Council (Consejo Supremo Electoral, CSE). These changes and inadequate funding brought confusion and increased partisanship to electoral boards nationwide. Anomalies plagued voter registration, the campaign, preparation and delivery of materials, polling place operation, voting, tabulation, and vote reporting. Ultimately the CSE threw out the votes from hundreds of precincts.

The Liberal Alliance triumphed by a margin that rendered the discarded presidential votes immaterial. AL presidential candidate Alemán (51 percent of the vote) beat the FSLN's Ortega (38 percent). With 86 percent turnout, the Liberals took 42 National Assembly seats (45 percent), the FSLN 36 seats, and 9 minor parties split 15. Ortega and another presidential candidate initially labelled the Liberal victory illegitimate, but later accepted the outcome.[59]

CONTEMPORARY NICARAGUAN POLITICS

The Alemán presidency (1997–2002) became an inflection point for the Nicaraguan political system. Policies enacted, political deals made, and external economic decisions set the nation on a course that paradoxically would improve the economy yet undermine democracy and lead to political turmoil. Political elites would demonstrate shrinking commitment to democratic rules of the game. Democratic breakdown ensued as caudillo-style leadership culture revived.

The Economy. Decades of war, economic embargoes, and disinvestment left Nicaragua with the weakest economy in Latin America by 1990. There it has remained for three decades, despite growth and recovery. Early signs for the post-revolutionary economy looked bleak when, late in 1998, hurricane Mitch unleashed widespread flooding, deaths, and infrastructure damage that worsened Nicaragua's already depressed economy. Much of country's north suffered heavily, especially areas producing most of the nation's basic grains and coffee. The storm killed 2,800 people, destroyed or damaged almost 42,000 homes, left 65,000 in shelters, and started a surge in emigration abroad in search of work.

Deep poverty and natural disaster, however, also helped initiate two decades of economic growth. GDP and per capita GDP growth would accelerate after 2000 (see Table A.1). Several factors accounted for this protracted economic improvement, which brought urban growth, extensive public works, and new private investment and commerce. In late 1997 government–FSLN negotiations resolved the thorny property issue to end a constitutional crisis. The Assembly enacted the Law of Urban and Rural Reformed Property after a brief debate. It guaranteed land titles for many smallholder beneficiaries of property distributions during the revolution and after, indemnified people who lost property, and required major beneficiaries of *la piñata* to pay for their confiscated houses.[60]

These changes helped begin a new economic era in Nicaragua by easing fears about the investment climate. Some Nicaraguan capital that had fled during the revolution began coming back. The International Monetary Fund (IMF) resumed previously suspended support. Hurricane Mitch's damage moved international organizations to provide reconstruction assistance. A multilateral group of countries and organizations pledged loans of $1.8 billion over four years to promote macroeconomic stability, the development of agriculture, and governability. Private foreign investment also surged in the early 2000s.

Nicaragua's poverty qualified it for several billion dollars in external debt forgiveness under multilateral and bilateral programs for heavily indebted poor countries (HIPC). This reduced burdensome foreign loan payments and lowered external debt from 649 percent of GDP in 1991 to 23 percent by 2011.[61] Remittances from Nicaraguans living abroad surged after the hurricane and eventually grew severalfold to reach 10.8 percent of GDP by 2018. Venezuela became an important bilateral benefactor by providing cheap petroleum after 2000 and importing Nicaraguan goods. Venezuela also directly underwrote social welfare programs managed by the FSLN after Daniel Ortega won re-election in 2007.

The resulting long boom eventually ended when Venezuela's political and economic fortunes fell beginning around 2016. Venezuela curtailed its financial aid to Nicaragua, and defaulted on payments for its Nicaraguan exports. Loss of these revenues caused Nicaragua a sharp economic slowdown and budget deficit in 2018–2019, and these problems fed political turmoil.

Politics and Pacts. Nicaraguan democracy's decline into semi-democracy by 2006 and then to autocracy by 2016, we believe, had its roots in the conflict between the Liberal party of the Somozas and Sandino. In the insurrection and revolution of the 1970s and 1980s the FSLN and its allies devastated the Liberals. Two decades of democracy after 1987 succumbed to neo-caudillismo among a recovering Liberal movement (vengeful and increasingly fractious) and the Sandinistas in the critical 1996–2006 decade. Old partisan antagonisms exacerbated newer ones driven by war and revolution. Deals forged between enemies for short-term advantage ultimately proved Daniel Ortega better at the political long game than were Arnoldo Alemán and the Liberals, and that neither movement embraced democratic principles. Nicaragua's young democracy became the loser.

President Alemán and his ALN plurality in the National Assembly sought to punish the FSLN, first by denying its leaders their rightful seats on the National Assembly's executive body. They then challenged Chamorro-era laws (previously negotiated with the FSLN), on the military, property, and the constitution. The Sandinistas and their allies responded with strikes, demonstrations, invective, renewed armed insurgency, FSLN boycotts of the National Assembly, and litigation. Secretive bargaining between the contending leaders under heavy international and domestic pressure forced a compromise, including resolution of property claims.[62]

The leaders of the ALN and FSLN each suffered personal scandals. Escalating rumors of corruption engulfed Alemán and saw him prosecuted and imprisoned. Meanwhile Ortega's 30-year-old stepdaughter accused him of many years of sexual abuse.[63] Each lost prestige, although Alemán delayed his legal difficulties until after leaving office and Ortega clung to his role as leader of the FSLN. Meanwhile Nicaragua's economic and political elite failed to unite under neoliberal globalist leaders as occurred elsewhere. This left two feuding capitalist coalitions. One was a modernizing, externally oriented group identified with the Central Bank, globalist think tanks, and US and multilateral financial institutions. The other included older agro-export interests "imbued in the traditional politics of partisan corruption and patronage."[64]

In 1999 Ortega and Alemán, the caudillos of the FSLN and ALN, unexpectedly conspired to their mutual benefit. They forged a pact to "reform" the constitution and electoral law. One provision guaranteed losing presidential candidates and the immediate ex-president seats in the Legislative Assembly, which conveyed immunity from criminal prosecution. The deal also packed the Supreme Court, strengthened each leader within his own party, and rewrote the electoral law to privilege their parties over all other political movements. Immediate effects included a reduction of smaller-party representation in the 2001–2006 Assembly and future elections. Many Sandinistas believed the pact undermined democracy and quit the party.[65]

In 2001 the Liberal Alliance nominated Alemán's vice president, businessman Enrique Bolaños Geyer, to run against FSLN presidential nominee Daniel Ortega. Bolaños benefitted from a Bush administration campaign labeling Ortega a terrorist following the September 11 terrorist attacks in the United States.[66] The United States also persuaded Conservatives to align with the Liberals to prevent ticket-splitting among rightists. Bolaños won 56.3 percent of the vote. The Sandinistas captured 38 Assembly seats to the ALN's comfortable majority of 51. The Conservative Party, once second to the Liberals, captured only one seat. The FSLN had definitively supplanted the Conservatives as the Liberals' opposition in an unstable post-revolutionary party system.

As part of his anti-corruption campaign, President Bolaños and the National Assembly worked to repeal the effective amnesty for ex-presidents in the Alemán–Ortega pact. In 2002 the Assembly stripped Alemán of immunity from prosecution. Detained under house arrest, he was charged with laundering $100 million to party candidates and embezzling $1.3 million for himself. In 2004 a court sentenced Alemán to 20 years in detention, but the Supreme Court overturned his conviction in January 2009.[67] Soon Bolaños himself was beset by charges of campaign-finance fraud that he called politically motivated revenge by Alemán's and Ortega's supporters.

Bolaños' prosecution of Alemán split the PLC, controlled by Alemán supporters. Bolaños quit the party and helped found the Alliance for the Republic (Alianza para la República, APRE), a center-right alternative, before the 2004 municipal elections. The FSLN benefited handsomely from this Liberal schism and won new municipal governments nationwide, including the prized mayoralty of Managua. Alemán's beleaguered PLC lost considerable ground and Bolaños' APRE also performed poorly. Voter abstention exceeded 50 percent.[68]

In November 2004 a PLC–FSLN alliance in the National Assembly passed constitutional changes that would punish President Bolaños by shifting to the Assembly itself the power to appoint government ministers, diplomats, and other executive appointees.[69] Bolaños resisted, producing an impasse between him and the Assembly's PLC–FSLN coalition that paralyzed the country.[70] The crisis ended when Bolaños agreed not to challenge the revisions if implementation were delayed until after the 2006 elections. The FSLN dropped its insistence that Bolaños be removed and allowed the Central American Free Trade Agreement (CAFTA) to pass.

The FSLN in 2006 again nominated Daniel Ortega for president, with former Contra Jaime Morales as his running mate. The odd pairing revealed a campaign strategy to soften Ortega's image and emphasize reconciliation (i.e., triangulate to capture some rightist votes). As in 2001, the Sandinistas eschewed their traditional red and black colors for pink, and campaigned on messages of peace, love, and God. Candidate Ortega secured the support of the Catholic Church by repairing his relationship with Cardinal Miguel Obando y Bravo and supporting a ban on therapeutic abortions just days before the elections.[71] In a campaign of contradictions, Ortega vowed to fight poverty while endorsing market forces and CAFTA.

The divided opposition included the fragmented right and the Sandinista Renovation Movement (MRS) of former Sandinistas. Eduardo Montealegre, Alemán's former minister of the presidency and foreign relations, broke from the PLC to run on a newly formed Nicaraguan Liberal Alliance (Alianza Liberal Nicaragüense, ALN) ticket in coalition with the Conservatives. The

PLC nominated José Rizo Castellón, Bolaños' former vice president, who emphasized Ortega's ties to Fidel Castro and Hugo Chávez.[72] Herty Lewites, a popular former FSLN mayor of Managua, was expelled from the FSLN and became the MRS presidential candidate. Lewites died in July 2006 before the election and was replaced by economist Edmundo Jarquín.[73]

The United States interfered aggressively in the 2006 election campaign. US ambassador Paul Trivelli all but publicly endorsed Montealegre. Various US sources warned of dire consequences should Ortega win. Venezuela took the other side, sending oil and fertilizer to FSLN-led municipalities.[74] Ortega prevailed with a scant 38 percent of the votes, 5 percent less than he had obtained while losing in 2001. Montealegre received 29 percent, Rizo (PLC) 26 percent—unified Liberals might have won–and Jarquín (MRS) 6 percent. Ortega thus owed his victory to the Liberal split and the electoral law's low threshold of votes (35 percent) required to avoid a runoff.[75] The FSLN took 38 Assembly seats, the PLC 25, the ALN-PCN alliance 24 seats, and the MRS 5.

Buoyed by economic growth, multilateral aid, and remittances from abroad valued at 10 percent of GDP, President Ortega used two tactics to strengthen his political standing. First, he aimed myriad social policies at reducing poverty, estimated by the United Nations Development Program (UNDP) to include 80 percent of Nicaraguans. During his first year back in office, Ortega instituted free education, health, and literacy programs, and low-interest microloans for women. The Zero Hunger program distributed livestock. Although popular, critics argued these initiatives lacked sufficient funding and transparency. The government also established neighborhood Citizens Power Councils (CPCs) to administer local anti-poverty programs.[76] These operated under the National Plan for Human Development (Plan Nacional para el Desarrollo Humano, PNDH), headed by the president's wife, Rosario Murillo. Proponents described CPCs as expressions of popular power, free of partisanship and promoters of citizen participation.[77] Critics said they undermined civil society and were political tools reminiscent of Sandinista Defense Councils (CDS) of the 1980s.[78] Opposition parties voted in the Assembly to nullify Ortega's decree establishing the CPCs, but the president vetoed the law, a move upheld by the Supreme Court.

The 2008 municipal elections took place against a backdrop of violent protests and reprisals against regime critics. The CSE disqualified the MRS and Conservative Party for not having met threshold requirements for public support in the previous election. This narrowed the field and immediately advantaged the larger parties.[79] Although Nicaragua had welcomed observers for all five elections since 1984, in 2008 the CSE refused to accredit international and independent domestic observers.[80] Public confidence in political parties, elections, and various institutions declined between 2004 and 2008.[81] Government intimidation of civil-society organizations curtailed civil-society activism.[82]

In the 2008 municipal elections, the FSLN prevailed in 105 of 146 and the PLC won 37. The FSLN captured 13 of 17 departmental capitals, including Managua and León. The opposition protested, alleging fraud, including excessive and improper annulment of ballots (7 percent of the total), CPC intimidation of voters and interference with opposition at polling places, undistributed voter-identification cards, early poll closures, and vote counts in excess of registered voters.[83] The few informal international observers who managed to be present reported no evidence of fraud. CSE tallies awarded the mayoralty of Managua to former boxing champion Alexis Argüello of the FSLN, despite opponent Eduardo Montealegre's claims of irregularities.[84] Several former Sandinistas leaders also alleged fraud.[85] The United States and European Union responded by freezing aid. Washington cited transparency of the 2008 election and cut $62 million from a $175 million Millennium Challenge Corporation program.[86]

Semi-democracy. We date Nicaragua's shift from democracy to semi-democracy to 2006, although the date is imprecise. The change occurred through multiple rule changes implemented between 2004 and 2009, mainly through court rulings and election administration. These actions reinforced the FSLN–PLC pact by allowing party caudillos Ortega and Alemán to control the courts and the electoral field. The flawed 2006 presidential election reinstated Ortega in office, and the 2008 municipal elections and machinations behind the scenes and irregularities in each vote revealed that elections were no longer reliably free and fair. Increasing intimidation of opposition by pro-Sandinista mobs made it increasingly risky to represent or support an opposition party or to express dissent.

With his conviction overturned, Arnoldo Alemán announced his intention to seek the presidency again in 2011. Meanwhile, Daniel Ortega had already moved to retain power. Nicaragua's constitution prohibited consecutive re-election for presidents and mayors, and limited presidents to two terms. Either condition would have blocked Ortega's eligibility in 2011. When the National Assembly would not amend the constitution, Ortega and more than 100 FSLN mayors petitioned the Constitutional Chamber of the Supreme Court. They argued that the no-consecutive-election and term-limits provisions did not apply to all elected offices (specifically, the

Assembly) and were thus discriminatory. On its authority to resolve disputes over constitutional issues—but following questionable and highly criticized procedures—the Constitutional Chamber ruled for the plaintiffs.[87] The CSE forthwith approved Ortega's presidential candidacy for 2011. The National Assembly later removed the constitution's prohibitions against multiple terms and self-succession.

In January 2010 President Ortega faced losing key supporters on the CSE and CSJ when their terms ended. He issued a decree allowing 25 high-ranking officials to retain their posts until successors had been chosen. The National Assembly's failure to compromise on new appointees sparked violent protests in April 2010. When the Assembly tried to meet to overturn Ortega's decree, FSLN activists blocked opposition lawmakers from entering the building. When the deputies convened instead at a hotel, protesters attacked, injured three legislators, and damaged property.[88] No replacement nominees were made, so Ortega's officials remained in office.

Polls revealed Daniel Ortega's popularity to have grown considerably since 2006, likely assisted by economic growth and domestic aid programs. This suggested that only a unified opposition could defeat him in 2011. Arnoldo Alemán, his corruption sentence dismissed on appeal, would run for the PLC. A 79-year-old radio journalist and station owner Fabio Gadea Mantilla led the PLI slate, joined by Edmundo Jarquín of the MRS as vice presidential candidate. Other political factions endorsed Gadea and Jarquín's slate under the Nicaraguan Unity for Hope (UNE) banner.

The CSE blocked electoral observation again in 2011. Most domestic observer teams were refused accreditation, though some conducted observation nonetheless.[89] Unlike 2008, several prominent international observer missions were invited to participate, but too late to observe all phases of the election process.[90] International observers ultimately reported various irregularities: problems getting on the voter rolls, delayed distribution of voter-identity cards, difficulty accessing polling places, and concerns about the CSE's neutrality.[91] The European Union's mission noted "deterioration in the democratic quality of Nicaraguan electoral processes, due to the lack of transparency and neutrality with which they were administered by the Supreme Electoral Council."[92]

The flawed process provided President Ortega an easy re-election with 63 percent of the votes. Gadea captured 31 percent and Alemán only 6 percent, clear evidence of fading influence. The FSLN won 63 seats in the National Assembly, enough to partially amend the constitution. The PLI captured 27 seats and the PLC 2. Women won 36 of 93 Assembly seats (33 of them

Sandinistas). Though the outcome was no surprise—months of polling indicated a strong lead for Ortega—Gadea and Alemán nevertheless denounced
the results. Post-election violence caused several protester deaths and police
injuries. The United States expressed its disapproval by cutting some $3 mil-
lion in bilateral aid.

The international response to Nicaraguan elections aside, popular support
for President Ortega and the FSLN had grown since 2010. An April 2012
Mitofsky survey pegged Ortega's approval at 61 percent, one of the highest
in the region. When polled about the state of Nicaraguan democracy under
Ortega, 58 percent said it had been strengthened.[93] Public trust in two key
institutions involved in the vote, the CSE and the Supreme Court, increased
markedly following the 2011 elections. Three-quarters of survey respondents
reported observing no irregularities in the 2011 voting.[94] While these perceptions often depended on party affiliation, public support for the FSLN had
increased dramatically since Ortega's return to power in 2007.

A strengthening economy and anti-poverty programs likely contributed
to these approval levels. As of 2012, Nicaragua entered the sixth year of an
11-year economic expansion (from 2006 to 2017) at an average 3.2 percent
annual growth in GDP per capita, buoyed by growing remittances. Public
revenues were rising, and public expenditures were increasing at almost 10
percent per year.[95] Moreover, Ortega maintained Nicaragua's agreements with
the IMF and CAFTA, and signed new trade and investment agreements with
Panama, Taiwan, Russia, Chile, and the Bolivarian Alliance for the Americas
(ALBA). The Assembly passed legislation after 2007 that accelerated investment and garnered business-sector praise for President Ortega. ALBA continued supplying cheap Venezuelan oil and technological assistance, including
generators for the electrical grid and a $3.5 billion refinery. Venezuela also pro-
vided bilateral aid and cheap short-term loans. In 2010, Nicaragua received
more than $500 million in oil discounts and aid from Venezuela (equal to 7.6
percent of GDP). Not content with discounted Venezuelan oil, the Ortega
administration vigorously pursued such renewable energy sources as wind and
hydroelectric power.

In foreign affairs, Nicaragua had previously sought advantage in an old
dispute by suing Colombia in the International Court of Justice (ICJ) over
the San Andrés islands and waterways. In 2012 the ICJ ruled to expand Nicaragua's maritime territory there at Colombia's expense, and Nicaragua quickly
initiated exploratory drilling for oil in its new territory. In 2013 Nicaragua
filed a new ICJ complaint over Colombia's continued patrols in the area and
Colombia recalled its ambassador from Managua.[96]

A border dispute also roiled relations with Costa Rica. A 2009 ICJ ruling on the San Juan River had affirmed Nicaragua's sovereignty over the waterway following the first dispute, but also guaranteed Costa Rica right of use. In October 2012, Nicaragua began dredging the San Juan. Costa Rica charged this damaged its wetlands. Rhetoric escalated and Costa Rica further accused Nicaragua of a military incursion. The ICJ eventually ruled Nicaragua could continue dredging, but that neither party should use security forces in the disputed territory.

On the domestic scene, Venezuelan aid continued supporting the popular social programs Ortega had initiated in his previous term. Three of them together cost US $95 million.[97] Plan Techo provided roofing materials to low-income families. Others supplied low-interest loans and shoes and backpacks to schoolchildren in low-income families to encourage school attendance. Survey data from 2012 suggested that FSLN sympathizers and middle-class Nicaraguans received more assistance than the rural poor.[98]

Nicaragua controlled crime better than its regional neighbors. Nicaragua's community-policing model helped hold down crime. The homicide rate, 11 per 100,000 in 2012, was a fraction of those of its northern neighbors and would remain so for the rest of the decade.[99] Nicaragua avoided the transnational gang problem plaguing other countries and proved adept at crime prevention by specifically targeting the country's youth. However, crime rates, including homicides, remained higher in the Caribbean area Autonomous Zones than elsewhere because of drug trafficking and organized crime.[100]

Nicaragua also made some progress—at least legislatively—on the enduring problem of violence against women and girls. Nicaragua had the highest rate of inter-partner violence in Central America. Many victims of sexual violence (including incest) were distressingly young. Amnesty International reported that between 1998 and 2007 over two-thirds of Nicaraguan rape victims were under 17. Between 2002 and 2009, the number of girls aged 10 to 14 giving birth increased 48 percent.[101] In January 2012 the National Assembly passed the Comprehensive Law against Violence Toward Women (Law 779). It addressed physical and structural forms of violence and set sentencing guidelines for violent crimes against women, including femicide.[102] Religious leaders protested the law, saying it undermined families and would be abused by women seeking revenge. Opponents of Law 799 law unsuccessfully challenged its constitutionality in the Supreme Court because it prohibited mediation between victim and abuser, but the National Assembly subsequently amended Law 799 to permit mediation, despite protests by women's groups.

The FSLN-dominated National Assembly approved several changes to the municipal elections law. These eliminated the re-election ban for mayors, tripled the number of municipal council members, and provided that half of municipal office candidates must be females. A year after Ortega's re-election, the FLSN further consolidated its electoral dominance in the November 2012 local elections by winning 134 of 153 municipalities. Strongly indicating the effective collapse of the Liberal movement nationwide, the PLI won only 13 municipalities, the PLC two, and the ALN one. Yapti Tasba Masraka Nanih Aslatakanka (YATAMA), a Miskitu indigenous party, captured three municipalities. The CSE rejected challenges by the PLC and PLI.[103] Although concerns persisted about the voter registry and the transparency of the CSE, the elections effectively consolidated the FSLN's hegemony.

In 2013 the FSLN introduced and the National Assembly passed 97 constitutional amendments. Several affected elections: the elimination of presidential term limits, presidential election by a simple plurality, elimination of runoffs, and a gender quota requiring that 50 percent of all elected offices be held by women. Others aimed at solidifying the FSLN's Sandinistas' commitment to participatory democracy on the community level. Some amendments, such as redefining the country's borders to include the recent ICJ decision, enjoyed popular support. Others drew withering criticism for consolidating FSLN power and further eroding democratic practices: decree powers for the president and allowing current military personnel to hold government appointments. The government consulted with members of the opposition, civil society, and the business community after unveiling the proposals.

The amendments became effective in 2014. Several new laws on public security followed, including providing the military a role in internal security, allowing the president to appoint and extend the appointment of the director of the National Police, and allowing police personnel to participate in political activity. The December 2015 Sovereign Security law could potentially allow militarization of the National Police. These reforms and changes to the constitution further consolidated power in the presidency.

The gender quotas and resulting appointments of women to high-ranking positions, such as the director of the National Police and minister of defense, significantly improved women's representation in public life. In 2015, nearly 60 percent of cabinet positions were held by women. Nearly 40 percent of Supreme Court judges were women in 2015. In 2014, Nicaragua was ranked sixth of 142 countries surveyed in the World Economic Forum's *Global Gender Gap Report*, which evaluated gender-based inequality. The 2014 Family Code covered several issues related to women's status within relationships, including divorce, parental leave, child protection, legal age for marriage, and inheritance. It effectively granted men and women the same rights in marriage. The Family Code also defined "family" as a male–female union and barred adoptions to heterosexual couples. It was denounced by LGBT groups. A subsequent law prohibited discrimination in health service provision based on sexual identity, though it was unclear how successfully that was being implemented. The government also created an ombudswoman for sexual diversity.

Despite greater political representation of women, women and girls still suffered from high rates of violence. As many as one of every two women reported experiencing violence in her lifetime.[104] Nicaragua has one of the highest teenage and adolescent pregnancy rates in Latin America. Nearly 30 percent of women give birth before age 18, and nearly half of those among girls aged 10 to 14, most caused by rape.[105] Women-only police stations, established in 1993 to encourage reporting of gender-based violence, all closed in 2016 due to budget cuts. In truth, there had been little political will to address gender-based violence. Women's right to be free from violence remained subordinate to their role in the family.[106]

Land Conflicts. In recent years, the Nicaraguan government's interests in capital investment projects, including mining and the interoceanic canal, have conflicted with community organizations over land and property. The Nicaraguan police, generally recognized as the most professionalized police force in Central America, have increasingly responded to resulting activism with repression. Promising jobs and investment, in 2012 President Ortega announced plans for an interoceanic canal with Hong Kong-based developer and Chinese billionaire Wang Jing and his company HKND. The National Assembly passed Law 800 in 2012, which made Nicaragua a 51 percent shareholder in the project and created a Nicaraguan Canal Authority to oversee the project, work with those affected by property expropriation, and address environmental issues.[107] But in June 2013, Law 830 replaced Law 800. It conceded the canal and all related projects to HKND and reduced Nicaragua to only 1 percent ownership at the outset plus an additional 10 percent each successive decade.[108] The Nicaragua Canal and Development Project Commission (Canal Commission) replaced the original authority.

Critics denounced the absence of economic or environmental impact studies on the viability of an interoceanic canal prior to passing the laws. As of 2019 the government had still not released an economic impact study. Some claimed that the concessions, effectively ceding Nicaraguan territory to a foreign developer, violated the constitution. Moreover, the proposed canal route, which changed several times, would require extensive dredging of Lake

Cocibolca.[109] Environmentalists worried that dredging would contaminate the region's largest fresh water source and destroy its ecosystem.[110]

While initially widely popular among Nicaraguans, the construction project could potentially displace as many as 100,000 people. The indigenous Rama and African-descended Kriol communities complained to the Inter-American Commission on Human Rights (IACHR) that concessions of their lands had been given without their consent. Though the government promised to compensate displaced residents, they feared eviction and the survey teams accompanied by armed security forces.[111] Protests throughout 2014 and 2015 brought clashes with police.[112] By 2019, there was no evidence of any significant construction on the $50 billion project. Wang reportedly lost most of his fortune in the volatile 2015–2016 Chinese stock market. Although HKND retained the concession, the company had closed its headquarters in 2018.

Indigenous communities experienced attacks elsewhere. During the past two decades, armed settlers known as *colonos* had moved into their territory, terrorizing and dislocating indigenous populations, clearing the land, and then selling it. More than 100 people were killed from 2005 to 2015, 54 of them in 2015 alone.[113] Residents of the Bosawás Biosphere Reserve along the northern border of Jinotega department, Central America's largest rainforest, claim the Sandinista government supports the colonos. Many colonos do support the Ortega government, and local officials have facilitated illegal land sales by providing fraudulent titles.[114] Global Witness reported that 11 land defenders were killed in Nicaragua in 2016. Of those, ten were indigenous people killed in conflicts with settler communities. In Waspam, east of Jinotega, some indigenous communities have obtained weapons from area drug traffickers. Several documented violent attempts to remove the settlers have brought about torture-fueled massacres in retribution, leading many indigenous to flee to neighboring Honduras.

The 2016 and 2017 Elections. With a simple plurality required to elect the president, Daniel Ortega's re-election became inevitable, especially absent effective opposition. Ortega enjoyed strong public support thanks to popular social programs and the long economic growth spurt. Attempting to offer some competition, the PLI assembled an opposition coalition ticket headed by Eduardo Montealegre. In June, Nicaragua's Supreme Court removed Montealegre as the PLI's leader, thus forcing its best-known figure out of the race.[115] Subsequently 16 PLI deputies were expelled from the National Assembly for refusing to accept the court-ordered replacement PLI leader. After years of infighting, the PLI had lost public support, was polling at under 6 percent and the playing field had tilted against it. Ultimately José del Carmen Alvarado became the PLI's presidential nominee. The Liberals appeared hopelessly fragmented by fielding two other efforts. The Liberal Constitutionalists nominated Máximo Rodríguez and the Nicaraguan Liberal Alliance nominated Saturnino Cerrato.

Unsurprisingly, Ortega won a third consecutive term with 72 percent of the vote. His wife, Rosario Murillo, became vice president. The PLC's Rodríguez won 15 percent of the vote and the PLI 4.5 percent (combined the Liberals took only 24 percent of the vote). The FSLN captured 70 seats of the 92 in the National Assembly, followed by the PLC (13 seats) and the PLI (2 seats). The CSE said turnout was 66 percent but civil society groups claimed it was much lower. The FSLN later won 135 of 153 mayoralties contested in November 2017 municipal elections. Ortega initially refused to allow domestic or international election monitoring, but later allowed an observation team from the Organization of American States (OAS) who were only present from mid-October. The OAS report cited no major irregularities and characterized voting centers as orderly and peaceful, but several people died and dozens received injuries in post-election violence.[116] Most of the violence occurred in the Caribbean Coast regions where FSLN and YATAMA supporters clashed.

2018. A decade of steady economic growth ended in 2017, causing a 5 percent contraction in GDP per capita and a 3 percent decline in government revenue in 2018. Foreign assistance from Venezuela had recently fallen as its economy slowed. Nicaragua's exports had declined, and unemployment had risen for only the second time in nine years. The national social security system was also operating in the red. These factors contributed to a 2 percent budget deficit in 2017 and suggested that fiscal reforms would be required.

In April 2018, a wildfire broke out in the Indio Maíz Biological Reserve in southeastern Nicaragua. The government failed to respond to the fire for three days. Dissatisfied with the slow response and a refusal of international assistance, students began peaceful protests urging action to save the reserve. Days later, the government announced reforms to Social Security Law. Students returned to the streets to protest, this time accompanied by unhappy pensioners, environmental and land rights activists, and civil opposition groups. Clashes between and protestors and police escalated quickly and, in response to the state's repression, protests spread across the country.

Nicaraguan police met the protests with uncharacteristic repression and conflict escalated. Students at the Nicaraguan Polytechnic University (UPOLI) occupied campus buildings and erected barriers as they fought off police with homemade Molotov cocktails. Dozens died in the early weeks of the protests,

mostly students.[117] In May an attempt at dialogue failed between t
ment and the Civic Alliance for Justice and Democracy, a coaliti
dents, business groups, farmers' organizations, and human rights acti
Ortega administration rejected demands for the president's resigna ᴖᴖ and
early elections. Weeks later, on Mother's Day, huge crowds gathered to march
peacefully in solidarity with the mothers who had lost children since the protests began. Violence erupted and by day's end at least 15 people had been
killed and 200 injured. Reports of snipers and heavily armed, un-uniformed
men accompanying police raised public alarm.

Barricades made from street pavers, or *tranques*, were erected by protestors
around the country. In some places the tranques sufficiently impeded transportation to cause shortages of food, medicine, and gasoline around the country.
Neighborhoods that once resisted Somoza's National Guard, such as Masaya
and Monimbó, had become anti-Ortega strongholds. Having failed to get
the barricades dismantled as a pre-condition for talks, in July the government
forcibly removed the barricades and laid siege to the National Autonomous
University of Nicaragua.[118] Social media videos showed parapolice working
alone or alongside the national police to detain and harass residents. Strike
mobs, often associated with Sandinista Youth, were also accused of coordinated violence. After the dialogue broke down, the government encouraged
FSLN supporters to take private land to retaliate against business leaders who
spoke out against Ortega. The Union of Agricultural Producers of Nicaragua
estimated that 8,800 acres were seized between May and July 2018.[119]

The IAHCR investigated these events. In its June 2018 report, the IACHR
called on the government to cease repression of demonstrators and respect
the right to protest. It also called on the government to create an investigative
body to assign responsibility for abuses. It further reported:

> State-perpetrated violence has been aimed at deterring participation in
> the demonstrations and … political dissent and that it follows a common
> pattern, marked by (a) the excessive and arbitrary use of police force, (b)
> the use of parapolice forces or shock groups with the acquiescence and
> tolerance of State authorities, (c) intimidation and threats against leaders
> of social movements, (d) a pattern of arbitrary arrests of young people and
> adolescents who were participating in protests, (e) irregularities in open-
> ing investigations into the killings and bodily injuries taking place …, (f)
> obstacles in accessing emergency medical care for the wounded …, (g) the
> dissemination of propaganda and stigmatization campaigns, [and] meas-
> ures of direct and indirect censorship.[120]

The Ortega administration rejected the report, labeled the protesters "terrorists" seeking to overthrow his government with US aid, and as a "murderous, coup-mongering satanic sect."[121] Vice president Murillo called demonstrators "vampires." In July, the government enacted a new law against money laundering and financing terrorism, expanded the definition of terrorism, and provided for sentences of up to 20 years. By July, the violence was harming the economy by impeding the movement of goods and slowing tourism.

In August a second international group, the Office of the UN High Commissioner for Human Rights (OHCHR) issued a report stating that the Nicaraguan police and their armed allies operated with "total impunity" in killing approximately 300 and injuring 2,000 people.[122] The OHCHR described a majority of protestors as peaceful and reported that the police and parapolice had responded with lethal force to nonlethal threats. The report offered a litany of severe abuses of detainees, disappearances and extrajudicial killings by police and parapolice, and violations of due process. The UN report also addressed protester violence, noting the destruction of infrastructure, the killings of 22 police officers, and episodes of violence against Sandinista supporters. The Nicaraguan government responded by expelling the UN human rights investigative delegation.

In September 2018, the National Police outlawed unauthorized marches and demonstrations. Attacks against the press and civil society intensified in December. The government revoked the legal status of several organizations, including the Nicaraguan Center for Human Rights (CENIDH), the country's leading human rights group. Police closed and occupied the television news station 100% Noticias, and charged its director, Miguel Mora, with fomenting violence and conspiring to commit terrorism.[123] Mora and fellow journalist Lucia Pineda Abau were held in isolation for months before their release. The police also raided the newspaper *El Confidencial*, and the television program "Esta Semana," featuring the country's most prominent opposition journalist, Carlos Fernando Chamorro. His popular news program was taken off air. In January 2019 Chamorro announced he was in exile in Costa Rica, though he returned in November 2019. He was one of more than 62,000 Nicaraguans who fled the country between April 2018 and April 2019.[124]

Daniel Ortega in December 2018 expelled both the Interdisciplinary Group of Independent Experts (GIEI) and the Special Follow-up Mechanism for Nicaragua (MESENI) of the IACHR from the country. Both had conducted investigations to which his government had consented. The GIEI report, scheduled for release the day after the group's expulsion, accused the government of crimes against humanity including extrajudicial killings, torture, sexual violence, arbitrary arrests and detentions, the criminalization of protest, and a failure to diligently investigate the deaths of citizens, among other abuses.[125] Negotiations between the government and the Civic Alliance resumed in February 2019, though talks collapsed weeks later when President Ortega again rejected early elections or an independent investigation of the crackdown. In March 2019, the government agreed to release political prisoners in hopes of restarting talks with the opposition and getting sanctions lifted. By June, several hundred had been released, including journalists Mora and Piñeda. Charges against some of those released were dropped under an amnesty law passed in June for crimes committed in the context of anti-government protests. Critics feared this would shield state actors from responsibility.[126] In September, the government blocked an OAS delegation from entering the country. At the time of this writing, targeted sanctions by the United States and European Union had not changed regime behavior.

CONCLUSIONS

Global economic forces following World War II brought development cooperation among Central American countries and the United States to spur Nicaragua's rapid economic growth under the CACM. But growing inequality and impoverishment, the OPEC embargo, the 1972 Managua earthquake, and the Somoza dictatorship worsened living conditions for working-class Nicaraguans. This mobilized protesters into the political arena. The Somoza regime's brutal response drove escalating resistance that coalesced behind the FSLN. This rebel coalition marshaled progressively greater resources while the regime's resources deteriorated, leading the revolutionaries to power.

The Nicaraguan revolution in 1979 became a critical fulcrum in Central American history. When the Sandinistas consolidated their domination over the revolution, they moved internal and external political forces across the isthmus—democratization efforts, counterrevolution, economic sanctions, insurrections in neighboring states, and escalated US intervention. Despite the revolutionary government's democratizing efforts in the mid- and late 1980s, the Contra war and embargoes eventually caused such misery that Nicaraguan voters replaced the revolutionary government with one acceptable to Washington and confirmed Nicaragua's transition to electoral democracy.

Corruption, political polarization, and self-serving deal-making among elites soon began to undermine the promise and performance of civilian democracy. The FSLN and PLC caudillos conspired to limit political space. The Liberal schism effectively collapsed political opposition and the Nicaraguan regime deteriorated into semi-democracy. FSLN policies benefited the poor, somewhat redressing their economic decline under prior administrations, while Nicaragua escaped the crime waves of its northern neighbors. As public support grew, the Ortega government solidified its hold on power with the 2011 election and implemented constitutional and legal changes concentrating executive power. Damage to election institutions and practices, the suppression and effective collapse of the opposition, increased executive power, and repression of regime critics constituted another regime change to civilian autocracy by 2016. Its governance by Daniel Ortega and FSLN by then resembled the Somoza-era regime in many respects. The resemblance deepened with the government's violent response to protests in 2018, events that echoed the mobilization of the 1970s and the tactics of the Somozas. In the March 2019 regional elections in the Autonomous Region of the North Caribbean Coast (Región Autónoma de la Costa Caribe Norte) and Autonomous Region of the South Caribbean Coast (Región Autónoma de la Costa Caribe Sur), voters went to the poll under a heavy military presence. The FSLN won a majority of seats in each. Whether Nicaragua recreates and consolidates an "Orteguista" version of Somocismo is a question that awaits history's answer.

Notes

1. Paul Levy, as quoted in Jaime Wheelock Román, *Imperialismo y dictadura: Crisis de una formación social* (México: Siglo Veintiuno Editores, 1975), p. 29.

2. John A. Booth and Thomas W. Walker, *Understanding Central America*, 3rd ed. (Boulder, CO: Westview Press, 1999)., Appendix, Table A.1.

3. For an extended discussion see ibid., pp. 69–76 and data in Appendix, Tables A.5, A.6, A.7, and A.8.

4. Centro de Investigaciones y Estudios de la Reforma Agraria (CIERA), *Informe de Nicaragua a la FAO* (Managua: Ministerio de Desarrollo Agropecuario y Reforma Agraria, 1983), pp. 40–41.

5. Mario A. DeFranco and Carlos F. Chamorro, "Nicaragua: Crecimiento industrial y empleo," in Daniel Camacho et al., *El F fracaso social de la integración centroamericana* (San José, Costa Rica: Editorial Universitaria Centroamericana, 1979), Cuadro 2.

6. John A. Booth, *The End and the Beginning: The Nicaraguan Revolution*, 2nd ed. (Boulder, CO: Westview Press, 1985), Ch. 5.

7. See Booth and Walker, *Understanding Central America*, 3rd ed., Appendix, Table 8. Note that computational methods vary across countries, so cross-national

unemployment rate comparisons should not be made. Trends within nations, however, are usefully disclosed.

8. Donaldo Castillo Rivas, "Modelos de acumulación, agricultura, y agroindustria en Centroamérica," in D. Castillo Rivas, ed., *Centroamérica: Más allá de la crisis* (Mexico City: Ediciones SIAP, 1983), pp. 202–205; Consejo Superior Universitaria Centroamericana (CSUCA), *Estructura agraria, dinámica de población, y desarrollo capitalista en Centroamérica* (San José, Costa Rica: Editorial Universitaria Centroamericana, 1978), pp. 204–254.

9. CIERA, *Informe de Nicaragua*, p. 41.

10. Jaime Wheelock Román, *Imperialismo y dictadura: Crisis de una formación social* (Mexico City: Siglo Veintiuno Editores, 1975), pp. 141–198; Amaru Barahona Porto-Carrero, *Estudio sobre la historia contemporánea de Nicaragua* (San José: Instituto de Investigaciones Sociales, Universidad de Costa Rica, 1977), pp. 33–44.

11. Material from Ricardo E. Chavarría, "The Nicaraguan Insurrection," in Thomas W. Walker, ed., *Nicaragua in Revolution* (New York: Praeger, 1982), pp. 28–29; Booth, *The End and the Beginning*, Ch. 6.

12. George Black, *Triumph of the People: The Sandinista Revolution in Nicaragua* (London: Zed Press, 1981), pp. 70–72; Centro de Información, Documentación y Análisis del Movimiento Obrero Latinoamericano (CIDAMO), "El movimiento obrero," in G. García Márquez et al., *Los Sandinistas* (Bogotá, Colombia: Editorial Oveja Negra, 1979), pp. 171–176.

13. Michael Dodson and Tommie Sue Montgomery, "The Churches in the Nicaraguan Revolution," in T.W. Walker, ed., *Nicaragua in Revolution*, pp. 163–174; Laura Nuzzi O'Shaughnessy and Luis H. Serra, *The Church and Revolution in Nicaragua*, Monographs in International Studies, Latin American Series, No. 11 (Athens, OH: Ohio University, 1986).

14. Thomas W. Walker, "Introduction," in Thomas W. Walker, ed., *Nicaragua: The First Five Years* (New York: Praeger Publishers, 1985), p. 20; Julio, López C. et al., *La caída del Somocismo y la lucha Sandinista en Nicaragua* (San José, Costa Rica: Editorial Universitaria Centroamericano, 1979), pp. 98–112.

15. Thomas W. Walker, *The Christian Democratic Movement in Nicaragua* (Tucson, AZ: University of Arizona Press, 1970).

16. Omar Cabezas, *Fire from the Mountain*, trans. Kathleen Weaver (New York: New American Library, 1986).

17. Booth, *The End and the Beginning*, Ch. 8.

18. Ibid., pp. 97–104; López C. et al., *La caída del Somocismo*, pp. 71–98.

19. "A Secret War for Nicaragua," *Newsweek*, November 8, 1982, p. 44. See also Peter Kornbluh, "The Covert War," in Thomas W. Walker, ed., *Reagan Versus the Sandinistas: The Undeclared War on Nicaragua* (Boulder, CO: Westview Press, 1987), p. 21.

20. Ariel C. Armony, *Argentina, the United States, and the Anticommunist Crusade in Central America, 1977–1984* (Athens, OH: Ohio University Center for International Studies, 1997).

21. Tayacán [the CIA], *Psychological Operations in Guerrilla Warfare: The CIA's Nicaragua Manual* (New York: Vintage Books, 1985).

22. Michael Isikoff, "Drug Cartel Gave Contras $10 Million, Court Told," *Washington Post*, November 26, 1991, pp. A1, A8. For more on how drug money was used to finance the Contras, see Peter Dale Scott and Jonathan Marshall, *Cocaine Politics: Drugs, Armies and the CIA in Central America* (Berkeley, CA: University of California Press, 1991).

23. See also Rose Spalding's *Capitalists and Revolution in Nicaragua: Opposition and Accommodation, 1979–1993* (Chapel Hill, NC: University of North Carolina Press, 1994).

24. E.g., a report by Latin Americanists, *The Electoral Process in Nicaragua: Domestic and International Influences* (Austin, TX: Latin American Studies Association, November 19, 1984); or Booth, *The End and the Beginning*, pp. 215–223.

25. For a balanced analysis of building governmental institutions in Sandinista Nicaragua and the 1987 constitution, see Andrew A. Reding, "The Evolution of Governmental Institutions," in Thomas W. Walker, ed., *Revolution and Counterrevolution in Nicaragua* (Boulder, CO: Westview Press, 1991), pp. 15–47. On the constitution see Kenneth J. Mijeski, ed., *The Nicaraguan Constitution of 1987: English Translation and Commentary* (Athens, OH: Ohio University Press, 1991).

26. Walker, ed., *Nicaragua in Revolution*, and *Nicaragua: The First Five Years*.

27. Michael Linfield, "Human Rights," in T.W. Walker, ed., *Revolution and Counterrevolution in Nicaragua*, pp. 275–294.

28. Lawyers Committee for International Human Rights, *Nicaragua: Revolutionary Justice* (New York: April 1985), pp. 33–40.

29. John Spicer Nichols, "*La Prensa*: The CIA Connection," *Columbia Journalism Review* 28, No. 2 (July–August 1988), pp. 34–35.

30. *Los Angeles Times*, June 27, 1986, p. 15.

31. Martin Diskin et al., "Peace and Autonomy on the Atlantic Coast of Nicaragua: A Report of the LASA Task Force on Human Rights and Academic Freedom," Part 2, *LASA Forum* 17 (Summer 1986), p. 15.

32. Americas Watch, *On Human Rights in Nicaragua* (New York: May 1982), pp. 58–80.

33. See Martin Diskin et al., "Peace and Autonomy on the Atlantic Coast of Nicaragua." Part 1, *LASA Forum* 17 (Spring 1986), pp. 1–16; and Part 2, pp. 1–16.

34. Americas Watch, *On Human Rights in Nicaragua*, pp. 58–80.

35. O'Shaughnessy and Serra, *The Church and Revolution in Nicaragua*; *Los Angeles Times*, June 27, 1986, p. 15, and June 30, 1986, p. 7; and *New York Times*, July 5, 1986, p. 2.

36. "Latin Presidents Announce Accord on Contra Bases," *New York Times*, February 15, 1989, pp. 1, 4; *New York Times*, February 16, 1989, pp. 1, 6; "Nicaragua Pins Hopes on Turning Bureaucrats into Farmers," *Dallas Morning News*, February 22, 1989, p. 12A; and author Booth's conversations with Mauricio Díaz of the Popular Social Christian Party and Pedro Joaquín Chamorro Barrios, former director of the Nicaraguan Resistance, Montezuma, New Mexico, February 1989.

37. Joseph R. Thome and David Kaimowitz, "Agrarian Reform," in T.W. Walker, ed., *Nicaragua: The First Five Years*; and Forrest D. Colburn, *Post-Revolutionary Nicaragua: State, Class, and the Dilemmas of Agrarian Policy* (Berkeley, CA: University of California Press, 1986)

38. Booth and Walker, *Understanding Central America*, 3rd ed., Appendix, Table A.9.

39. John Weeks, "The Industrial Sector," and Michael E. Conroy, "Economic Legacy and Policies: Performance and Critique," in T.W. Walker, ed., *Nicaragua: The First Five Years*; and interviews by Booth with COSEP members in León, August 1985.

40. Booth and Walker, *Understanding Central America*, 3rd ed., Appendix Table 5.

41. Latin American Studies Association (LASA), Commission to Observe the 1990 Nicaraguan Elections, *Electoral Democracy Under International Pressure* (Pittsburgh, PA: LASA, March 15, 1990), p. 19.

42. [United Nations] Comisión Económica para América Latina y el Caribe, "Balance preliminar de la economía de América Latina y el Caribe, 1990," *Notas Sobre la Economía y el Desarrollo*, Nos. 500–501 (December 1990), p. 27.

43. Data on the human cost of the war provided to author Walker by the Nicaraguan Ministry of the Presidency in January 1990.

44. LASA Commission, *Electoral Democracy*, pp. 24–26.

45. Eric Weaver and William Barnes, "Opposition Parties and Coalitions," in T.W. Walker, ed., *Revolution and Counterrevolution in Nicaragua*, pp. 117–142.

46. An unidentified US official quoted in "Chamorro Takes a Chance," *Time*, May 7, 1990, p. 43; William I. Robinson, *A Faustian Bargain: U.S. Involvement in the Nicaraguan Elections and American Foreign Policy in the Post–Cold War Era* (Boulder, CO: Westview Press, 1992).

47. Coauthor Thomas Walker served as a member of the LASA Commission to Observe the 1990 Nicaraguan Elections in the war zone of northern Nicaragua in late 1989 and early 1990.

48. As quoted in "Ortega Livens up San José Summit," *Central America Report* 16, No. 43 (November 3, 1989), p. 340.

49. Thomas W. Walker, ed. *Nicaragua Without Illusions: Regime Transition and Structural Adjustment in the 1990s* (Wilmington, DE: Scholarly Resources, 1997).

50. Booth and Walker, *Understanding Central America*, 3rd ed., Appendix, Tables A.1 and A.6.

51. Cited in Nitlápan-Envío Team, "President Alemán: First Moves, First Signals," *Envío*, 16, No. 187–188 (February–March 1997), pp. 3–4.

52. William I. Robinson, *Transnational Conflicts: Central America, Social Change, and Globalization* (London and New York: Verso, 2003), pp. 78–79.

53. Ibid., p. 79.

54. See "Nicaragua: Atlantic Coast Groups Rearm," *Central America Report* 25, No. 22 (June 11, 1998), p. 3.

55. J. Mark Ruhl, "Curbing Central America's Militaries," *Journal of Democracy* 15, No. 3 (July 2004), p. 141.

56. Shelly A. McConnell, "Institutional Development," pp. 45–64 in T.W. Walker, ed., *Nicaragua without Illusions*.

57. "William Grigsby: 'Refounding' the Sandinista Movement." *Envío* 225 (April 2000).

58. Coauthors interviewed various Nicaraguan political leaders during June–July of 1998, including Víctor Hugo Tinoco, FSLN National Assembly deputy; Dora María Téllez, professor, former minister of health, and leader of the MRS; René Núñez, an official of the FSLN; Mariano Fiallos, professor and former head of the CSE; Alejandro Bendaña, author and former foreign ministry official in the Ortega administration; Antonio Lacayo, businessman, farmer, and former minister of the presidency in the UNO government; and Dr Rigoberto Sampson, mayor of León. They offered striking uniformity in their assessment of the FSLN.

59. John A. Booth and Patricia Bayer Richard, "The Nicaraguan Elections of October 1996," *Electoral Studies* 16, No. 3 (1997), pp. 386–393; John A. Booth, "Election Observation and Democratic Transition in Nicaragua," in Kevin J. Middlebrook, ed., *Electoral Observation and Democratic Transitions in Latin America* (La Jolla, CA: Center for US-Mexican Studies of the University of California, San Diego, 1998); *Envío* 15 (December–January, 1996–1997); and Thomas W. Walker, Epilogue, in T.W. Walker, ed., *Nicaragua without Illusions*, pp. 305–311.

60. Nitlápan-Envío Team, "An Accord Besieged by Discord," *Envío* 16, No. 196 (November 1997), pp. 3–4.

61. John A. Booth, Christine J. Wade, and Thomas W. Walker, *Understanding Central America: Global Force, Rebellion and Change*, (Boulder, CO: Westview Press, 2015), Appendix Table A.1.

62 Nitlápan-Envío Team, "An Accord Besieged by Discord," *Envío2* 16, No. 196 (November 1997), pp. 3–4.

63. On Alemán's scandal see David Close and Kalowatie Deonandan, eds., *Undoing Democracy: The Politics of Electoral Caudillismo* (Lanham, MD: Lexington Books, 2004); on Ortega's scandal see Juan Ramón Huerta, *El silencio del patriarca* (Managua: Litografía El Renacimiento, 1998); and "Extractos del testimonio desgarrador de Zoliamérica," *Confidencial* 2 (May 24–30, 1998), pp. 1, 9–11.

64. Robinson, *Transnational Conflicts*, p. 83; see also pp. 82–87.

65. Vilma Núñez de Escorcia, "The FSLN Leadership's Disintegration Goes Way Back," *Envío* 222 (January 2000).

66. "No aceptan Ortega," *La Prensa Libre*, February 28, 2001, and "Garza tajante contra el FSLN," *El Nuevo Diario*, April 6, 2001.

67. The Court ruled out Alémán's sentence on the grounds that "no evidence was found to ratify either the original sentence in December 2002 or the Appeals Court's 2007 decision to uphold it." See Nitlápan-Envío Team, "Abuse as Usual Means Many Accounts to Settle," *Envío* 330 (January 2007).

68. Ibid.

69. Latin American Database, "Nicaraqua's Legislature Looks to Limit Presidential Powers; Aleman Could Rescue Bolanos," *NotiCen*, January 13, 2005.

70. See Shelley McConnell, "Can the Inter-American Democratic Charter Work? The 2004–05 Constitutional Crisis in Nicaragua," paper presented at the International Studies Association meeting, February 28–March 3, 2007; and Council on Hemispheric Affairs, "Nicaragua: A Three-Way Political Ground," COHA Memorandum to the Press, July 20, 2005.

71. Max Blumenthal, "The Kinder, Gentler Daniel Ortega," *The Nation*, January 19, 2007.

72. Latin American Database, "Nicaragua's Far Right Presidential Candidate Running against the Regional Tide," *NotiCen*, July 27, 2006.

73. Latin American Database, "FSLN Seeks to Stop Another Sandinista Revolution," *NotiCen*, March 10, 2005.

74. Shelley McConnell, "Ortega's Nicaragua," *Current History* (February 2007), pp. 83–88.

75. Ibid.

76. James C. McKinley Jr., "Nicaraguan Councils Stir Fear of Dictatorship," *New York Times*, May 4, 2008.

77. Latin American Database, "Ortega's First 100 Days as Nicaragua's President," *NotiCen*, April 26, 2007.

78. Asier Andres Fernández, "CPCs: A Sandinista Tool?" *Central America Report*, May 23, 2008; James Smith, "CPCs Get Judicial Seal of Approval," *Central America Report*, December 7, 2007; Asier Andres Fernández, "Dubious Court Rulings at One Year Mark," *Central America Report*, January 25, 2008.

79. Asier Andrés Fernández, "Court Dashes Third Party Hopes in Municipal Elections," *Central America Report*, June 27, 2008; Asier Andres Fernández, "A Murky Pact between Liberals and Sandinistas," *Central America Report*, July 18, 2008.

80. See William Booth, "Democracy in Nicaragua in Peril, Ortega Critics Say," *Washington Post*, November 20, 2008, A–12; Roger Burbach, "Et Tu, Daniel? The Sandinista Revolution Betrayed," *NACLA Report on the Americas*, April 6, 2009; "How to Steal an Election," *The Economist*, November 13, 2008.

81. See Chapter 9.

82. Ibid. See also Tina Rosenberg, "The Many Stories of Carlos Fernando Chamorro," *New York Times*, March 22, 2009.

83. Instituto para el Desarrollo y la Democracia (IPADE), *Elecciones muncipales 2008/2009* (Masaya, Nicaragua: IPADE, May 2009); Nitlápan-Envío team, "Nicaragua Is the Municipal Elections' Big Loser," *Envío* 328 (November 2008); Kitty Monterrey, "These Elections Were Won by Both Fraud and Theft," *Envío* 329 (December 2008); Ethics and Transparency Civil Group, "Looking at the Ruins of a Defiled Electoral Process," *Envío* 332 (March 2009).

84. Argüello, who had a history of depression and substance abuse, committed suicide on July 1, 2009.

85. Marc Lacey, "Sandinista Fervor Turns Sour for Former Comrades of Nicaragua's President," *New York Times*, November 24, 2008.

86. Matthew Lee, "US Cuts Aid to Nicaragua," *Washington Post*, June 11, 2009.

87. Coauthor interviews in Managua, Nicaragua, June 2011; Supreme Court of Justice, Constitutional Chamber, Exp. No. 602–09, Judgment No. 504; see also www. nytimes.com/2009/11/16/world/americas/16nicaragua.html; http://findarticles.com/p/ articles/mi_go1655/is_2011_Feb_3/ai_n56893409/?tag=content;col1.

88. NotiCen, May 6, 2010.

89. No accreditation meant these groups had no access to polling stations or vote-counting locations.

90. "Carter Center Statement on November 6 Elections in Nicaragua," September 9, 2011, www.cartercenter.org/news/pr/nicaragua-090911.html.

91. Organization of American States, "OAS Permanent Council Hears Reports by Electoral Missions in Guatemala and Nicaragua," (November 15, 2011), www.oas. org/en/media_center/press_release.asp?sCodigo=E–958/11; Unión Europea, "Misión de observación electoral Nicaragua 2011: Elecciones presidenciales, legislativas y al parlacen," Declaración preliminar, Managua 8 de Noviembre 2011, www.eueom.eu/ files/pressreleases/other/moeue-nicaragua-preliminar-08112011_es.pdf.

92. European Union Election Observation Mission, "Nicaragua Final Report: General Elections and Parlecen Elections 2011," p. 3, www.eueom.eu/files/dmfile/ moeue-nicaragua-final-report-22022012_en.pdf.

93. Arturo Cruz-Sequeria, "Political Reform in Central America: Are Democratic Institutions at Risk?" *Inter-American Dialogue*, (July 2013), p. 7, http://thedialogue.org/uploads/Cruz071213publishedversion.pdf.

94. John A. Booth and Mitchell A. Seligson, "Political Culture of Democracy in Nicaragua and in the Americas, 2012: Towards Equality of Opportunity," *Latin American Public Opinion Project, Vanderbilt University*, 2013, p. 149, 274.

95. World Bank Group, Indicators, https://data.worldbank.org/indicator, September 11, 2019.

96. International Court of Justice, "Territorial Dispute and Maritime Delimitation (Nicaragua v. Colombia) Summary of the Judgment of November 19, 2012," November 19, 2012, www.icj-cij.org/docket/files/124/17180.pdf.

97. Cruz, p. 6, http://thedialogue.org/uploads/Cruz071213publishedversion.pdf.

98. Booth and Seligson, p. 264.

99. Yader Luna, "Disminuyen homicidios," *El Nuevo Diario*, May 30, 2013, www.elnuevodiario.com.ni/nacionales/287550-disminuyen-homicidios.

100. Elizabeth Romero, "RAAN urge más atención," *La Prensa*, July 31, 2013, www.laprensa.com.ni/2013/07/31/ambito/156812-raan-urge-más-atención.

101. Ben Witte, "Nicaragua's Femicide Law Slow to Produce Results,"*NotiCen*, May 13, 2013.

102. Maria Teresa Blandon, "Comments on the Integral Laws against Violence against Women," *Nicaragua Dispatch*, March 9, 2012, www.nicaraguadispatch.com/news/2012/03/comments-on-the-integral-law-against-violence-against-women/2720; Ipas, "Rapporteur for Women's Rights Visits Nicaragua, Urges Reforms to Address Sexual Violence and Unsafe Abortion," July 16, 2012, www.ipas.org/en/News/2012/July/Rapporteur-for-womens-rights-visits-Nicaragua-urges-reforms-to-address-sexual-violence-an.aspx; Latin American Database; "Cash-Strapped Femicide Law Takes Effect in Nicaragua," *NotiCen*, July 26, 2012.

103. CINCO, "Elecciones municipales 2012 en Nicaragua," November 26, 2012, www.cinco.org.ni/noticia/373; Ben Witte, "Sandinistas Dominate Municipal Elections in Nicaragua," *NotiCen*, November 15, 2012, http://ladb.unm.edu/noticen/2012/11/15–078810; Organization of American States, "Statement of the OAS Mission on the Municipal Elections in Nicaragua," November 5, 2012, www.oas.org/en/media_center/press_release.asp?sCodigo=E–399/12.

104. Mary Ellsberg, et al."Candies in Hell: Women's Experiences of Violence in Nicaragua," *Social Science & Medicine* 51, No. 11 (2000): 1595–1610.

105. Edilberto Loaiza and Mengjia Liang, *Adolescent Pregnancy: A Review of the Evidence*. United Nations Population Fund (New York: UNPFA, 2013), www.unfpa.org/sites/default/files/pub-pdf/ADOLESCENT%20PREGNANCY_UNFPA.pdf; IPAS, "Embarazo impuesto por violación: Niñas-madres menores de 14 Años."

Ipas Centroamérica, Managua, Nicaragua; 2016. https://ipas.azureedge.net/files/
ESTUDIO2016-EmbarazoImpuestoporViolacioin.pdf; Shuka Kalantari, "Nicaragua's
teen pregnancy rate soars," *Public Radio International*, August 17, 2016, www.pri.org/
stories/2016-08-17/nicaraguas-teen-pregnancy-rate-soars.

106. Pamela J. Neumann, "In Nicaragua, A Failure to Address Violence
Against Women," *NACLA*, April 28, 2017, https://nacla.org/news/2017/04/28/
nicaragua-failure-address-violence-against-women.

107. Ley No 800 del régimen jurídico del Gran Canal Interoceánico de Nicaragua,
http://legislacion.asamblea.gob.ni/SILEG/Iniciativas.nsf/0/1c79b32dfa494
db906257a14007fb07f/$FILE/Ley%20No.%20800%20El%20Gran%20Canal.
pdf.

108. Ley No 840. "La ley especial para el desarrollo de infraestructura y
transporte Nicaragüense," http://legislacion.asamblea.gob.ni/SILEG/Gacetas.nsf/
5eea6480fc3d3d90062576e300504635/f1ecd8f640b8e6ce06257b8f005bae22/
$FILE/Ley%20No.%20840.pdf.

109. Jonathan Watts, "Land of Opportunity–And Fear—Along Route of
Nicaragua's Giant Canal," *The Guardian*, January 20, 2015, www.theguardian.com/
world/2015/jan/20/-sp-nicaragua-canal-land-opportunity-fear-route.

110. Paula Leighton, "Canal Could Turn Lake into 'Dead Zone,'" SciSevNet,
August 1, 2015, www.scidev.net/global/water/news/canal-dredging-lake-nicaragua-
dead-zone.html.

111. "Nicaragua's Transoceanic Canal Survey Leaves Residents Fearful of
Losing Homes," *The Guardian*, August 27, 2014, www.theguardian.com/world/
2014/aug/27/residents-fearful-nicaragua-trans-oceanic-canal-surveys-hknd-group;
"Nicaragua Starts Survey on $40 Billion Canal; Some Residents Worried
about Evictions," *The Tico Times*, August 29, 2014, www.ticotimes.net/2014/
08/29/nicaragua-starts-survey-on-40-billion-canal; David Boddiger, "Nicaragua's
Canal Survey off to Rocky Start Marked by Fear and Mistrust," *The Tico Times*,
September 4, 2014, www.ticotimes.net/2014/09/04/nicaragua-canal-survey-off-to-
rocky-start-marked-by-fear-and-mistrust.

112. Nina Lakhani, "Amnesty Condemns 'Campaign of Harassment' Against
Nicaragua Canal Protestors," *The Guardian*, August 2, 2017, www.theguardian.com/
world/2017/aug/03/daniel-ortega-nicaragua-canal-human-rights-violation.

113. Ray Downs, "Violent Land Invasions on Nicaragua's Atlantic Coast – 'Just
Like the Spaniards,'" *Vice*, December 8, 2015, www.vice.com/en_us/article/ywjbpv/
violent-land-invasions-on-nicaraguas-atlantic-coast-just-like-the-spaniards.

114. Laura Hobson Herlihy, "The New Colonization of Nicaragua's Caribbean
Coast," *NACLA*, September 6, 2016, https://nacla.org/news/2016/09/06/new-
colonization-nicaragua's-caribbean-coast.

115. "La Corte Suprema de Nicaragua quita partido a la principal coalición opositora," *EFE*, June 8, 2016, www.efe.com/efe/america/politica/la-corte-suprema-de-nicaragua-quita-partido-a-principal-coalicion-opositora/20000035-2950307.

116. "Preliminary Report of the Electoral Observation Mission of the Organization of American States in Nicaragua," November 7, 2017, www.oas.org/documents/eng/press/preliminary-report-electoral-observation-mission-nicaragua-2017.pdf.

117. Lori Hanson and Miguel Gomez, "Deciphering the Nicaraguan Student Uprising," *NACLA*, June 15, 2018, https://nacla.org/news/2018/07/03/deciphering-nicaraguan-student-uprising-descifrando-el-levantamiento-estudiantil.

118. Amnesty International, "Nicaragua: Government Steps Up 'Ruthless' Crackdown during 'Clean-up' Operation," October 18, 2018, www.amnesty.org.uk/press-releases/nicaragua-government-steps-ruthless-crackdown-during-clean-operation.

119. Tim Rogers, "Amid Unrest, Nicaragua's Ruling Party Organizes a Series of Land Grabs," *McClatchy*, July 25, 2018, www.mcclatchydc.com/news/nation-world/world/article215489355.html.

120. "Gross Human Rights Violations in the Context of Social Protests in Nicaragua," Inter-American Commission on Human Rights, June 21, 2018, www.oas.org/en/iachr/reports/pdfs/Nicaragua2018-en.pdf.

121. Tom Phillips, "Nicaragua: Ortega Blames 'Satantic Sect' for Uprising Against His Rule," *The Guardian*, July 20, 2018, www.theguardian.com/world/2018/jul/20/nicaragua-latest-daniel-ortega-satanic-sect-protests-uprising.

122. Office of the United Nations High Commissioner for Human Rights (OHCHR), "Human Rights Violations and Abuses in the Context of Protests in Nicaragua: 18 April–August 18, 2018," www.ohchr.org/Documents/Countries/NI/HumanRightsViolationsNicaraguaApr_Aug2018_EN.pdf.

123. Teresa Mioli and Silvia Higuera, "Nicaraguan Journalists Jailed Incommunicado as Ortega Government Continues Targeting of Independent Media," January 3, 2019, https://knightcenter.utexas.edu/blog/00-20454-nicaraguan-journalists-jailed-incommunicado-ortega-government-continues-targeting-inde.

124. Sylvia Higuera, "Nicaraguan Journalist Carlos Chamorro Goes into Exile in Costa Rica as Repression of the Press Grows in His Country," January 22, 2019, https://knightcenter.utexas.edu/blog/00-20523-nicaraguan-journalist-carlos-chamorro-goes-exile-costa-rica-repression-press-grows-his.

125. GIEI, "Report on the Violent Events That Took Place Between April 18th and May 30th, 2018" [in Nicaragua], OAS and IACHR, https://gieinicaragua.org/giei-content/uploads/2019/05/GIEI_REPORT_ENGLISH_72dpi.pdf.

126. Ismael Lopez, "Nicaraguan Congress Approves Ortega-Backed Amnesty Law," *Reuters*, June 8, 2019, www.reuters.com/article/us-nicaragua-amnesty/nicaraguan-congress-approves-ortega-backed-amnesty-law-idUSKCN1TA00U.

RECOMMENDED READINGS AND RESOURCES

Babb, Florence. 2001. *After Revolution: Mapping Gender and Cultural Politics in Neoliberal Nicaragua*. Austin, TX: University of Texas Press.

Baracco, Luciano. 2011. *National Integration and Contested Autonomy: The Caribbean Coast of Nicaragua*. New York: Algora Press.

Booth, John A. 1985. *The End and the Beginning: The Nicaraguan Revolution*, 2nd ed. Boulder, CO: Westview Press.

Close, David. 1999. *Nicaragua: The Chamorro Years*. Boulder, CO: Lynne Rienner Publishers.

Close, David. 2013. "Nicaragua." In Diego Sánchez-Ancochea and Salvador Martí Puig, editors *Handbook of Central American Governance*. London: Routledge, pp. 432–446.

Close, David and Kalowatie Deonandan. 2004. *Undoing Democracy: The Politics of Electoral Caudillismo*. Lanham, MD: Lexington Books.

Colburn, Forrest D. 1986. *Post-Revolutionary Nicaragua: State, Class, and the Dilemmas of Agrarian Policy*. Berkeley, CA: University of California Press.

Gonzalez Rivera, Victoria. 2011. *Before the Revolution: Women's Rights and Right-Wing Politics in Nicaragua, 1821–1979*. University Park, PA: Pennsylvania State University Press.

Kinzer, Stephen and Merilee S. Grindle. 2007. *Blood of Brothers: Life and War in Nicaragua*. Cambridge, MA: David Rockefeller Center Series on Latin American Studies.

O'Shaughnessy, Laura Nuzzi. 2009. *Nicaragua's Other Revolution: Religious Faith and Political Struggle*. Chapel Hill, NC: University of North Carolina Press Enduring Editions.

Pastor, Robert. 2002. *Not Condemned to Repetition: The United States and Nicaragua*, 2nd ed. Boulder, CO: Westview Press.

Prevost, Gary and Harry E. Vanden, eds. 1997. *The Undermining of the Sandinista Revolution*. London: Macmillan.

Robinson, William I. 1992. *A Faustian Bargain: US Involvement in the Nicaraguan Elections and American Foreign Policy in the Post–Cold War Era*. Boulder, CO: Westview Press.

Spalding, Rose. 1994. *Capitalists and Revolution in Nicaragua: Opposition and Accommodation, 1979–1993*. Chapel Hill, NC: University of North Carolina Press.

Vanden, Harry and Gary Prevost. 1993. *Democracy and Socialism in Sandinista Nicaragua*. Boulder, CO: Lynne Rienner Publishers.

Vilas, Carlos. 1989. *State, Class and Ethnicity in Nicaragua*. Boulder, CO.: Lynne Rienner Publishers.

Walker, Thomas W. 1982. *Nicaragua in Revolution*. New York: Praeger.

Walker, Thomas W., ed. 1991. *Revolution and Counterrevolution in Nicaragua*. Boulder, CO: Westview Press.

Walker, Thomas W., ed. 1997. *Nicaragua Without Illusions: Regime Transition and Structural Adjustment in the 1990s*. Wilmington, DE: Scholarly Resources.

Walker, Thomas W. and Christine J. Wade. 2017. *Nicaragua: Emerging from the Shadow of the Eagle*, 6th ed. New York: Taylor and Francis.

6

El Salvador

To many visitors, El Salvador's overpopulation registers as its most striking characteristic. Some argue the tiny country lacks the resources to support its teeming populace, but other densely populated countries (the Netherlands, Japan) manage to feed their people. El Salvador's real problem, as in the rest of northern Central America, is maldistribution of resources brought about by centuries of external dependence and elite control.[1]

After 12 violent years of brutal civil war in the 1980s and early 1990s, El Salvador's warring factions in 1992 agreed to adopt formal civilian democracy. The country became more stable, and more quickly, than most observers expected. Given the historical record of El Salvador's elites, its government's embrace of conservative economic policies, and the nation's role in the world economy, the country appeared likely to indefinitely maintain debilitating socioeconomic inequalities and external dependency. Yet by the early twenty-first century El Salvador was politically quieter than at any time in the previous century, but had again become dangerous and unsettled by crime.

HISTORICAL BACKGROUND

During most of a century after independence in 1823, a Liberal elite controlled El Salvador. Guatemalan intervention occasionally imposed Conservative rulers, but they were exceptions. Like their regional counterparts, Salvadoran Liberals advocated free enterprise and economic modernization to link the country to the world economy. They promoted economic and service modernization to increase agricultural exports. The elite regarded the mestizo and indigenous masses simultaneously as obstacles to progress and an essential labor supply.

El Salvador's nineteenth-century economy revolved around the production, extraction, and export of indigo dye. By the mid-nineteenth century, cheaper European chemical dyes sharply cut international demand for the deep-blue colorant, forcing El Salvador's elite to turn to coffee, best cultivated on the higher, volcanic terrain previously disdained by large landowners. The mountain slopes, however, were occupied by mestizo and indigenous communal farmers whose ancestors had been displaced from the valley floors by the Spanish.

The would-be coffee growers used their control of government to appropriate good coffee land. In 1856, the state required indigenous communes to plant at least two-thirds of their lands in coffee or forfeit them. This wiped out many communes lacking the considerable capital necessary to buy and plant coffee trees and wait years for a crop. Communes that survived the 1856 law vanished in the early 1880s when legislation banned communal holdings. Wealthy coffee farmers bought the newly available land. The government also passed "vagrancy" laws that forced the now landless peasants to work on the coffee plantations. Outraged by this legalized land taking and forced labor, peasants several times rebelled—unsuccessfully—in the late nineteenth century. Coffee's promoters prevailed, and the privileged classes brought El Salvador into the twentieth century with one of the most unequal land-distribution systems in Latin America. A coffee-growing elite, thereafter known (inaccurately) as the "fourteen families," controlled most of the country's resources. Coffee cultivation continued expanding into the twentieth century. In 1929, for instance, the socially conscious editor of *La Patria* wrote:

> The conquest of territory by the coffee industry is alarming. It is now descending into the valleys displacing maize, rice and beans. It is extended like the conquistador, spreading hunger and misery, reducing former proprietors to the worst conditions—woe to those who sell![2]

The situation became critical when the Great Depression lowered demand and prices for Salvadoran exports in the 1930s. Coffee growers cushioned this blow by cutting workers' already miserable wages. Popular hopes for justice momentarily rose during an aberrant period of democratic reform in 1930–1931 but crashed when General Maximiliano Hernández Martínez established another reactionary dictatorship. The turmoil and economic travail spawned an ill-coordinated peasant uprising in January 1932. The government and landowners crushed it by massacring over 30,000 peasants (but few actual insurgents). The revolt's promoter, charismatic Marxist intellectual Augustín Farabundo Martí, was captured before the revolt, then shot and beheaded in its wake. His memory, like Sandino's in Nicaragua, would linger decades later.

The five decades following the rise of General Hernández Martínez and the 1932 massacre (known to this day as *la Matanza*—"the Slaughter") forms an epoch in Salvadoran history. Previously the Liberal elite had normally ruled through civilian dictators drawn from among themselves, but they now entrusted government to an uninterrupted series of military regimes. Hernández Martínez protected the coffee elite and promoted modernization. Post-World War II demands for reform from labor and middle-class elements and from within the military ended the Hernández Martínez dictatorship in 1944. In 1948 the armed forces restructured the regime by establishing a military-dominated party, the Revolutionary Party of Democratic Unification (Partido Revolucionario de Unificación Democrática, PRUD). The party promoted neither revolution, democracy, or unity but instead provided "an impressive machine of patronage and electoral mobilization."[3] In 1960 the PRUD was replaced by its own clone, the National Conciliation Party (Partido de Conciliación Nacional, PCN).

After 1948 the Salvadoran military, supported by much of the bourgeoisie, ruled essentially on its own behalf and became increasingly powerful and corrupt. Military rule developed a cycle of "change" that maintained the status quo. Responding to popular unrest and national problems, young military officers who pledged to make reforms would overthrow an increasingly repressive regime. Then conservative army elements backed by the agrarian oligarchy would reassert themselves and abandon reforms. This would provoke civil unrest, followed by increased repression, disaffection by another reformist military faction, and a new coup.[4]

One such cycle produced the PRUD between 1944 and 1948, and another brought the PRUD's restructuring itself into the PCN in 1961. In January of 1961, a conservative coup encouraged by the outgoing Eisenhower administration occurred in El Salvador, just after John F. Kennedy's inauguration as

US president. Kennedy recognized the new government, but also employed the Alliance for Progress to pressure the interim junta to implement mild democratic and social reforms.

The US-created Alliance for Progress and the Central American Common Market (CACM) promoted rapid economic growth. The government developed infrastructure while domestic and foreign capitalists invested in manufacturing and commerce. Reformist rhetoric in the mid-1960s sparked popular hopes for change. During this period the Christian Democratic Party (Partido Demócrata Cristiano, PDC) formed. Its popular leader, José Napoleón Duarte, advocated gradual reformism of the sort supported by the Alliance. Duarte twice won the mayoralty of San Salvador.[5]

This tentative process of political transition, aided by rapid economic growth, soon vanished in the familiar way. The mild reforms and the PDC's progress alarmed the oligarchy. El Salvador's establishment press labeled President Kennedy a "Communist" for promoting agrarian reform. When the PDC's Duarte apparently won the 1972 presidential election, the military overthrew the election, installed rightist Colonel Arturo Armando Molina as president, and arrested, tortured, and exiled Duarte.

GLOBAL FORCES AND INSURRECTION

Effects of Rapid Economic Growth

Under the CACM, gross domestic product (GDP) per capita grew over 2 percent annually between 1962 and 1978. But as in Nicaragua, the benefits were very unevenly distributed. Consumer prices in El Salvador inflated at a mild rate of about 1.5 percent per year from 1963 to 1972. The OPEC (Organization of Petroleum Exporting Countries) oil-price shock, however, drove inflation up to an average of 12.8 percent annually from 1973 through 1979.[6]

Unlike prices, real working-class wages in El Salvador declined after 1973, losing about one-fifth of their real purchasing power by 1980. Salvadorans' median income was already consistently the second lowest in Central America. Taking into account the maldistribution of income, the disposable annual income of the poorest half of the population probably amounted to no more than a US dollar or two per day. Meanwhile, food and clothing costs resembled those in the more prosperous United States. Thus even for those employed throughout the CACM boom, officially fixed wages steadily lost purchasing power.

Despite industrialization and productivity growth, the capital-intensive production of consumer goods generated relatively few new jobs for the growing workforce—the opposite of what CACM and Alliance promoters hoped.

Meanwhile changes in the agrarian economy increased joblessness by pushing hundreds of thousands of peasants off the land. Estimates placed unemployment in El Salvador at around 16 percent in 1970 but by 1978 it reached 21 percent, driven upward by oil-price increases and investor fears generated by the insurrection in Nicaragua. After 1980, unemployment accelerated because of El Salvador's own developing insurrection. Nervous investors closed some plants and disrupted regional trade closed others.[7]

After 1950 much of the best agricultural land was converted to capital-intensive cultivation of export crops, especially cotton, replacing subsistence farming by tenants, squatters, and smallholders. During the 1960s, pressure on the land continued increasing; the overall number of farms grew by 19 percent while cultivated land shrank by 8 percent. The 1965 agricultural minimum-wage law lowered the number of *colonos* and *aparceros* (peasants cultivating for subsistence a plot of land donated by the owner) to one-third of the 1961 level by 1971, and the amount of land so employed to one-fifth of the earlier level.[8]

Thus, in the 1960s changing rural class relations greatly increased rural poverty. Rental and ownership of farms of less than 2 hectares increased sharply while the average area of these small plots shrank. Despite a numerical increase in small plots, the number of landless peasants more than tripled between 1961 and 1971. Large farms (over 50 hectares) also shrank in number and size as their owners sold part of their holdings for capital to invest elsewhere. Many members of the rural bourgeoisie moved some of their wealth into the fast-expanding industrial sector during the 1960s and 1970s. They invested in modern, capital-intensive industries that generated large profits. Industrial production and industrial worker productivity grew rapidly, but real industrial wages and employment levels declined.

Wealth continued concentrating in fewer hands during the 1970s.[9] Workers' share of the burgeoning national income shrank while production and investment became more centralized.[10] Major coffee growers invested roughly four times more in industry than any other Salvadoran group, forging joint ventures with about 80 percent of the foreign capital invested in the country. Industrial output more than doubled between 1967 and 1975 while the number of firms producing goods diminished by 10 percent, concentrating wealth and income among industries' owners.[11] On observer noted:

The old saying that "money follows money" was never truer than in El Salvador. These investment patterns not only contributed to an ever-greater concentration of wealth, but confirm that the traditional developmentalist assumption that wealth will "trickle down" in developing nations is groundless.[12]

good to wealthy

Another agreed: "The majority of Salvadorans, excluded from the benefits of that growth, were prevented from adequately satisfying their basic needs."[13]

Although El Salvador's capitalist elite grew relatively and absolutely wealthier during the mid-1970s, this trend ended abruptly in 1979. The Sandinista revolution in nearby Nicaragua combined with the onset of popular mobilization within El Salvador in 1978 to reduce Salvadoran investment and economic growth. Falling coffee prices and the breakdown of Central American trade due to the exhaustion of the CACM import-substitution growth model accelerated the recession. El Salvador's rapid GDP growth of the mid-1970s reversed into a 3.1 percent *decline* in production and a 5.9 percent *drop* in GDP per capita in 1979. This severe economic contraction persisted for years, harmed the country's coffee producers and industrialists, and caused massive layoffs of their employees.[14]

In summary, the development model followed El Salvador state under the CACM at first increased production and the share of wealth controlled by the national capitalist class. The working classes became relatively and absolutely poorer during the 1970s; their purchasing power as wage earners declined rapidly from 1973 on. Joblessness and underemployment rose steadily during much of the 1970s and accelerated late in that decade. Living standards eroded badly during this period. Most Salvadorans measured this adversity in terms how much food they could put on the table each day. Their impoverishment gave them powerful political grievances.

Popular Mobilization

Although the military's PRUD-PCN Party controlled the government, several new opposition parties appeared during the 1960s.[15] Early signs of growing opposition came in 1959–1960 with two new reformist parties: the social democratic National Revolutionary Movement (Movimiento Nacional Revolucionario, MNR) and the Christian Democratic Party (Partido Demócrata Cristiano, PDC). The Democratic National Union (Unión Democrática Nacionalista, UDN), a leftist coalition, formed in 1967.[16] The PDC and MNR briefly formed a legislative coalition with dissident PCN deputies in the late 1960s. In 1972 a major push for reform developed the National Opposition Union (Unión Nacional Opositora, UNO), an electoral coalition of the PDC, MNR, and UDN. UNO's presidential nominee, José Napoleón Duarte, apparently won the 1972 election but was denied the office by fraud. UNO reportedly also won the 1977 presidential election, but again lost to electoral fraud.

Myriad organizations—unions, self-help groups, peasant leagues—developed during the late 1960s and the 1970s, many promoted by the Church and new political parties. Cooperatives multiplied from 246 to 543 between 1973 and 1980.[17] Labor-union membership among blue-collar and middle-class workers rose steadily, reaching 44,150 in 1970 and 71,000 by 1977. Several unions, especially among public employees, became increasingly militant.[18] The number and frequency of strikes rose dramatically from 1974 on as inflation eroded living standards.

Development programs sponsored by the PDC, Catholic Church, and even the US Agency for International Development (USAID) swelled the number of working-class organizations in El Salvador during the 1960s and early 1970s. Catholic Christian base communities (CEBs) spread through urban and rural poor neighborhoods. In the 1970s CEBs increasingly demanded political and economic change on behalf of the poor. Many peasant organizations also developed during this period, in part encouraged by the Molina regime's mid-1970s land-reform proposals. Peasant leagues demanded access to land and higher wages. The United Popular Action Front (Frente de Acción Popular Unida, FAPU), a coalition of labor, peasant, and university student organizations, and the Communist Party of El Salvador (Partido Comunista de El Salvador, PCS) formed in 1974. FAPU was the first of several similar coalitions that together would eventually build a broad opposition network.

Between 1970 and 1979 five guerrilla organizations arose to present an armed challenge to the PCN (see Table A.4). Each forged a coalition with unions and other popular organizations. These broad-front coalitions enhanced opposition capability and resources, facilitating strikes and mass demonstrations while providing material resources for the armed opposition.

Government Repression and the Opposition

After 1970, successive military regimes escalated repression against swelling popular mobilization.[19] A rightist paramilitary organization directly tied to public security forces formed in the late 1960s, the Nationalist Democratic Organization (Organización Democrática Nacionalista, ORDEN). Its acronym spells the Spanish word for "order." ORDEN recruited tens of thousands of peasants from among former military conscripts. The anti-Communist militia mainly sought to suppress peasant organization. It built a grisly record by attacking and killing striking teachers in 1968, and thereafter murdering organizers of workers, peasants, or political opposition.

President Molina (1972–1977) and his handpicked successor Carlos Humberto Romero (1977–1979), both closely linked to the agrarian oligarchy, staunchly opposed political and economic reform. As early guerrilla actions occurred and labor and peasant organizations grew after 1973, regular security forces openly escalated repression. In 1974 National Guard and ORDEN forces murdered six peasants and "disappeared" several others affiliated with a Church–PDC peasant league. On July 30, 1975, troops killed at least 37 students protesting the Miss Universe pageant being held in San Salvador. Regular soldiers in the capital massacred an estimated 200 UNO supporters among protesters of fraud in the 1977 presidential election. "Death squads," a misnomer employed to disguise political terror by regular security forces and ORDEN,[20] became increasingly active from 1975 on. (As discussed elsewhere, their use in El Salvador is just one example of US-sanctioned death-squad activity throughout the Americas beginning in 1969.)[21] Beginning with the public assassination of opposition legislator and labor leader Rafael Aguiñada Carranza in 1974, death squads attacked Church property and assassinated and kidnapped dissidents, Catholic social activists, and priests. Eighteen Catholic clergy and religious personnel, including Archbishop Oscar Arnulfo Romero, were murdered between 1977 and 1982.[22] Romero, assassinated on March 24, 1980 while delivering mass, was made a saint in October 2018.

Official mortality statistics began to reflect the wave of state terror in the late 1970s. After labor disputes increased in 1977–1979, two separate violence indicators shot upward. The government's own official statistical abstracts reported that violent deaths rose from normal background levels of an average of 864 murders per year for 1965–1966 to 1,837 in 1977, and then to 11,471 violent deaths in 1980.[23] A Catholic human rights agency reported that political murders rose from an average of about 14 per year for 1972–1977, to 1,030 by 1979, 8,024 in 1980, and 13,353 in 1981.[24]

Statistics fail to convey the intensity of government assaults on human rights in El Salvador. The following became commonplace: searches of persons and residences on a massive scale; arbitrary, unmotivated, and unappealable arrests by secret police/military agencies; widespread, systematic physical and psychological torture; kidnappings; arbitrary and indefinite retention of prisoners (often without charges); "confessions" extracted through torture or intimidation; official refusal to provide information about detainees; judicial corruption; abysmal prison conditions; systematic impunity for human rights violators; government antagonism toward humanitarian, human rights, and relief agencies; and intimidation and harassment of prisoners, released prisoners, and their families. Common types of torture by the military and police of El Salvador were the following:

> Lengthy uninterrupted interrogations during which the prisoner is denied food and sleep; electrical shocks; application of highly corrosive acids to the prisoner's body; hanging of prisoners by the feet and hands; hooding prisoners [for long periods]; introduction of objects into the anus; threats of rape; disrespectful fondling and rape; threats of death; simulation of death of the prisoner by removing him from the cell, blindfolded and tied, late at night, and firing shots [toward the prisoner but] into the air; all manner of blows; . . . [and] threats of rape, torture, and murder of loved ones of the prisoner. Among the thousands of murdered detainees, the signs of torture reach uncommon extremes of barbarism: dismemberment [of various types], mutilation of diverse members, removal of breasts and genitals, decapitation . . . and leaving of victims' remains in visible and public places.[25]

After this escalation of government repression, four large opposition coalitions formed. Each linked various labor, peasant, and student groups to one of the guerrilla organizations. FAPU formed in 1974, the Revolutionary Popular Bloc (Bloque Popular Revolucionario, BPR) in 1975, the 28th of February Popular Leagues (Ligas Populares 28 de Febrero, LP-28) in 1978, and the Popular Liberation Movement (Movimiento de Liberación Popular, MLP) in 1979. By allying with each other and with armed rebels, their constituent groups committed themselves to revolutionary action. Together they mobilized hundreds of thousands of supporters to demonstrate or strike, and raised funds and recruited for the guerrillas. Guerrilla groups accumulated large war chests by kidnapping wealthy Salvadorans for ransom. After mid-1979 arms flowed to the insurgents from private dealers in Costa Rica. Other arms briefly passed through Nicaragua during 1980 and early 1981.[26]

Growing opposition mobilization, the escalation of regime and rebel violence, the Romero government's incapacity to address national problems, career frustration among certain groups of military officers, and apprehension about the Sandinistas' victory in Nicaragua in July 1979 led to another major regime change in El Salvador. Disgruntled senior officers and reformist younger officials ousted President Romero on October 15, 1979. The coup temporarily allied these military factions with opposition social democrats of the MNR, the Christian Democrats (PDC), and some business factions. The Carter administration gambled that the junta's reformist inclinations might

stem the revolutionary tide. It immediately endorsed the coup and the reformist military regime it established.[27] The coup and new junta also made more
palatable resumed US arms transfers to El Salvador.

This new regime allowed new civilian players (the MNR, PDC) and
ousted some others (especially the PCN's Romero and his allies) and, with
US encouragement, proposed socioeconomic reforms. The new junta nevertheless failed to contain escalating official violence. Rightist elements soon
asserted themselves and expelled some reformers in early 1980. The MNR and
most Christian Democrats then abandoned the junta. However, the support
of the United States added a crucial new element to the political game and
continued the pressure for socioeconomic reform. The coup thus ushered in a
reformist military regime that "signaled the exhaustion of traditional forms of
political control and the search for a more viable system of domination. The
old power apparatus was severely shaken."[28]

The October 1979 coup briefly raised opposition hopes for change, but
the restructured junta and rising official violence soon alienated much of the
center and left and changed opposition tactics. Further opposition unification came in early 1980 when the five guerrilla groups jointly formed the
Farabundo Martí National Liberation Front (Frente Farabundo Martí para
la Liberación Nacional, FMLN) to increase their political and military coordination. Opposition forces also created the Revolutionary Coordinator of
the Masses (Coordinadora Revolucionaria de Masas, CRM) in January 1980
and continued massive strikes, protests, and guerrilla warfare. Several parties
and mass coalitions, including the MNR and much of the PDC, then united
into the Revolutionary Democratic Front (FDR). The FDR and FMLN soon
allied to form the joint political-military opposition organization FMLN-
FDR, which coordinated overall revolutionary strategy, fielded 4,000 troops
and 5,000 militia, and controlled several areas of the country.

The FMLN-FDR adopted a platform for a revolutionary government, established governmental structures in their zones of control, and began planning
to assume ruling power.[29] Embracing this powerful challenge to the regime's
sovereignty, Mexico and France increased the rebels' legitimacy by recognizing
the FMLN-FDR as a belligerent force. FMLN-FDR representatives operated
openly in Panama, Nicaragua, Mexico, Colombia, and even the United States.

Outcome of the Challenge to Sovereignty

Momentum favored the Salvadoran opposition in 1979 and 1980. The October coup had momentarily linked the major opposition parties, a reformist
military faction, and key middle-sector proponents of democracy to pursue

major structural reforms and curtail government violence. When rightist elements pushed moderates from the junta and escalated violence, it undercut the reformists' power and blocked reforms. This closed a key, less-violent path to change and convinced much of the moderate center-left to ally with the armed opposition. On January 30, 1980, Guillermo Ungo and other moderates resigned from the junta and cabinet. The rebels had built a cooperative popular base and acquired financing and mobilized several thousand men and women under arms. When the junta reconstituted itself with more conservative elements of the Christian Democrats and government violence continued, the FDR formed (April 1980), followed by the FMLN (October 1980). By late 1980, guerrilla troops had seized effective control of much of Morazán, La Unión, and Chalatenango departments, so that "1981 opened with the army badly stretched and the undefeated FMLN poised for a major offensive."[30]

The government found itself in disarray. The first junta, internally divided, lacked support from either mass organizations or the private sector. When the conservative remnant of the Christian Democrats joined the junta in 1980, the major organization representing Salvadoran capital, the National Association of Private Enterprises (Asociación Nacional de Empresas Privadas, ANEP) boycotted the government. Rightist elements inside and outside the military tried several times to overthrow the junta. The poor battlefield performance of the military's 15,000 ill-trained troops throughout 1980 appeared to foretell imminent doom for the regime.

Help for the junta came from the US government, which provided military aid to the failing Salvadoran military and thus altered the balance of forces between regime and insurgents. Military aid and advice and economic assistance worth $5.9 million sent during the waning days of the Carter administration began rescuing the Salvadoran regime. The incoming Reagan administration then greatly boosted US technical assistance and financing. By 1985, US military aid to El Salvador reached $533 million. Over the 12 years of the Salvadoran civil war, US aid (military plus civilian) totaled about $6 billion.[31]

The Reagan administration supported the PDC's Duarte, helped contain rightist opposition to the government, and provided aid for programs ranging from agrarian reform to constituent assembly elections.[32] US training, arms, munitions, aircraft, and intelligence held the Salvadoran army together long enough to increase its size and capability to effectively fight the FMLN. Unlike Nicaragua, where American aid was withdrawn, US assistance in El Salvador rescued the official armed forces. This prolonged the conflict.

The principal reason for the extended nature of the war was the capacity of the junta to hold its piecemeal military apparatus together . . . to ward off guerrilla offensives [and hold] the population in a state of terror . . . It could only have achieved this or, indeed, survived for more than a few weeks with the resolute support of the US, which Somoza was, in the last instance, denied.[33]

The government after 1979 depended heavily upon several interacting forces—hard-liners in control of the armed forces, major business interests, extremist anti-Communist ideologues like Roberto D'Aubuisson and his Nationalist Republican Alliance Party (Alianza Republicana Nacionalista, ARENA), and the Carter, Reagan, and first Bush administrations. US pressure brought another regime transformation. These Salvadoran actors agreed to replace the junta with a transitional civilian-led government along with constitutional reform and elections. The war went badly for the military during the early 1980s, but massive US economic, military, and technical assistance held off the FMLN.

The right fiercely opposed most reforms and wished to exclude moderates, but their dependence on US aid undermined their resistance. Throughout most of the 1980s, the United States championed José Napoleón Duarte's PDC faction as the only political force that could legitimize the struggle against the armed opposition. Backed by the immense resources of the United States, Duarte was installed in the presidency and the PDC won a majority of the legislative seats in the 1984 presidential and 1985 legislative elections—both of very dubious quality.[34] This shaky civilian transitional government would eventually provide the institutional and legal foundation for greater democracy. The short-term goal of the United States in 1984 was to establish new political rules with civilian leadership and a broader spectrum of participants. This liberalization would provide enough political space to keep moderates from aligning with the FMLN. Although detested as a "Communist" by the right and distrusted by the military, US-backed Duarte was the key to the US aid to required avoid defeat. US pressure on the military and right protected the Duarte/PDC civil government, but could neither control radical rightist forces nor compel them to permit social reform. In effect, Duarte formally held the presidency without ever really taking power.

US involvement during the Duarte period thus created an unstable and artificial coalition among incompatible elements. President Duarte exercised no control over the security forces or the war.[35] The Salvadoran military and the United States blocked Duarte's attempts to negotiate with the FMLN-FDR because both wished to win the war rather than negotiate a settlement. The constitution written in 1982 and 1983 barred agrarian-reform programs that might have eased the social pressures contributing to the rebellion. The transitional government mustered no support from the business community or conservative parties for needed economic austerity measures. Duarte's base of mass support, the PDC's allied labor unions, grew increasingly frustrated and uncooperative in the late 1980s. The inefficacy and growing corruption of the PDC, aggravated by internal divisions, led to its defeat by ARENA in the 1988 legislative elections. On March 19, 1989, moderate-appearing ARENA candidate Alfredo Cristiani won the presidential election, with party strongman Roberto D'Aubuisson discreetly in the background.

Presiding over this second administration in El Salvador's civilian transitional government, President Alfredo "Freddy" Cristiani came from a wealthy family. A graduate of Georgetown University, fluent in English and diplomatic by nature, Cristiani was quickly embraced by the US government and media as a worthy ally, despite his affiliation with ARENA. Cristiani in action proved more moderate than many expected. His ARENA credentials helped him with the armed forces. With the assistance of the Central American Peace Accord and US acquiescence, he negotiated for peace with the FMLN. However, Cristiani failed to improve elections or clean up judicial corruption.[36]

War and Peace

The Salvadoran conflict became a bloody stalemate during the 1980s. The rebels held their own against increasingly powerful and sophisticated military pressure until 1984–1985. FMLN troop strength rose to around 10,000 by 1984. However, US training, aid, and intelligence helped the regime's forces steadily gain ground in the mid-1980s as transport, logistics, and tactics improved. By 1986, government troop strength rose to 52,000 from the 1980 level of 15,000. By 1985–1986 the government's advantages reduced the rebels effective strength to about 5,000, where it remained into the late 1980s.[37] Growing government air power eroded rebel troop numbers, shrank guerrilla-controlled zones, and increased civilian casualties in rebel-held zones. In 1988 and 1989 the guerrillas shifted operations in urban areas. When the ARENA-led Legislative Assembly refused to postpone the March 1989 presidential election in response to an FMLN offer to return to peaceful civic competition, the FMLN tried to disrupt the election by causing widespread power outages and attacking transportation.

A dispassionate summary of some of the horrors of El Salvador's civil war includes the following: virtually all objective observers attribute at least

80 percent of the country's 70,000 deaths between 1979 and 1992 to the military, the police, and ORDEN.[38] The Reagan administration, worried about retaining US Congressional funding for the Salvadoran government, pressured the country's military, police, and ORDEN to curtail sharply deaths and disappearances in 1983 and 1984. Despite such efforts—in themselves revealing how much repression emanated directly from the security forces—increasing combat operations kept the casualty rate high into the mid-1980s. The violence caused over a sixth of Salvadorans to flee the country. Even for those untouched by personal losses, the war, migration, and capital flight deepened the nation's economic depression and human misery. From 1980 through 1987 the economy slowed by almost 10 percent of its 1980 per capita production level.[39]

The Central American Peace Accord, signed in Esquipulas, Guatemala, in August 1987, raised hopes for a negotiated settlement of the Salvadoran war, yet little progress came until the early 1990s. Starting in late 1982, the rebels had pushed for a compromise settlement rather than outright victory. In their opinion, to capture ruling power would have brought the type of US-sponsored surrogate war and economic strangulation they observed inflicted on Nicaragua's Sandinista revolution.[40] Throughout the 1980s, however, the United States and the Salvadoran right opposed a negotiated settlement and pressed for outright victory. Accordingly, the Salvadoran government sporadically engaged in show negotiations that brought no real progress. Indeed, the Esquipulas agreement even triggered an upswing in the number of murders by the "death squads"—security forces.

In early 1989 the FMLN offered to participate in the upcoming presidential elections if the government would postpone them for six months so democratic safeguards could be put in place. The government, however, refused. ARENA candidate Alfredo Cristiani, who campaigned on peace and economic recovery, easily defeated Christian Democrat Fidel Chávez Mena and began the first of four successive ARENA presidencies. Cristiani immediately began neoliberal reforms, starting with banking and financial reforms.

The rebels, frustrated by the refusal to delay the elections, escalated military operations in outlying areas to demonstrate their strength and convince the government to negotiate seriously. When this also failed, the FMLN in late 1989 mounted a major military offensive in the capital city, San Salvador. The military responded by murdering many noncombatants it believed sympathetic to the rebels. Most shocking were the murders of six prominent Jesuit priest-intellectuals, their housekeeper, and her daughter at the Central American University on November 16, 1989. High-ranking officers, including the

(handwritten margin note: • warnings by rebels • they wanted negotiations)

chief of staff of the army and the head of the air force, authorized this atrocity by a unit of the US-trained Atlacatl Battalion.[41] The guilty generals all went free, but two years later a colonel and lieutenant who had acted on superiors' orders became the first Salvadoran officers convicted of human-rights violations in the war's 12-year history.

The guerrilla offensive, the embarrassment of the Jesuit massacre and other atrocities, and the Cold War's end apparently convinced the United States to opt for a negotiated settlement in El Salvador. As a Rand Corporation specialist wrote, "the security concerns that impelled the policy have all but evaporated along with the East–West contest . . . 'Winning' in El Salvador no longer matters much. A negotiated solution, or even 'losing' would no longer carry the same ominous significance."[42] President George H.W. Bush embraced the peace process. This cleared the way for an ultimately successful effort to bring the warring parties together by outgoing United Nations Secretary-General Javier Pérez de Cuellar. Toward the end, US diplomats such as UN Ambassador Thomas Pickering and Assistant Secretary of State Bernard Aronson pushed the Salvadoran government to make concessions. Even ARENA founder Roberto D'Aubuisson—in a last public gesture before dying of cancer—endorsed the peace proposal.

EL SALVADOR SINCE THE PEACE ACCORD

The 1992 peace agreement changed El Salvador politics by establishing a civilian democracy, permitting participation by a broad ideological spectrum of groups. This encouraged important social change, beginning with a quarter-century of weak economic recovery.

Economics

The unrest beginning in the late 1970s in El Salvador caused a 6 percent initial slump in GDP per capita in 1978 that ballooned to a net 34 percent downturn by 1982. Ten ensuing years of capital flight, disinvestment, and labor unrest caused a depression from which GDP per capita did not recover for three decades. Two major forces would contribute to gradual recovery. First, the civil war ended in 1992. This calmed economic relations, attracted back some investment, and moved many from waging war into productive work. Second, the war had driven hundreds of thousands of Salvadorans to emigrate, especially to the United States, and this outflow continued in peacetime. Emigres sent home funds (remittances) to their families, which contributed increasingly to growth. In 1980 remittances constituted only 1.4 percent of

GDP, but that rose steadily to 20.4 percent by 2017 (about ten times the value of foreign direct investment that year). Remittances alone thus drove much of El Salvador's post-war economy.[43]

Another unanticipated consequence of war- and disaster-related emigration was crime. Allowed to work in the United States under temporary protected immigration status, Salvadorans built lives there. In some cities, most notoriously Los Angeles, children of immigrants joined street gangs, sometimes forming their own for protection from extant gangs. When caught in the US judicial system, US policy mandated their deportation to El Salvador, where they lacked resources. Gangs such as the Mara Salvatrucha and 18th Street thus reorganized in country, adding a corrosive social force as they operated protection rackets, dealt drugs, and fought each other for territory.[44] The resulting criminality overwhelmed the government's ability to provide security to citizens and became a motivation for more Salvadorans to emigrate.

Politics Under ARENA Leadership

Under UN supervision from 1992, the government drastically reduced the army's size and somewhat depoliticized the services by retiring and reassigning senior officers and reforming military education. It dismantled its infamous US-trained rapid-deployment forces, the Treasury Police, and the National Guard.[45] The government replaced the National Police with a new National Civil Police (Policía Nacional Civil, PNC). Under civilian authority, it drew personnel from both the FMLN and government ranks.[46] A truth commission investigated the civil war. In 1993 it attributed 95 percent of the human rights abuses after 1980 to the armed forces and death squads. The Legislative Assembly immediately passed a general amnesty law barring both criminal or civil recourse for crimes committed during the war.[47]

The FMLN demobilized by early 1993 and moved openly into electoral politics. In 1994 the "election of the century" marked the first truly democratic vote in El Salvador's history. Parties from across the political spectrum vied for seats in the Assembly, mayoralties, and the presidency. The FMLN joined a center-left coalition with Democratic Convergence (Convergencia Democrática, CD) in the presidential election. While CD candidate Rubén Zamora managed to force a runoff, ARENA's Armando Calderón Sol prevailed in the second round of voting. ARENA won 39 Legislative Assembly seats, nearly double those won by the FMLN (see Tables A.6 and A.7).

President Calderón Sol intensified neoliberal reforms by privatizing the telecommunications and energy sectors and reducing tariffs. Slowing growth in the mid-1990s produced tensions between the industrialists and agrarian elites within ARENA, and neoliberalism had not addressed poverty, unemployment, or the growing crime problem. Discontent with neoliberal policies helped the FMLN make significant gains in the 1997 legislative and municipal elections. ARENA's share of Assembly seats declined from 39 to 28 while the FMLN won 6 new seats for a total of 27. The FMLN alone or in coalition also won 54 mayoralties, including San Salvador. Tensions within ARENA also aided the right-wing PCN, which increased its Assembly representation to 11 seats in 1997, up from 4 in 1994. The Christian Democrats posted significant losses, dropping from 18 to 10 seats—a downward trend that would leave them with zero deputies in 2012.

Growing electoral successes prompted an internal debate within the FMLN over policy and strategy. *Renovadores* favored modernizing the party and compromising with the neoliberals. The *ortodoxo* faction argued that the FMLN's potency at the ballot box warranted rejecting neoliberal economic policies. Following a long, heated convention, the FMLN nominated former guerrilla and renovador Facundo Guardado as its presidential candidate for 1999. ARENA's nominee Francisco Flores easily defeated Guardado 52 to 29 percent in the presidential election. This sizable loss divided the FMLN. Guardado blamed the ortodoxos for the loss, whereas they blamed his abandonment of the socialist platform. Guardado resigned as the party's general coordinator and the ortodoxos took over the party.[48]

Implementing Neoliberalism

Privatization stalled in 1999 when plans to privatize the health sector caused a five-month strike by health-care workers. Flores' unwillingness to negotiate with the workers played poorly during the 2000 legislative campaign. According to one poll, only 37 percent rated Flores as doing a good job and a majority said that the economy and crime had worsened during the first year of his administration.[49]

The FMLN again benefited from the unpopular ARENA policies by becoming El Salvador's largest party in the 2000 municipal and legislative elections. The FMLN gained four seats in the Assembly and won mayoralty of San Salvador. The PCN took advantage of ARENA's losses, gaining three seats in the legislature and 15 mayoralties. ARENA's 2000 municipal election losses caused the party to reshuffle its executive committee. Many Salvadorans chose not to vote in 2000, when turnout fell to 38 percent from 45 percent in 1997.[50]

ARENA's poor election showing and nearly stagnant growth in 2000–2001 did not derail Flores' commitment to neoliberalism. In a controversial move, in January 2001 he "dollarized" the economy (substituted the US dollar for its former currency the *colón*), a move that initially benefitted the wealthy but hurt the poor. Two major earthquakes also struck in January and February. This overwhelmed hospitals and other services and exposed the prior neglect of social services under the neoliberal program. The government again suggested privatizing certain health services before the 2003 municipal and legislative elections. Health-care workers again struck throughout the campaign. The FMLN maintained its 31 seats in the Legislative Assembly in the 2003 legislative elections, while ARENA lost two seats. The FMLN retained control of the mayoralty of San Salvador despite losing its popular two-time incumbent Hector Silva.

President Flores' tenure thus saw two prolonged health-care worker strikes, economic stagnation, growing dependence on remittances from abroad, and growing trouble with gangs. Combined with the FMLN's momentum from the 2003 elections, ARENA appeared weakened entering the 2004 presidential election campaign. To toughen its image, the Flores government pushed for harsh anti-gang measures. The legislation, known as *mano dura* (effectively an "iron fist"), criminalized gang membership and created police anti-gang units. Domestic and international human rights advocates decried the policy, and Salvadoran courts eventually released most of those arrested merely for gang association.

Both gangs and remittances wrought changes in Salvadoran society. During the civil war Salvadoran emigration, primarily to the United States, increased dramatically and it continued rising afterward.[51] By 2004 an estimated 1.5 million Salvadorans lived in the United States. Most were young, and about half were women.[52] Remittances they sent to their families increased to $2.5 billion in 2004, well over 15 percent of GDP, and roughly 100 times larger than annual US aid and ten times greater than foreign direct investment that year (see Table A.1). Despite its economic benefits, some analysts believed emigration increasingly undermined Salvadoran families and left their youths vulnerable to the growing gang culture. (US repatriation of gang members to El Salvador beginning in the mid-1990s fueled the rise in post-war violence.)[53] These factors, along with high youth unemployment and socioeconomic marginalization, fed the country's burgeoning gangs. The politicization of both issues increasingly dominated electoral campaigns.

Controlled by the ortodoxos in 2004, the FMLN again failed to follow its recent legislative and municipal gains with a presidential win. Its nomination of former commander and Communist Party leader Shafick Handal for president drew criticism both at home and abroad. The United States expressed strong misgivings because Handal vowed to withdraw Salvadoran troops from Iraq and adamantly opposed the Central American Free Trade Agreement (CAFTA). Former US ambassador Rose Likins predicted worsened US–Salvadoran relations should Handal win.[54] Several US congressmen suggested that an FMLN victory would bring a review or end of temporary protected status (TPS) for Salvadorans living in the United States and a reconsideration of remittance policies.[55] ARENA's candidate, former sportscaster Antonio "Tony" Saca, exploited these potential ruptures by emphasizing the country's dependence on remittances.

The 2004 presidential elections were the most polarized in a decade. ARENA invoked Cold War imagery and rhetoric and lambasted Handal as a terrorist bent on turning El Salvador into another Cuba. Handal's unpopularity and US interference eventually thwarted the FMLN. ARENA's Saca easily won by 57 percent to 36 percent. Former San Salvador mayor Hector Silva ran on the United Democratic Center (Centro Democrático Unido, CDU) coalition ticket with the Christian Democrats, but the CDU-PDC won only 3.9 percent of the vote. Surprisingly, the election's outcome had little effect on the ortodoxos' control of the FMLN; Handal remained head of the party. For its part, Saca's resounding victory bolstered ARENA with its fourth successive presidency despite its virtually unknown candidate.

President Saca's administration sought to distinguish itself from prior ARENA administrations by creating poverty alleviation programs while continuing neoliberal policies. The Common Health Fund (Fondo Solidario para la Salud, FOSALUD) and Solidarity Network (Red Solidaria) targeted some of the poorest municipalities in the country. But years of slow growth, a regressive tax system, and growing public debt severely constrained the president's ability to fund these programs. By the end of Saca's term, the general perception was that poverty had increased. Ironically, the most effective tool for reducing poverty and inequality was remittances, which offset El Salvador's trade imbalance and represented the single greatest source of foreign exchange. By 2006, remittances—received by a quarter of households—exceeded exports and foreign investment combined and demonstrably reduced poverty and inequality.[56]

President Saca strengthened his predecessor's *mano dura* policies as the crime wave continued. When the Supreme Court declared the original law unconstitutional in April 2004, Saca soon proposed an enhanced "*super mano dura*" replacement law.[57] The new policy led to the arrests of some 11,000 alleged gang members in a single year.[58] These arrests, however, did not reduce the country's crime wave, and homicides actually *increased*. The violence was costly in lives taken, infringed human rights, and economic activity. A 2005

United Nations Development Program (UNDP) study estimated that violence cost El Salvador nearly 12 percent of its GDP.[59] Crime also provided authorities an excuse to crack down on popular protest. In October 2006, the Salvadoran government approved the Special Anti-Terrorism Law (Ley Especial contra Actos de Terrorismo), which criminalized common protest techniques including demonstrations, marches, occupying buildings, and street blockades.

Crime continued front and center in the 2006 legislative and municipal elections. The FMLN emphasized rising insecurity and failed *mano dura* policies, whereas ARENA repeatedly suggested the FMLN and gangs were in cahoots.[60] Although some speculated Shafik Handal's death from a heart attack a few weeks before the elections might help the FMLN, the results were mixed. The FMLN won one additional (32) Assembly seat, but lost 14 mayoralties, including five of seven departmental capitals, and won by only 44 votes the mayoralty of San Salvador which it had held since 1997. In contrast, ARENA improved its fortunes in legislative and municipal elections after a decade of losses, gaining seven legislative seats and increasing its control of municipal governments from 111 to 147.

In 2007 El Salvador conducted its first census since 1992. It counted only 5.7 million citizens, significantly lower than the previous 7.1 million estimate. Possible reasons for the gross overestimations included increased out-migration, declining birth rates, and errors in the 1992 census. [61] The consequences of this adjustment meant that some of El Salvador's indicators, such as per capita income, improved while others worsened. Already the most violent country in the hemisphere, El Salvador's homicide rate adjusted upward from 55 to 67 per 100,000.

Salvadoran democracy reached a major crossroad with the 2009 elections. For the first time since 1994 all presidential, legislative, and municipal elections would be held concurrently. Without explanation, the electoral tribunal set the municipal and legislative elections two months before presidential elections (all were traditionally held the same day). ARENA, with legislative help from conservative parties, had governed for 20 years, despite the widespread public dissatisfaction reflected in steady FMLN electoral gains. In 2009 the FMLN increased its share of Assembly seats to 35 from 32. It gained a few municipalities, but it lost San Salvador, which it had held since 1997. ARENA lost two seats in the Assembly (down to 32) but won San Salvador, which apparently augured well for the presidential elections because ARENA's alliance with the PCN could salvage a working majority in the next Assembly.

After infighting, President Saca's preferred presidential nominee prevailed—Rodrigo Avila, former director of the national police, and vice-minister of security. Attempting to rebrand itself, the FMLN selected popular journalist Mauricio Funes. Considered a moderate, his candidacy somewhat deflected the charges of radicalism that had plagued prior FMLN nominees Guardado and Handal. His running mate, former guerrilla commander Salvador Sánchez Cerén, however, evoked suggestions that FMLN hard-liners would ultimately rule.[62]

ARENA's campaign again invoked Cold War rhetoric and attempted to tie the FMLN to Hugo Chávez, Fidel Castro, and Colombia's leftist guerrillas.[63] They suggested US relations would suffer and remittances might dry up should the FMLN win. Addressing the American Enterprise Institute, Salvadoran Foreign Minister Marisol Argueta claimed an FMLN victory would endanger US security interests. Although numerous members of the US Congress pledged neutrality, Congressman Dana Rohrabacher renewed his threats from 2004. He called the FMLN a "pro-terrorist party" and "an ally of Al-Qaeda and Iran," and claimed the FMLN trafficked arms to Colombia's rebels. He called for lifting temporary protected status for Salvadorans in the United States should the FMLN win, a threat to remittances.[64] Unlike the Bush administration in 2004, the Obama administration pledged neutrality and vowed to work with whoever won.

The FMLN's Funes proclaimed himself the candidate of change.[65] His slogan, "This time is different," referred both to his candidacy and the possibility of victory. He distanced himself from previous FMLN platforms by vowing to retain dollarization and CAFTA membership. Funes led widely in early polls, but the gap narrowed after the municipal and legislative elections when the PCN, the PDC, and other parties withdrew their presidential nominees and endorsed ARENA. On election day, 5,000 election observers fanned out throughout the country. They reported some minor incidents but no evidence of systematic fraud. Funes won 51.3 to 48.7 percent. Voter turnout declined 5 percent from 2004, to 61 percent.

Politics Under FMLN Leadership

The importance of the 2009 ruling party change can hardly be overstated. Within the defeated ARENA, former president Cristiani returned to head the party's directorate, whereas former president Saca was expelled from the party. Saca and 12 ARENA defectors in the Assembly then founded a new party, the Grand Alliance for National Unity (Gran Alianza por la Unidad Nacional, GANA) in January 2010. GANA then forged a working coalition with the

FMLN in the Assembly. President Funes signaled his intention to govern from the center by appointing a cabinet with several centrists, including San Salvador's popular ex-mayor Héctor Silva, as well as several FMLN ortodoxos.

The new government's most pressing problem was the ongoing crime wave. Shortly after entering office, Funes deployed the military into high-crime neighborhoods, continuing the militarization of public security begun by his predecessors. Yet another anti-gang law was passed in September 2010, again criminalizing gang membership and setting stiff prison sentences (up to six years for members, ten for leaders). This had little effect except provoking retaliatory gang violence.[66] In 2011, the homicide rate was 70 per 100,000 with no sign of abating. In a controversial move, Funes appointed former generals David Munguía Payés and Francisco Salinas, respectively, as minister of justice and public security and as director of the National Civilian Police. Critics argued their appointments violated the 1992 peace accords, which separated the military from the civilian police.[67] The National Police inspector general, Zaira Navas, resigned in early 2012 to protest that the military had gained too much influence in the police.

In a stunning development in March 2012, leaders of the warring MS-13 and 18th Street gangs announced a truce (purportedly brokered by El Salvador's chief army and police chaplain, Monsignor Fabio Colindres, and former FMLN guerrilla and legislator, Raúl Mijango). Gang leaders ordered that killings stop in exchange for transfers from maximum- to medium-security prisons, conjugal visits, and cell phone use. The truce provided for reintegration and vocational training, and designated "peace zones" (violence-free municipalities). Homicides quickly declined to 42 per 100,000, but public opinion remained skeptical. Almost 90 percent of respondents to a 2012 poll distrusted the truce, and 65 percent felt it had not reduced crime.[68] Some also questioned the effectiveness of the truce because, while homicides declined, disappearances seemed to increase.[69]

The truce and Funes' policies toward violence became problematic when questions arose concerning the government's involvement in the deal. Although the Funes administration had repeatedly tried to distance itself from the truce, it emerged that it was undertaken with the administration's full knowledge.[70] In addition, in 2013 the Constitutional Chamber of the Supreme Court ruled Munguía Payés' and Salinas' appointments unconstitutional because they violated the law against military serving in civilian security positions. Their subsequent removal increased concerns about the truce, which collapsed by the end of 2013 as homicides increased.[71] In addition to El Salvador's youth gang problem, drug traffickers and organized crime were also contributing to violence.

Social and Legal Issues

Violence against women reached epidemic levels in El Salvador. President Funes in 2009 announced the Ciudad Mujer (City for Women) project. Coordinated by the first lady, the program established numerous centers to provide women such social services as health care for women and children, domestic-violence counseling, and financial counseling.[72] The Legislative Assembly advanced gender equality by passing in 2011 the Law of Equality, Equity, and the Eradication of Violence against Women. Among other things, it guaranteed equal access to education, equal pay, and established femicide as a crime. Violence against LGBT persons was also widespread, though reliable data are difficult to obtain. El Salvador's Ministry of Social Inclusion reported some 600 LGBT persons were killed between 1993 and 2017.[73] Many in the LGBT community suffered violence at the hands of security forces.[74] In 2010 Funes issued a presidential decree banning discrimination based on sexual orientation and gender identity in the public sector. Pignato and Funes also created the Sexual Diversity Division under the Secretary of Social Inclusion to assist with policy formation and later established a hotline to provide assistance to the LGBT community in 2013.

Despite such actions, violence and discrimination against women in El Salvador remained endemic. In a 2017 national survey, 67 percent of Salvadoran women over the age of 15 reported being victims of violence.[75] Despite its femicide law, by 2019 El Salvador still had one of the highest femicide rates in the world. Some laws attempted to address women's issues, such as the creation of a new unit to oversee crimes against women, girls, and LGBT persons in 2018. Others, however, contributed to them. For example, in 2006 El Salvador enacted one of the world's strictest abortion bans. It provided no exceptions, including risk to the life of the mother. It criminalized abortions and imposed jail sentences for the woman, provider, and any accomplices.[76] The ban not only increased dangerous "back alley" abortions, but women seeking medical attention for pregnancy problems were prosecuted for aggravated homicide, which carried a much harsher sentence than having an abortion. Several women who reported miscarriages at emergency rooms were subsequently arrested and convicted of having abortions.[77] Between 2000 and 2014, 147 women were convicted and sentenced to up to 40 years under the country's abortion law. Others died incarcerated after being denied due process and medical care following miscarriages.[78] In 2013, the story of a young woman named "Beatriz" captured international attention. Suffering from lupus and kidney failure, she petitioned the Supreme Court for an exception to the abortion ban to save her own life and because the fetus showed life-threatening anomalies.[79] The Court ultimately permitted Beatriz to have a cesarean delivery, not an abortion. The baby, born anencephalic, died within hours of delivery. In another well-publicized case, Evelyn Hernández served three years of a 30-year sentence before being retried and acquitted in 2019. She had been convicted of aggravated homicide after she gave birth to a still-born baby. Days after her acquittal, prosecutors announced that they planned to seek a *third* trial in Hernández's case, underscoring the virulent pursuit of women accused in such matters and in stark contrast to other crimes.

Constitutional Crises

In June 2011 the Assembly passed and Funes signed Decree 743, which required unanimous rulings of the Constitutional Chamber of the Supreme Court to declare a law unconstitutional. Critics argued the law weakened the judiciary and would effectively prevent the Court from challenging the constitutionality of legislation, especially the Amnesty Law that exempted the military from punishment for crimes during the civil war. The FMLN and many civil-society organizations announced their opposition to Decree 743.[80] Public protests ensued—so massive that the Assembly repealed the law in July 2011.

The second crisis also pitted the legislature against the judiciary. Following the 2012 elections but before the new Assembly had been seated, the outgoing Assembly appointed new justices to the Supreme Court. The Constitutional Court overruled these appointments and retroactively overturned those the Assembly made in 2006 as unconstitutional because each session was only permitted one round of appointments.[81] The FMLN and GANA, who had collaborated on the appointments, challenged that ruling in the Central American Court of Justice, which ruled for the Assembly. A settlement ultimately mediated by Funes let the judges elected in 2009 retain their positions and allowed the re-election of the 2006 and 2012 Supreme Court judges.[82]

Elections 2012

These legislative and municipal elections could reasonably be interpreted as a referendum on the Funes administration. High crime, an economy stagnant except for remittances, and the decree brouhaha were fresh on voters' minds as they headed to the polls. In results, ARENA recuperated most of its earlier losses to GANA defections by taking 33 Assembly seats. The FMLN followed with 31 seats, down four from 2009. ARENA interpreted the results as a major triumph. FMLN spokesmen rationalized that things could have been worse. Former President Saca's new GANA won 11 seats, establishing itself as the largest of the legislature's smaller parties. Older parties generally lost seats (see Table A.7). ARENA also won the most mayoralties with 116; the FMLN captured 95 (10 in coalition races), followed by the CN with 26, and GANA with 18. The FMLN lost several long-held mayoralties, again including the capital San Salvador. The 2012 elections brought two innovations in the election system: first, the traditional party-list ballot was replaced with a new one listing individual candidates, and second, independent candidates were allowed to run for the first time in 2012. These changes contributed to a rise in the number of Assembly candidates.

President Funes broke with past administrations on human rights violations by becoming the first president to acknowledge or apologize for government abuses during the war. On January 17, 2012, during twentieth-anniversary commemoration of the peace accords, Funes apologized for the 1981 massacre at El Mozote and named those responsible.[83] In December 2012, the Inter-American Commission for Human Rights ruled that the Amnesty Law violated international law, did not exempt crimes committed during the war, and ordered the government to investigate the El Mozote massacre.[84] Months later the Human Rights Institute of the Central American University challenged the Amnesty Law in the Supreme Court, and the Attorney General's office in September 2013 agreed to open investigations into El Mozote. The possibility of criminal prosecutions and overturning the Amnesty Law unsettled some. Tutela Legal, the Archbishop's human rights and legal aid office, established by Archbishop Romero in 1977, closed without warning, raising alarm among human rights advocates. The office had documented more than 50,000 cases of abuses during and since the war. Shortly after Tutela Legal's closing, armed gunmen ransacked files and set fire to the offices of Pro Búsqueda, an organization that searched for children who disappeared during the war. The chilling incident occurred days after adult children represented by that organization testified before the Supreme Court about their parents' murders.[85] In December 2013, however, the Archdiocese created a new human rights office, Tutela de Derechos Humanos, to carry on Tutela Legal's mission.[86]

The 2014 Presidential Election

The 2014 presidential elections would determine whether the FMLN would retain power after its first term or lose to ARENA. Despite many challenges, President Funes maintained significant public support throughout his presidency, some garnered from his handling of the 2012 constitutional crisis.[87] His approval rose to 86 percent in one 2013 poll, including 68 percent of ARENA supporters.[88] Despite Funes' popularity, some FSLN factions regarded him

as too centrist. Indicating an impending leftward tack, the FMLN nominated a former FPL guerrilla—vice president and education minister, Salvador Sánchez Cerén—for president. ARENA nominated San Salvador major
Norman Quijano, and former President Saca ran on the UNIDAD ticket, a
coalition of GANA, PES, and the CN.

Saca's candidacy aroused controversy. El Salvador's constitution allows
for a second, non-consecutive term, and Saca became the first former president to seek re-election. His defection from ARENA threatened to split
that party's vote. Various complaints were filed in vain attempts to disqualify
him—unconstitutionality, fraud, and conflict of interest. Meanwhile, corruption allegations dogged the ARENA and UNIDAD candidates: Quijano
was under investigation for the misuse of funds, for instance, and the public
learned his personal wealth had grown fifteenfold to $10.5 million while in
office.[89] Moreover, prosecutors arrested several officials of the Flores administration (1999–2004, authors of dollarization and the first *mano dura*). Former
president Flores himself came under investigation for the misuse of disaster
relief donations from Taiwan.[90]

The campaigns focused on the economy and violence. Sanchez Cerén
pledged to continue social programs, deepen socioeconomic reforms, and
continue supporting the gang truce. Quijano opposed the truce and advocated resuming the failed hardline law-and-order strategy. GANA's Saca
embraced many FMLN social programs, such as Ciudad Mujer, opposed the
truce, and pledged to promote employment and the agricultural sector. All
three campaigned in US cities with large Salvadoran populations because for
the first time Salvadorans living abroad could vote.[91] This change enfranchised
the approximately 200,000 expatriate Salvadorans.

As expected, Saca's candidacy forced a presidential runoff. Sánchez Cerén
narrowly lost the first round (48.9 percent of the vote). ARENA's Quijano
won 38 percent and GANA's Saca 11 percent of the vote. Only 1,909 Salvadorans abroad voted. In the March 2014 runoff, despite favorable polls
Sánchez Cerén narrowly prevailed by only 6,364 votes, the closest presidential election in Salvadoran history. ARENA's runoff campaign had relentlessly
promoted fears El Salvador would succumb to turmoil like Venezuela's should
the FMLN win. Perhaps owing to such fears, turnout *increased* slightly in the
runoff, a rarity. It was later revealed that officials from both ARENA and
the FMLN had paid gang members to deliver votes in the election. During
the truce trial in 2017, a gang leader testified that the FMLN had paid $250,000
and ARENA had paid $100,000 to gangs to vote for their party and, in some
cases, suppress turnout or confiscate voter identification cards.[92]

Extraordinary Measures

Salvador Sánchez Cerén took office amid growing violence. With the collapse of the gang truce, homicides increased almost 60 percent in 2014. In February 2015, Sánchez Cerén announced Plan El Salvador Seguro (Plan Safe El Salvador), which focused primarily on crime prevention. It appeared to break significantly from past security plans, but he also announced the creation of new military battalions to fight crime. Emphasizing the contradiction, the police director told officers who used their weapons against criminals to "do so with complete confidence."[93] Gangs began targeting security personnel, killing dozens early in 2015. In response Sánchez Cerén transferred gang leaders back to maximum security prisons, a change from the lower-security facilities they had enjoyed during the truce. Gangs retaliated by unleashing a wave of violence throughout San Salvador in mid-2015. This brought a bus strike that snarled transportation around the capital. By the end of the year homicides had risen to 104 per 100,000, the highest in the world by far.

The administration took an increasingly aggressive stance against gangs. In August, the attorney general began trying gang members under the country's 2006 anti-terror law. In 2016, the government passed a series of "extraordinary measures" that restricted imprisoned gang members' privileges, including visitation rights and telecommunications within prisons. Gangs began targeting security forces who retaliated with extrajudicial killings. In August 2019, the Human Rights Ombudsman's office released a report that the police had executed 116 people between 2014 and 2018.[94] The report also described police coverups of the killings, which included tampering with crime scenes and evidence. Evidence surfaced of death squads operating within security forces, and extrajudicial killings were going unpunished. As of June 2018, no security personnel had been convicted of extrajudicial killings. A case in point is the 2015 San Blas massacre, where police were charged with killing eight people and tampering with evidence, yet all officers were acquitted because the court could not identify the specific triggerman.[95]

Corruption and Other Legal Issues

Former presidents Francisco Flores, Antonio Saca, and Mauricio Funes were all embroiled in corruption scandals. Flores (1999–2004) died in 2016 while awaiting trial on charges that he diverted $15 million in earthquake aid from Taiwan to personal and party accounts. Saca (2004–2009) pleaded guilty to charges of money laundering and embezzlement of more than $300 million and received a ten-year prison sentence. He subsequently pled guilty to bribing

judicial officials. Funes was accused of embezzling and laundering more than
$350 million, much of it moved in black trash bags.[96] In 2016 he fled to
Nicaragua to evade justice, using twitter to proclaim his innocence and attack
his opponents. In July 2019 Nicaragua granted him citizenship, effectively
blocking his extradition.

Attorney General Douglas Meléndez had earned a reputation for prosecuting high-profile corruption cases, such as those against the former presidents. He also brought corruption charges against his predecessor, former
attorney general Luis Martínez, and against prominent businessman Enrique
Rais for defrauding the justice system.[97] In December 2018, the legislature
failed to renew Meléndez's term, instead appointing Raúl Melara, a member
of ARENA with no criminal prosecutorial experience.

In 2016 the Constitutional Chamber ruled that the country's 1993
amnesty law was unconstitutional. It also ordered an investigation into war
crimes and crimes against humanity during the civil war, as well as a comprehensive reparations program for victims. The courts reopened investigations
into the 1980 murder of Archbishop Oscar Romero, the 1989 murder of
six Jesuit priests and their housekeeper and her daughter, and the 1981 El
Mozote massacre. In 2017, President Sánchez Cerén announced the creation
of the National Commission on the Search for Adult Persons Disappeared in
the Context of the Armed Conflict in El Salvador (CONABUSQUEDA), a
commission charged with locating victims of forced disappearances during
the civil war.

In its 2016 ruling, the Constitutional Chamber ordered the Legislative
Assembly to create a new ad hoc commission to draft a law on national reconciliation by July 2019. More than two years later, the commission presented a draft National Reconciliation Law in February 2019. Among the
commission's five deputies were four directly involved in the conflict. Rodolfo
Parker, who chaired the commission, had been cited by the Truth Commission for complicity in the cover up of the murders of Jesuit priests of the
Central American University. The draft bill, widely criticized by civil society,
human rights groups, and victims groups, proposed halting existing prosecutions, such as the El Mozote massacre, and forbidding future prosecutions.[98] It
was suspended in May 2019 under pressure from domestic and international
rights groups.

In March of 2008 the Saca administration had placed a moratorium
on mining, after which the international mining firm Oceana Gold sued
El Salvador for $75 million, claiming consequent losses. The litigation
evolved into a $250 million case in the World Bank's International Center

for Settlement of Investment Disputes that El Salvador eventually won in 2016. Meanwhile, between 2009 and 2011 four anti-mining activists were killed and dozens of others attacked or threatened.[99] The Salvadoran government claimed the murders were unrelated to mining activities and no one has been prosecuted. In 2016, the international tribunal ruled in El Salvador's favor, a major victory for a tiny country. In 2017 El Salvador became the first country in the world to ban metal mining in a unanimous vote of all legislators present.[100]

The 2018 and 2019 Elections

Unrelenting crime and corruption took their toll on the electorate. In 2018 and 2019, Salvadorans punished the two main parties at the polls. Former Nuevo Cuscatlán and San Salvador mayor, Nayib Bukele, urged voters to boycott the 2018 legislative and municipal elections. The results devastated the FMLN, which lost eight seats in the National Assembly and 44 percent of its vote share from the previous election. While ARENA gained Assembly seats and won key municipalities, including San Salvador, it also lost vote share. Null votes cast increased 150 percent to 226,000, more than won by the third largest party. It was a dire omen for the March 2019 presidential elections. A November poll by the University of Central America's Institute of Public Opinion (IUDOP) revealed that more than 75 percent of voters expressed little to no interest in the upcoming presidential elections.[101]

Bukele, who had been expelled from the FMLN in 2017, formed his own political party, Nuevas Ideas, in preparation for the 2019 presidential elections. When his party was not registered in time, he first attempted to run on the CD ticket, also later disqualified. Bukele then made a last-minute deal with GANA leadership to run as their candidate, a move many considered opportunistic. The FMLN nominated former foreign minister Hugo Martínez, while ARENA nominated US-educated businessman and political unknown Carlos Calleja. Throughout his campaign Bukele hammered on corruption, promising to establish an anti-impunity and corruption body similar to Guatemala's CICIG. He also promised pragmatic approaches to crime and the economy, though all candidate proposals were short on details.

Bukele won a resounding victory—53.1 percent of the vote, the most ever in the first round of presidential voting. He won all of El Salvador's 14 departments, as well as the vote from abroad, and 195 of 262 municipalities. As the first third-party candidate to win since the peace accords, he effectively broke the country's two-party dominant system. Some even referred to it as El Salvador's "first postwar election."[102] The FMLN and ARENA won a combined 46 percent of the vote, with the FMLN taking only 14.4 percent—a loss of more than 1.1 million votes, most of which went to Bukele. But big victories come with big expectations. It remained to be seen whether Bukele could deliver on his promises to root out corruption, reduce crime, and reinvigorate the economy with GANA holding only 10 of 84 National Assembly seats.

CONCLUSIONS

Following the peace accords, El Salvador changed markedly. Foreign assistance smoothed the transition to civilian democracy, encouraged the formation of hundreds of civil-society organizations, and trained former combatants for new occupations. The peace process restructured the armed forces, dismantled several state security organizations, and established a new civilian police force. The FMLN contested elections and won Assembly seats, mayoralties, and successive presidencies in 2009 and 2014. The FMLN and ARENA had successfully and peacefully transferred power between them for 25 years, an important step in the consolidation of democracy in El Salvador. But the 2019 presidential elections upended the country's two-party dominant system when Nayib Bukele and GANA won a landslide first round victory. Bukele, who capitalized on widespread discontent over previous administrations' failure to reduce epidemic violence and corruption, announced the creation of an anti-impunity commission in September 2019. But he faced major challenges: low economic growth, public and external debt, the looming termination of TPS, a wave of outward migration, and insecurity.

In 2019, El Salvador remained one of the world's most violent countries, though premilinary police data indicated a significant drop in violence for that year. Much of the violence was driven by gangs who now had a presence in 184 of the country's 262 municipalities. A 2013 study by the Public Opinion Institute at the Central American University in San Salvador (UCA) estimated that between 250,000 and 400,000 Salvadorans were connected to the country's gangs somehow.[103] Criminal violence and corruption continued to undermine El Salvador's institutions, as illustrated by extrajudicial killings. Crime was also driving many Salvadorans to leave the country. In 2017 nearly 300,000 Salvadorans were internally displaced by violence.[104] More than 25 years after the signing of El Salvador's peace accords, the country remained mired in intractable conflict.

NOTES

1. Tommie Sue Montgomery, *Revolution in El Salvador: Origins and Evolution* (Boulder, CO: Westview Press, 1982); and Enrique Baloyra-Herp, *El Salvador in Transition* (Chapel Hill, NC: University of North Carolina Press, 1982).

2. Quoted in Montgomery, *Revolution in El Salvador*, p. 46.

3. Baloyra-Herp, *El Salvador in Transition*, p. 35.

4. Tommie Sue Montgomery, "El Salvador: The Roots of Revolution," in Steve C. Ropp and James A. Morris, eds., *Central America: Crisis and Adaptation* (Albuquerque, NM: University of New Mexico Press, 1984), p. 78.

5. See Stephen Webre, *José Napoleón Duarte and the Christian Democratic Party in Salvadorean Politics: 1960–1972* (Baton Rouge, LA: Louisiana State University Press, 1979).

6. For an extended discussion on the CACM boom in El Salvador, see John A. Booth and Thomas W. Walker, *Understanding Central America*, 3rd ed. (Boulder, CO: Westview Press, 1999), Ch. 7 and Appendix.

7. See ibid., Appendix, Table A.8; Hugo Molina, "Las bases económicas del desarrollo industrial y la absorción de fuerza de trabajo en El Salvador," in Daniel Camacho et al., *El fracaso social de la integración centroamericana* (San José, Costa Rica: Editorial Universitaria Centroamericana, 1979), pp. 245–254; Phillip L. Russell, *El Salvador in Crisis* (Austin, TX: Colorado River Press, 1984), pp. 76–78; Victor Antonio Orellana, *El Salvador: Crisis and Structural Change*, Occasional Paper Series No. 13 (Miami: Latin American and Caribbean Center, Florida International University, 1985), pp. 5–9; Victor Bulmer-Thomas, *The Political Economy of Central America since 1920* (Cambridge: Cambridge University Press, 1987), pp. 175–229.

8. Dirección General de Estadística y Censos (DGEC–El Salvador), *Anuario estadístico 1981, tomos III-V* (San Salvador, El Salvador: Ministerio de Economía, 1983), Cuadros 311–01, 311–02; Bulmer-Thomas, *Political Economy of Central America*, pp. 201–207.

9. Tommie Sue Montgomery, *Revolution in El Salvador*; Donaldo Castillo Rivas, "Modelos de acumulación, agricultura, y agroindustria en Centroamérica," in D. Castillo Rivas, ed., *Centroamérica: Más allá de la crisis* (México: Ediciones SIAP, 1983), pp. 204–207; and James Dunkerley, *The Long War: Dictatorship and Revolution in El Salvador* (London: Junction Books, 1982), pp. 87–118.

10. Orellana, *El Salvador: Crisis*, pp. 5–10; Molina, "Las bases económicas," pp. 245–254.

11. Orellana, *El Salvador: Crisis*, pp. 5–7.

12. Montgomery, *Revolution in El Salvador*, pp. 94–95.

13. Orellana, *El Salvador: Crisis*, pp. 6–7.

14. Booth and Walker, *Understanding Central America*, 3rd ed., Tables 1.1, Appendix A.6.

15. Montgomery, *Revolution in El Salvador*; Dunkerley, *The Long War*, pp. 90–102; Jorge Cáceres Prendes, "Radicalización política y pastoral en El Salvador: 1969–1979," *Estudios Sociales Centroamericanos* 33 (September–December 1982), pp. 97–111.

16. Russell, *El Salvador in Crisis*, pp. 71–78; Tomás Guerra, *El Salvador en la hora de su liberación* (San José, Costa Rica, 1980), pp. 103–108; Baloyra-Herp, *El Salvador in Transition*, pp. 43–52.

17. DGEC–El Salvador, *Anuario estadístico, 1981*, tomos III–V.

18. Rafael Menjívar, *Formación y lucha del proletariado industrial salvadoreño* (San José, Costa Rica: Editorial Universitaria Centroamericano, 1982), pp. 115–162; Russell, *El Salvador in Crisis*, p. 71.

19. See Michael McClintock, *The American Connection, Volume 1: State Terror and Popular Resistance in El Salvador* (London: Zed Books, 1985), pp. 156–209, for details on the rise of repression in El Salvador; see also Inforpress Centroamericano, *Central America Report*, January 20, 1984, p. 23.

20. McClintock, *The American Connection*, pp. 174–177.

21. Even in 2004 certain US officials, veterans of the anti-Communist crusade in Central America, advocated using death squads against insurgents in Iraq, see Michael Hirsh and John Barry, "The Salvador Option," *Newsweek*, January 10, 2005, https://globalpolicy.org/component/content/article/153-expansion-a-intervention/26186.html.

22. Tommie Sue Montgomery, "El Salvador: The Roots of Revolution," in Ropp and Morris, eds., *Central America: Crisis and Adaptation* pp. 86–90.

23. Taken from DGEC-El Salvador, *Anuario estadístico* for years 1965, 1966, 1968, 1969, 1971, 1977, 1980, and 1981; the figure reported is the total number of "homicides" plus other, unexplained violent deaths.

24. Data reported in Baloyra-Herp, *El Salvador in Transition*, p. 190; and Richard Alan White, *The Morass: United States Intervention in Central America* (New York: Harper and Row, 1984), p. 44; and Inforpress Centroamericano, *Central America Report*, January 20, 1984, p. 23.

25. Comisión de Derechos Humanos de El Salvador (CDHES), *Primer Congreso de Derechos Humanos en El Salvador* (San Salvador, El Salvador: CDHES, November 1984), pp. 30–31, authors' translation.

26. It is unclear whether the Sandinistas knew arms were coming through their territory. When confronted with that charge by US ambassador Lawrence Pezzullo, Daniel Ortega of the Nicaraguan junta promised to stop the flow The Department of State then certified that it had stopped. Though no credible evidence of significant

subsequent arms flow from Nicaragua was ever presented, the Reagan and Bush administrations kept making the charge until the US media accepted it as fact.

27. Philip J. Williams and Knut Walter, *Militarization and Demilitarization in El Salvador's Transition to Democracy* (Pittsburgh, PA: University of Pittsburgh Press, 1997), pp. 100–113.

28. Ibid., p. 113.

29. Montgomery, *Revolution in El Salvador*, pp. 140–157.

30. Dunkerley, *The Long War*, p. 175.

31. Benjamin C. Schwarz, *American Counterinsurgency Doctrine and El Salvador: The Frustration of Reform and the Illusion of Nation Building* (Santa Monica, CA: Rand Corporation, 1991), p. v.

32. Baloyra-Herp, *Salvador in Transition*; José Z. García, "El Salvador: Recent Elections in Historical Perspective," in John A. Booth and Mitchell A. Seligson, eds., *Elections and Democracy in Central America* (Chapel Hill, NC: University of North Carolina Press, 1989), pp. 60–89.

33. Dunkerley, *The Long War*, p. 163.

34. For discussions of problems with the US-backed elections in El Salvador in 1982, 1984, and 1985, see Terry Karl, "Imposing Consent: Electoralism vs. Democratization in El Salvador," in P. Drake and E. Silva, eds., *Elections and Democratization in Latin America* (La Jolla, CA: Center for Iberian and Latin American Studies, Center for US-Mexican Studies, University of California, San Diego, 1986), p. 21; Edward S. Herman and Frank Brodhead, *Demonstration Elections* (Boston, MA: South End Press, 1984), pp. 93–152; and García, "El Salvador: Recent Elections," pp. 60–89.

35. See, for instance, Karl, "Imposing Consent," pp. 18–34; and Clifford Krauss, "El Salvador Army Gains on the Guerrillas," *Wall Street Journal*, July 30, 1986, p. 20.

36. On elections see Enrique A. Baloyra-Herp, "Elections, Civil War, and Transition in El Salvador, 1982–1994: A Preliminary Evaluation," in Mitchell A. Seligson and John A. Booth, eds., *Elections and Democracy in Central America, Revisited* (Chapel Hill, NC: University of North Carolina Press, 1995), pp. 45–65. On the military and peace negotiations, see Williams and Walter, *Militarization and Demilitarization in El Salvador*, Chs. 6 and 7; and Ricardo Córdova Macías, "El proceso de diálogo-negociación y las perspectivas de paz," in *El Salvador: Guerra, política, y paz, 1979–1989* (San Salvador: Cinas-Cries, 1988), pp. 195–219; and Ricardo Córdova Macías, *El Salvador: Las negociaciones de paz y los retos de la postguerra* (San Salvador, El Salvador: Instituto de Estudios Latinoamericanos, 1989).

37. Karl, "Imposing Consent."

38. Comisión de la Verdad, *De la locura a la esperanza: La guerra de doce años en El Salvador*. Informe de la Comisión, published in *Estudios Centroamericanos* (San

Salvador, El Salvador) no. 158 (March 1993); Booth and Walker, *Understanding Central America*, 3rd ed., Appendix, Table A.11.

39. Booth and Walker, *Understanding Central America*, 3rd ed., Appendix, Table A.1.

40. Interviews of three FMLN spokespersons by members of the Central American Task Force of the United Presbyterian Church's Council on Church and Society in Managua in November 1992. Coauthor Walker attended.

41. Written Statement of Representative Joe Moakley, chairman of the Speaker's Task Force on El Salvador, November 18, 1991; see also the account in Comisión de la Verdad, *De la locura a la esperanza*.

42. Schwarz, *American Counterinsurgency Doctrine*, pp. v, vi.

43. Data from World Bank Group, Indicators, accessed May 13, 2019, https://data.worldbank.org/indicator/BX.KLT.DINV.WD.GD.ZS?locations=SV.

44. See Washington Office on Latin America (WOLA), *Youth Gangs in Central America; Issues in Human Rights, Effective Policing and Prevention* (Washington, DC: WOLA, 2006); Ana Arana, "How the Youth Gangs Took Central America." *Foreign Affairs* 84, 3 (2005), pp. 98–110.

45. See Philip J. Williams and Knut Walter, *Militarization and Demilitarization*, pp. 151–182.

46. On police reform: Jack Spence, *War and Peace in Central America: Comparing Transitions Toward Democracy and Social Equity in Guatemala, El Salvador and Nicaragua* (Boston, MA: Hemisphere Initiatives, November 2004), pp. 59–62.

47. On these reforms under Cristiani and Calderón Sol; Jack Spence, David Dye, Mike Lanchin, and Geoff Thale, *Chapultepec: Five Years Later* (Boston, MA: Hemisphere Initiatives, January 16, 1997). See Margaret Popkin, *Peace Without Justice. Obstacles to Building Rule of Law in El Salvador* (University Park, PA: The Pennsylvania State University Press, 2000).

48. Guardado and several others were expelled from the FMLN in 2001.

49. Instituto Universitario de Opinión Pública (IUDOP), *Evaluación del primer año del gobierno de Francisco Flores* (San Salvador, El Salvador: Universidad Centroamericana José Simeon Cañas, 2000).

50. Tribunal Supremo Electoral de El Salvador.

51. See Cecilia Menjívar, *Fragmented Ties: Salvadoran Immigration Networks in America.* (Berkeley, CA: University of California Press, 2000); Carlos Cordova, *The Salvadoran Americans.* (Westport, CT: Greenwood Press, 2005).

52. See United Nations Development Program, *Informe sobre desarrollo humano, El Salvador 2005: Una mirada al nuevo nosotros, El impacto de las migraciones* (San Salvador, El Salvador: UNDP, 2005).

53. Coauthor Wade interviews in San Salvador, El Salvador, October–November 2006; see Arana, "How the Youth Gangs Took Central America."

54. "Embajadora E.U.A. advierte contra FMLN," *La Prensa Gráfica*, June 4, 2003; "Peligraría la inversión americana; Entrevista: Rose M. Likins," *La Prensa Gráfica*, June 4, 2003; "Diferencias con FMLN: Noriega pide tomar la mejor decisión," *El Diario de Hoy*, February 7, 2004.

55. In place since the 1980s, TPS is a concession by the United States allowing many Salvadoran citizens to live and work the United States (there are hundreds of thousands of them). Its maintenance guarantees continuation of the remittance flow from US-based Salvadorans to their families, a mainstay of the economy. In January 2018 President Trump ordered suspension of TPS for Salvadorans and others. Under suit, in October 2018 a federal court enjoined the administration from enforcing the policy until further resolution of the case. "Disturbing Statement out of El Salvador," *Congressional Record*, March 17, 2004, pp. E394–E395; "El Salvador," *Congressional Record*, March 17, 2004, p. E402; "Election in El Salvador," *Congressional Record*, March 17, 2004, p. E389; Maya Rhodan, "200,000 Salvadorans Have Lived in the U.S. for Decades. The Trump Administration Says They Have to Leave," (January 8, 2018), http://time.com/5092645/salvador-temporary-protected-status-donald-trump/.

56. Christine Wade, "El Salvador: Contradictions of Neoliberalism and Building Sustainable Peace," *International Journal of Peace Studies* 13, No. 4 (August–Winter 2008), pp. 24–25. The Gini coefficient, a measure of inequality of income, ranges from 0 (no inequality) to 100 (complete inequality); the Gini coefficient for those who received remittances was 44, as opposed to 52 for non-recipients.

57. "No Place to Hide: Gang, State and Clandestine Violence in El Salvador," International Human Rights Clinic, Human Rights Program, Harvard Law School, February 2007, http://law.harvard.edu/programs/hrp/documents/Final ElSalvadorReport(3–6–07).pdf.

58. USAID, "Central America and Mexico Gang Assessment, Annex1: El Salvador Profile," April 2006, http://usaid.gov/locations/latin_america_caribbean/democracy/els_profile.pdf.

59. United Nations Development Program, "*¿Cuánto cuesta la violencia en El Salvador?*" (San Salvadore: UNDP El Salvador, 2005).

60. William Grigsby, "The 2006 Elections: A Contradictory Outcome," *Envío* 297 (April 2006), accessed at http://Envío.org.ni/articulo/3252.

61. Edith Portillo, "Somos un millón menos … y un poco más violentos," *El Faro*, July 9, 2007, http://elfaro.net/secciones/Noticias/20070709/noticias6_20070709.asp.

62. Joaquín Villalobos, "¿Quién gobernaría, Funes o el FMLN?" *El Diario de Hoy*, December 30, 2008, http://elsalvador.com/mwedh/nota/nota_opinion.asp?idCat=6350&idArt=3182935.

63. *Fuerza Solidaria* sponsored much of the negative advertising. The organization was founded by Venezuelan Alejandro Peña Esclusa, a vocal opponent of Hugo Chávez.

64. Rep. Dana Rohrabacher, "Extension of Remarks, El Salvador Election," March 11, 2009, http://rohrabacher.house.gov/UploadedFiles/elsalvador_extension_of_remarks.PDF.

65. So much so that the Obama administration had to request that he stop using his image in the campaign.

66. In fact, gangs responded to the passage of the anti-gang law by burning a passenger bus in Mejicanos, killing 17 people.

67. "WOLA Expresses Concern About Naming of New Justice and Security Minister in El Salvador", Washington Office on Latin America, November 22, 2011, http://wola.org/news/wola_expresa_profunda_preocupacion_por_el_nombramiento_del_nuevo_ministro_de_justicia_y_segurid.

68. IUDOP, "Los salvadoreños y salvadoreñas evalúan la situación del país a finales de 2012," *Boletín de Prensa Año* XXVII, No.4, December 12, 2012, http://uca.edu.sv/publica/iudop/archivos/boletin4_2012.pdf.

69. Jessel Santos, "Hallazgos de osamentas aumentaron 81% en 2013," *La Prensa Gráfica*, March 8, 2013, http://laprensagrafica.com/hallazgos-de-osamentas—aumentaron-81—en–2013; and Daniel Valencia Caravantes, "Los desparacidos que no importan," *El Faro*, January 21, 2031, http://salanegra.elfaro.net/es/201301/cronicas/10773/?st-full_text=0.

70. Oscar Martinez, "Making a Deal with Murders," *The New York Times*, October 5, 2013, http://nytimes.com/2013/10/06/opinion/sunday/making-a-deal-with-murderers.html?pagewanted=1&_r=3&hp.

71. Nelson Rauda Zablah, "Perdomo: Pandillas están en guerra," *La Prensa Gráfica*, November 21, 2013, http://laprensagrafica.com/2013/11/21/perdomo-pandillas-estan-en-guerra; and Geoff Thale, "Public Security in El Salvador: Civilan Leadership and the Challenges Ahead," *Washington Office on Latin America*, May 21, 2013, http://wola.org/commentary/public_security_in_el_salvador_civilian_leadership_and_the_challenges_ahead.

72. "In El Salvador, Women's Rights Come to the Forefront," May 28, 2013, http://worldbank.org/en/news/feature/2013/05/28/derechos-de-la-mujer-pasan-a-primer-plano; and "Cuidad Mujer: City of Hope for Salvadoran Women," June 6, 2011, http://iadb.org/en/news/webstories/2011–06–06/ciudad-mujer-hope-for-salvadoran-women,9369.html.

73. Andrea Fernández Aponté, "Left in the Dark: Violence Against Women and LGBTI Persons in Honduras and El Salvador," *Latin American Working Group*, March 7, 2018. https://lawg.org/wp-content/uploads/storage/documents/Between_Dangers_Part_8.pdf.

74. International Human Rights Law Clinic, "*Sexual Diversity in El Salvador: A Report on the Human Rights Situation of the LGBT Community*" (Berkeley, CA:

University of California, July 2012), https://law.berkeley.edu/files/IHRLC/LGBT_
Report_English_Final_120705.pdf.

75. United Nations, "Un 67% de las mujeres ha sufrido algún tipo de violencia in El Salvador," April 17, 2018, https://news.un.org/es/story/2018/04/1431372.

76. Jack Hitt, "Pro-Life Nation," *New York Times*, April 9, 2006. Accessed at http://nytimes.com/2006/04/09/magazine/09abortion.html?pagewanted=all&_r=0.

77. Tim Rogers, "El Salvador High Court Upholds Abortion Ban as 'Beatriz' Challenges Law," *Christian Science Monitor*, May 30, 2012, http://csmonitor.com/World/Americas/2013/0530/El-Salvador-high-court-upholds-abortion-ban-as-Beatriz-challenges-law; Luisa Cabal, "El Salvador Abortion Controversy Shows Lack of Progress on Cairo Agenda," *The Guardian*, July 5, 2013, http://theguardian.com/global-development/poverty-matters/2013/jul/05/el-salvador-abortion-womens-rights.

78. "Center for Reproductive Rights Files Case Revealing the Horrifying Reality of El Salvador's Abortion Ban," Center for Reproductive Rights, March 21, 2012, http://reproductiverights.org/en/press-room/center-for-reproductive-rights-files-case-revealing-the-horrifying-reality-of-el-salvador.

79. Tim Rogers, "El Salvador High Court Upholds Abortion Ban as 'Beatriz' Challenges Law," *Christian Science Monitor*, May 30, 2012, http://csmonitor.com/World/Americas/2013/0530/El-Salvador-high-court-upholds-abortion-ban-as-Beatriz-challenges-law.

80. Gabriela D. Acosta, "Funes' Broken Promises," *Council on Hemispheric Affairs*, June 24, 2011, http://coha.org/funes-broken-promises/http://coha.org/funes-broken-promises/; and Washington Office on Latin America, "El Salvador: Troubling Attacks on the Independence of the Judiciary," June 29, 2011, www.wola.org/commentary/el_salvador_troubling_attacks_on_the_independence_of_the_judiciary.

81. Geoff Thale, "Tensions Rise between El Salvador's National Assembly and the Supreme Court: Understanding (and Misunderstanding) the Salvadoran Constitutional Crisis," *Washington Office on Latin America*, July 18, 2012, http://wola.org/commentary/tensions_rise_between_el_salvador_s_national_assembly_and_the_supreme_court_understanding.

82. Transparencia Activa, "Partidos políticos llegan a acuerdo en Casa Presidencial que pone fin a conflicto sobre Corte Suprema de Justicia," August 19, 2012, http://transparenciaactiva.gob.sv/partidos-politicos-llegan-a-acuerdo-en-casa-presidencial-que-pone-fin-a-conflicto-sobre-corte-suprema-de-justicia/.

83. Ben Witte, "El Salvador President Funes Irks Armed Forces with Emotional El Mozote Apology," *NotiCen*, July 4, 2012.

84. Elisabeth Malkin, "El Salvador: Court Orders Investigation of 1981 Massacre," *The New York Times*, December 10, 2012, http://nytimes.com/2012/12/11/world/americas/el-salvador-court-orders-investigation-of-1981-massacre.html?_r=1&.

85. Lynette Wilson, "El Salvador: Human Rights, Justice Organizations Weary in Face of Attacks," *Episcopal News Service*, November 18, 2013, http://episcopaldigitalnetwork.com/ens/2013/11/18/el-salvador-human-rights-justice-organizations-weary-in-face-of-attacks/.

86. "Arzobispado mantiene en su custodio archivos Tutela Legal," *La Prensa Gráfica*, October 21, 2013, https://laprensagrafica.com/elsalvador/Arzobispado-mantiene-bajo-custodia-archivos-Tutela-Legal-20131021-0037; "Arzobizpado anuncia creación de Tutela de Derechos Humanos," *La Prensa Gráfica*, December 23, 2013, https://laprensagrafica.com/elsalvador/Arzobispado-anuncia-creacion-de-Tutela-de-Derechos-Humanos-20131223-0066.html.

87. "Funes eleva popularidad tras papel de mediador en crisis," *El Mundo*, July 29, 2012, http://elmundo.com.sv/funes-eleva-popularidad-tras-papel-de-mediador-en-crisis.

88. "Funes Wins Stratspheric Approval Rating," *Latin News*, http://latinnews.com/component/k2/item/6198-el-salvador-funes-wins-stratospheric-approval-rating.html; "76% de los salvadoreños aprueba la imagen de Funes," *La Pagina*, May 16, 2013, http://lapagina.com.sv/nacionales/81719/2013/05/15/76-de-los-salvadorenos-aprueba-la-imagen-de-Funes.

89. Gabriel Labrador, "Ganancias de las empresas de Saca se multiplicaron hasta por 16 cuando fue president," *El Faro*, November 19, 2013, http://elfaro.net/es/201311/noticias/13936/.

90. Marcos Alemán, "Former President of El Salvador Francisco Flores Dead at 56," Associated Press, January 31, 2016, https://businessinsider.com/ap-former-president-of-el-salvador-francisco-flores-dead-at-56-2016–1.

91. "Asamblea aprueba voto en el exterior," *Contra Punto*, January 24, 2013, www.contrapunto.com.sv/gobierno/asamblea-aprueba-voto-en-el-exterior.

92. Oscar Martínez, Carlos Martínez, and Efren Lemus, "Relato de un fraude electoral, narrado por un pandillero," *El Faro*, August 11, 2017, https://elfaro.net/es/201708/salanegra/20737/Relato-de-un-fraude-electoral-narrado-por-un-pandillero.htm; Héctor Silva Ávalos, "After El Salvador Gang Truce Trial, 5 Doubts Remain," *InSight Crime*, August 17, 2017, https://insightcrime.org/news/analysis/after-el-salvador-gang-truce-trial-5-doubts-remain/.

93. David Gagne, "El Salvador Police Chief Targets Rising Gang Violence," *InSight Crime*, January 21, 2015, https://insightcrime.org/news/brief/el-salvador-police-commander-green-light-gangs/.

94. Nelson Rauda Zablah and Gabriela Cáceres, "PDDH: La Policía ejecutó 116 personas entre 2014 y 2018," *El Faro*, August 28, 2019, https://elfaro.net/es/201908/el_salvador/23592/PDDH-La-Polic%C3%ADa-ejecutó-a-116-

personas-entre-2014-y-2018.htm?utm_campaign=Central%20American%20
News&utm_medium=email&utm_source=Revue%20newsletter.

95. Roberto Valencia, Óscar Martínez, and Daniel Valencia Caravantes, "La
Policía macacró en la finca San Blas," *El Faro*, July 22, 2015, http://salanegra.elfaro.
net/es/201507/cronicas/17205/La-Polic%C3%ADa-masacró-en-la-finca-San-Blas.
htm.

96. Héctor Silva Ávalos, "El Salvador Ex-President Funes' Trash Bags Full of
Money," *InSight Crime*, June 13, 2018, https://insightcrime.org/news/analysis/el-
salvador-ex-president-funes-trash-bags-money/.

97. Felipe Puerta, "El Salvador AG's Office Escalates Efforts Against Corruption,"
InSight Crime, October 17, 2018, https://insightcrime.org/news/analysis/el-salvador-
ags-office-escalates-efforts-against-corruption/.

98. Ray Bonner, "El Salvador Considers Amnesty Law for Those Accused of Crimes
During Its Civil War," *ProPublica*, March 21, 2019, https://propublica.org/article/
el-salvador-considers-amnesty-for-those-accused-of-crimes-during-its-civil-war.

99. Christine J. Wade, *Captive Peace: Elites and Peacebuilding in El Salvador*
(Athens, OH: Ohio University Press, 2016), pp. 182–185.

100. Gene Palumbo and Elisabeth Malkin, "El Salvador, Prizing Water Over
Gold, Bans All Metal Mining," *The New York Times*, March 29, 2017, https://
nytimes.com/2017/03/29/world/americas/el-salvador-prizing-water-over-gold-bans-
all-metal-mining.html?_r=0.

101. "Evaluación del país a finales de 2017 y perspectivas electorales para 2018,"
Instituto Universitario de Opinión Pública, XXXII, no. 1, (2018), http://uca.edu.sv/
iudop/wp-content/uploads/BOLETIN_118.pdf.

102. Christine J. Wade, "Big Victory Comes With Big Expectations for El
Salvador's Young New President," *World Politics Review*, February 11, 2019,
https://worldpoliticsreview.com/articles/27407/big-victory-comes-with-big-
expectations-for-el-salvador-s-young-new-president.

103. Instituto Universitario de Opinión Pública (IUDOP), Universidad
Centroamericana "José Simeón Cañas" (UCA), "The Situation of Security and
Justice 2009–2014—Between Expectations for Change, Heavy-Handed Military
and Gang Truces," 2014, www.uca.edu.sv/iudop/wp-content/uploads/Resumen-
Ejecutivo-english.pdf.

104. Cristosal, "Informe sobre desplazamiento interno forzado por violencia en
El Salvador 2017," http://centroamerica.cristosal.org/wp-content/uploads/2018/05/
Visibilizar-lo-invisible.-Informe-sobre-desplazamiento-forzado-por-violencia-en-El-
Salvador.pdf.

RECOMMENDED READINGS AND RESOURCES

Almeida, Paul D. 2008. *Waves of Protest: Popular Struggle in El Salvador, 1925–2005.* Minneapolis, MN: University of Minnesota Press.

Anderson, Thomas. 1971. *Matanza: El Salvador's Communist Revolt of 1932.* Lincoln, NE: University of Nebraska Press.

Baloyra, Enrique. 1982. *El Salvador in Transition.* Chapel Hill, NC: University of North Carolina Press.

Boyce, James K., ed. 1996. *Economic Policy for Building Peace: The Lesson of El Salvador.* Boulder, CO: Lynne Rienner Publishers.

Byrne, Hugh. 1996. *El Salvador's Civil War: A Study in Revolution.* Boulder, CO: Lynne Rienner Publishers.

Ching, Erik. 2016. *Authoritarian El Salvador: Politics and the Origins of the Military Regimes, 1880-1940.* Notre Dame, IN: University of Notre Dame Press.

Clements, Charles. 1984. *Witness to War: An American Doctor in El Salvador.* New York: Bantam Books.

Dunkerley, James. 1982. *The Long War: Dictatorship and Revolution in El Salvador.* London: Verso.

Ladutke, Larry. 2004. *Freedom of Expression in El Salvador: The Struggle for Human Rights and Democracy.* Jefferson, NC: MacFarland.

Lindo Fuentes, Hector. 1990. *Weak Foundations: The Economy of El Salvador in the Nineteenth Century.* Berkeley, CA: University of California Press.

McClintock, Cynthia. 1998. *Revolutionary Movements in Latin America: El Salvador's FMLN and Peru's Shining Path.* Washington, DC: US Institute of Peace.

Montgomery, Tommie Sue. 1995. *Revolution in El Salvador: Origins and Evolution.* Boulder, CO: Westview Press.

Moodie, Ellen. 2010. *El Salvador in the Aftermath of War.* Philadelphia, PA: University of Pennsylvania Press.

Pelupessy, Wim. 1997. *The Limits of Economic Reform in El Salvador.* New York: St. Martin's.

Popkin, Margaret. 2000. *Peace Without Justice: Obstacles to Building the Rule of Law in El Salvador.* University Park, PA: The Pennsylvania State University Press.

Spence, Jack. 2004. *War and Peace in Central America: Comparing Transitions Toward Democracy and Social Equity in Guatemala, El Salvador and Nicaragua.* Boston, MA: Hemisphere Initiatives.

Stanley, William. 1996. *The Protection Racket State: Elite Politics, Military Extortion, and Civil War in El Salvador.* Philadelphia, PA: Temple University Press.

Wade, Christine J. 2016. *Captured Peace: Elites and Peacebuilding in El Salvador.* Athens, OH: Ohio University Press.

Williams, Philip J. and Walter, Knut. 1997. *Militarization and Demilitarization in El Salvador's Transition to Democracy.* Pittsburgh, PA: University of Pittsburgh Press.

Wolf, Sonia. 2017. *Mano Dura: The Politics of Gang Control in El Salvador.* Austin, TX: University of Texas Press.

Wood, Elisabeth Jean. 2003. *Insurgent Collective Action and Civil War in El Salvador.* New York: Cambridge University Press.

7

GUATEMALA

GUATEMALA'S LONG, VIOLENT PASSAGE FROM MILITARY authoritarianism to electoral democracy differed from Nicaragua's but resembled El Salvador's, though rapid economic change and repression drove turmoil and regime change in all three. In Guatemala, as in El Salvador, rebels and power holders fought a protracted civil war marked by three regime changes, the last of which established a democracy, curtailed military power, and permitted former rebels into the political arena. Unlike El Salvador, Guatemala's military governments had largely kept rebels at bay without much visible involvement by the United States.

HISTORICAL BACKGROUND

Although Guatemala stands apart from the rest of modern Central America in its large, only partly integrated indigenous population, it shares historical legacies with nineteenth-century Nicaragua and El Salvador. In each, consolidation of Liberal control followed early Liberal–Conservative conflict. The Liberals' "reforms" produced profound socioeconomic realignments and shaped contemporary social and political problems.

191

Liberals took control of Guatemala in 1871 and with minor exceptions held power until the 1940s. Liberal dictator-president Justo Rufino Bárrios (1873–1885) modernized by building roads, railways, a national army, and a more competent national bureaucracy. He promoted the new crop, coffee, and encouraged foreign investment. Barrios opened Church and indigenous communal lands to cultivation by large landowners (latifundistas). By 1900 coffee accounted for 85 percent of Guatemala's exports. Landownership concentrated increasingly in the hands of latifundist coffee growers, who also dominated Guatemalan economics and politics. Forced from their land, indigenous Guatemalans fell prey to debt-peonage and "vagrancy" laws, enacted and enforced by the coffee-grower-dominated government, which coerced them to labor on coffee plantations.

In the late nineteenth century, the construction of an Atlantic coast railroad also created the banana industry. Early in the twentieth century, the US-based United Fruit Company (UFCO), formerly mainly a shipper/exporter, squeezed out Guatemalan banana growers. UFCO eventually owned key public utilities and vast landholdings. The Liberal development program continued in the twentieth century. In politics, Manuel Estrada Cabrera's brutal dictatorship (1898–1920) inspired Nobel laureate Miguel Angel Asturias's chilling novel of state terror, *El Señor Presidente*. Big coffee plantations, many foreign owned, displaced small-scale subsistence farmers.

The world depression of 1929 slashed Guatemala's exports. Worker unrest grew. President Jorge Ubico assumed dictatorial powers in 1931 and violently suppressed unions, Communists, and other political activists while centralizing power in the national government. Ubico continued promoting government and infrastructure development (banks, railways, highways, telephones, telegraph, and electrical utilities). Although originally an admirer of European Fascists Mussolini and Franco, Ubico seized the opportunity provided by World War II to confiscate over $150 million in German-owned properties, mainly coffee plantations. He amended vagrancy laws to require the indigenous to work a certain number of days per year for the state, effectively converting the government into Guatemala's labor contractor.

Labor unrest, middle-class democratization pressures, and a loss of US support caused Ubico to resign in 1944. Student- and labor-backed military reformers called for elections for later that year. Educator and former exile Juan José Arévalo Bermejo, a self-styled "spiritual socialist," won the presidency. During his five-year term, Arévalo began numerous reforms: social security, a labor code, professionalization of the military, rural education, public health promotion, and cooperatives. Arévalo vigorously encouraged union and peasant organization and open elections. His economic policies, described as an "explicit attempt to create a modern capitalist society,"[1] did not address the extreme maldistribution of land—a legacy of the "liberal" reforms—that underlay the country's social problems.

In 1950 Guatemalans elected a young army officer, Jacobo Arbenz Guzmán, to succeed Arévalo. Arbenz promoted deeper social reforms, despite growing conservative and US opposition. In 1951 he legalized the Communist Party (Guatemalan Labor Party, Partido Guatemalteco del Trabajo, PGT). The PGT began actively organizing labor and promoting agrarian reform. Over 500 peasant unions and 300 peasant leagues formed under the Arbenz government.[2] The 1952 Agrarian Reform Law began confiscation and redistribution of farmland to 100,000 peasants.

Arbenz's reforms and multiplying peasant and worker organizations threatened the rural labor supply by shifting economic power toward workers and peasants and away from latifundists and employers. These threatened interests took action when Arbenz nationalized land belonging to United Fruit and offered compensation at its previously declared tax value. This troubled several high Eisenhower administration officials with ties to UFCO. The nationalization, some PGT personnel in the government, and Guatemala's purchase of light arms from Czechoslovakia prompted the United States to label the Arbenz government Communist. In 1953 the United States undertook to destabilize Arbenz's administration with financial sanctions, diplomatic pressure in the Organization of American States (OAS), and Central Intelligence Agency (CIA) disinformation and covert actions. The CIA engineered a conspiracy with a rightist army faction. In June 1954 the tiny, CIA-supported National Liberation Army, led by Colonel Carlos Castillo Armas, invaded Guatemala. The military refused to defend the government and President Arbenz had to resign.[3]

Colonel Castillo Armas, head of the National Liberation Movement (Movimiento de Liberación Nacional, MLN), seized the presidency with US and Catholic Church backing. With ferocious anti-Communist propaganda, the counterrevolution dismantled the labor and peasant movements, killed and jailed thousands, repressed political parties, revoked the Agrarian Reform Law, and returned confiscated lands to their former owners. Castillo's regime suppressed working- and middle-class and pro-revolutionary organizations and pursued "a continuing … promotion of upper-sector interests."[4] Military and business sectors gained influence within the government. Foreign policy aligned closely with the United States, and US and multilateral aid programs promoted economic growth by financing extensive infrastructure development.

The MLN became a political party during the late 1950s, drawing together coffee planters, municipal politicians and bureaucrats, owners of midsized farms, and certain military elements united in anti-Communism and in their hostility toward the 1944–1954 revolution. Confusion followed Castillo's assassination in 1957, and the army imposed General Miguel Ydígoras Fuentes as president. His government endorsed Guatemala's participation in the Central American Common Market (CACM), permitted CIA-backed anti-Castro Cuban forces to train in Guatemala for the Bay of Pigs invasion of 1961, and continued police terror against supporters of the revolution and labor and peasant leaders.

Continued violence and corruption under Ydígoras prompted an abortive coup by reformist army officers in 1960. Escaped plotters then formed the nucleus of the first of several rebel groups. The leaders of the Revolutionary Armed Forces (Fuerzas Armadas Revolucionarias, FAR) and the 13th of November Revolutionary Movement (Movimiento Revolucionario del 13 de Noviembre, MR-13) eventually adopted a Marxist-Leninist ideology and guerrilla war strategy patterned after Fidel Castro's in Cuba. US military aid poured in, but early operations against the guerrillas proved ineffective. Military dissatisfaction and a desire to block the next election culminated in Colonel Enrique Peralta Azurdia's overthrow of Ydígoras in 1963, and rapidly expanded counterinsurgency operations.

In 1965 the military nominally returned the government to civilians, and the 1966 election campaign was generally free and open.[5] The Revolutionary Party (Partido Revolucionario, PR) candidate, Julio César Méndez Montenegro, who denounced the 12-year counterrevolution, won the presidency. After Méndez took office, however, counterinsurgency accelerated and military control of politics deepened despite the civilian president. The army's 1968 Zacapa campaign, heavily US-backed and trained, killed an estimated 10,000 civilians, dealt the guerrillas a severe blow, and earned its commander, Colonel Carlos Arana Osorio, the sobriquet of "the Butcher of Zacapa."

One decade of reform/revolution followed by another of counterrevolution left Guatemalan society deeply polarized. Some rightists feared the 1966 election would end the counterrevolution and took drastic action. Several right-wing "death squads" formed and commenced terrorizing persons vaguely associated with the left and reformist politics. Regular national security forces (army and police), government-armed peasant irregulars in insurgent areas, and rightist terrorist groups permitted and encouraged by the regime conducted a terror campaign against and effectively demobilized and disarticulated much of the political opposition (although many victims were apolitical).

Under these circumstances the 1970 presidential election—though conducted cleanly—resulted in victory for Colonel Carlos Arana Osorio, the nominee of both the MLN and the military's own Institutional Democratic Party (Partido Institucional Democrático, PID). With US aid at its historic peak, Arana consolidated the military's power and deepened its corruption. An aggressive economic modernization program created huge public-sector enterprises and projects (some under army control) to bolster the financial autonomy of the armed forces and the graft available to top officers. Terror against unions, political parties, and suspected regime critics escalated anew.

GLOBAL FORCES AND CONFLICT

The political situation of the late 1960s, with a counterinsurgency-oriented military regime confronting an ongoing insurgency, seemingly offered poor prospects for economic growth. Much of the violence, however, occurred in Guatemala's indigenous highlands or lowland jungles and away from urban areas. This allowed parts of Guatemala to experience rapid economic growth driven by CACM and Alliance for Progress policies.

Economy

Income and Employment. Under the military-business partnership, Guatemala's economy grew rapidly, as in Nicaragua and El Salvador. Per capita gross domestic product (GDP) rose an average of 3 percent annually from 1962 through 1971, and 2.6 percent from 1972 through 1980. During the CACM boom, per capita GDP in constant 1986 dollars rose 70 percent, the second-highest growth rate in Central America.[6]

Guatemalan economic growth did not increase the income of the poor. The average annual change in consumer prices was only 0.7 percent from 1963 through 1972, but rose to 12.3 percent per annum for 1973–1979. Real wages badly lagged inflation. Working-class wages peaked in 1967 then declined throughout the 1970s losing a fourth of their 1967 value by 1979.[7] Income distribution became markedly more unequal during the CACM boom. Between 1970 and 1984 income concentrated increasingly in the hands of the wealthiest fifth of the people, whose national income share rose from 46.5 to 56.8 percent between 1970 and 1984. The income share of Guatemala's poorest fifth shrank from 6.8 to 4.8 percent for the same years. The middle three-fifths of income earners also lost ground, from 46.7 percent in 1970 to 38.4 percent in 1984.[8]

Official statistics indicate a steady growth of Guatemala's unemployment even during the fastest CACM-induced GDP growth. Official unemployment rates rose from 4.8 percent in 1970 to 5.5 percent in 1980 and then to 10.0 percent by 1984. Estimated *underemployment rates rose* steadily from 24.5 percent in 1973 to 43.4 percent in 1984.[9]

Wealth. Guatemalan wealth distribution data are scarce, but some studies permit inferences.[10] Land has long been unequally distributed. The agrarian census of 1950 reported that farms smaller than five manzanas (roughly 3.5 hectares) made up 75.1 percent of the farms but only occupied 9.0 percent of the cultivated land.[11] The 1.7 percent of farms larger than 64 manzanas (45 hectares) made up 50.3 percent of the cultivated land. The 1979 agricultural census revealed land ownership inequality in Guatemala was the greatest in Central America. Rapid rural population growth shrank the amount of arable land per capita from 1.71 hectares/capita in 1950 to less than 0.79 by 1980.[12]

In the late 1970s, indigenous agrarian unemployment began rising while wages deteriorated. Ladinos (mestizos) were reportedly appropriating communally and privately held land in the indigenous highlands. Land-ownership concentration caused highland people to relocate to cities or public lands newly opened in Petén and Izábal. However, military officers and politicians amassed land in those departments by driving many small-holders off their new plots in the region.[13] In 1976 an earthquake devastated the western highlands and worsened the poverty of tens of thousands of indigenous peasants.

Worker productivity in manufacturing grew steadily from the 1950s through the 1970s, but real wages and the working- and middle- class shares of national income declined during the 1970s. Increasing productivity thus benefitted mainly foreign and national investors.[14] Simultaneously the ownership of the means of industrial production became more concentrated among fewer firms. Private-sector pressure-group organization became more extensive and sophisticated.[15] In some industries modernization of production and ownership concentration efficiencies displaced many workers.

Guatemala's upper classes prospered during the 1970s from the industrialization boom and relatively high coffee prices, but conditions deteriorated as output declined from 1981 through 1985. Causes of this recession included declining commodity prices, political unrest elsewhere in Central America, and capital flight. Guatemala's general recession (as distinct from deteriorating real working-class wages) lagged four years behind a similar one in Nicaragua *general economic recession*

and two years behind El Salvador's. It eroded the economic elites' position sufficiently that some criticized the economic management of successive military
presidents and reconsidered their commitment to the regime.

Popular Mobilization

Reformists under Guatemala's democratic governments of 1944 to 1954 suffered badly after the 1954 coup. The MLN government's and military's demobilization campaign decimated reformist politicians, unionists, and indigenous
people who had supported the Arévalo and Arbenz governments. Marxist guerrilla opposition to the regime first appeared in 1962 but was set back greatly by
heavy repression and intense counterinsurgency in the late 1960s.[16]

Popular mobilization rekindled during the 1970s as real wages and income
distribution worsened. Mobilization in Guatemala, however, lagged behind
that in Nicaragua and El Salvador because of heavier repression and ethnic divisions.[17] Increased unionization and industrial strikes during the government
of General Eugenio Kjell Laugerud García (1974–1978) followed a decline in
manufacturing wages in the early 1970s. When Laugerud momentarily relaxed
repression of unions in 1978, a wave of strikes ensued. The 1976 earthquake's
devastation of lower-class housing mobilized slum dwellers into two confederations. These civil society groups pressed for housing assistance and in 1978
organized a transport boycott protesting increased bus fares. The FAR resurfaced and two new, indigenous-based guerrilla organizations—the Guerrilla
Army of the Poor (Ejército Guerrillero de los Pobres, EGP) and the Organization of the People in Arms (Organización del Pueblo en Armas, ORPA)—also
appeared. All grew rapidly and began overt military activity in the late 1970s.

During the 1960s and 1970s the Christian Democratic Party (Partido
Demócrata Cristiano de Guatemala, PDCG) promoted hundreds of agrarian
cooperatives and a labor union movement to build a constituency. As in El
Salvador and Nicaragua, Christian base communities (CEBs) appeared across
poor rural and urban Guatemala during the early 1970s. CEBs organized
community and labor groups among Guatemala's long-quiescent indigenous
populace. Despite military rule and repression, civil society and opposition
parties multiplied. The PDCG and other centrist and leftist parties including the Democratic Socialist Party (Partido Socialista Demócrata, PSD) and
the United Front of the Revolution (Frente Unido de la Revolución, FUR)
demanded reforms and competed for office. Citizens organized, but also lost
confidence in elections because the military regime fraudulently manipulated
several presidential elections. Abstention among registered voters rose from 44
percent in 1966 to 64 percent in the 1978 election.[18]

centrist & leftist parties ran in campaigns, but military regime

State Response and Opposition

During the post-1954 counterrevolution, Guatemalan rulers intensely repressed union activists, students, peasant groups, indigenous peoples, opposition parties, and other dissidents. Somewhat relaxed during the early 1960s, repression of these groups escalated sharply from 1966 on. In that year both private and public security-force death-squad terrorism began taking dozens of lives a month. The army's 1968–1970 counterinsurgency campaign decimated the Revolutionary Armed Forces (FAR) and the Edgar Ibarra Guerrilla Front (Frente Guerrillera Edgar Ibarra, FGEI) guerrilla movements.

In the turmoil of the 1978 election, all parties again nominated military officers as presidential candidates. After General Fernando Lucas García won the vote, government forces crushed Guatemala City bus-fare protests. As opposition parties grew in 1978 and 1979, security-force death squads extra-judicially murdered dozens of national and local leaders of the Democratic Socialist and Christian Democratic parties and of the reformist FUR. Hundreds of union leaders, university faculty, and student leaders also disappeared or were assassinated during the Lucas government.

Campesino organizations led by the Peasant Unity Committee (Comité de Unidad Campesina, CUC) stepped up organizing. The CUC staged a major strike against sugar planters in 1980. In 1978 and 1979 the regrouped FAR and ORPA began military activity in the western highlands. Soon afterward the Guerrilla Army of the Poor (Ejército Guerrillero de los Pobres, EGP), also with strong indigenous support, resumed combat in the highlands. Estimates placed the number of guerrilla troops at around 4,000 by 1982; the rebels' popular support was widespread. Counterinsurgency escalated and included massacres of indigenous villagers to discourage support for the guerrillas.

From 1960 on, the US embassy tracked Guatemalan political murders, most committed by government security forces and rightist death squads.[19] The average political murder rate, mainly in urban areas, rose from about 30 per month in 1971 to 75 per month in 1979 and to a nearly 303 per month by 1982.[20] Some experts believe that army counterinsurgency operations in rural areas killed even many more Guatemalans than urban violence. Despite such massive human rights violations, Guatemala continued receiving economic assistance from the United States that totaled over $60 million from 1979 through 1981.[21] Guatemala's truth commission, the Historical Clarification Commission, later referred to the period from 1978 to 1985 as the "most violent and bloody period of the confrontation." Deaths likely totaled 200,000.[22]

The armed forces, the backbone of the Lucas regime, faced three critical problems in 1982. First was the extensive indigenous support for the guerrillas in the western highlands and growing rural unrest elsewhere. Second, the economy slowed—GDP per capita contracted nearly 8 percent from 1980 to 1982. Third, the Lucas government lost allies. When news leaked that Lucas had perpetrated another election fraud in 1982, younger army officers overthrew him and installed General Efraín Ríos Montt as president. This coup began a gradual process of regime changes that took 14 years to complete.

The coup leaders pursued a dual strategy of increasing repression to crush the rebels and demobilize growing opposition while also slowly reforming the political rules of the game with elections and eventual civilian rule under military tutelage. In the first phase, President Ríos Montt annulled the electoral law and 1965 constitution, dissolved Congress, suppressed political parties, and imposed a state of siege. Pursuing a political reform agenda largely obscured by the regime's de facto nature, a Council of State decreed a new electoral law and called July 1984 elections for an assembly to draft a new constitution.

On the military agenda, repression escalated with a new counterinsurgency campaign in indigenous zones. Ríos Montt's press secretary Francisco Bianchi justified the campaign:

The guerrillas won over many Indian collaborators. Therefore, the Indians were subversives, right? And how do you fight subversion? Clearly, you had to kill Indians because they were collaborating with subversion. And then they would say, "You're massacring innocent people." But they weren't innocent. They had sold out to subversion.[23]

The army massacred numerous villages and committed other atrocities against suspected guerrilla sympathizers. It forced the relocation and concentration of indigenous people, many pressed into work on modern, army-owned farms producing vegetables to export to the United States. The military formed army-controlled, mandatory "civil self-defense patrols" involving virtually all the adult rural males. Estimates of the rural counterinsurgency's toll range up to 150,000 dead between 1982 and 1985. US embassy statistics often overlooked such massacres because staff could not easily verify the incidents.[24] The war displaced at least 500,000 persons, mostly indigenous, internally or abroad.[25] Robinson contends that this dislocation of the indigenous population produced a new supply of cheap labor to support Guatemala's embrace of the neoliberal economic model.[26]

Unable to detect meaningful political reform under Ríos Montt, centrist political activists hunkered down or fled, while the leftist opposition built coalitions to enhance their power and resource base.[27] The Democratic Front Against Repression (Frente Democrático Contra la Represión, FDCR) appeared in 1979; it linked numerous unions, the PSD, and the FUR. Two years later, several of the FDCR's more radical elements—including the peasant federation CUC—split with the FDCR and formed the January 13th Popular Front (Frente Popular 13 de Enero, FP-13). In 1982 the FP-13 and the FDCR endorsed yet another coalition, the Guatemalan Committee of Patriotic Unity (Comité Guatemalteco de Unidad Patriótica, CGUP). Guerrilla groups forged the Guatemalan National Revolutionary Union (Unidad Revolucionaria Nacional Guatemalteca, URNG) in 1982; their revolutionary manifesto challenged the regime's sovereignty.

The URNG's drive for a broader coalition became bogged down, possibly a victim of the regime's efforts to re-establish civilian rule. Labor unions remained reluctant to form political links that might jeopardize their legal status—even with legal political parties.[28] The government curtailed rightist terrorism in urban areas after 1982, despite intensifying rural counterinsurgency. When President Ríos Montt's increasingly erratic public behavior embarrassed the military reformists, they replaced him with General Oscar Humberto Mejía Victores in August 1983. Political reforms advanced—the electoral registry was reformed and voter registration redone. The constituent assembly, elected in 1984, produced a new constitution that took effect in May 1985. President Mejía called for elections, and the regime allowed some long-suppressed political forces of the center and left to resurface.

Elections for president, Congress, and municipalities took place in late 1985. Although military pressure excluded leftist parties, centrist parties participated. Despite its backdrop of three decades of brutal demobilization, this election was generally free from terrorism against opposition parties. The Christian Democrats, led by Vinicio Cerezo Arévalo, won the presidency and a majority of the Congress in clean elections in late 1985.[29] Party spokesmen affirmed that they participated in the 1984 and 1985 elections and the constituent assembly because they believed the military seriously intended to reduce its role in governing.[30] This opening to civilian politicians in the mid-1980s dissuaded some opposition parties from allying with the revolutionary left.

The 1985 election brought Guatemala's second critical regime change in the lengthy military-managed liberalization. It established a civilian-transitional regime with new electoral rules and institutions and admitted more actors into the political arena. Powerful economic sectors, once military allies, contemplated a half decade of miserable economic performance and embraced the prospect of civilian economic and governmental management.

Citizens showed their hopes for an end to Guatemala's long political nightmare by voting at much higher rates—78 percent in 1984 and 69 percent in 1985—especially in urban areas with less violence and more political freedom.

THE CIVILIAN TRANSITIONAL REGIME AND THE CIVIL WAR

Main duties for new civ.- trans. regime

The civilian-transitional regime needed first to end the civil war, but President Cerezo and successors held limited influence over the armed forces or rebels. A second need was to consolidate civilian rule and progress toward democracy. To accomplish this, any settlement would have to pacify the rebels and curtail the military's enormous power. Constituencies that supported war would have to accept peace and civilian constitutional rule. Third, Guatemala needed economic recovery, but the economy remained desultory. Progress on each front was halting. During the Cerezo administration, however, globally oriented capitalists, intent on modernizing the economy by reducing the power of the traditional agro-export elite, coalesced around several economic organizations and think tanks, actively encouraged by a US Agency for International Development (USAID) program of Private Enterprise Development.

> The emerging New Right groupings began to explore the development of the transnational project in Guatemala and to gain an instrumental hold over the state in policy development... At the behest of this emerging private sector bloc, the government approved a series of liberalization and deregulation measures.[31]

President Cerezo actively embraced the August 1987 Central American Peace Accord, which proposed political reconciliation, dialogue, and formal democratization. Efforts to end the civil war, however, stagnated because the military and rebels failed to cooperate fully. The war intensified in late 1987 as the URNG and the army sought to improve their positions. Cease-fire talks in Madrid fell apart and other dialogue between government and other political and economic forces remained limited.[32]

The balance of resources between the warring parties began shifting in the government's favor. Although economic and military assistance from the United States remained a tiny fraction of that to El Salvador (see Table A.3), Guatemala's military and governmental institutional capabilities remained fairly high. Political reform isolated the rebels from a broader coalition. The rural counterinsurgency program increasingly denied rebels access to indigenous supporters. Economic performance improved after 1987. Moreover, the military's retreat from executive power, the election of a new government, and some progress on the abysmal human rights situation (enactment of habeas corpus and other individual rights protections embodied in *amparo* laws;[33] a human rights ombudsman; and judicial reforms) increased the government's domestic and external legitimacy.

Despite a promising beginning, the Cerezo administration performed poorly in many areas. Business groups, opposition parties, and labor criticized Cerezo and the PDCG for corruption, indecision, policy errors, economic problems, inattention to the poor, and failing to improve human rights. Social mobilization increased. External human rights monitors and the government's own rights ombudsman denounced continuing army and police abuses of labor activists, union members, homeless street children, students, human rights advocates, religious workers, political party leaders, and foreigners.[34]

Peace talks commenced in Oslo, Norway, but too late to benefit Cerezo and the PDCG. Before negotiations commenced, the URNG changed its goal from military victory to a negotiated settlement. In the early 1990s, several factors reinforced that decision, including the difficulty of fighting while cut off from its indigenous base and potential moderate allies, the Soviet bloc's collapse, and the electoral defeat of Nicaragua's Sandinistas. The army's new willingness to negotiate reflected its eroding support among the bourgeoisie, increasing criticism of military human rights violations, and the attrition of the war. The negotiations progressed little during Cerezo's term.

The president's dismal record handicapped the Christian Democrats in the 1990 election. Parties of the old right (landed oligarchy and military) such as the MLN and PID declined. New parties appeared, several representing transnationally oriented economic elites who had been gaining influence. These included the Union of the National Center (Unión del Centro Nacional, UCN), the Solidarity Action Movement (Movimiento de Acción Solidaria, MAS), and the National Advancement Party (Partido del Avance Nacional, PAN). The 1990 vote was relatively free and clean despite the left's exclusion. Barely half of Guatemala's dispirited electorate turned out in both rounds of the elections—a major decline from 1985. Voters rejected the discredited PDCG, which effectively vanished thereafter. The presidential runoff matched two new-right conservatives, newspaper publisher PAN's Jorge Carpio Nicolle and engineer MAS's Jorge Serrano Elías. Serrano, a Protestant with a populist flair who promised to push the peace negotiations, won.[35]

President Serrano, a former minister in Ríos Montt's cabinet, appointed numerous military officials to his government. He addressed himself to human rights violations with unexpected vigor by detaining and prosecuting military officials, and energetically pursued peace negotiations. However, when the economy slumped further in 1991, Serrano imposed a package of tough neoliberal structural adjustment measures informed by the transnational capitalist sector and its think tanks.[36] Adversely affected popular groups protested widely, and the security forces replied with a typical barrage of human rights abuses.

Serrano plunged Guatemala into crisis on May 25, 1993, when (apparently supported by part of the military) he attempted an *autogolpe* ("self-coup"). He illegally dissolved the Supreme Court and Congress, censored the press, restricted civil liberties, and sought to rule by decree. Citizens, civil society organizations, and governmental institutions energetically protested the "Serranazo." The United States, the OAS, and other external actors quickly warned Guatemalan political actors, military included, that the international financial institutions so essential to Guatemala's economic recovery would disapprove of this deviation from constitutional practice.[37]

Combined internal and external pressure undermined the Serranazo and kept the civilian-transitional regime on track. The Court of Constitutionality (Corte de Constitucionalidad, CC), backed by an institutionalist military faction, removed Serrano from office under provisions of the 1985 constitution. Congress elected Ramiro de León Carpio, the human rights ombudsman, to finish Serrano's presidential term. President de León, unaffiliated with a political party but backed by a broad array of civil organizations, pushed through Congress several further constitutional reforms that Guatemalans ratified by referendum in January 1994. This initiated the election of a new Congress in August 1994 to serve out the rest of the term.[38]

Peace negotiations progressed in 1994 under the mediation of the United Nations (UN).[39] A January "Framework Accord" established a timetable and provided for an Asamblea de la Sociedad Civil (Assembly of Civil Society, ASC) made up of most political parties and diverse nongovernmental organizations, including women's and indigenous groups, to advise negotiators. Progressing, negotiators in March 1994 signed a human rights accord to establish a UN monitoring mission that went to work in November. There followed agreements on refugee resettlement, a historical clarification commission to study the long-term violence (June 1994), and indigenous rights (March 1995).[40]

As negotiations continued, national elections took place in 1995. Guatemala City mayor Alvaro Arzú of the National Advancement Party (PAN) announced his candidacy, as did Efraín Ríos Montt of the right-wing populist Republican Front of Guatemala (Frente Republicano de Guatemala, FRG).

Ríos' candidacy prompted a legal battle because the constitution barred the presidency to participants in prior de facto regimes. The election tribunal ruled against the former dictator. The left signified growing confidence in its ability to participate safely when several leftist groups coalesced into a new party, the New Guatemala Democratic Front (Frente Democrático Nueva Guatemala, FDNG) to contest the election. The URNG suspended military actions during the final weeks of the campaign. In the November 1995 election the FDNG took 6 of 80 seats in Congress, the PAN 43, and the FRG 21, with higher turnout than in 1990. The FDNG and various indigenous civic committees won several mayoral races. Arzú, a businessman active in the new transnationally oriented coalition, narrowly won the presidency in a January 1996 runoff (see Tables A.6 and A.7).[41]

Alvaro Arzú took office under worsening political portents,[42] but moved decisively toward peace by reorganizing the army high command and police, meeting rebel leaders, and embracing negotiations. There followed an indefinite cease-fire between the URNG and the army in March 1996, an accord on socioeconomic and agrarian issues (May 1996), and another to increase civilian control of the armed forces, limit military authority to external defense, and replace the violent and corrupt national police (September 1996).

THE PEACE ACCORDS AND AFTERMATH

On December 29, 1996, the government and URNG signed the Final Peace Accord in Guatemala City and ended 36 years of civil war.[43] This signal event continued to shape Guatemala's politics positively and negatively for more than a decade. Forces aligned for and against political and economic change battled to control the state and its policies. Meanwhile powerful global pressures combined with venality to worsen corruption and crime. The country would continue to have the stingiest state in Central America. Despite moderate economic growth, Guatemala consistently had, per capita, the smallest budget in the region and spent the least on its citizens' education and health. It distributed what little it did provide very unequally across the Ladino–indigenous racial divide.

One persistent trait of the post-peace accord era was the near disappearance of stable political parties with predictable programs, replaced by competition among personalities elevated to the public eye by personal wealth or notoriety of some sort rooted in the long civil war or by media influence. Nineteen presidential nominees competed in 1995, and from 10 to 20 or more did in subsequent elections through 2019. More parties won seats in

Congress in each election from 1995 on as the number of seats increased from 80 to 158. By 2015 14 parties held seats in Guatemala's Congress. Only once since then, under the conservative FRG (1999–2003), would any party hold an outright majority of Congress' seats (see Tables A6 and A.7).

Post-Accord Politics

The peace accord signed by Arzú provided new political rules (an electoral democratic regime) and subsumed the previously negotiated accords. The military came under increased civilian authority and found its responsibilities curtailed. Police reforms began. URNG rebels, many groups of the left, the new FDNG, and indigenous peoples—previously repressed or otherwise excluded—entered the political system as legal players. The URNG agreed to demobilize and participate within the constitutional framework. Many civil society organizations, including bourgeoise elements previously ambivalent about peace and democratization, embraced the new regime. Guatemala's political party situation—hardly a system—became increasingly unstable.

President Arzú's neoliberal economic program (privatization of electricity and telecommunications, budget cuts, fiscal reforms, trade and foreign exchange liberalization, and reduced regulation) was designed to promote new economic growth, but at the cost of worsening poverty and income distribution.[44] Indeed, no matter the specific programs, several successive governments would maintain this very conservative approach to the economic role of the state despite Guatemala's economic growth being increasingly driven by remittances (11 percent of GDP by 2017), not by investment inspired by neoliberal policies.

Violent forces pushed hard against democracy and reforms. Nothing more clearly revealed the challenges to democratic consolidation than the fate of Auxiliary Archbishop Juan Gerardi Conedera on April 26, 1998. He was bludgeoned to death two days after the Catholic Church's Human Rights Office issued its report on civil war political violence to Guatemala's Historical Clarification Commission (Comisión para el Esclarecimiento Histórico, CEH). Bishop Gerardi was one of its authors. A death squad connected to the presidential guard claimed credit for the murder and began intimidating Catholic human rights workers.[45] In June 2001 the ensuing investigation blamed, and a court convicted, two army captains and a sergeant and a priest for Gerardi's murder.[46] Following appeals, Guatemala's Supreme Court ultimately upheld their convictions.[47]

In 1999 the CEH report, *Guatemala: Memory of Silence*, found that over 200,000 persons had died in the war and roughly 1.5 million were displaced. The report attributed 93 percent of the war's acts of violence—most intense from 1978 to 1984—to the army and state security forces.[48] It described the killings as genocidal because 83 percent of the victims were indigenous, and the attacks upon them a deliberate strategy to deny the rebels support.[49] The report attributed 626 massacres of Mayan communities to the state,[50] and found that US military assistance to Guatemala "had significant bearing on human rights violations during the armed conflict."[51] Shortly after the report's publication, US president Bill Clinton publicly apologized for Washington's role in supporting Guatemala's state security forces during the war.[52]

Despite early progress on implementing the peace accord, President Arzú later downplayed the CEH's findings and recommendations on preservation of memory, victim compensation, national reconciliation, and strengthening democracy and human rights. He rejected CEH recommendations to investigate and purge army officers for acts of violence, and claimed the military had already investigated itself and "purified" its forces. The peace process hit another roadblock in 1999 when voters by 56 percent defeated a referendum on constitutional reforms (including judicial and military reform) required to implement some provisions of the peace accords.

Growing social violence and socioeconomic woes became the main issues of the 1999 elections. The conservative FRG nominated Alfonso Portillo after the party's leader, retired General Efraín Ríos Montt was ruled ineligible for the presidency for his role in the 1982 coup. Portillo failed to win a majority in the first round election, but easily defeated PAN candidate and Guatemala City mayor Oscar Berger in the runoff. The FRG also dominated Congress with 63 of 113 seats, and selected Ríos Montt as Congress president.[53] The leftist New Nation Alliance (Alianza Nueva Nación, ANN), which included the URNG, outperformed expectations, winning 11 percent of the congressional vote (ten seats). The UNRG, however, would never approach the electoral successes of the FSLN in Nicaragua or El Salvador's FMLN.

President Portillo fared little better than Arzú in addressing Guatemala's persistent socioeconomic problems. His populist initiatives to reduce poverty, such as increasing the minimum wage, antagonized the Guatemalan business community. In 2002 Portillo established the National Compensation Program for war victims. The $400 million program would have included possible payments to some 400,000 former members of the militias known as Patrullas de Autodefensa Civil (PAC), many of them forcibly recruited during the war. Although later ruled unconstitutional, the payments issue highlighted continuing tensions within society.[54]

military
duties ; budget *increased*

Portillo's scant reformist advances were tempered by failures to combat rising crime, especially attacks on human rights workers, and to further implement the peace accords. Rather than shrink and reform the military, Portillo and Ríos Montt replaced Arzú-appointed reformist officers with others more sympathetic to the FRG administration. "Contrary to the regional trend, the corrupt FRG government also significantly increased the military's budget and duties," giving command of the military to "an unsavory trio of discredited former army officers allegedly associated with past human rights abuses and organized crime."[55] Portillo's government also became notorious for corruption.[56] In 2003 the US government decertified Guatemala for failing to contain the narcotics trade, which reduced US aid. Under Portillo, Guatemala's cocaine seizures plummeted, despite evidence that transshipments actually increased. The US Drug Enforcement Administration (DEA) estimated that Guatemala's corrupt Department of Anti-Narcotic Operations stole more than twice what it reported confiscated in 2002.[57]

The 2003 presidential campaign was tumultuous, but the pendulum swung back toward reform. In May 2003, the FRG nominated Ríos Montt, but he was again blocked from running because of his role in the 1982 coup. The Supreme Electoral Tribunal (Tribunal Supremo Electoral, TSE) denied Ríos' appeals. When blocked by the Supreme Court of Justice (Corte Supremo de Justicia, CSJ), he further appealed to the Court of Constitutionality (Corte de Constitucionalidad, CC), which ordered the TSE to instate his candidacy. When the CSJ suspended voter registration to protest the CC decision, Ríos Montt arranged a violent protest by thousands of demonstrators, many bused in from the countryside, to demand his reinstatement. Many, including by the US government, condemned the protest, but Ríos Montt appeared on the ballot. He ran a distant third with 20 percent of the vote.[58] This forced a runoff between two moderates—National Unity of Hope (Unidad Nacional de la Esperanza, UNE) candidate Alvaro Colom and Great National Alliance (Gran Alianza Nacional, GANA) candidate Oscar Berger. With turnout below 50 percent, Berger defeated Colom in the runoff, 52.8 to 47.2 percent. GANA also won 49 of 158 congressional seats (FRG received 41 seats, UNE 30, and PAN 17), leaving incoming President Berger without a majority in Congress.

Berger had campaigned on job creation and renewed support for the peace accords. He swiftly appointed indigenous rights activist and Nobel Peace laureate Rigoberta Menchú to oversee the implementation of the peace accords and noted human rights attorney Frank La Rue to head the president's human rights office. Speaking on the fifth anniversary of the truth commission, Berger apologized for the war and pledged to compensate victims.[59]

Berger

The Supreme Court's final rulings in the Bishop Gerardi murder trials somewhat refocused attention on peace and human rights. Additionally, Berger replaced problematical military commanders and pledged to reduce the size and budget of the military.[60]

As in other Central American countries, Guatemala's violence surged *after* the civil war. In the first six months of 2004, nearly 2,000 people were murdered. Berger replaced the interior minister and the chief of police, but also ordered 1,600 soldiers to join the police in combating crime, a violation of the peace accords.[61] One horrific national trend was the murders of more than 1,183 young women between January 2002 and June 2004.[62] Many were raped and horribly tortured. Government and media sources attributed many of these killings to gangs, but few were ever investigated.[63] To curb gangs, Berger signed an agreement with El Salvador, Honduras, and Nicaragua that allowed warrants issued in one country to be shared with all signatories. Gang members retaliated by pinning a note on a decapitated victim warning Berger against anti-gang laws.

Youth gangs committed many crimes, but crime syndicates and clandestine security organizations also increasingly contributed.[64] Homicide statistics revealed that regions with the most murders were not those with the most gang activity, nor were they poor or indigenous municipalities.[65] Rather, murder victims routinely included human rights activists, unionists, journalists, and protestors, presumably because they threatened business, political, or bureaucratic interests. Younger murder victims often bore evidence of torture. Death squads existed within the Interior Ministry and National Police. Many of their members were allegedly Protestant evangelicals who aimed to rid Guatemala of "evil" undesirables (gang members, prostitutes, and homosexuals) through so-called social cleansing (*saneamiento social*).[66] Thus the roots of post-conflict violence in Guatemala linked back to the war. That era's clandestine security organizations were never fully dismantled.[67] They morphed into organized crime networks that infiltrated the military, police, other state agencies, and political parties, which provided them impunity for drug trafficking, extortion, and money laundering.

In February 2007 three Salvadoran representatives to the Central American Parliament (PARLACEN), were murdered and their car torched in Guatemala.[68] Authorities quickly arrested four Guatemalan policemen, including the head of the organized-crime unit, as suspects. The suspects were soon murdered in their maximum-security cells at El Boquerón prison before they could be interrogated by the US Federal Bureau of Investigation (FBI) (invited to assist with the inquiry). Further investigation initially implicated a former UNE congressman and Jutiapa mayor, Manuel Castillo Medrano, who was apprehended in August 2007. Investigators later determined that a disgraced Salvadoran politician had contracted the murders to avenge ARENA for lifting his immunity from prosecution.[69]

The case highlighted the deep infiltration of criminal networks within Guatemala's security apparatus. In response, Berger sacked the minister of the interior, national police chief, and 1,900 police officers.[70] The PARLACEN killings also advanced Berger's fight against impunity for rights violations. In 2006 the government and the UN agreed to establish the International Commission against Impunity in Guatemala (Comisión Internacional contra la Impunidad en Guatemala, CICIG).[71] Approved by Congress in 2007, CICIG began its original two-year mandate in 2008, later repeatedly extended through 2019. Its responsibilities were to "investigate and dismantle violent criminal networks," assist in prosecutions, and recommend policies. CICIG could also file complaints against civil servants who might interfere with its mandate.[72] CICIG helped prosecute 20 high-profile cases through October 2013, including corruption, impunity, smuggling, and narco-trafficking. Prosecutors charged former president Portillo with embezzling more than $15 million while in office. He fled to Mexico in February 2004 after being stripped of his immunity from prosecution. Mexico eventually extradited Portillo to Guatemala, where he was acquitted in 2011. Portillo was then extradited to the United States in May 2013 to face charges of money laundering in New York.[73]

Violence marred the 2007 election season. With reformist elements ascendant, the fluid party system offered 14 presidential candidates, and 15 parties sought seats in Congress. Politics remained Guatemala's blood sport. More than 50 congressmen, candidates, and activists were killed in pre-election violence.[74] About one-quarter of the victims were from the reform-oriented party UNE, including a congressman's 14-year-old daughter. UNE nominee Alvaro Colom narrowly won the first round of voting to face Otto Pérez Molina of the conservative Patriot Party (Partido Patriota, PP) in a runoff. Pérez Molina, a retired general, had participated in counterinsurgency during the civil war. Rigoberta Menchú headed the ticket of the new Encounter for Guatemala (Encuentro por Guatemala, EG) but won only 3 percent of the first-round vote. In the Congressional elections UNE won 52 two seats, PP 29, the Grand National Alliance (Gran Alianza Nacional, GANA) 37, and FRG 14. Women won 19 seats, including four indigenous women. Voter turnout was 60 percent, the highest since the end of the war.

In the runoff campaign, Colom claimed a Pérez Molina victory would represent a return to civil war. Colom, a candidate twice before, pledged to increase social investment and to fight impunity and corruption. Pérez Molina, whose campaign symbol was a fist, argued Guatemala needed more order and vowed to use the military to restore it.[75] Each man charged the other with organized crime and drug cartel links (a claim that had plagued the UNE in recent years). Colom defeated Pérez Molina in the runoff, 53 percent to 47 percent, with runoff turnout falling to 53 percent.

Controversy and rising violence marked Colom's first year in office. The crime wave escalated; homicides increased 9 percent to 6,292. Public bus drivers became targets for extortion—in 2008 criminals murdered 175 bus drivers, attendants, and company owners.[76] Frustrated with poor official response to rampant crime, Guatemalan vigilante mobs lynched numerous suspected criminals as well as municipal and police officials.[77] From 2002 to 2004 femicides (murders of women because they are women) increased 57 percent, more than twice the rate of murders of men.[78] In 2007, 722 femicides were reported, almost 10 percent of all reported homicides that year. Only a fraction of these crimes resulted in convictions.

In 2008 the Congress approved the Law Against Femicides and Other Forms of Violence Against Women, unanimously supported by all 19 congresswomen.[79] The law criminalized all violence against women whether economic, sexual, psychological, or physical.[80] Congress also passed the Arms and Ammunitions Act, which banned arms trafficking, required a psychological test for a gun license, and limited to three the number of arms owned by an individual. The UN estimated that there were 1.5 million illegal arms in Guatemala.

President Colom also especially emphasized human rights. He ordered declassification of military archives accidentally discovered in a munitions depot in July 2005.[81] The army refused to obey the order as unconstitutional, but the Constitutional Court disagreed and granted a petition from the Human Rights Ombudsman for the production of the documents. Colom significantly increased reparations payments made by the Berger administration. By May 2009, the administration had delivered almost 10,500 reparations checks to survivors. Colom, whose uncle was murdered by death squads, also sent letters to victims' families asking for forgiveness for the state's offenses.[82]

Rumors of coup conspiracies swirled around Colom. When hidden microphones and video cameras were discovered in the presidential offices and residence in September 2008, Colom fired the attorney general. Soon after, the 2009 murder of prominent attorney Rodrigo Rosenberg threatened to destabilize Colom's government. In a bizarre videotape recorded before his death, Rosenberg blamed Colom for his demise, and alleged drug-related conspiracies among the directors of the Rural Development Bank and anti-poverty programs run by Colom's wife.[83] Colom's opponents and supporters demonstrated for days and observers speculated the affair was an attempt to force Colom from office.[84] Colom requested that CICIG and the FBI investigate. They ultimately found that Rosenberg orchestrated his own death to implicate Colom, whom he blamed for the murder of his married lover.[85]

In 2009 the Inter-American Court on Human Rights ruled that Guatemala's 1996 amnesty law did not bar prosecution of crimes against humanity. Shortly thereafter, prosecutors issued warrants for soldiers accused of participating in certain massacres. In 2010, President Colom appointed Claudia Paz y Paz as Guatemala's attorney general. She implemented a new evaluation system for prosecutors that caused the retirement of almost 80 percent of prosecutors.[86] Paz y Paz prosecuted drug cartels and organized crime figures, and former President Portillo for corruption. But the prosecution of crimes committed during the war drew international attention. In 2011 warrants were issued for both former dictator Oscar Mejía Victores and former head of the armed forces Hector Mario López Fuentes, though both were ruled too ill to stand trial. By 2011 Guatemalan courts had tried and convicted several lower-ranking participants (civil-defense-patrol members and army officers) in civil war atrocities.[87]

Despite some progress prosecuting criminals, Guatemala remained a haven for drug traffickers and organized crime.[88] Mexico's Sinaloa Cartel and Zetas operated with relative impunity. In 2010, Colom's administration declared a state of siege in Alta Verapaz where the Zetas preyed upon the local population, and another in Petén following the massacre of dozens of workers and children at the Los Cocos ranch.[89] Troubling but not surprising evidence surfaced that the very members of the military that had been tasked with fighting the traffickers were instead colluding with them.[90] In addition to the Mexican cartels, dozens of other traffickers operated in the country. In July 2011 an Argentine folk singer died in an ambush targeting a Nicaraguan music promoter, all orchestrated by Costa Rican drug traffickers operating in Guatemala.

CONTEMPORARY SOCIETY AND POLITICS

The Economy

Guatemala's overt political violence obscures the ubiquitous hardships caused by dependent development and poverty. To understand Guatemala's political problems it helps to take stock of the Guatemalan economy in the twenty-first century. As we have repeatedly stated, the dominant fact of Guatemalan society is its divide between Ladinos and indigenous people. Since Spaniards arrived five centuries ago, Ladino elites have exploited and repressed the indigenous peoples, yet neglected their education, well-being, and communities. Data here and elsewhere on the last 20 years emphasize the country's poverty and inequality, but still partially obscure how the Ladino–indigenous divide always works against indigenous Guatemalans.

The National Statistical Institute reported in 2006 that over half of Guatemalans lived below the poverty line, 13 percent in extreme poverty. Poverty was much worse in rural areas in the country's north and west, and among indigenous populations it was 56 percent compared to Ladinos' 44 percent.[91] Guatemala has consistently over decades been the most economically unequal country in the region by a host of measures (see Tables 1.1, 2.1, and 2.2). Recent data reveal that in Central America, Guatemala has the worst sanitary conditions, highest infant mortality, and lowest life expectancy, literacy, and educational attainment. Ladinos in Guatemala often blame indigenous for these conditions, but Table A.5 reveals the real reason for these discrepancies— chronic underinvestment in human capital. Over four decades, Guatemala's government has been proportionately the region's smallest and has spent the least on education and health. Guatemalan poverty statistics would be much worse if not for the remittances from citizens working abroad. Guatemala has become increasingly dependent on remittances,[92] which have increased steadily since the 1990s. In 1990 remittances accounted for only 1.6 percent of Guatemala's GDP, but this increased to 11.2 percent of GDP by 2017, an amount roughly six times greater than foreign direct investment and all foreign aid combined that year.[93] To subtract this critical stream of income to many Guatemalan families would sharply increase poverty and plunge the economy into recession.

Poverty and inequality increasingly pitted business-elite interests against the poor majority. Social protest erupted in 2005 over controversial government policies, such as mining and the Central American Free Trade Agreement (CAFTA). Small-scale agricultural producers, unions, and others feared CAFTA's removing trade barriers and opening markets to foreign goods, firms, and capital. There were numerous anti-CAFTA demonstrations demanding the issue be decided by referendum.[94] In the end, business interests prevailed in Congress, passing by 126 to 12; most opposing votes came from the URNG. Protests continued after ratification, resulting in one death and several injuries caused by the army.[95]

Politics

The 2011 elections again saw high levels of campaign violence, high levels of spending, and low voter morale.[96] Three dozen activists, mostly local candidates, were assassinated before the September elections.[97] Despite ten presidential candidates, some felt that the elections merely reaffirmed elite interests. Allegations accused several candidates of ties to drug traffickers.[98] The PP again nominated Otto Pérez Molina, former general and director of army intelligence. An early leader in polls, he campaigned on *mano dura* policies that had failed elsewhere. First Lady Sandra Torres divorced President Alvaro Colom and tried to run but was disqualified, leaving UNE with no candidate.[99] Manuel Baldizón of the Renewed Democratic Liberation Party (LIDER) emerged as a strong contender. A wealthy businessman, he had served in Congress and been a member of both PAN and UNE before forming LIDER in 2008 with other UNE defectors. His running mate was the ex-wife of former president Vinicio Cerezo. Both major candidates promised to get tough on crime. Baldizón's style and rhetoric assumed a populist tone, emphasizing social programs, suggesting public executions, and promising to get Guatemala's soccer team to the World Cup.

Pérez Molina failed to win a majority in the first round of voting, winning 36 percent to Baldizón's 23 percent. The Patriotic Party performed well, gaining 25 seats more Congress seats than in 2007 for 56 total. UNE won 48, down three from 2007. LIDER and UCN each captured 14 seats (see Table A.7). Women won 13 seats, including three indigenous women. Only seven women won mayoral races. Indigenous candidates won 20 seats. Although his military past—including allegations of participation in genocide—troubled some, many Guatemalans perceived Pérez Molina's military background as an asset for combatting crime.[100] He won the November runoff, 54 to 46 percent. He became the first ex-military president since 1986 and his vice president, Roxana Baldetti, became the first woman to occupy that office.

In 2013 former president General Efraín Ríos Montt and his intelligence chief, José Mauricio Rodríguez Sánchez, stood trial on charges of genocide and crimes against humanity in the 1982 Dos Erres massacre of 1,771 Ixil people, and the rape of nearly 1,500 women and girls.[101] The pretrial hearings and trial were contentious. Ríos Montt's supporters mounted a sometimes menacing campaign against the trial.[102] On May 10, Ríos Montt was convicted of genocide and crimes against humanity and sentenced to 80 years in prison, the first time a former head of any state had been convicted of genocide in a national court. Ten days later, the Constitutional Court cited procedural errors, partially annulled the verdict, and ordered

the original trial to resume at the point when Ríos Montt's attorney had
been expelled from court. Testimony from the original trial would stand but
closing arguments would now be given before a new tribunal.[103] Another
uncertainty was whether President Pérez Molina would face trial for crimes
he allegedly committed during the war once his immunity from prosecution
expired upon leaving office.[104] The Constitutional Court's removal of attorney general Claudia Paz y Paz several months before the end of her official
term on a technicality also raised questions about institutional commitments
to justice and human rights.

The homicide rate declined significantly between 2009 and 2012, from 46
to 24 per 100,000. Though somewhat higher in 2013, homicides remained
well below the rates of neighboring Honduras and El Salvador.[105] Yet Guatemala remained the most violent country in the region for women, with
the third-highest femicide rate in the world.[106] Murders of women declined
9 percent between 2011 and 2012, but also appeared to increase slightly in
2013. Despite improving murder rates, many Guatemalans did not view Pérez
Molina positively. Although his May 2013 approval rating was 58 percent,
70 percent viewed his administration as the same or worse than the previous
administration.[107] Guatemalans remained concerned about unemployment
and the economy. Social programs implemented by his administration, such
as Hambre Cero (Zero Hunger), accomplished little to reduce food insecurity.
More than half of Guatemalans still lived below the poverty line and chronic
malnutrition among children was endemic. Corruption, which plagued previous administrations, remained a serious problem.[108] Concerns grew about
infringement of basic rights as repression of journalists and trade unions
increased.[109] The use of the military to combat crime, a trend throughout the
region, also posed a threat to human rights. In October 2012, seven indigenous people were killed and dozens injured during a protest over an electricity
rate hike in Totonicapán. One army colonel and eight soldiers were ordered to
stand trial in the massacre.[110]

Indigenous Guatemalans

Self-identified Mayan indigenous peoples constitute roughly 42 percent of
Guatemalans.[111] The nation's Ladinos, long a minority, have traditionally
endeavored to control the labor, movement, and political behavior of the indigenous. Over 80 percent of the dead from the civil war were indigenous, and
most of the violence and massacres took place in indigenous areas. Civil war
terror disrupted indigenous communities, and many migrated abroad or to
the cities. Their communities and leaders have thus mobilized very cautiously.

The CEH viewed the treatment of Guatemala's Mayan people as so central to the problem of returning Guatemala to peace that it encouraged the government especially to promote their political participation, incorporate indigenous professionals in the public sector, teach the public tolerance, and provide reparations for the injuries done during the violence. As noted, voters in 1999, defeated several constitutional reforms required to implement the accords.

How different are the political behavior and attitudes of Guatemala's Ladino and indigenous populations? As in 1995 and 2008 surveys,[112] Guatemala's indigenous citizens in 2012 were significantly poorer and less educated than Ladinos. In 2012, 80 percent of Guatemala's indigenous people lived in poverty and nearly 60 percent of indigenous children suffered from chronic malnutrition. Poor access to schools in rural communities and too few bilingual instructors posed impediments to young indigenous Guatemalans, particularly at the primary-school level.[113] The 1995 survey revealed few other differences between the indigenous and Ladino populations. By 2012, however, the picture had changed considerably. Indigenous persons still remained badly underrepresented in public offices (only ten won seats in Congress in the 2011 elections and only one served in Pérez Molina's cabinet).

Surveys in 2012 revealed no significant difference between indigenous and Ladino Guatemalans on diffuse political system support and agreement that "one should support the political system." Indigenous Guatemalans expressed greater confidence than Ladinos that the political system "protects basic rights" and greater pride in the system. No significant differences appeared in left–right ideological orientation or democratic attitudes. (Survey results from 2008 and 2012 had shown the indigenous supported democratic norms less than did Ladinos, so this new parity of democratic values is notable.) In political participation, indigenous respondents reported contacting officials more than did Ladinos, and resorted much more to civil society activism, but evinced no difference in voting or party and campaign activism. Overall, this picture suggests that, despite their economic disadvantages, indigenous Guatemalans have become more integrated into the system—more supportive and as politically active or more so than Ladinos. One difference stands out—despite protesting less than Ladinos, indigenous people supported confrontation and rebellion more. Greater willingness to consider confrontation or rebellion are not surprising, given Guatemala's history of victimizing its indigenous people. On balance, the indigenous populace displays considerable social capital and robust political engagement.[114]

The 2015 Elections. In April 2015 sustained protests erupted throughout the country in response to revelations that dozens of public officials, including

President Otto Pérez Molina and Vice President Roxana Baldetti Elías, had been implicated in a $200 million corruption scandal involving the customs authority. The scandal, called La Linea, prompted the resignations and arrests of Pérez Molina and Baldetti, as well as nearly two dozen other public officials, in August and September 2015. It was only the first of numerous corruption allegations against Pérez Molina and Baldetti as subsequent investigations later revealed that the two had established multiple corruption networks.[115] Alejandro Maldonado, who had been serving as vice president since Baldetti's resignation, became president in September. In June 2016, prosecutors charged Pérez Molina and Baldetti with money laundering and the illegal financing of political parties.

While some questioned whether the scheduled September elections should be postponed due to the crisis, elections were held five days after Pérez Molina resigned the presidency. Fourteen candidates vied for the presidency, including Zury Ríos Sosa, daughter of Efraín Ríos Montt. In July 2015, the Supreme Court approved her presidential candidacy despite a constitutional ban on relatives of coup leaders or dictators running for president. The National Convergence Front (FCN), a party created by former military officers, selected television comedian and political unknown Jimmy Morales as its candidate. Morales, who ran a single-issue campaign under the slogan, "not corrupt, nor a thief," led the first round of voting with 24 percent of the vote. He was followed by former first lady Sandra Torres (UNE).

Morales won the October runoff against Torres with 67 percent of the vote. In Congressional races, LIDER won 45 seats, followed by UNE with 32 seats, and the PP and Todos with 18 seats each. The remaining 45 seats were distributed among nine other parties. Women candidates continued to make small gains in 2017, winning 24 congressional seats. Sandra Morán (Convergence) became the country's first openly gay legislator. Indigenous candidates won 18, down two, seats in Congress and 113 out of 333 mayoral races. As with prior elections, campaign violence occurred throughout the 2015 campaign with as many as 20 people murdered in election-related violence.

CICIG and the Fight Against Corruption

In April 2016, Morales extended CICIG's mandate through for another three-year period. But Morales' anti-corruption pledge would soon be tested as both his son and brother were investigated for possible involvement in the previous administration's corruption network. Both were acquitted in 2019. A 2015 CICIG report revealed that Guatemala's political parties received about half of their financing for the 2011 and 2015 elections through unreported donations, including sources such as state contractors, business elites, and organized crime.[116] Legislation including stronger oversight of campaign financing and reporting passed in 2016. In addition to penalizing parties for violations, the electoral commission created a new unit to monitor spending in 2018.

In August 2017, CICIG and the attorney general revealed evidence that President Morales and his party had received some $825 million in illicit financing during the 2015 campaign and announced that they were seeking to repeal his immunity from prosecution. Two days later, Morales ordered the expulsion of CICIG head, Iván Velasquez.[117] Though Morales' immunity remained intact and the Constitutional Court overturned the expulsion order, the episode presaged things to come.

In April 2018, the attorney general and CICIG announced that Morales and his party may have received over $1 million in illegal campaign contributions.[118] When the CICIG and attorney general petitioned to lift Morales's immunity for a third time in August, Morales made a public announcement, surrounded by dozens of members of the military, including Kaibiles Special Forces, that he would not renew CICIG's mandate. He accused CICIG of "sowing judicial terror" in Guatemala.[119] During his announcement, military vehicles rolled through the capital past CICIG offices and foreign embassies. He then banned Velásquez from re-entering the country and later revoked the visas of foreign nationals working for CICIG.[120] While the Constitutional Court overruled these expulsions, Morales simply ignored multiple court decisions and attempted to impeach several judges in what one analyst described as a "slow motion coup."[121]

CICIG's mandate expired in September 2019. The United States, which had initially supported the commission, largely ignored Morales' attacks against the anti-graft body.[122] With US support it might have been saved. During its 12 years, CICIG worked to strengthen the attorney general's office, proposed dozens of legal reforms, identified more than 60 criminal networks, prosecuted nearly 700 people, and won convictions in more than 300 cases related to graft and corruption.[123] Another report credited CICIG with driving down the country's homicide rate, which declined from 46 per 100,000 in 2008 to 22.4 in 2018.[124] Through its work, CICIG became the most trusted institution in the country with a 72 percent approval rating in 2019.[125]

Justice and Legal Issues

Investigations into past crimes from the country's civil war continued. Rios Montt, whose genocide conviction was overturned by the Constitutional Court ten days after it was issued, died in April 2018 without returning to trial. But other trials moved forward. In 2016, two military officers were convicted of crimes against humanity on counts of murder, rape, and enslavement in Sepur Zarco. The case, which was brought by 11 surviving indigenous Q'eqchi' women from the village, was the first involving sexual violence from the war to be prosecuted. In 2018, a former member of the Kaibiles was convicted of 171 counts of murder in the 1982 Dos Erres massacre, which had left more than 200 dead. Also in 2018, four high-ranking military officials were convicted and sentenced in the disappearance of 14-year-old Marco Antonio Molina Theissen and the rape of his sister Emma Guadalupe in 1981. But not all outcomes were so positive. In September 2018, Guatemala's High Risk Court B found that the state of Guatemala and the Guatemalan army had committed genocide and crimes against humanity against Maya Ixil, but failed to convict Ríos Montt's director of military intelligence, José Mauricio Rodríguez Sánchez.[126]

While courts continued to make slow, but important, progress on crimes committed during the war, indigenous Guatemalans continued to be persecuted. Indigenous communities routinely clashed with development projects, particularly in the mining and hydroelectric sectors. Environmental and land activists, the majority of whom were indigenous, continued to be targeted with impunity. According to Global Witness, Guatemala was the most dangerous country in the world in 2018 for land and environmental activists, more than two dozen of whom were killed in 2018 alone.[127] Land conflicts and repression combined with climate change to create a dangerous situation for many indigenous communities. As severe drought led to crop failure, food insecurity drove growing numbers of Guatemalans to attempt to migrate to the United States[128]

In 2018, Guatemala had the third highest femicide rate in the world after El Salvador and Honduras. According to Guatemala's National Institute of Forensics, there were more than 7,200 femicides (averaging 15 per week) from 2009 to 2017.[129] As with other countries in the region, little had improved since the implementation of the country's femicide law in 2008. An analysis of cases showed that while reporting had improved, impunity had not.[130]

2019 Elections

The 2019 elections were held against a backdrop of pessimism and uncertainty. In the months prior to the election several candidates, including two of the top three contenders, were forced out of the race. In March, a judge issued an arrest warrant for former attorney general (2014–2018) Thelma Aldana on charges of illegal hiring, embezzlement, and tax fraud, among other charges. In May, the court ruled her ineligible to run for president.

Aldana, who had been the frontrunner in the polls and was the only leading candidate to openly support CICIG, vigorously denied the charges and claimed they were politically motivated. In May, the Constitutional Court ruled that the candidacy of Zury Rios was—unlike 2015—prohibited by the constitution. Another candidate, Mario Estrada (National Change Union), was arrested in Miami on charges that he planned to use drug money to assassinate rivals.[131]

Despite their exits, voters still faced a field of 19 presidential candidates, including indigenous rights activist Thelma Cabrera (MLP). The UNE again nominated former first lady and 2015 runner-up Sandra Torres. Torres faced high negatives, with more than half of voters saying they would never vote for her.[132] Despite this, Torres won the first round of voting with nearly 26 percent of the vote, followed by Alejandro Giammattei of Vamos with 14 percent. Giammattei, the former director of the penitentiary system, ran on a tough-on-crime platform. Cabrera came in fourth with almost 10.4 percent. UNE won 54 of 160 seats in Congress, followed by Vamos with 16 and UCN with 12 (see Table A.7). The remainder of the seats were divided amongst 17 other parties, leaving no party with a potential majority. Women won 31 seats, up 5 percent from 2015. Winaq's Aldo Dávila, one of two openly gay candidates in legislative races, became the first openly gay man and first HIV-positive member of Congress. Giammattei won the August runoff with nearly 58 percent of the vote. Just days after the election, authorities arrested Torres on campaign finance violation charges pending from the 2015 elections. It was a tumultuous end to a tumultuous campaign season.

CONCLUSIONS

Guatemala's 36-year civil war left some 200,000 dead, and many more missing and displaced. The 1996 peace accords and formal democratization notwithstanding, turmoil of many kinds continued to plague Guatemala and democratic consolidation remained elusive. Although the creation of the anti-impunity agency CICIG and legislative reforms passed during the Colom administration signaled some positive changes, much remained to be done to stabilize the political system, curtail social violence, and improve the lot of the very numerous poor. Likewise, though important elements of the 1996 peace accords have not yet been implemented, and there seems little likelihood that they ever will be, prosecutions of crimes committed during the civil war give some hope for some measure of justice for Guatemalans. Little has been done to address the rights of Guatemala's indigenous population, and marginalization and systemic racism persist. The indigenous community, however, is politically more active and organized than Ladinos.

Just as the Guatemalan legal system was reckoning with the country's past of rampant official abuses, voters were embracing politicians who promised to get tough on crime. The election of Otto Pérez Molina in 2011 revealed an electorate more concerned about rising violent crime than past abuses. Although there was some notable success in reducing Guatemala's homicide rate by 2012, drug traffickers and organized crime networks undermined public security and the economy, and deepened already severe corruption. "Social cleansing" and clandestine security organizations underscored the impunity and corruption that characterized the Guatemalan state.

Twelve years of CICIG's assistance brought meaningful advancements to the fight against corruption, strengthened judicial institutions, and reduced crime. The La Linea case brought down a president, vice president, and dozens of other public officials. But CICIG also threatened powerful actors who had a vested interest in its demise. President Morales, who assumed the presidency pledging to fight corruption, ultimately fought to shutter the commission in a bid to save himself. By 2019, CICIG's time in Guatemala was over. The future of the fight against corruption was uncertain.

NOTES

1. George Black, et al., *Garrison Guatemala* (New York: Monthly Review Press, 1984), p. 13.

2. Jerry L. Weaver, "Guatemala: The Politics of a Frustrated Revolution," in Howard J. Wiarda and Harvey F. Kline, eds., *Latin American Politics and Development* (Boston, MA: Houghton Mifflin, 1979), p. 337; Piero Gleijeses, *Shattered Hope: The Guatemalan Revolution and the United States* (Princeton, NJ: Princeton University Press, 1991).

3. Richard H. Immerman, *The CIA in Guatemala: The Foreign Policy of Intervention* (Austin, TX: University of Texas Press, 1982), pp. 2–7; Gleijeses, *Shattered Hope.*

4. Richard Newbold Adams, *Crucifixion by Power: Essays on the Guatemalan National Social Structure, 1944–1966* (Austin, TX: University of Texas Press, 1970), p. 195.

5. John Sloan, "*The Electoral Game in Guatemala*," Ph.D. dissertation, University of Texas at Austin, 1968.

6. See Tables A.1 and A.2, in John A. Booth and Thomas W. Walker, *Understanding Central America*, 3rd ed. (Boulder, CO: Westview Press, 1999).

7. Ibid., Tables A.5 and A.6.

8. Inforpress Centroamericana, *Guatemala: Elections 1985* (Guatemala City: n.p., 1985), p. 19.

9. Booth and Walker, *Understanding Central America*, 3rd ed., Appendix, Table A.8.

10. Ibid.; Thomas P. Anderson, *Politics in Central America: Guatemala, El Salvador, Honduras, and Nicaragua* (New York: Praeger, 1982), pp. 19–62; "Guatemala," *Mesoamérica*, May 1982; Consejo Superior Universitaria Centroamericana (CSUCA), *Estructura agrária, dinámica de población, y desarrollo capitalista en Centroamérica* (San José, Costa Rica: Editorial Universitaria Centroamericana, 1978), pp. 77–132; Technical Commission of the Great National Dialogue, *Economic and Social Policy Recommendations to the Head of State* (Guatemala City: Technical Commission of the Great National Dialogue, 1985); Lars Schoultz, "Guatemala: Social Change and Political Conflict," in Martin Diskin, ed., *Trouble in Our Backyard* (New York: Pantheon, 1983), pp. 178–183; Brockett, *Land, Power, and Poverty*, pp. 99–123; and Susanne Jonas, *The Battle for Guatemala: Rebels, Death Squads, and US Power* (Boulder, CO: Westview Press, 2000), p. 5.

11. Julio Castellano Cambranes, "Origins of the Crisis of the Established Order in Guatemala," in Steve C. Ropp and James A. Morris, eds., *Central America: Crisis and Adaptation* (Albuquerque, NM: University of New Mexico Press, 1984), pp. 119–152.

12. Mitchell A. Seligson et al., *Land and Labor in Guatemala: An Assessment* (Washington, DC: Agency for International Development, Development Associates, 1982), pp. 1–18.

13. Black et al., *Garrison Guatemala*, pp. 34–37; Schoultz, "Guatemala," p. 181; Seligson et al., *Land and Labor*.

14. Gustavo A. Noyola, "Integración centroamericana y absorción de mano de obra: Guatemala," in Daniel Camacho, Mario A. de Franco, and Carlos F. Chamorro, *El fracaso social del la integración centroamericana: Capital, tecnología, empleo* (San José, Costa Rica: Educa, 1979), pp. 276–319.

15. Adams, *Crucifixion by Power*; Black et al., *Garrison Guatemala*, pp. 48–51.

16. John A. Booth, "A Guatemalan Nightmare: Levels of Political Violence, 1966–1972," *Journal of Interamerican Studies and World Affairs* 22 (May 1980), pp. 195–225.

17. Gabriel Aguilera Peralta, Romero Imery, et al., *Dialéctica del terror en Guatemala* (San José, Costa Rica: Editorial Universitaria Centroamericana, 1981); Americas Watch, *Human Rights in Guatemala: No Neutrals Allowed* (New York, 1982), and *Little Hope: Human Rights in Guatemala, January 1984–1985* (New York, 1985); John A. Booth et al., *The 1985 Guatemalan Elections: Will the Military Relinquish Power?* (Washington, DC: International Human Rights Law Group, Washington Office on Latin America, 1985); see also Gordon L. Bowen, "The Origins and Development of State Terrorism," in Donald E. Schulz and Douglas H. Graham, eds., *Revolution and Counterrevolution in Central America and the Caribbean* (Boulder, CO:

Westview Press, 1984), pp. 269–300; and "Guatemala," *Mesoamérica,* July–August 1982, pp. 2–4; Jonas, *The Battle for Guatemala,* Ch. 5–7; Brockett, *Land, Power, and Poverty,* pp. 112–119; Black et al., *Garrison Guatemala,* pp. 61–107; Anderson, *Politics,* pp. 19–60; Inforpress Centroamericana, *Guatemala: Elections 1985,* pp. 8–11; Jonathan Fried et al., *Guatemala in Rebellion: Unfinished History* (New York: Grove, 1983), pp. 151–316.

18. Héctor Rosado Granados, *Guatemala 1984: Elecciones para Asamblea Nacional Constituyente* (San José, Costa Rica: Instituto Centroamericano de Derechos Humanos-Centro de Asesoría y Promoción Electoral, 1985), p. 41; "Guatemala," *Mesoamérica,* March 1982, pp. 2–4; Margaret E. Roggensack and John A. Booth, *Report of the International Human Rights Law Group and the Washington Office on Latin America Advance Election Observer Mission to Guatemala* (Washington, DC: International Human Rights Law Group, Washington Office on Latin America, 1985), Appendix B.

19. Data for selected periods drawn from US Embassy–Guatemala reports from 1966 through 1984, Booth, "A Guatemalan Nightmare," and US Department of State, *Country Report on Human Rights Practices* (Washington, DC: US Government Printing Office, February 2, 1981), p. 441; later data came from Inforpress Centroamericana, *Central America Report,* February 1, 1985, p. 31; November 22, 1985, p. 357; and January 21, 1988, p. 12.

20. For 1982 and after, see US Embassy–Guatemala, "A Statistical Comparison of Violence (1982–1985)," Guatemala City, xerox, 1985. Later studies confirm the extent of violence; see Francisco Mauricio Martínez, "Guatemala, Never More: 55,000 Human Rights Violations," and "URNG Committed 44 Massacres," both from *La Prensa Libre* (Guatemala City), April 14, 1998, translated into English in *Human Rights News Clips,* Foundation for Human Rights in Guatemala, www.fhrg. org/042098.htm//G, accessed July 13, 1998, pp. 1–3.

21. Lars Schoultz, "Guatemala: Social Change and Political Conflict," in Diskin, ed., *Trouble in Our Backyard,* pp. 188–189.

22. Historical Clarification Commission (CEH), *Guatemala: Memory of Silence* (Guatemala City, 1999), p. 1, section 27.

23. Quoted by Allan Nairn in "Guatemala Can't Take 2 Roads," *New York Times,* July 20, 1982, p. 23A; US Department of State, "Bureau of Inter-American Affairs," *Background Notes: Guatemala* March 1998, www.state.gov/www/background_notes/ guatemala_0398_bgn.html, pp. 3–4.

24. Booth's conversation with US Embassy personnel, Guatemala City, September 1985.

25. Booth's field observations in Guatemala in 1985; Americas Watch, *Human Rights in Guatemala* and *Little Hope;* Booth et al., *The 1985 Guatemalan Elections;* Inforpress Centroamericana, *Guatemala: Elections 1985;* British Parliamentary Human

Rights Group, *"Bitter and Cruel . . .": Report of a Mission to Guatemala by the British Parliamentary Human Rights Group* (London: House of Commons, 1985); and Black et al., *Garrison Guatemala*, pp. 61–113. Much of the volume (55,000 deaths) and responsibility (80 percent military, 20 percent URNG) for human rights abuses are confirmed by the human rights office of the Archdiocese of Guatemala; see Martínez, "Guatemala, Never More," and "URNG Committed."

26. William I. Robinson, *Transnational Conflicts: Central America, Social Change, and Globalization* (London: Verso, 2003), pp. 106–108.

27. Black et al., *Garrison Guatemala*, pp. 107–109.

28. Interviews with Guatemalan labor sources, September–October 1985 and April–May 1987, Guatemala City; see Booth et al., *The 1985 Guatemalan Elections*, pp. 39–40, and David Carliner et al., *Political Transition and the Rule of Law in Guatemala* (Washington, DC: International Human Rights Law Group, Washington Office on Latin America, January 1988), pp. 7–8. For confirmation see also Jonas, *The Battle for Guatemala*.

29. Booth et al., *The 1985 Guatemalan Elections*.

30. Interviews with spokesmen for various parties, September–October 1985, Guatemala.

31. Robinson, *Transnational Conflicts*, quote pp. 111–112, and see pp. 110–113.

32. Latin American Studies Association (LASA), *Extraordinary Opportunities . . . and New Risks: Final Report of the LASA Commission on Compliance with the Central America Peace Accord* (Pittsburgh, PA: LASA, 1988), pp. 15–20; Booth's interviews in Guatemala, September 1988; "Año de tumulto en Guatemala," *Excelsior* (Mexico City), December 30, 1988, p. 4A; *Christian Science Monitor*, February 14, 1989, p. 3.

33. U.S. Department of State, *Background Notes: Guatemala*, Bureau of Inter-American Affairs, March 1998, www.state.gov/www/background_notes/guatemala_0398_bgn.html. *Amparo* and habeas corpus are court orders for the government to cease violating constitutional rights, helpful against abuses of power such as wrongful detention.

34. Killed were US citizens Diana Ortiz, a nun, and businessman Michael Devine, and Salvadoran Social Democratic Party leader Héctor Oqueli. On counterinsurgency and indigenous, see Washington Office on Latin America, *Who Pays the Price? The Cost of War in the Guatemalan Highlands* (Washington, DC, April 1988). See also Carliner et al., *Political Transition*; LASA, *Extraordinary Opportunities . . . and New Risks*, pp. 15–20; April, May, June, July, August, October, and November 1990, and January 1991 sections on Guatemala, in *Mesoamérica*; "Four Guatemalan Troops Charged in Killings," *Boston Globe*, September 30, 1990, pp. 1–2; and "Amnesty International Reports Guatemalan Police and Private Sector Forces Torture and Murder Street Children," *Excelsior* (Mexico City), November 10, 1990, p. 2A.

35. Robinson, *Transnational Conflicts*, p. 112.

36. Ibid., p. 113; Guatemala, section of *Mesoamérica*, April, May, June, August, and September 1991; Katherine Ellison, "Celebrity of Guatemalan Rights Activists Could Save His Life," *Miami Herald*, November 22, 1990, p. 20B; "Guatemalan Troops Said to Kill 11 Protesting Raid," *New York Times*, December 3, 1990, p. 8A; "Government Accuses Death Squads of Wave of Killings, Denies Connections to Armed Forces," *Excelsior*, August 5, 1991, p. 2A; Haroldo Shetemul, "National Blackout in Guatemala: Police Chief Assassinated," *Excelsior*, August 6, 1991, p. 2A; "Attacks on Journalists Condemned by President Serrano Elias," *Excelsior*, September 1, 1991, p. 2A.

37. Susanne Jonas, "Electoral Problems and the Democratic Prospect in Guatemala," and John A. Booth, "Introduction: Elections and Democracy in Central America: A Framework for Analysis," both in Mitchell A. Seligson and John A. Booth, eds., *Elections and Democracy in Central America, Revisited* (Chapel Hill, NC: University of North Carolina Press, 1995), pp. 35–36, p. 1.

38. Susanne Jonas, "The Democratization of Guatemala through the Peace Process," in Christopher Chase-Dunn, Susanne Jonas, and Nelson Amaro, eds., *Globalization on the Ground: Postbellum Guatemalan Democracy and Development* (Lanham, MD: Rowman and Littlefield, 2001), pp. 49–82; and US Department of State, *Background Notes: Guatemala*, pp. 4–5.

39. See Susanne Jonas, *Of Centaurs and Doves: Guatemala's Peace Process* (Boulder, CO: Westview Press, 2000) and Jonas's "The Democratization of Guatemala."

40. The indigenous rights accord, a landmark in this country profoundly marked by anti-indigenous racism, called Guatemala a multiethnic, multicultural, and multilingual society and provided for education reform and indigenous representation in governmental structures; see Kay B. Warren, "Pan-Mayanism and Multiculturalism in Guatemala," paper presented at the Symposium on Development and Democratization in Guatemala: Proactive Responses to Globalization, Universidad del Valle, Guatemala City, March 18, 1998, pp. 1–5.

41. Ibid., pp. 4–5; and US Department of State, *Guatemala: Background Notes*, p. 5; "Mayans Win Local Representation," *Cerigua* (Peace Net), *Weekly Briefs*, No. 3, January 18, 1996; Tim Johnson, "Maya Mayor Triumphs over Entrenched Racism," *Miami Herald*, January 15, 1996, p. 1A; Robinson, *Transnational Conflicts*, p. 112.

42. "FDNG Activists Assassinated," *Cerigua* (Peace Net) *Weekly Briefs*, No. 2 (January 11, 1996); "Human Rights Violations Continue to Rise," *Cerigua* (PeaceNet) *Weekly Briefs*, No. 5 (February 1, 1996); Michael Riley, "Refugees Outside Looking In," *Christian Science Monitor*, January 10, 1996, p. 5; Larry Rohter, "Specter in Guatemala: Iron-Fisted General Looms Large Again," *New York Times*, January 10, 1996, p. 4A; "Arzú Greeted by Strikes and Protests," *Central America Report* (Guatemala City), January 19, 1996, p. 3.

43. Jonas, *Of Centaurs and Doves*; US Department of State, *Background Notes: Guatemala*, pp. 10–11; J. Mark Ruhl, "Curbing Central America's Militaries," *Journal of Democracy*, 15, No. 3 (July 2004), pp. 137–151.

44. See Table 1.1 and Table 2.2. See also US Department of State, *Background Notes: Guatemala*, pp. 5–8; Jonas, *Of Centaurs and Doves*; "Uncertain Future: Social Watch Evaluates Guatemala," *Cerigua Weekly Briefs*, June 4, 1998; "President Accused of 'Killing the Media,'" *Central America Report*, March 26, 1998, p. 1; Celina Zubieta, "Victims of Death Squads or Gang Warfare?" *InterPress Service* (Peace Net), March 31, 1998; Mike Lanchin, "Death Squad Claims Responsibility for Bishop's Death," *National Catholic Reporter*, May 22, 1998, p. 2; Francisco Mauricio Martínez, "Progress towards Peace Evaluated," *La Prensa Libre*, www.prensalibre.com, December 28, 1998.

45. "CEH Pressured to Denounce Genocide," *Central America Report*, May 21, 1998, p. 5; Lanchin, "Death Squad Claims," p. 12.

46. The three military officers received sentences of 30 years and Father Orantes, who had been Gerardi's cook, received a 20-year sentence for assisting in the crime.

47. Another closely watched trial was that of Colonel Juan Valencia Osorio for the murder of anthropologist Myrna Mack in 1990. Convicted by the trial court in 2002, his conviction was overturned on appeal but in January 2004 reinstated by the Guatemalan Supreme Court—the first conviction of a ranking officer for rights abuses.

48. CEH, *Guatemala, Memoria del silencio*, Ch. 2, Section 82.

49. See Victoria Sanford, *Buried Secrets: Truth and Human Rights in Guatemala* (New York: Palgrave Macmillan, 2003) for a complete discussion of this issue.

50. CEH, *Memoria*, Ch. 2, Section 86.

51. CEH, *Memoria*, Ch. 1, Section 13.

52. Charles Babington, "Clinton: Support for Guatemala Was Wrong," *Washington Post*, March 11, 1999.

53. The PAN won 37 seats.

54. The Berger administration planned to continue the payments to ex-PAC members, but the payments were deemed unconstitutional by the Constitutional Court in 2004; Latin American Database, "PAC holds Guatemala's Feet to Fire; They Want Their Money," *NotiCen*, July 1, 2004.

55. Ruhl, "Curbing Central America's Militaries," p. 144; see pp. 144–146.

56. In early 2004 Guatemala's Constitutional Court stripped ex-president Portillo and his vice president Francisco Reyes López of their immunity from prosecution, enjoyed as members of the Central American Parliament. Portillo fled to Mexico, whereas Reyes López was arrested on corruption charges. See "Accused in Corruption Case, Ex-President Leaves Country," *Miami Herald*, February 20, 2004; "Guatemala Former Vice President Arrested for Graft," Reuters, July 28, 2004.

57. According to the DEA, cocaine seizures fell from 9.2 and 10.05 metric tons in 1998 and 1999 to 1.4, 4.1, and 2.8 metric tons in subsequent years. US Drug Enforcement Administration, *Drug Intelligence Brief, Country Brief: Guatemala*, www.dea.gov/pubs/intel/03002/03002.htm, April 2003.

58. URNG candidate Rodrigo Asturias won less than 3 percent of the vote.

59. "Guatemalan President Apologizes for Civil War," *U.N. Wire*, February 27, 2004, www.unwire.org/UNWire/20040227/449_13525.asp.

60. Latin American Database, "Guatemala: Government Backs Away from Truth Commission Recommendations," *NotiCen*, April 15, 1999.

61. Frank Jack Daniel, "Guatemala Calls in Troops to Fight Crime Wave," *Reuters*, July 26, 2004.

62. Jo Tuckman, "Land Where Women Are Killers' Prey," *The Observer*, June 6, 2004, www.guardian.co.uk/gender/story/0%2C11812%2C1232430%2C00.html; and Marion Lloyd, "Guatemala Activists Seek Justice As Women Die," *Boston Globe*, June 14, 2004, www.boston.com/news/world/latinamerica/articles/2004/06/14/guatemala_activists_seek_justice_as_women_die/?rss_id=Boston.com+/+News.

63. United Nations Economic and Social Council, "Integration of the Human Rights of Women and the Gender Perspective: Preliminary Note on the Mission to El Salvador and Guatemala," submitted by Special Rapporteur on Violence Against Women, Yakin Erturk, United Nations document number E/CN.4/2004/66/Add.2.

64. Washington Office on Latin America (WOLA), *The Captive State: Organized Crime and Human Rights in Latin America* (Washington, DC: WOLA, October 2007).

65. WOLA, *Transnational Youth Gangs in Central America, Mexico and the United States* (Washington, DC: WOLA, 2007); United Nations Development Program Guatemala, *Informe estadístico de la violencia en Guatemala* (Guatemala: Programa de Seguridad Cuidadana y Prevención de la Violencia del PNUD Guatemala, December 2007), www.pnud.org.gt/data/publicacion/Informe%20Estad%C3%ADstico%20de%20la%20Violencia%20en%20Guatemala%20final.pdf.

66. James Mckinley, Jr., "In Guatemala, Officers' Killings Echo Dirty War," *New York Times*, March 5, 2007; "Congressman's Murder: Rogue Death Squads Run Amok," *Central America Report*, March 9, 2009.

67. WOLA, *The Captive State: Organized Crime and Human Rights in Latin America*, pp. 7–8.

68. Eduardo D'Aubuisson was the son of ARENA founder and death-squad leader Roberto D'Aubuisson.

69. "Fiscal guatemalteco acusa a Silva Pereira de asesinato de diputados," *El Faro*, February 23, 2009, www.elfaro.net/secciones/Noticias/20090223/noticias4_20090223.asp.

70. United Nations, *Promotion and Protection of all Human Rights, Civil, Political, Economic, Social and Cultural Rights, Including the Right to Development,* Report of the Special Rapporteur on extrajudicial, summary or arbitrary executions, Philip Alston, Addendum, Follow-up to Country Recommendations-Guatemala (May 2009), www2.ohchr.org/english/bodies/hrcouncil/docs/11session/A.HRC.11.2.Add.7.pdf.

71. The CICIG was actually the second attempt to create an international body to investigate impunity for criminal behavior by public officials. The first was ruled unconstitutional in 2004.

72. International Commission Against Impunity in Guatemala (CICIG), "One Year Later," September 2008, http://huwu.org/Depts/dpa/docs/CICIG1reportEn. pdf.

73. Bob Van Voris and Patricia Hurtado, "Ex-Guatemala President Portillo Enters Not Guilty Plea," *Bloomberg News*, May 28, 2013, www.bloomberg.com/news/2013–05–28/ex-guatemalan-president-portillo-enters-not-guilty-plea.html.

74. Marc Lacey, "Drug Gangs Use Violence to Sway Guatemala Vote," *New York Times*, August 4, 2007; Luis Solano, "Political Violence Takes a New Twist," *Central America Report*, October 19, 2007.

75. Manuel Roig-Franzia, "Choosing a Future from Tainted Pasts," *New York Times*, November 4, 2007.

76. Robert Lummack, "Growing Bloodshed Rocks Guatemala," *NACLA*, December 15, 2008.

77. "Report Highlights Widespread Societal Violence," *Central America Report*, March 6, 2009.

78. Ginger Thompson, "Guatemala Bleeds in Vise of Gangs and Vengeance," *New York Times*, January 1, 2006.

79. Louise Reynolds, "Congress Approves Law Against Femicide," *Central America Report*, April 18, 2008.

80. Accessed at www2.ohchr.org/english/bodies/hrcouncil/docs/11session/A. HRC.11.2.Add.7.pdf.

81. Anne-Marie O'Connor, "The Emerging Secrets of Guatemala's Disappeared," *The Washington Post*, April 11, 2009.

82. Anne-Marie O'Connor, "Payments and Apologies for Victims of Guatemala's Civil War," *The Washington Post*, May 6, 2009.

83. Marc Lacey, "Guatemalan Leaders Under Pall in Lawyer's Killing," *New York Times*, May 22, 2009; "Rosenberg Case Divides Political Spectrum," *Central America Report*, May 29, 2009.

84. "Killing of Prominent Lawyer: A Plot to Oust Alvaro Colom?" *Central America Report*, May 15, 2009; "The Rosenberg Case: A State Orchestrated Murder or a Coup Plot?" *Central America Report*, May 22, 2009.

85. David Grann, "A Murder Foretold," *The New Yorker*, April 4, 2011, www. newyorker.com/reporting/2011/04/04/110404fa_fact_grann.

86. Louisa Reynolds, "The Woman Who Reduced Impunity of Guatemala," *InterPress Service*, November 5, 2013, www.ipsnews.net/2013/11/the-woman-who-reduced-impunity-in-guatemala/.

87. See, for example, BBC News, "Guatemala Dos Erres Massacre Soldier Given 6,060 Years," March 13, 2012, www.bbc.co.uk/news/world-latin-america-17349774, accessed December 4, 2012.

88. On the origins and transformation of organized crime in Guatemala, see Julie Lopez, "Guatemala's Crossroads: The Democratization of Violence and Second Chances," *Woodrow Wilson International Center for Scholars*, Working Paper Series of Organized Crime in Central America, December 2010, www.wilsoncenter.org/sites/default/files/Lopez.Guatemala.pdf.

89. Hannah Stone, "Guatemala Imposes State of Siege in Wake of Massacre," May 17, 2011, www.insightcrime.org/news-analysis/guatemala-imposes-state-of-siege-in-wake-of-massacre.

90. James Bargent, "US Report Shows Zetas Corruption of Guatemala's Special Forces," November 8, 2013, www.insightcrime.org/news-briefs/us-report-shows-zetas-corruption-of-guatemalas-special-forces.

91. Latin American Database, "Hardly a Dent in Guatemalan Poverty," *NotiCen*, October 4, 2007.

92. Unlike Salvadorans and Nicaraguans, Guatemalans are ineligible for temporary protected status under US immigration law and thus immediately deportable if apprehended, making their income stream to Guatemala very vulnerable.

93. World Bank Group, *Indicators*, https://data.worldbank.org/indicator/, accessed May 23 2019; authors calculations.

94. Latin American Database, "Guatemala's Congress Ratifies, and the Masses Reject, CAFTA," *NotiCen*, March 17, 2005.

95. Xuan-Trang Ho, "Return to the Bad Old Days? Guatemala and CAFTA," *Counterpunch*, March 31, 2005, www.counterpunch.org/ho03312005.html, accessed June 11, 2009.

96. Mike Allison, "Most Guatemalans Unhappy with Options in This Weekend's Presidential Election," *Christian Science Monitor*, September 9, 2011.

97. Louisa Reynolds, "Otto Pérez Molina Leads the Polls ahead of Guatemala's Presidential Election," *NotiCen*, September 1, 2011, https://ladb.unm.edu/noticen/2011/09/01–078289.

98. Chris Arsenault, "Narco Elite vs Oligarchy: Guatemala Votes," *Al Jazeera*, September 11, 2011, www.aljazeera.com/indepth/features/2011/09/2011911184355644496.html.

99. "Registro de ciudadanos niega inscripción a Torres, por fraude de ley," *Prensa Libre*, June 30, 2011, www.prensalibre.com/decision_libre_-_actualidad/RC-niega-inscripcion-Torres-fraude_0_508749142.html.

100. Damien Cave, "Desperate Guatemalans Embrace an 'Iron Fist,'" *The New York Times*, September 9, 2011, www.nytimes.com/2011/09/10/world/americas/10guatemala.html?pagewanted=1&_r=2&ref=Americas.

101. He was acquitted of all charges.

102. Mike Allison, "Guatemala: Ríos Montt Genocide Trial Ends in Historic Verdict," *Al Jazeera*, May 15, 2013, www.aljazeera.com/indepth/opinion/2013/05/201351591259267287.html.

103. "Guatemala Ríos Montt Genocide Trial to Resume in 2015," *BBC News*, November 6, 2013, www.bbc.co.uk/news/world-latin-america-24833642.

104. Mica Rosenberg and Mike McDonald, "New Guatemala Leader Faces Questions About Past," *Reuters*, November 10, 2011, www.reuters.com/article/2011/11/10/us-guatemala-perez-idUSTRE7A93OP20111110.

105. On the 2013 increase in homicides, see Eylssa Pachico, "Explaining the Jump in Guatemala's Murder Rate," May 9, 2012, www.insightcrime.org/news-analysis/explaining-the-jump-in-guatemala-murder-rate.

106. Geoffery Ramsey, "Guatemala on Course for 10 Percent Drop in Femicides," October 30, 2012, www.insightcrime.org/news-briefs/femicides-guatemala-10-drop.

107. "Aprobación de gestión presidencial de Otto Pérez baja 20 por ciento," *El Periodico*, May 23, 2013, http://elperiodico.com.gt/es/20130523/pais/228683/.

108. Louisa Reynolds, "Administration of Guatemalan President Otto Pérez Molina Scores Badly in Recent Poll," *Noticen*, August 2, 2013.

109. Anna-Claire Bevan, "Guatemala: The Worst Place in the World to be a Trade Unionist," August 26, 2013, www.ticotimes.net/More-news/News-Briefs/Guatemala-The-worst-place-in-the-world-to-be-a-trade-unionist_Monday-August–26–2013.

110. Louisa Reynolds, "Guatemalan Army Colonel, Eight Soldiers Will Stand Trial for Totonicapán Massacre," *NotiCen*, February 14, 2013, https://ladb.unm.edu/noticen/2013/02/14–078895.

111. Estimates for indigenous population in Guatemala vary. The UNDP estimated it 66 percent in 2003: United Nations Development Program, *Human Development Report 2004: Cultural Liberty in Today's Diverse World* (New York: United Nations Development Program, 2004), http://hdr.undp.org/en/media/hdr04._complete.pdf. Another places the indigenous at 40 percent: Central Intelligence Agency, "Guatemala: People," *The World Factbook*, www.cia.gov/library/publications/the-world-factbook/geos/GT.html, accessed June 19, 2009. The Latin American Public Opinion Project Americas Barometer survey for 2012 asked Guatemalans to classify themselves by ethnic group: 42 percent of adults identified themselves as indigenous.

112. John A. Booth, "Global Forces and Regime Change: Guatemala in the Central American Context," *Journal of Interamerican Studies and World Affairs* 42, No. 4 (Winter 2000), pp. 59–87, Table 5.

113. "Education System Accused of Racism," *Central America Report*, January 5, 2007.

114. John A. Booth and Patricia Bayer Richard, *Political Culture and Public Opinion in Latin America*, (Washington, DC: Congressional Quarterly Press, 2014), Chapter 7.

115. Michael Lohmuller, "Guatemala's Government Corruptions Scandals Explained," *InSight Crime*, June 21, 2016, www.insightcrime.org/news/analysis/guatemala-s-government-corruption-scandals-explained/.

116. CICIG, "Financiamiento de la política en Guatemala," July 15, 2015, www.cicig.org/uploads/documents/2015/informe_financiamiento_politicagt.pdf.

117. "Guatemala Congress to Weigh Lifting Morales' Immunity," *Al Jazeera*, September 4, 2017, www.aljazeera.com/news/2017/09/guatemala-request-lift-morales-immunity-proceed-170904215031343.html.

118. Miguel Barrientos, Glenda Sánchez, and Natiana Gándara, "Partido FCN-Nación ocultó al TSE Q15 millones," *Prensa Libre*, April 15, 2018, www.prensalibre.com/guatemala/justicia/cicig-revela-caso-corrupcion-mp-financiamiento-electoral-ilicito-fcn-nacion-evento–2/.

119. Sofia Menchú, "Guatemala Not Renewing Mandate of U.N. Anti-Corruption Body," *Reuters*, August 31, 2018, www.reuters.com/article/us-guatemala-corruption/guatemala-not-renewing-mandate-of-u-n-anti-corruption-body-idUSKCN1LG2KC.

120. Adam Isacson, "The Army's Role in the Anti-CICIG Backlash is a Setback for Guatemala's Civil-Military Relations," *Washington Office on Latin America*, September 24, 2018, www.wola.org/analysis/guatemala-army-cicig-backlash/.

121. Lauren Carasik, "Guatemala's 'Slow-Motion Coup' Rolls Onward," *Foreign Policy*, January 26, 2019, https://foreignpolicy.com/2019/01/26/guatemalas-slow-motion-coup-rolls-onward/.

122. Mary Beth Sheridan, "How U.S. Apathy Helped Kill A Pioneering Anti-Corruption Campaign in Guatemala," *The Washington Post*, June 15, 2019.

123. CICIG, 11th Annual Work Report of CICIG, November 12, 2018, www.cicig.org/press-release-2018/11th-annual-work-report-of-cicig/?lang=en.

124. International Crisis Group, "Saving Guatemala's Fight Against Crime and Impunity." October 24, 2018, www.crisisgroup.org/latin-america-caribbean/central-america/guatemala/70-saving-guatemalas-fight-against-crime-and-impunity.

125. CICIG, "Opinion Poll Shows That 72% of Guatemalans Support CICIG's Work," April 5, 2019, www.cicig.org/citizen-support/opinion-poll-shows-that-72-of-guatemalan-people-support-cicigs-work/?lang=en.

126. Jo-Marie Burt and Paulo Estrada, "Court Finds Guatemalan Army Committed Genocide, but Acquits Military Intelligence Chief," *International Justice Monitor*, September 28, 2018, www.ijmonitor.org/2018/09/court-finds-guatemalan-army-committed-genocide-but-acquits-military-intelligence-chief/.

127. John Vidal, "How Guatemala is Sliding into Chaos in the Fight for Land and Water," *The Guardian*, August 19, 2018, www.theguardian.com/world/2018/aug/19/guatemala-fight-for-land-water-defenders-lmining-loging-eviction.

128. Jonathan Blitzer, "How Climate Change is Fueling the U.S. Border Crisis," *The New Yorker*, April 3, 2019, www.newyorker.com/news/dispatch/how-climate-change-is-fuelling-the-us-border-crisis; World Food Program, *Food Security and Emigration: Why People Flee and the Impact on Family Members left Behind in El Salvador, Guatemala, and Honduras*, August 2017, https://docs.wfp.org/api/documents/WFP-.0000022124/download/?_ga=2.175857894.550599162.1568487626-979225673.1568487626.

129. "At Least 62 Women Killed Every Month in Guatemala: Report," *Telesur*, November 3, 2017, www.telesurenglish.net/news/At-Least-62-Women-Killed-Every-Month-in-Guatemala-Report-20171103-0028.html.

130. Héctor Ruiz, "No Justice for Guatemalan Women: An Update Twenty Years After Guatemala's First Violence Against Women Law," *Hastings Women's Law Journal* 29, 1 (2018), pp. 101–124.

131. Sofia Menchú, "Guatemalan Presidential Candidate Arrested in Miami in Drug-Trafficking Plot," *Reuters*, April 17, 2019, www.reuters.com/article/us-guatemala-politics/guatemalan-presidential-candidate-arrested-in-miami-in-drug-trafficking-plot-idUSKCN1RU007.

132. Ana Lucía Ola, "La mitad de los encuestados nunca votaría por Sandra Torres," *Prensa Libre*, April 4, 2019, www.prensalibre.com/tribuna/plus/la-mitad-de-los-encuestados-nunca-votaria-por-sandra-torres/.

RECOMMENDED READINGS AND RESOURCES

Adams, Richard N. 1970. *Crucifixion by Power: Essays on Guatemalan National Social Structure, 1944–1966.* Austin, TX: University of Texas Press.

Anderson, Thomas P. 1982. *Politics in Central America: Guatemala, El Salvador, Honduras, and Nicaragua.* New York: Praeger.

Burrell, Jennifer. 2013. *Maya After War: Conflict, Power and Politics in Guatemala.* Austin, TX: University of Texas Press.

Carliner, David, Joseph Eldridge, Margaret Roggensack, and Bonnie Teneriello. 1988. *Political Transition and the Rule of Law in Guatemala.* Washington, DC: International Human Rights Law Group, Washington Office on Latin America.

Chase-Dunn, Christopher, Susanne Jonas, and Nelson Amaro. 2001. *Globalization on the Ground: Postbellum Guatemalan Democracy and Development*. Lanham, MD: Rowman and Littlefield.

Garrard-Burnett, Virginia. 2011. *Terror in the Land of the Holy Spirit: Guatemala under General Efraín Ríos Montt 1982–1983*. New York: Oxford University Press.

Gleijeses, Piero. 1991. *Shattered Hope: The Guatemalan Revolution and the United States, 1944–1954*. Princeton, NJ: Princeton University Press.

Goldman, Francisco. 2007. *The Art of Political Murder*. New York: Grove Press.

González, Pablo. 2013. "Guatemala." In Diego Sánchez-Ancochea and Salvador Martí I Puig, eds. *Handbook of Central American Governance*. London: Routledge, pp. 400–419.

Grandin, Greg. 2000. *The Blood of Guatemala: A History of Race and Nation*. Durham, NC: Duke University Press.

Historical Clarification Commission. 1999. *Guatemala: Memory of Silence*. Guatemala City: Historical Clarification Commission. http://shr.aaas.org/guatemala/ceh/report/english/toc.html.

Immerman, Richard H. 1982. *The CIA in Guatemala: The Foreign Policy of Intervention*. Austin, TX: University of Texas Press.

Jonas, Susanne. 1991. *The Battle for Guatemala: Rebels, Death Squads, and US Power*. Boulder, CO: Westview Press.

Jonas, Susanne. 2000. *Of Centaurs and Doves: Guatemala's Peace Process*. Boulder, CO: Westview Press.

Little, Walter E., and Timothy J. Smith, eds. 2009. *Mayas in Postwar Guatemala: Harvest of Violence Revisited*. Tuscaloosa, AL: University of Alabama Press.

McAllister, Carlota, and Diane Nelson, eds. 2013. *War by Other Means: Aftermath in Post-Genocide Guatemala*. Durham, NC: Duke University Press.

Menchú, Rigoberta. 1984. *I, Rigoberta Menchú: An Indian Woman in Guatemala*. London: Verso.

Nelson, Diane M. 2009. *Reckoning: The Ends of War in Guatemala*. Durham, NC: Duke University Press.

Sanford, Victoria. 2003. *Buried Secrets: Truth and Human Rights in Guatemala*. New York: Palgrave Macmillan.

Schirmer, Jennifer. 1999. *The Guatemalan Military Project: A Violence Called Democracy*. Philadelphia, PA: University of Pennsylvania Press.

Schlesinger, Stephen, and Stephen Kinzer. 2005. *Bitter Fruit: The Story of the American Coup in Guatemala*. Cambridge, MA: David Rockefeller Center for Latin American Studies.

Short, Nicola. 2007. *The International Politics of Post-Conflict Reconstruction in Guatemala*. New York: Palgrave Macmillan.

Stanley, William. 2013. *Enabling Peace in Guatemala: The Story of MINUGUA.* Boulder, CO: Lynne Rienner.

Stoll, David. 1999. *Rigoberta Menchú and the Story of All Poor Guatemalans.* Boulder, CO: Westview Press.

Weld, Kristen. 2014. *Paper Cadavers: The Archives of Dictatorship in Guatemala.* Durham, NC: Duke University Press.

8

HONDURAS

HONDURAS EXPERIENCED THE CENTRAL AMERICAN COMMON
Market growth boom and the resulting turmoil of the 1980s and 1990s. Governed by the armed forces well into the 1980s, it shared many similarities to
pre-insurrection El Salvador, Guatemala, and Nicaragua. Honduras nevertheless mostly escaped the violent upheavals of its authoritarian neighbors by
adopting a strategy similar to Costa Rica's. The government embraced policies that somewhat mitigated eroding popular living standards and avoided
or ameliorated brutal political repression. Subsequently external pressures
brought its economic policy under neoliberal rules as elite groups sympathetic
to these pressures rose to political prominence. In June 2009, after nearly
three decades of civilian rule, a constitutional crisis and coup d'état derailed
Honduras' democratic regime. Despite a return to civilian rule, the coup left
lasting legacies on politics.

HISTORICAL BACKGROUND

Honduras is an unusual and paradoxical country. A geological quirk left its
soil without the rich volcanic material prevalent elsewhere in the isthmus.
Geographically isolated, with broken terrain and poor transportation facilities,

Honduras developed no exports in the nineteenth century and relied instead on subsistence production. Although ordinary Hondurans were poorer than their Nicaraguan, Salvadoran, or Guatemalan counterparts, Honduran history reveals little rebellion or unrest until the 1970s. Party and military elites—often under pressure from such foreign actors as the United States—and not the masses, have intermittently roiled Honduran political waters.

Several factors contributed to this relative stability in the face of mass poverty. Honduras never really developed so coherent or privileged an elite as its immediate neighbors. Of course, there have always been rich Hondurans, but their wealth remained regionally based. Unlike the rest of Central America, coffee became a significant export crop for Honduras only after World War II; it thus did not drive wealth redistribution or greatly shape social classes there. Foreigners, not Hondurans, developed commercial banana production in the early twentieth century. Located mainly along the sparsely populated northern coast, bananas displaced few peasants or indigenous communities. Indeed, though generally poor, land was nearly always plentiful. Poor peasants could usually find free or cheap land to farm. Land shortages arose only in the mid-twentieth century, when foreign markets led wealthier Hondurans to begin concentrating landownership.

These economic developments had other ramifications.[1] First, absent an angry, dispossessed rural working class, the army remained weak into the twentieth century. Landed and political elites regularly battled among themselves for control of government, causing chronic instability.[2] Second, banana production shaped labor relations differently than in neighboring nations. Because banana companies were foreign owned, Honduran governments felt little pressure to suppress their workers' wages, while rising pay increased basic consumption and helped Honduran entrepreneurs. Moreover, because banana production was less labor intensive than coffee, companies could absorb higher wages. Banana companies made wage concessions more easily in Honduras than in other countries or other crops. Thus, although labor unions only became legal in 1954, they had operated informally for decades. Honduras eventually developed a larger and politically more potent organized workforce than neighboring countries.

In another contrast with its neighbors, the Liberal–Conservative debate began later in Honduras. In the nineteenth century, a succession of non-ideological caudillos succeeded each other by force. Party development began under President Marco Aurelio Soto (1876 to 1883). True to Liberalism of the era, Soto began modernizing, built a service infrastructure and state apparatus, and attracted foreign investors. By the twentieth century the Honduran Liberal

Party (Partido Liberal de Honduras, PLH) had consolidated and dominated politics until the 1930s. The conservative National Party (Partido Nacional, PN) appeared in 1923, and first captured power when the PLH split in the 1932 election. National Party caudillo Tiburcio Carías Andino was elected in 1932 and remained president until 1949, giving Honduras its longest period of political stability.

Following Carías' retirement, Liberal–National conflict intensified. The Liberal Party's electoral strength recovered as the labor movement grew in the 1950s. PN efforts to deny the Liberals power prompted the army in 1956 to seize power to end the dispute. When the military relinquished power a year later, PLH candidate Ramón Villeda Morales swept the 1957 election. Villeda's government signed the Central American Common Market (CACM) accords and passed several modernizing social policies, including social security, labor, and agrarian reform laws. Despite such progressive legislation, Honduras remained the poorest country in Central America.

From the mid-twentieth century onward, Honduras' problems and patterns grew more like those elsewhere in Central America. Land hunger intensified during this period as larger-scale landholders appropriated peasant-occupied lands to increase commodity production for export. Further, population growth increased due to improved public health conditions and practices developed during World War II. Rapidly increasing demand for land in the 1950s and 1960s led to greater tension between classes and to growing peasant mobilization.

During this era Honduras militarized its political system. With the advent of the Cold War, labor unrest in the banana plantations was labeled "Communist agitation." Seeking to contain "communism," the United States "concluded several agreements to train and equip the loosely organized armed forces of Honduras. From the early 1950s through 1979 more than 1,000 Honduran personnel received US training."[3] Although during this period there was virtually no guerrilla opposition in Honduras, US training emphasized counterinsurgency and "national security." Between 1973 and 1980 US aid (especially military) to Honduras rose sharply (see Table A.3).

Increasing factionalism and conflict within and between the Liberal and National parties left power and leadership vacuums. This and the military's growing strength drew the armed forces deeper into politics. Even though civilian caudillos had run the country for the first half of the twentieth century, for four decades after the 1956 coup the military ruled the nation directly or powerfully influenced civilian rulers from just offstage. The Honduran military behaved somewhat better, although not well, than its counterparts in neighboring states until the 1980s. It served more as an arbiter between other political groups than as an agent of a ruling class. It tolerated labor, peasant, and political party organizations, and allowed Catholic clergy to carry the "social gospel" to the poor and to build grassroots organizations. After the birth of the Alliance for Progress and CACM, it encouraged discussion of basic socioeconomic reforms, some promoted by military governments.

In 1963 Air Force Colonel Oswaldo López Arellano overthrew Villeda Morales to rule in coalition with National Party figures. The regime began repressing labor and peasant activism and strengthening the armed forces. Conservative economic policies, disadvantageous trade relations built into the CACM, and the brief 1969 war with El Salvador (over Salvadorans' land invasions in Honduran territory along the shared border) led to growing public unrest as López's presidency ended. The failure of the successor National–Liberal coalition to manage growing turmoil prompted López Arellano, now a wealthy general, to seize power again. This time, supported by labor, peasant groups, and other progressive elements, he implemented populist programs, including an agrarian reform.

Military participation in rule evolved in the late 1970s. Embarrassed by a bribery scandal, López in 1975 transferred power to Colonel Juan Alberto Melgar Castro, the first of two military dictators who abandoned López's populist reforms and curtailed civilian participation in national administration. Colonel Policarpo Paz García overthrew Melgar in 1978. Despite the rapid leadership changes, the military continued promoting economic development but de-emphasized social programs. Although the Melgar and Paz regimes largely ignored social justice, they remained relatively respectful of basic human rights and permitted certain civil and political liberties. There were no death squads, no systematized tortures, and no rash of disappearances. The press remained relatively free and boisterously critical of the military governments.

The Honduran armed forces proved themselves inept rulers. By 1980 corruption scandals, deepening economic difficulties, the Somoza regime's fall in Nicaragua, and pressures from spurned civilian politicians created powerful incentives for the military to abandon power. Although the Carter administration never severed military assistance to Honduras, it pressured General Paz to relinquish power. Ceding to these pressures, the military in 1980 called elections for an assembly to rewrite the constitution. In November 1981, presidential elections were held.

Liberal candidate Roberto Suazo Córdova won easily and became president in January 1982. The Liberal victory surprised many who believed the armed forces would interfere in favor of its erstwhile PN allies. Colonel Gustavo

Alvarez Martínez became head of the armed forces. The Reagan administration strongly pressured Honduras to assist US efforts against Nicaraguan and Salvadoran guerrillas operating in Honduras. A US military spokesman summarized the US appraisal of the situation: "Honduras is the keystone to our policy down there."[4] Suazo and Alvarez accepted US troops on continuous "maneuvers," the construction and expansion of military bases and facilities, and even US training of Salvadoran troops within Honduras. Honduras gave sanctuary and overt cooperation to the Contra army the United States was developing to attack Nicaragua's Sandinista government. Honduras thus became the active ally of the US military strategy for Nicaragua and El Salvador.[5] Wags described the country as an aircraft carrier—the "*USS Honduras.*" In exchange, Honduras received hundreds of millions of dollars in US assistance—especially military aid (see Table A.3).

This American military assistance rapidly expanded the Honduran military's size and power, which in turn enabled defense chief Alvarez to intimidate the civilian president and Congress. Relations with Nicaragua deteriorated. By 1984 Contra forces operating inside Honduras began to rival in number the Honduran military, and disrupted order along the Nicaraguan border. By 1983 Honduras developed death squads, including elements of public security forces and Nicaraguan exiles. Political disappearances and murders became more frequent. As repression grew and domestic political tensions rose, several small leftist guerrilla groups—a novelty in Honduras—appeared and began operations. Though weak and fragmented, the guerrilla movement grew in the 1980s. In the next section we will explain why such problems did not push Honduras into civil war as had occurred in Nicaragua, El Salvador, and Guatemala.

WEATHERING GLOBAL FORCES

In the late 1970s, Honduras seemed mired in Central America's past. Economic growth there was certainly the slowest of the five CACM nations. Much new investment went into agriculture. Honduras' agricultural sector remained the largest in the isthmus, having declined only modestly between 1960 and 1980 (see Table A.1). While manufacturing workforce and gross domestic product (GDP) share both expanded between 1960 and 1980, the Honduran industrial sector remained the region's smallest.

Despite lagging development, Honduras experienced sustained overall economic growth of almost 1.5 percent per year of GDP per capita between 1962 and 1971. A consumer rather than exporter of manufactured consumer goods, Honduras developed trade imbalances with other CACM nations, especially neighboring rival, El Salvador. These imbalances and resulting economic difficulties worsened after the 1969 war with El Salvador. Economic growth slowed to only 0.4 percent from 1972 through 1979. Overall, per capita GDP in Honduras (in 2010 constant dollars, see Table A.1) rose from $1,096 in 1960 to $1,590 by 1980. Thereafter, however, the economy stagnated—per capita GDP declined slightly to $1,561 in 1990 and to $1,620 in 2000.

Income

Our theory about rebellion in Central America argues that severe declines in real working-class wages and living conditions play an important role in mobilizing labor, political, and protest organization and activity. Because many wage earners in Central America live on incomes that provide them little or no margin of safety, a drop in their real earnings (wages corrected for inflation) can catastrophically affect their ability to survive. Rapidly eroding life chances can provide a powerful motive to join political or labor groups seeking to redress such problems.

Honduran wage workers lost ground relative to other income earners in the mid-1970s, but then recovered much of their purchasing power by 1978–1979. Wages fluctuated somewhat but experienced no sustained declines like those occurring in Guatemala, El Salvador, and Nicaragua at the same time. Honduran working-class wages fell in 1974 and 1975, recovered in 1976, fell again in 1977, and then rose to above 1973 levels again in 1978 and 1979. Real working-class wages in Honduras declined again in 1981, recovered in 1982, but then declined every year afterward into the early 1990s, sparking considerable labor unrest in the 1990s. In sum, working-class earnings and living standards declined in Honduras during the mid-1970s, but less severely than those in neighboring countries.[6]

Income Distribution

Another economic disparity in Honduras involved shifting income distribution among classes. One measure of changing income inequality patterns during the 1970s is the share of national income paid out as employee compensation. A decrease in overall employee compensation would indicate a relative shift of income away from salaried and wage-earning workers and toward investors and entrepreneurs. Between 1970 and 1975, the employee compensation share of Honduran income fluctuated somewhat, but overall tended to increase. Honduran employee compensation improved markedly in the early 1970s.[7] Overall, it appears that wages and salaries in Honduras continued to rise until the early 1980s.

In summary, Honduras during the 1970s and 1980s presented a clear contrast to Nicaragua, El Salvador, and Guatemala in both relative and absolute income trends. Hondurans' wages fluctuated but tended to recover within a year or two after declines. As we have shown, however, in the other three countries during this period, real and relative income for working-class citizens suffered sustained and severe declines.

Wealth

Honduras also avoided the marked increases in wealth inequality observed in Nicaragua, El Salvador, and Guatemala during the 1970s. Although Honduras was a member of the CACM and experienced the rapid energy-driven consumer price increases of the mid-1970s, this affected wealth distribution in Honduras (and Costa Rica) less than in the rest of the isthmus.

The least industrialized nation in the CACM, Honduras underwent less socioeconomic structural transformation in the first two decades of the Common Market. During the 1970s its income inequality changes were smaller and slower than in Guatemala, El Salvador, and Nicaragua.[8] As noted above, working-class wages tended to recover from inflation in the late 1970s, and income distribution did not sharply disfavor wage and salary earners. Honduran governments vigorously encouraged export agriculture in the 1960s and 1970s, and colonizable agricultural land continued to be available for peasants until the late 1970s. Both factors helped to prevent a rapid growth of rural unemployment. Peasant organization and mobilization during the 1960s and 1970s led the government to implement an ambitious agrarian reform program.[9] From 1975 to 1979 it distributed some 171,480 hectares to roughly 10 percent of Honduran landless and land-poor campesino families.[10] The reform distributed about one-fourth of its goal and was criticized as insufficient, but nevertheless constituted a major transfer of wealth toward campesinos. After 1980 peasant organizations, facilitated by the 1970s reform legislation, invaded much additional land in an informal or quasi-legal redistribution program.[11] Efforts by the government of Rafael Leonidas Callejas to curtail land transfers in 1991 provoked violent clashes between peasants and the government. The government quickly restored the program.

Popular Mobilization

In Honduras,[12] popular movements increased during the 1960s and 1970s.[13] The already large union movement expanded. The greatest growth involved peasant wage workers and landless peasants as several federations organized land occupation movements. The Catholic Church promoted some rural mobilization in the 1960s but retreated from it in the 1970s. The Liberal Party remained out of power during military rule from 1963 through 1981. The National Party collaborated with the first López Arellano regime in the 1960s but was frozen out afterward. Two small centrist parties appeared during the 1970s—the Christian Democratic Party of Honduras (Partido Demócrata Cristiano de Honduras, PDCH) and the Innovation and Unity Party (Partido de Inovación y Unidad, PINU). When elections resumed in 1979, however, neither PINU nor the Christian Democrats took many votes from the Liberal or National parties.

Private-sector organizations also multiplied and exerted more policy demands upon the state during the 1960s and 1970s. Although its relative underdevelopment had heretofore left Honduras without a unified bourgeoisie or dominant upper-class sector, economic elites became more politically active in politics in the 1980s. Robinson argues that, spurred by the United States Agency for International Development (USAID) and a decade of heavy US presence in the country, bourgeois groups linked to the emergent transnational economy began to influence the main national parties and the military. In the process, "clusters came together, penetrated, and largely captured both [Liberal and National] parties by the 1990s, but without the coherence" between business and political organizations of El Salvador or Guatemala.[14]

Several small leftist guerrilla groups appeared in Honduras during the 1970s and early 1980s (see Table A.4).[15] In 1960 a pro-Castro splinter from the Honduran Communist Party (Partido Comunista de Honduras, PCH) formed the guerrilla Morazán Front for the Liberation of Honduras (Frente Morazanista para la Liberación de Honduras, FMLH), sporadically active in the 1960s and 1970s. In 1978, the PCH spun off more dissidents, who formed the Popular Movement for Liberation (Movimiento Popular de Liberación, MPL), known as the Chichoneros. The MPL's most spectacular action was the taking hostage of 80 San Pedro Sula business leaders in 1982. The Lorenzo Zelaya Popular Revolutionary Forces (Fuerzas Populares Revolucionarias "Lorenzo Zelaya," FPR), founded by a pro-Chinese faction of the PCH, appeared in 1981 and staged various urban attacks. The Revolutionary Party of Central American Workers of Honduras (Partido Revolucionario de Trabajadores Centroamericanos de Honduras, PRTCH), the Honduran branch of a regional revolutionary group, appeared in 1977. In 1983 these guerrilla groups formed a National Directorate of Unity (Dirección Nacional de Unidad, DNU) to coordinate their revolutionary activities. Despite the rise of armed opposition, insurgent violence in Honduras remained low compared to neighboring nations.

One new guerrilla group, the Army of Patriotic Resistance (Ejército de Resistencia Patriótica, ERP-27), appeared in 1989. However, reconciliation efforts and a government amnesty program for political prisoners and exiles brought the release of more than 300 persons from jail in 1991. Several exiled guerrilla leaders returned from exile, and four Chichoneros abandoned armed struggle to form a new political party.[16]

Overall, then, the levels of popular and elite mobilization increased in Honduras during the 1970s and continued into the 1980s. Indeed, protest and violence against regime policies developed to include incipient guerrilla struggle by various leftist factions, but revolutionary efforts eventually stalled.

Government Response to Popular Mobilization

Honduras' military authoritarian regime of the 1960s and 1970s included elements with developmentalist and populist orientations. It sought to control fewer aspects of national life than the military regimes of El Salvador and Guatemala. General Oswaldo López Arellano's second government (1971–1975) accommodated burgeoning campesino mobilization and developed a populist agrarian reform program. A conservative military faction of led by Colonel Juan Alberto Melgar Castro deposed López for the second time in 1975. Labor repression then increased, marked by a massacre of 14 protesters at Los Horcones in 1975. Yet in an astounding departure from a likely outcome in neighboring nations, the government employed civilian courts to prosecute, convict, and imprison army officers implicated in the massacre.[17]

Violent regime repression of opponents (illegal detentions, disappearances, and murders) rose significantly in Honduras in the early 1980s, but remained moderate by Central American standards.[18] For instance in 1982, a year when Guatemala and El Salvador each had over 10,000 political disappearances and murders, Honduran human rights activists reported a total of only 40 assassinations and "permanent disappearances."[19] Political parties, unions, peasant leagues, and a free press operated openly and likely helped restrain human rights violations by vigorously denouncing government abuses of authority.[20]

Honduran security forces took numerous measures to curtail armed opposition, including stepped up counterinsurgency and forming rural militias called Civil Defense Committees (Comités de Defensa Civil, CDCs) in several areas. Rightist elements, apparently involving Nicaraguan exiles with military complicity, began to kidnap, torture, and murder suspected subversives and government critics in the early 1980s. By 1982, "extra-judicial action [had become] standard operating procedure for the Honduran armed forces in dealing with violent opposition. The methods include[d] disappearances, torture, use of clandestine detention centers, and . . . execution of prisoners."[21]

A distinctive feature of the Honduran case was how the armed forces returned formal power to civilians. Despite the growing strength of the military during the 1960s and 1970s, the Honduran armed forces never controlled the state apparatus so much as did the militaries of neighboring countries. Moreover, as the punishment of military officials for the Los Horcones massacre revealed, the Honduran military never fully evaded accountability to the law and constitution.

In a clear indication of how leaders' choices can avert catastrophe, the military authoritarian regime headed by General Policarpo Paz García voluntarily undertook political reform rather than choosing the massive repression practiced by Honduras' three immediate neighbors. Popular unrest had grown in the mid- and late 1970s, and its repression by the army and military-dominated police, the Public Security Forces (Fuerzas de Seguridad Pública, FUSEP) brought increasing pressure for reforms from the Carter administration. The military government's corruption became increasingly embarrassing, and the military's traditional National Party allies became disaffected from the regime. Finally, developments elsewhere in the isthmus in 1979 troubled the military leadership: Nicaraguan revolutionaries ousted the repressive despot Somoza, destroyed his National Guard, and began a revolution. Popular mobilization and growing violence in El Salvador portended similar problems there.

Rather than risk civil war, revolution, or destruction of the military, General Paz and the senior military officers' council decided to return power to civilians, ushering in a brief reformist military regime. General Paz called a constituent assembly election in 1980. The Liberal Party, long mistrusted by the armed forces, captured a near majority of the assembly. With Paz holding the provisional presidency to maintain military ascendancy, the Liberals drafted a new constitution, which set elections for a civilian government for 1981.

Confounding many expectations, the military permitted both traditional parties (including the Liberals' social democratic left wing) and the new PINU and Christian Democrats to participate in a generally free 1981 election. And again contrary to expectations, the military did not rig the 1981 elections on behalf of its long-time PN allies. Liberal candidate Roberto Suazo Córdova won a clear majority in a clean election, and General Paz relinquished the presidency in early 1982.[22]

So began the transitional civilian democratic regime in Honduras, engineered by the armed forces to prevent civil war and institutional damage to the military itself. For over a decade the military, resisting civilian control and feared by civilian politicians, would remain powerful in the new regime. Military power largely eluded civilian control until the mid-1990s, thus blocking full transition to formal democracy. Indeed, during the 1980s, the Honduran military's power and resources increased somewhat, despite having relinquished the formal power. US military assistance to Honduras during the 1980s ballooned from $3.1 million per year for 1977–1980 to $41.5 million annually for 1981–1984 and eventually hit $57.7 million per year for 1985–1988 (see Table A.3). The United States provided this military aid (and copious economic assistance) in exchange for the Honduran military's help in containing revolutionary movements in neighboring El Salvador and Nicaragua. In trade for effectively ceding control over much of southern Honduras to the Nicaraguan Contras, cooperating with the US-advised Salvadoran armed forces against the FMLN, and allowing heavy US military presence, the Honduran military waxed rich in US-built bases, equipment, and training. Human rights abuses by the army and FUSEP increased during the mid-1980s.

The prospects for civilian rule appeared to dim in the early 1980s. US military assistance expanded the power of the armed forces and permitted General Alvarez to overshadow and intimidate the civilian president and congress.[23] Opposition violence and repression rose under Alvarez's leadership. But in 1984 senior armed forces officers unexpectedly ousted Alvarez from his command for deepening Honduras' role in the US–Nicaragua imbroglio, allowing Salvadoran troops to train in Honduras, and disregarding the military's tradition of corporate decision making. In another poor augury for democratic prospects, in 1985 President Suazo himself precipitated a constitutional crisis by seeking to retain power. The armed forces, labor movement, and United States, however, applied counter-pressure and blocked Suazo's efforts to amend the constitution.

The military's adherence to constitutional rule helped save the trappings of civilian democracy in 1985, but the civilian transition remained wobbly. Liberal nominee José Azcona Hoyos won the 1986 presidential election. Azcona represented a new modernization-oriented agro-industrial and manufacturing faction of the Liberal Party, the Popular Liberal Alliance (Alianza Liberal Popular, ALIPO). Protests over Honduran support for the US-backed Contras grew during Azcona's term. Other obstacles to effective civilian rule were the military's power, elites' uneven commitment to democracy, and continued military and FUSEP human rights violations. Economic troubles accumulated: expected cutbacks in US assistance, a sharp contraction in GDP per capita (1989–1991), rapid consumer price increases, and declining real wages.[24]

The Liberals lost a clean election in 1990, and President Azcona transferred power to Rafael Callejas of the National Party. Callejas led a reformist faction of urban businessmen and economic technocrats and represented the neoliberal wing of the National Party. The economy had suffered considerable capital flight, but had been buoyed up by heavy US aid. This had allowed Honduras to avoid the full neoliberal structural adjustment regime imposed elsewhere in the region. But when the end of the Sandinista revolution in Nicaragua foretold reduced US aid to Honduras, pressures mounted to embrace neoliberalism. Callejas agreed in March 1990 to the first of three major structural adjustment programs negotiated with the International Monetary Fund (IMF), USAID, and other international lenders. Two more such packages promoting economic austerity, free markets, non-traditional exports, tourism, free trade zones, and assembly plant manufacturing (*maquiladoras*) would follow for two successive administrations.[25]

The peaceful transfer of power from incumbents to a victorious opponent in 1990 was a step toward democracy, but prospects for full transition to a civilian democratic regime remained in question. After the Contras left Honduras in 1990 and 1991 following the 1990 Nicaraguan election and peace accord, anger about their abuses faded. A 1991 amnesty law allowed members of armed insurgent groups to abandon violent opposition; some eventually rejoined legal politics. This effectively dismantled the tiny revolutionary left. The Callejas administration's embrace of neoliberal reforms attracted new foreign capital and dozens of assembly plants. Callejas' austerity measures and devaluation of the lempira, however, spawned hardship, labor unrest, and popular protest. Security forces often harshly repressed such mobilization, but the military and government continued exercising relative restraint. In late 1990 the military high command chose a new commander who curtailed and punished abusive military behavior and reconciled with guerrilla, peasant, and labor leaders.[26]

The opposition Liberals won Honduras' 1993 presidential and congressional elections. President Carlos Roberto Reina, a human rights leader, campaigned on a promise to curtail military power and corruption. Again, an incumbent government relinquished power to a victorious opponent, another step toward democratic consolidation. However, the military commander, General Luis Discua, immediately showed displeasure with Reina's proposals to end the draft, cut the military budget, and transfer the police agency FUSEP to civilian control. Despite military objections, Reina and Congress passed and ratified the constitutional reform transferring FUSEP. In a sad irony, as in El Salvador and Guatemala, the police reform contributed to a crime wave. Congress also revised the military draft law, allowed the draft to lapse, and reduced force levels. Civilians curtailing military power signaled a critical political-game rule change and effectively reduced the military's political role. We believe these changes marked 1996 as the year of Honduras' transition to civilian democracy.[27]

Reina's successor, Liberal Carlos Roberto Flores Facussé, took office in January 1998 after yet another clean election (see Tables A.6 and A.7). Despite campaign rhetoric critical of IMF policies, Flores' economic plan proposed to strengthen the neoliberal model through the expansion of the *maquila* industry, increased tourism, and expanding the agro-export sector.

The neoliberal reforms exacerbated decades of such environmental degradation through deforestation and soil erosion. Many Hondurans migrated to the cities seeking work.[28] In October 1998 Hurricane Mitch struck; it killed 11,000 people and left two million homeless.[29] Many victims were recent migrants who had settled in crowded neighborhoods that washed away from the hillsides surrounding Tegucigalpa. The hurricane caused nearly $4 billion in losses and devastated the agricultural and shrimping sectors. The World Bank's Heavily Indebted Poor Countries (HIPC) initiative allowed Honduras to suspend payments on its $4.4 billion debt, which had consumed 46 percent of its annual budget. Creditors canceled $900 million of Honduras' debt.

This restructuring of Honduras' debt and the extension of additional loans required the Flores administration to pursue structural adjustment policies while pledging to reduce poverty. After selling the airports, political resistance stymied Flores' effort to privatize telecommunications. The IMF froze Honduras' loans and demanded an acceleration of privatization and poverty reduction programs. These requisites contradicted each other because neoliberalism reduced state resources just as poverty and unemployment escalated after Hurricane Mitch.

Oddly, the hurricane disaster helped consolidate civilian rule in Honduras. The military responded incompetently to Mitch, undermining its stature. Moreover, the military's power eroded as President Flores' constitutional amendments subjected the armed forces to direct control of the civilian president for the first time since 1957. Some army officers plotted to overthrow Flores, but the coup never occurred. Flores then demonstrated his authority over a divided military when in 1999 he dismissed its uniformed commander and most of the army's top echelon. The military refrained from interfering in governance for the next decade.[30]

Human rights and indigenous groups denounced the human rights abuses of the 1980s and 1990s with increasing energy. The government began investigating past military rights abuses. A civilian judge seized military intelligence and counterintelligence services' files that implicated numerous high-ranking officers. Evidence of serious ongoing human rights problems nevertheless persisted, including renewed activity by death squads and the assassination in February 1998 of Ernesto Sandoval, a leader of the country's most prominent human rights organization, the Human Rights Committee of Honduras (Comité de Derechos Humanos de Honduras, CODEH).[31]

Two Liberal administrations managed the early transition to democracy but failed to address mounting socioeconomic problems. After controversy regarding his eligibility, the National Party's Ricardo Maduro, a former central bank president, won the 2001 presidential elections. The PN won only 61 of 128 seats, the first time in two decades the governing party did not control Congress. The PN later allied with the Christian Democrats to provide the party a 64 to 55 vote edge over the Liberals. Maduro pledged to crack down on crime and corruption. He reduced government perks by selling off hundreds of government luxury vehicles. Initial attempts to reduce the number of elected officials failed, as did his effort to limit immunity for crimes and human rights abuses.

Crime

Honduras' prolonged crime wave became a major theme of the 2001 elections. In 2000, the murder rates in Tegucigalpa and San Pedro Sula were 51 and 95 per 100,000, respectively, making Honduras one of the most violent countries in the hemisphere.[32] Much of the crime originated with the gangs that had proliferated since 1990. Gang violence hurt business as firms and factories relocated to avoid a rash of kidnappings of foreign businessmen. An estimated 500 gangs, including the infamous Mara Salvatrucha and Mara 18, had more than 100,000 members. President Maduro, whose son died in a bungled kidnapping, continued his predecessors' militarization of the police force. Operación Guerra Contra la Delincuencia, sent 10,000 officers into the streets and appointed a military official as the head of security.[33] Maduro's hard line spawned retaliation. In December 2004 gang members attacked a public bus in San Pedro Sula, killing 28 people and proclaiming the act was to protest a possible reimposition of the death penalty.

Extrajudicial killings of youth, primarily street children presumed to be involved in gangs, constituted another part of the crime wave. Between 1998 and 2002 more than 1,500 youths were murdered, mostly young males.[34] Human rights organizations labeled some of these deaths "social cleansing" by state and private security forces. A United Nations report denounced Honduras' widespread failure to investigate and prosecute the crimes.[35] Mounting criticism eventually forced the government to commission its own study, which implicated police and security forces in a small percentage of the killings. Evidence of social cleansing by security forces also extended into prisons, which held many suspected gang members. Several prison massacres, including fires at prisons in El Porvenir (2003) and San Pedro Sula (2004), killed over 100 gang members and suggested deliberate official efforts to exterminate mara inmates.[36]

President Maduro's economic plan intensified Honduran social unrest. After contentious negotiations with the IMF, the technocratic administration pledged to reinvigorate the privatization of government-owned firms. Yet meeting international demands to shrink government while reducing poverty and violent crime proved self-contradictory as the latter required more, not less, government. Maduro tried to trim the number of elected officials and bureaucrats, but resisted a general reduction in public employment. Civil society increasingly protested privatizing state-owned utilities and government services. In 2003 25,000 people protested proposed civil-service reforms and privatization of water systems.[37]

CONTEMPORARY HONDURAN POLITICS

Economy

Between 1984 and 2017, Honduras' GDP per capita (2010 dollars) roughly tripled, with a plateau for a few years following the devastating Hurricane Mitch of 1998, but afterward little slowing down even during the world recession of 2008. This growth arose mainly from growing remittances from Hondurans living abroad, which grew from 1.3 percent of GDP in 1990 to 18.7 percent in 2005. Remittances then shrank to 15.8 percent in 2012, but recovered to 18.8 percent by 2017. In contrast, for the same period foreign direct investment was erratic. Agriculture remained dominant in GDP and employment share, but manufacturing grew throughout (see Table A.1). Debt relief under the HIPC agreement eased Honduras' external burden, and during the first decade after 2000 Venezuela provided considerable aid. Writ large, other than inflation economic troubles might not have generated much political turmoil. However, consumer price rises averaging above 5 percent a year after 2000 consumed much of the nominal economic growth.

Politics

In 2005 crime, not the economy, again dominated the election campaign. National Party nominee Porfirio Lobo Sosa ran on a pro-business, tough-on-crime platform and vowed to reinstate capital punishment. Liberal candidate

José Manuel Zelaya Rosales also pledged to reduce crime but to institute gang rehabilitation programs as well. His "citizen power" campaign promised decentralization and transparency, while emphasizing his "rural roots."[38] With turnout at only 46 percent, Zelaya won by less than 4 percent, the closest margin in Honduran history. The Liberals captured 62 of 128 seats in Congress (see Tables A.6 and A.7). Finally, electoral law reform allowed Hondurans for the first time to vote directly for candidates instead of party lists.

As many as 200 protests marked President Zelaya's first year in office.[39] His media relations were so fraught that he mandated that all private television stations broadcast 20 hours of content on his administration's programs.[40] This drew comparisons to populist Venezuelan president Hugo Chávez, to whom Zelaya grew increasingly close. Zelaya's policies offended broadly across the ideological spectrum, alienating him from various social sectors—the opposition, his own party, the media, and the United States. His embrace of neoliberal projects and populist rhetoric led him to support ratification of the US-backed Central American Free Trade Agreement (2006), but also to membership in the Bolivarian Alternative for the Americas (Alternativa Bolivariana para las Américas, ALBA) in 2008 which sought to counter US-backed policies.[41] His unpopular ties to Venezuela's Chávez and Bolivia's president Evo Morales eroded his own Liberal Party's support.

Good economic news came when the IMF's HIPC initiative relieved Honduras of $3.7 billion in foreign debt in 2008. Although the macro economy grew steadily during Zelaya's term, borrowing abroad continued and rising inflation undercut the benefits for many.[42] The cost of the basic food basket increased 18 percent during Zelaya's first two years in office, which convinced him to freeze basic goods prices in late 2007.[43] In 2008 Honduras joined the PetroCaribe Agreement, by which Venezuela in 2005 supplied oil to members on preferential terms. In December 2008, President Zelaya further alienated business elites and his own party by raising the minimum wage 60 percent. By this time remittances from abroad exceeded 20 percent of GDP.

Rising prices reinforced the country's growing dependence on remittances while out-migration rose steeply in the early 2000s. Hurricane Mitch had deepened reliance on the cash Hondurans abroad sent home to their families. One report estimated remittances reduced the number of families living in extreme poverty by 20.5 percent.[44] During 2006 to 2008, however, a national economic crunch hit Hondurans' pocketbooks as inflation roughly doubled to over 11 percent while remittances shrank by more than 21 percent.[45] Political strains began to show.

Ongoing high violent crime rates eroded the public's security during President Zelaya's term. Ineffective *mano dura* policies were supplemented by short-term joint operations among police, armed forces, and private security forces. This privatization of security deepened human rights problems because private security firms were unregulated and more numerous than the police.[46] Though gang violence declined somewhat, international organized crime increased.[47] By 2009 Honduras' Caribbean coast had become a major transshipment location for drug trafficking, and organized enterprise had infiltrated the government itself. One former security minister estimated that 30 percent of police officers had organized crime ties and over half of Police Investigative Unit officers belonged to Mexican narcotics cartels.[48]

These problems provided the backdrop for a presidential primary election in November 2008. Once again, the candidates pledged to address poverty and crime. The National Party renominated Porfirio Lobo Sosa. The Liberal Party's former vice president Elvin Ernesto Santos Ordóñez defeated Roberto Micheletti, the National Congress' president and a fierce opponent of President Zelaya.[49] Presidential elections were to be held in November 2009, but a plethora of problems arose among national elites that would undermine democracy before then.

The Coup and Its Aftermath

In March 2009 President Zelaya called for a June 2009 national referendum on whether to convene a constituent assembly to rewrite and update the Honduran constitution. Opponents viewed the proposed poll as similar to measures in Venezuela and Bolivia—ultimately intended to extend the president's tenure in office—despite Zelaya's never mentioning presidential term limits.[50] Congress then challenged the constitutionality of the referendum and promptly banned referenda within the six months prior to an election.[51] An administrative court ruled the poll illegal and enjoined it. The Supreme Court sustained that ruling and declared the proposed June referendum illegal.[52] The head of the Honduran armed forces, General Romeo Vásquez, then refused the military's assistance to conduct it, and the Supreme Electoral Tribunal ordered confiscation of all ballot boxes.

Hemmed in by these laws and rulings, President Zelaya summarily fired armed forces head, General Vásquez, which the constitution clearly allowed (Article 280). The Supreme Court quickly overturned Vásquez's dismissal and ordered his reinstatement.[53] Zelaya and several hundred supporters then escalated the conflict by retrieving the election materials from a military storage facility. The Honduran constitution made no provision for the impeachment and removal of a president, even for illegal or unconstitutional actions. Honduras was thus virtually assured a political crisis should a president act unconstitutionally or illegally, as the Honduran Supreme Court had just ruled.

The crisis became a coup d'état on June 28, 2009, when the armed forces overstepped the Supreme Court order to arrest President Zelaya—instead detaining him at home at night and summarily expelling him to Costa Rica. The expulsion of the president manifestly violated the constitution's Article 102 that "no Honduran may be expatriated."[54] The armed forces then presented the National Congress with a forged "resignation" letter purportedly from Zelaya. Congress then embraced the coup, accepted the fake resignation, and immediately swore in its presiding officer, Roberto Micheletti, Zelaya's rival and critic, as president.

The de facto government suspended civil liberties and initiated a curfew after protests demanded Zelaya's return and reinstatement. Others demonstrated in support of the coup. The international community condemned the coup and the Organization of American States (OAS) suspended Honduras after the de facto government refused to reinstate President Zelaya. The European Union withheld more than $90 million in aid, and the United States ultimately cut $33 million in military and economic assistance. Costa Rican president and Nobel peace laureate Oscar Arias agreed to mediate the conflict in hopes of securing Zelaya's return to office to complete his term. Micheletti and others maintained their action was constitutional. They instead cast it as saving democracy from a would-be demagogue. The de facto government quickly hired Washington lobbyists and public relations specialists to press its cause with US policymakers and the international media. Though some policymakers proclaimed the crisis ended, negotiations in San José, Costa Rica, failed to forge a solution to restore constitutional government.[55] One important outcome of the San José Accords, however, was the establishment of a Truth and Reconciliation Commission charged with investigating the coup. Micheletti and his backers in the business elite and government resisted all efforts to reinstate Zelaya for the final months of his term.[56] The period following the coup was characterized by extensive violation of civil liberties, random curfews, and the brutal police suppression of protestors and political opponents. Journalists, human rights workers, and civil society organizations reported harassment and threats; some were killed. The Interamerican Commission on Human Rights (IACHR) found evidence of serious human rights violations and widespread impunity following the coup.[57]

In this environment Hondurans went to the polls in November 2009 to elect their next president from among five candidates.[58] The PN's Porfirio

Lobo won with 56.6 percent of the vote. The PLH's Elvin Santos Lozano, Zelaya's vice president, won 38 percent, and three minor parties won about 2 percent each. The PN also won the most seats in Congress, 71, followed by the PLH with 45. The 12 remaining seats were divided among three small parties. Not surprisingly, voter turnout remained low at 49 percent. Following his inauguration in January 2010, Lobo faced significant challenges: Honduras was deeply divided, many countries refused to recognize its government, the economy was weak, and criminals had used the power vacuum to escalate their activities.

Venezuelan president Hugo Chávez and Colombian president Juan Manuel Santos sponsored talks in April 2011 in hopes of resolving the crisis. In May, Lobo and Zelaya signed the Cartagena Accords which allowed Manuel Zelaya to return to Honduras without fear of prosecution and provided recognition of his new National Popular Resistance Front (Frente Nacional de Resistencia Popular, FRNP). The agreement affirmed citizens' right to modify the constitution through referendum, the chief issue precipitating the coup. The OAS readmitted Honduras in June 2011. The following month the Truth and Reconciliation Commission released its report on the coup. It called Zelaya's removal from office a coup, and Micheletti's interim government illegal. That said, the Commission also blamed the crisis on Zelaya's push for a referendum, thus attributing responsibility for the coup among all parties. The Commission also blamed the military for at least a dozen deaths following the coup. Despite this, no one has been charged in relation to the coup and it appears unlikely that anyone ever will face charges. A Supreme Court ruling against the prosecution of six generals charged with exiling Zelaya ended the only attempt at prosecuting the coup makers.

As if Honduras' political crisis were insufficient woe, drug traffickers, organized crime, and transnational gangs increased their activity. The 2012 homicide rate was 86 per 100,000, the highest in the world. Most murders were never investigated, nor murderers brought to trial. The Lobo administration approached growing crime by increasingly militarizing Honduras' thoroughly corrupt police forces. President Lobo in May 2012 appointed a controversial new police chief, Juan Carlos Bonilla, allegedly involved with a police death squad. Bonilla, also known as *El Tigre* (The Tiger), initiated a widespread purge of the notoriously corrupt police force shortly after assuming his post.[59] The United States attempted to skirt human rights concerns and maintain assistance by directing police aid to officers below Bonilla. Bonilla, however, claimed no officers functioned beyond his control.[60]

In December 2012, Congress precipitated another major constitutional crisis by voting to remove four of five Supreme Court justices in response to rulings on recent legislation. The first rejected the Special Police Purge Law, passed in May 2012, which required officers to undergo tests, including a polygraph examination, to establish their suitability for their jobs. The constitutional division of the Supreme Court rejected the law on several counts, including the absence of an appeal process. An angry President Lobo accused the justices of taking the side of criminals, which provoked a response from the Court, emphasizing judicial independence. Days later, Congress removed the four justices. An outcry ensued over the removal, which many characterized as illegal.[61] The justices appealed their firings to a special court, which voted 13–2 against their appeal.[62]

By early 2013, Honduras seemed on the brink of disaster. The budget deficit and foreign debt made it impossible to even pay bills.[63] Teachers were on strike because they had received no pay in months; pay to soldiers and other government workers was sporadic, and even surveillance cameras were shut off.[64] Remittances, which declined after the 2009 coup, had yet to return to their pre-coup levels, thus further hamstringing the economy. With a compliant Supreme Court, Congress passed several new laws, including an amended police purification law and a law establishing Employment and Economic Development Zones (ZEDE), commonly referred to as the Model Cities law, also struck down by the previous Court.[65] Congress also enacted a law empowering itself to remove any elected official, and to bar citizens from challenging the constitutionality of laws.[66] Overwhelmed by crime and stymied by the slow pace of police purges, the Honduran government increasingly relied on the military to address the country's devastating security problem.[67] In 2013, Congress authorized the creation of a new security organization, the Military and Public Order Police (Policía Militar y de Orden Público, PMOP) and combined the ministries of defense and security. This action raised further concerns about the militarization of Honduran society.[68]

Hondurans returned to the polls in 2013 to elect a new government. The campaign was contentious—new political forces appeared and violence flared. Following the 2009 coup political parties proliferated and the Liberals split. Eight parties competed, including the traditionally dominant National and Liberal parties. Juan Orlando Hernández, the president of Congress, won a hotly contested primary to become the PN nominee. The Liberals selected Mauricio Villeda, son of former president Ramón Villeda Morales (1957–1963). Two new parties broadened the field. Vying for disgruntled Liberals' votes was former president Manuel Zelaya's new party, Liberty and Refoundation (Partido

Libertad y Refundación, LIBRE), which nominated Zelaya's wife, Xiomara Castro. The Anti-Corruption Party (Partido Anti-Corrupción, PAC) selected sportscaster Salvador Nasralla as its candidate. Security and corruption themes again dominated the campaign. Hernández emphasized his support for military participation in fighting crime. Castro pushed an assembly to reform the constitution, the very issue that had caused her husband's ouster. Indeed, the 2009 coup haunted the campaign trail, as Zelaya was routinely present in Castro's campaign. Assassinations of numerous party activists and candidates, most from LIBRE including two killed on election-day morning, marred the electoral process.

While the European Union and OAS election observer missions deemed the elections relatively "free and fair," other observers reported interference by immigration officials and difficulty entering polling stations.[69] The military maintained a notable presence throughout the country. At one point the military surrounded Radio Globo's station, which had been attacked following the coup. Observers noted various irregularities throughout the day, ranging from problems with voter lists to vote buying to errors in reporting vote counts to the Supreme Electoral Tribunal's (TSE) offices. Both frontrunners Hernández and Castro rushed to declare a winner and pronounce the elections clean, each claiming victory with only a quarter of the vote counted. Premature calls of congratulation from world leaders came in for Hernández days before the TSE announced official results. The subsequent reporting delays occasioned accusations of fraud. Castro and the LIBRE officially challenged the results. When the recount failed to change the outcome, LIBRE unsuccessfully demanded that the elections be annulled.[70]

Official results gave the National Party's Hernández 36.8 percent, followed by LIBRE's Castro with 28.8 percent. In congressional elections, the PN won 48 seats, followed by LIBRE's 37, and the Liberal Party's 27. The Anti-Corruption Party captured 13, and PINU, PUD, and the Christian Democrats took one apiece (see Table A.6 and A.7). While Castro's claims of fraud garnered the most attention, the election results told another very important story: the longstanding duopoly of the National and Liberal parties had fractured. LIBRE had shattered the old PLH and had emerged as a "second force" in Honduran politics.[71] With only 38 percent of the deputies in Congress, the National Party and its new president would need at least 18 votes of members of other parties to enact laws, and 39 from other parties to reach the required two-thirds majority to amend the constitution.[72] As in Costa Rica and Nicaragua, the ancient Liberal–Conservative (National) party duopoly was vanishing.

Corruption and the State

In 2015 news broke that government officials had participated in a kickback scheme that drained the Honduran Social Security Institute (IHSS) of more than $300 million. Some of the funds went to President Hernández's National Party and his 2013 election campaign. The scheme had deprived thousands of Hondurans of medicines and brought mass protests around the country. For months tens of thousands of protestors, called the *Indignados* (Indignants), marched weekly to demand Hernández's resignation. Civil society groups demanded creation of an anti-corruption agency like Guatemala's CICIG. In mid-September the government responded by agreeing to establish an OAS-supported Mission to Support the Fight Against Corruption and Impunity in Honduras (MACCIH). Unlike CICIG, MACCIH lacked independent investigative or prosecutorial powers, and was underfunded and hampered by government machinations to protect impunity.[73] Still, MACCIH promoted some legal reform and empowered the attorney general's office in high-profile cases. One such case still unfolding at this writing, dubbed "Pandora," implicated at least 176 politicians in an embezzlement scheme, influencing elections, and vote buying in Congress.[74] In August 2019 came a first anti-corruption conviction—former first lady Rosa Elena Bonilla de Lobo, for fraud and embezzlement.

But it would take more than MACCIH to root out Honduras' endemic corruption. Its scope and complexity are vast. Corruption and links to organized crime (particularly drug trafficking) permeate virtually all Honduran state institutions, from local government to police to high-ranking politicians, including the office of the president. A 2019 US Department of State report on persons implicated directly in or facilitating corruption named a former president and his wife, current cabinet members, former congressmen and women, the former vice president of the National Congress, mayors, a former Supreme Court president, and judges. Charges included fraud, illicit enrichment, embezzlement, money laundering for drug traffickers, drug trafficking, and arms trafficking.[75] Corruption in Honduras was, as Sarah Chayes described it, "the operating system."[76]

Corruption infected every institution in Honduras, including the police, known to engage in extrajudicial killings, drug trafficking, and organized crime.[77] Police and security forces play a vital role in sustaining the government's kleptocratic networks. A researcher described the police role:

> Its most visible manifestation is an inept and criminalized police force that a former security minister once called "air traffic control men" for drug flights coming into the country. Parts of this police force also work as

custodians and assassins for criminal groups; rob drugs and resell them to the underworld; and, for a price, they can attack client's rivals and disrupt criminal investigations.[78]

Between 2012 and 2016 there were three separate attempts to purge the Honduran police, yet corruption and death squads persisted. Indeed, the very police chief in charge of the 2012 purge effort was himself accused for forced disappearances and extrajudicial killings.[79] In 2016 leaked documents confirmed the existence of a police hit squad dedicated to intimidating law enforcement. Its targets included the anti-drug chief and the former head of the anti-narcotics commission, who had denounced police infiltration by criminal elements. Documents revealed a cover-up of the murders and the internal investigation files.[80] In response, the government created the Special Commission for the Purging and Reform of the National Police. Since 2016, some 5,000 members of the Honduran National Police have been removed from duty by the commission because of corruption and abuse, including dozens of high-ranking police officers, the National Police commissioner, and other commanders accused of ties to drug trafficking networks and organized crime. Most were permitted voluntary resignations.[81] In 2018, during the middle of the commission's work, José David Aguilar Morán was appointed police chief. Within days of his appointment, it was revealed that Aguilar Morán had personally facilitated the shipment of nearly a ton of cocaine while the director of national intelligence in 2013, yet he remained in his post at the time of this writing.[82]

Absent effective domestic mechanisms, the United States pursued drug traffickers under a 2012 extradition law. As of September 2019, US authorities had extradited 20 high-profile criminals, including drug lord Carlos "El Negro" Lobo. In 2017, former investment minister, Yani Rosenthal, was convicted for laundering money on behalf of the Los Cachiros drug trafficking organization.[83] In 2018, a US court convicted former director of the Honduran National Police, Carlos Alberto Valladares García, of conspiring to import cocaine into the US. In November 2018 following a multi-year investigation, US authorities arrested in Miami the president's brother and former congressman, Juan Antonio "Tony" Hernández, on drug trafficking and weapons charges. According to the US Drug Enforcement Agency (DEA), Hernández "bribed law enforcement officials for sensitive information to protect drug shipments and solicited large bribes from major drug traffickers."[84] In August 2019, President Hernández was accused of drug conspiracy by US prosecutors in documents related to his brother's upcoming trial.[85] Weeks later, a US federal court charged Hernández's cousin and former police officer, Mauricio Hernández Pineda, with conspiring to import cocaine and firearms into the United States. In October, Tony Hernandez was convicted of drug trafficking and related charges. During the trial, witnesses implicated the Honduran president in receiving drug money for his presidential campaigns.

Violence

Honduras' endemic corruption and impunity generated growing violence in the post-coup era. Gang violence remained a serious problem in some communities, but it became increasingly clear that organized crime and drug trafficking, sociopolitical violence, and interpersonal violence were also deeply problematic. Honduras' homicide rate declined from its peak in 2012, reaching 40 per 100,000 in 2018. Despite the impressive decline, this remained one of the world's highest homicide rates (four times the World Health Organization's standard for a homicide epidemic). Local homicide hot spots persisted—in San Pedro Sula in 2016 it was 107 per 100,000, nearly double the national average.

Honduras, like El Salvador, is one of the deadliest countries in the world for women. As had homicides, femicides dramatically increased following the 2009 coup. In 2016, there were 466 reported femicides, a rate of 10.2 per 100,000. For comparison, the 2016 femicide rate in Mexico, another country experiencing a femicide epidemic, was 4.6. Despite recent laws on femicide and domestic violence, there existed little political will to address the problem.[86] According to the Centro de Derechos de Mujeres (Women's Rights Center), of over 400 cases of femicide in 2016, Honduran officials investigated only 3 percent and only two cases led to convictions. Inter-partner violence is high, but least half of the women in Honduras are killed by gang or drug traffickers. Femicides in Honduras stand out for their brutality. According to the Violence Observatory at the National Autonomous University of Honduras, 41 percent of women and girls killed in 2017 showed signs of mutilation and disfigurement.[87]

Violence has grown against the LGBT community in recent years. In 2018, the IACHR reported 177 murders of LGBT people in the previous five years, producing 65 investigations and no convictions.[88] Honduras reportedly had the highest number of transgender murders per capita in the world, more than double the rate of the second highest country.[89]

Environmental activists became frequent targets of state and parastatal security as they challenged development projects. In 2017, Global Witness named Honduras as the most dangerous country in the world for environmental activists. More than 120 environmental rights activists had been killed since the 2009 coup.[90] In March 2016 indigenous and environmental activist Berta Cáceres was murdered. The 2015 Goldman Environmental Prize winner, a member of the Lenca community, had co-founded and coordinated the Council of Popular and Indigenous Organizations of Honduras (COPIHN). She had been protesting the Agua Zarca Dam project at the Gualcarque River at the time of her murder. In November 2018, a Honduran court convicted seven individuals of her murder, including two former military officers and employees of Desarrollos Energéticos SA, a private hydroelectric dam company. Cáceres' family and activist communities believed that the intellectual authors of her murder were still at large.[91]

Land rights defenders were also targeted. Residents of the Bajo Aguán Valley suffered decades of violence as they battled to regain land they claim was illegally transferred to agribusiness firms including Dinant, owned by Miguel Facussé, uncle of former president Carlos Flores Facussé and one of the country's wealthiest businessmen. Paramilitaries have killed 120 people in land disputes since the 2009 coup, many of them members of the Unified Peasant Movement (MUCA). The Garifuna population (Caribbean coastal people of Afro-indigenous descent) were also targeted and forcibly displaced, as tourism and development projects encroached upon their lands.[92]

The 2017 Elections

In 2015 the Constitutional court, packed with candidates selected by Hernández, ruled that constitution's prohibition of presidential re-election was unconstitutional and held that the president could seek re-election. This was highly controversial given the 2009 coup that had removed Manuel Zelaya from office. In the presidential race Hernández faced Salvador Nasralla from the Anti-Corruption Party (PAC) and Luiz Zelaya from the Liberal Party. Six other smaller parties ran candidates as well. Nasralla allied with the Liberty and Refoundation party (LIBRE), with former first lady Xiomara Castro as his running mate. Throughout the campaign, Nasralla shared considerable media time with former president Zelaya, the head of LIBRE and Castro's husband.

Voters anxiously awaited election results after the polls closed, but no preliminary results were released until early the next morning. With 57 percent of the polling stations accounted for, Nasralla led by 5 percentage points. Observers inside and outside Honduras concluded that the election had produced a historic upset. Late the following day, the TSE announced a multi-day delay in final results. That afternoon, a TSE magistrate reported that Nasralla's lead was irreversible. Liberal Party candidate Luis Zelaya, who polled third, conceded and congratulated Nasralla on his victory.

When the TSE resumed its vote count updates days later, Hernández had somehow taken the lead and the final count gave him the victory. The likely fraud spawned protests nationwide. International observer groups urged calm. More than 20 people died and at least 60 received injuries in weeks of post-election violence. The UN's Office of the High Commissioner for Human Rights (OHCHR) reported that government security forces used excessive and lethal force in dispersing the protests, including live ammunition against unarmed protestors.[93] Hernández decreed a state of emergency and issued a ten-day curfew on December 1. Under the curfew, many protestors participated in pot-banging protests (*cacerolazos*) from their homes.[94] According to the OHCHR, more than 1,300 were arrested for violating the curfew. Electoral observers from the OAS called for new elections, citing an "abundance of irregularities and errors."[95]

On December 17, the TSE declared Hernández the winner with 42.6 percent followed by Nasralla with 41.4 percent. While the OAS had called for new elections, the US Trump administration recognized and congratulated Hernández on his "victory." Hernández's National Party won 61 seats in Congress, followed by Libre (20), and the PL (26), with 11 others distributed among five smaller parties. Only one indigenous representative and no Afro-Hondurans won seats in Congress. Only 27 women were elected to Congress, down 4 percent from the previous session, and women won only 23 of 298 mayoral elections.

Hernández's second term was marked by corruption scandals, some detailed above. Months-long nationwide protests erupted again in May 2019, first over the proposed privatization of health services and then over revelations that Hernández was being investigated as a co-conspirator in his brothers case. The government responded with repression, again using live ammunition against protestors.[96] Corruption and political and criminal violence drove Hondurans to emigrate in record numbers. Apprehensions of Hondurans at the southern US border more than doubled between 2017 and 2019.[97]

CONCLUSIONS

During the 1970s Honduras at least partly ameliorated growing impoverishment of working-class victims of rapid economic change, while employing only moderate repression. We emphasize that the Honduran armed forces exercised only *comparative* restraint. Their 1,000 victims during the 1980s and 1990s paled in comparison to the combined toll of over 300,000 lives taken by the security forces of Somoza's Nicaragua, and by military regimes in El

Salvador and Guatemala during the 1970s and 1980s. Modest socioeconomic reforms, some restraint in repression, and accommodative political reforms saved Honduras from as much violence as its three neighbors, and kept it relatively politically stable. The military's transfer of nominal control of executive and legislative power to a constitutional regime in 1981 began a process political reform that eventually led to electoral democracy.

As in other Central American nations, Honduras adopted neoliberal economic policies by 2000. This undermined the state-led programs that had been critical to political stability. Neoliberalism thus restricted Honduras' ability to respond to economic strains. Despite economic growth maintained by remittances of a growing number of Hondurans abroad, inflation eroded living standards and crime proliferated, breeding insecurity in an already vulnerable population. "Iron fist" anti-crime policies failed, partly because they misunderstood the changing nature of crime. The street gang threat was increasingly displaced by organized crime related to drug trafficking, which infiltrated and undermined Honduras' fragile institutions.

Having avoided civil war, Honduras progressed toward formal democracy for two decades, but then backslid. Institutional and economic performance remained poor enough that in 2008 Hondurans reported the lowest satisfaction with their institutions, democracy, and economic performance in Central America. The 2009 coup that toppled Zelaya—the first post-Cold War coup in the region—demonstrated that strong anti-democratic tendencies remained among the country's elites. The breakdown of law and order that followed the coup brought more crime, poverty, and inequality. According to the World Bank, Honduras had become the most unequal country in Latin America and the sixth most unequal in the world since the coup.[98]

Honduran elite behavior during the coup of 2009 and beyond reflected poor commitment to democratic norms and constitutional rule. The coup weakened such critical institutions as the courts, electoral tribunal, and law enforcement. This kicked opened the door to public corruption at all levels, drug trafficking, and organized crime. By 2019, Honduras had become a civilian-autocratic regime and a kleptocratic "narco-state."

NOTES

1. See James A. Morris, "Honduras: The Burden of Survival in Central America," in Steve C. Ropp and James A. Morris, eds., *Central America: Crisis and Adaptation* (Albuquerque, NM: University of New Mexico Press, 1984), pp. 189–223; James A. Morris, *Honduras: Caudillo Politics and Military Rulers* (Boulder, CO: Westview Press,

1984); and Darío Euraque, *Reinterpreting the Banana Republic: Region and State in Honduras, 1870–1972* (Chapel Hill, NC: University of North Carolina Press, 1996).

2. From the end of the Central American Republic in 1839 through 1972, Honduras had 62 heads of state, 28 of them presidents, 34 interims (18 acting, 8 provisional, 2 juntas, 5 councils of ministers, and 2 military chiefs of state). Average tenure of presidents was four years, of interims of any sort 1.4 years. Wikipedia, "List of Presidents of Honduras," https://en.wikipedia.org/wiki/List_of_presidents_of_Honduras.

3. James A. Morris, "Honduras: A Unique Case," in Howard J. Wiarda and Harvey F. Kline, eds., *Latin American Politics and Development* (Boston, MA: Houghton Mifflin, 1979), p. 349.

4. As quoted in "Commentary: The Region," *Mesoamérica*, September 1982, p. 1.

5. Eva Gold, "Military Encirclement," in Thomas W. Walker, ed., *Reagan Versus the Sandinistas: The Undeclared War on Nicaragua* (Boulder, CO: Westview Press, 1987), pp. 39–56.

6. Booth and Walker, *Understanding Central America*, 3rd ed., Appendix, Table A.6; see also Victor Bulmer-Thomas, *The Political Economy of Central America since 1920* (New York: Cambridge University Press, 1987), Table 10.7, p. 219.

7. Booth and Walker, *Understanding Central America*, 3rd ed., Appendix, Table A.7.

8. Thomas P. Anderson, *Politics in Central America: Guatemala, El Salvador, Honduras, and Nicaragua* (New York: Praeger, 1982), pp. 109–147.

9. Discussion of Honduras drawn from Victor Meza, *Honduras: La evolución de la crisis* (Tegucigalpa: Editorial Universitaria, 1980); Victor Meza, *Historia del movimiento obrero hondureño* (Tegucigalpa: Editorial Guaymuras, 1980), pp. 123–167; Anderson, *Politics*, pp. 109–121; Mario Posas, *El movimiento campesino* (Tegucigalpa, Honduras: Editorial Guaymuras, 1981); James A. Morris, "Government and Politics," in James D. Rudolph, ed., *Honduras: A Country Study* (Washington, DC: American University Foreign Area Studies Series, US Government Printing Office, 1984), pp. 168–193; Rosa María Pochet Coronado, "El reformismo estatal y la iglesia en Honduras 1949–1982," *Estudios Sociales Centroamericanos* 33 (September–December 1982), pp. 155–188; and J. Mark Ruhl, "Agrarian Structure and Political Stability in Honduras," *Journal of Inter-American Studies and World Affairs* 26 (February 1984), pp. 33–68.

10. Castillo Rivas, "Modelos," pp. 199–201; Mario Posas, *El movimiento campesino hondureño*, pp. 34–42.

11. Author Booth's conversation with Lucas Aguilera, member of the executive committee, Union Nacional Campesina, Tegucigalpa, and members of the Unión Maraíta cooperative farm, Departamento Francisco Morazán, August 21, 1985.

12. Victor Meza, *Historia del movimiento obrero hondureño*, pp. 123–167, and Meza, *Honduras: La evolución*, pp. 14–41; Anderson, *Politics*, pp. 109–121; Posas, *El movimiento campesino*.

13. James A. Morris, "Government and Politics," in James D. Rudolph, ed., *Honduras: A Country Study*, 1984 pp. 168–193; Rosa María Pochet Coronado, "El reformismo estatal y la iglesia en Honduras 1949–1982," *Estudios Sociales Centroamericanos 33* (September–December 1982), pp. 155–188.

14. William I. Robinson, *Transnational Conflicts: Central America, Social Change, and Globalization* (London: Verso, 2003), p. 128.

15. Steve C. Ropp, "National Security," in Rudolph, James D., ed., *Honduras: A Country Study*, pp. 391–396.

16. "Honduras," *Mesoamérica*, April 1990, p. 9; "Honduras," *Mesoamérica*, February 1991, pp. 10–11; "Honduras," *Mesoamérica*, May 1991, p. 12; "Honduras," *Mesoamérica*, June 1991, p. 2; *Excelsior*, January 13, 1991, p. 2A.

17. Richard L. Millett, "Historical Setting," in Rudolph, James D., ed., *Honduras: A Country Study*, p. 47.

18. *Washington Report on the Hemisphere*, October 28, 1987, pp. 1, 60.

19. Ramón Custodio, "The Human Rights Crisis in Honduras," in Mark Rosenberg and Phillip Shepherd, eds., *Honduras Confronts Its Future* (Boulder, CO: Lynne Rienner Publishers, 1986), pp. 69–71.

20. US Department of State, *Country Reports on Human Rights*, p. 46; Morris, "Government and Politics," pp. 192–193, and James A. Morris, "Honduras: The Burden of Survival in Central America," in Steve C. Ropp and James A. Morris, eds., *Central America*, pp. 217–219; Charles W. Anderson, *Politics and Economic Change in Latin America: The Governing of Restless Nations* (New York: Van Nostrand Reinhold, 1967), pp. 116–132.

21. Americas Watch, *Review of the Department of State's Country Reports on Human Rights Practices for 1982: An Assessment* (New York, February 1983), p. 55. The discrepancy between this figure and the number of 40 cited earlier arises from different reporting agencies involved, which report on somewhat different phenomena. The two are likely roughly congruent.

22. James A. Morris, "Honduras: The Burden of Survival in Central America," in Steve C. Ropp and James A. Morris, *Central America*, pp. 201–204.

23. Donald E. Schulz and Deborah Sundloff Schulz, *The United States, Honduras, and the Crisis in Central America* (Boulder, CO: Westview Press, 1994).

24. Data from Booth and Walker, *Understanding Central America*, 3rd ed., Appendix, Tables A.1, A.4, A.5, and A.6. See also Mark Rosenberg, "Can Democracy Survive the Democrats? From Transition to Consolidation in Honduras," in John A. Booth and Mitchell A. Seligson, eds., *Elections and Democracy in Central America* (Chapel Hill, NC: University of North Carolina Press, 1989); Latin American Studies Association (LASA), *Extraordinary Opportunities . . . And New Risks: Final Report of the LASA Commission on Compliance with the Central American Peace Accord* (Pittsburgh, PA: LASA, 1988), pp. 20–26.

25. Robinson, *Transnational Conflicts*, p. 129.

26. "Honduras," *Mesoamérica*, April 1990, pp. 8–9; "Honduras," *Mesoamérica*, January 1991, pp. 9–10; "Honduras," *Mesoamérica*, February 1991, p. 10; "Honduras," *Mesoamérica*, May 1991, p. 12; "Honduras," *Mesoamérica*, June 1991, p. 2; "Honduras," *Mesoamérica*, September 1991, pp. 8–9; *Excelsior*, December 12, 1990, p. 2A; *Miami Herald*, December 15, 1990, p. 24A; and *Miami Herald*, December 2, 1990, p. 22A; Robinson, *Transnational Conflicts*, p. 129.

27. J. Mark Ruhl, "Honduras: Militarism and Democratization in Troubled Waters," paper presentation, 21st Congress of the Latin American Studies Association, Chicago, September 25, 1998.

28. Jeff Boyer and Aaron Pell, "Mitch in Honduras: A Disaster Waiting to Happen," *NACLA Report on the Americas*, September–October 1999, pp. 36–43.

29. Latin American Database, "Hurricane Mitch Recovery Moving Slowly After One Year," *NotiCen*, November 4, 1999.

30. J. Mark Ruhl, "Curbing Central America's Militaries," *Journal of Democracy* 15, No. 3 (July 2004), p. 143.

31. Edward Orlebar, "Honduran President Faces Battle with His Own Military," *Los Angeles Times*, December 18, 1993, p. 2A; "Demilitarization Runs into Problems," *Central America Report*, November 21, 1996, p. 1; "Transfer of Police from Military to Civil Power Ratified," *Central America Report*, January 10, 1997, p. 6; "Honduras," *Mesoamérica*, June 6, 1997, p. 4; Thelma Mejía, "Vice President Implicated in Disappearances," *Interpress Service/Spanish* (PeaceNet), January 23, 1998; "Military Files Confiscated," *Central America Report*, February 12, 1998, p. 3; "New Government Seeks to Broaden Support," *Central America Report*, January 29, 1998, p. 7; Thelma Mejía, "Extra-Judicial Executions on the Rise," *Interpress Service/Spanish* (PeaceNet), February 4, 1998; "Death Squads Assassinate Human Rights Leader," *Interpress Service/Spanish* (PeaceNet), February 11, 1998; Thelma Mejía, "The Army Wants You!" *InterPress Service/Spanish* (PeaceNet), January 21, 1997; "Honduran Death Squads Active Again, Report Says," *Houston Chronicle*, January 15, 1998, p. 19A.

32. Latin American Database, "Honduras: Security Minister Gautama Fonseca under Fire as Crime Rates Soar," *NotiCen*, June 14, 2001.

33. Ismael Moreno, S.J., "A New President and Cracks in the Two-Party Structure," *Envío* (January–February 2002), pp. 37–43.

34. Latin American Database, "Honduras: President Ricardo Maduro Promises Action on Killings of Children," *NotiCen*, October 10, 2002.

35. United Nations Report of the Special Rapporteur, *Civil and Political Rights, Including the Question of Disappearances and Summary Executions* (New York: United Nations Economic and Social Council Commission on Human Rights, 2003).

36. Tom Weiner, "Cover-Up Found in Honduras Prison Killings," *New York Times*, May 20, 2003; Freddy Cuevas, "Fire in Honduran Prison Kills 103: Anti-Gang Laws Blamed for Overcrowding in Old Facilities," *Washington Post*, May 18, 2004.

37. Ismael Moreno, S.J., "The March on Tegucigalpa: 'It's Our Water'," *Envío* 266 (September 2003), pp. 46–51.

38. Latin American Database, "Honduras Primaries Yield Polar Opposites for President in 2006," *NotiCen*, February 24, 2005.

39. "Rocky First Year for Zelaya," *Central American Report*, February 16, 2007.

40. Latin American Database, "Honduras' President Takes on Media Moguls for Access to the People," *NotiCen*, June 28, 2007.

41. Other ALBA members include Venezuela, Nicaragua, Bolivia, and Cuba.

42. To attract investment to Choluteca, devastated by Hurricane Mitch, the government, developers, and labor unions agreed to wages below the minimum for five to ten years to guarantee a profit for developers. See Pamela Constable, "Hondurans Ride Winds of Change Blown in by Mitch," *New York Times*, July 1, 2007.

43. Latin American Database, "Honduras Takes Action to Relieve Economic Pressure Points," *NotiCen*, November 29, 2007.

44. State of the Nation: Region Program, "Informe Estado De La Región," *Program State of the Nation, Costa Rica* (November 2008), p. 262. www.estadonacion.or.cr/estadoregion2008/regional2008/capitulosPDF/Cap06.pdf.

45. World Bank Group, *Indicators,* https://data.worldbank.org/indicator/BX.TRF.PWKR.DT.GD.ZS?locations=HN, accessed June 8, 2018.

46. Thelma Mejía, "Honduras: A Violent Death Every Two Hours," October 30, 2006, http://ipsnews.net/news.asp?idnews=35275; Thelma Mejía, "In Tegucigalpa, the Iron Fist Fails," *NACLA Report on the Americas* (July–August 2007), pp. 26–29.

47. Matthew Brooke, "President Zelaya Says Government Is Powerless to Stop Violence," *Central America Report*, February 29, 2008.

48. Ismael Moreno, "Insecurity, Criminality, Hidden Powers and Visible Roots," *Envío Digital*, 312 (July 2007), www.envio.org.ni/articulo/3607.

49. Santos had to resign in order to run for president. His chief party rival Micheletti tried to block him from the primaries by literally locking the legislature's doors. "Elvin Santos on the Rise," *Central America Report*, January 30, 2009.

50. This accusation was problematic because, despite possible favorable votes, the hypothesized assembly could not have proposed a new constitution until after Zelaya's term would have ended in January 2010. However, the Honduran constitution forbade revision of the term of the president, so that any proposal to extend the president's term would have violated the constitution.

51. "Sin condiciones para romper constitución," *La Prensa*, March 14, 2009, www.laprensahn.com/Pa%C3%ADs/Ediciones/2009/03/15/Noticias/Sin-

condiciones-para-romper-Constitucion; "Artículos Pétreos No Pueden Reformarse Ni Con Plebiscito Ni Referendo," *La Prensa*, May 26, 2009, www.laprensahn.com/Ediciones/2009/05/26/Noticias/Articulos-petreos-no-pueden-reformarse-ni-con-plebiscito-ni-referendo.

52. The Supreme Court documents related to Zelaya's removal were available online at the Honduran Supreme Court official Web site, www.poderjudicial.gob.hn/NR/rdonlyres/87E2BFFC-AF4D-44EA-BFC5-D93730D8D81C/2413/Expediente Judicial1.pdf, accessed August 17, 2009.

53. The constitutionality questions were complicated: Article 280 of the constitution allows the president to "appoint and remove" the head of the armed forces. The Supreme Court, however, later ruled that General Vásquez's removal was unconstitutional and reinstated him. A provision supporting Vásquez's restitution is Article 323, providing that no government civilian or military functionary is obliged to carry out an illegal order. Congress had just legislated against a referendum, and an administrative court and the Supreme Court had ruled that to have conducted it would be illegal. See *Constitución de 1982 con reformas hasta 2005*, accessed August 16, 2009, http://pdba.georgetown.edu/Constitutions/Honduras/hond05.html.

54. Ibid. The military also arrested and deported foreign minister Patricia Rodas; see Toni Solo, "Honduras: A Defining Moment: The West Discredited, ALBA Vindicated," *Scoop*, www.scoop.co.nz/stories/HL0907/S00079.htm, accessed July 7, 2009.

55. See also Geoff Thale, "Behind the Honduran Coup," *Foreign Policy in Focus*, July 1, 2009, www.fpif.org/fpiftxt/6225; Larry Birns, "Caudillismo in Action: Looking Back on Honduras' Plight," *Council on Hemispheric Affairs*, July 7, 2009, www.coha.org/2009/07/caudillismo-in-action-looking-back-on-honduras; Secretary of State Hillary Rodham Clinton, "Breakthrough in Honduras," *U.S. Department of State*, October 30, 2009, https://2009-2017.state.gov/secretary/20092013clinton/rm/2009a/10/131078.htm/.

56. Tyler Bridges, "Honduras' Interim Leader: Manuel Zelaya Must Face Charges," *Miami Herald*, August 18, 2009, www.miamiherald.com/news/americas/story/1190592.html.

57. Inter-American Commission on Human Rights, "Honduras: Human Rights and the Coup D'état", *Organization of American States, OEA/Ser.L/V/II. Doc. 55*, December 30, 2009.

58. Note that the Carter Center, European Union, and OAS canceled their 2009 Honduras observer missions.

59. "Vicepresidente del Congress, 40 por ciento de la policía está infiltrada por el crimen," *Proceso*, July 19, 2011, http://proceso.hn/2011/07/19/Termómetro/Vicepresidente.del.Congreso/40028.html; Frances Robles, "Honduras Becomes Murder Capital of the World," *Miami Herald*, January 23, 2012, www.miamiherald.

com/2012/01/23/2603338_p3/honduras-becomes-murder-capital.html; and Edward Fox, "Dynamics of Honduran Police Corruption Narrow Chance for Reform," *InsightCrime*, January 31, 2012, www.insightcrime.org/news-analysis/dynamics-of-honduran-police-corruption-narrow-chance-for-reform.

60. Miriam Wells, "We Will Support Honduran Police But Ignore Their Director: US," *InsightCrime*, March 29, 2013, www.insightcrime.org/news-briefs/support-honduran-police-but-ignore-director-us; and Miriam Wells, "Honduran Police Chief Interview Reveals US Dilemma," *InsightCrime*, November 5, 2013, www.insightcrime.org/news-briefs/honduras-police-chief-interview-reveals-us-aid-dilemma.

61. Chapter XII of the Honduran Constitution of 1982, Article 309, provides judges may be removed (by implication, by Congress which appoints them) only for due cause as specified in law; Constitution of Honduras, accessed December 1, 2013, www.constitutionnet.org/files/Honduras%20Constitution.pdf.

62. "Pleno especial rechaza recursos a favor de magistrados destituidos," *El Heraldo*, February 6, 2013, www.elheraldo.hn/Secciones-Principales/Pais/Pleno-rechaza-amparo-de-exmagistrados.

63. "Lobo dejará una economía desastrosa, según economistas," *La Prensa*, January 23, 2013, www.laprensa.hn/csp/mediapool/sites/LaPrensa/Honduras/Apertura/story.csp?cid=328201&sid=267&fid=98.

64. "Honduran Government in Chaos, Can't Pay Its Bills, Neglects Basic Services," *Washington Post*, January 24, 2013, www.washingtonpost.com/business/honduran-government-in-chaos-cant-pay-its-bills-neglects-basic-services/2013/01/24/1a5950de-6686-11e2-889b-f23c246aa446print.html.

65. The "Model Cities" law allowed creating private cities outside of the control of the Honduran Constitution, raising questions about sovereignty.

66. "Congreso de Honduras aprobó medida que permite destituir presidentes," *Telesur*, January 23, 2013, www.telesurtv.net/articulos/2013/01/23/congreso-de-honduras-aprobo-medida-que-permite-destituir-presidentes-4837.html.

67. "Congreso crea 1,000 nuevas plazas en FF AA," *El Heraldo*, June 11, 2013, www.elheraldo.hn/content/view/full/154713?utm_source=feedburner&utm_medium=feed&utm_campaign=Feed:+elheraldo_pais+(El+Heraldo+-+Pa%C3%ADs)&utm_content=Google+Reader.

68. Dana Frank, "In Honduras Military Takes over with US Blessing," *Miami Herald*, September 11, 2013, www.miamiherald.com/2013/09/10/3618867/in-honduras-military-takes-over.html.

69. European Union Election Observation Missions, "Honduras: Final Report General Elections, 2013," http://eeas.europa.eu/archives/eueom/missions/2013/honduras/pdf/final-report-eueom-honduras-2013_en.pdf, accessed June 9, 2019; Lauren Carasik and Azadeh Shahshahani, "Honduras' Presidential Election Demands an Investigation,"

November 28, 2013, *Digital Commons, Western New England University School of Law*, https://digitalcommons.law.wne.edu/cgi/viewcontent.cgi?referer=&httpsredir=1&article=1036&context=media.

70. Nicholas Phillips and Elizabeth Malkin, "New Left-Wing Party in Honduras Cries Foul," *New York Times*, November 25, 2013, www.nytimes.com/2013/11/26/world/americas/honduras-presidential-race.html?_r=2&pagewanted=all&.

71. "Libre, segunda fuerza parlamentaria de Honduras," *Confidencial*, December 4, 2013, www.confidencial.com.ni/articulo/15155/libre-segunda-fuerza-parlamentaria-de-honduras.

72. Impeaching the president would require a three-quarters (96 vote) majority.

73. Christine J. Wade, "By Design, Honduras' Anti-Graft Mission Won't Actually Fight Corruption," *World Politics Review*, November 4, 2015, www.worldpoliticsreview.com/articles/17124/by-design-honduras-anti-graft-mission-won-t-actually-fight-corruption. See also Charles Call's blog *Monitoring MACCCIH and Anti-Impunity Efforts in Honduras*, www.american.edu/centers/latin-american-latino-studies/monitoring-maccih.cfm.

74. Jeff Ernst, "A Pandora's Box of Corruption in Honduras," *Univision News*, August 6, 2019, https://pulitzercenter.org/reporting/exclusive-pandoras-box-corruption-honduras

75. US Department of State, "Report to Congress on Corruption in El Salvador, Guatemala and Honduras," May 2019, www.insightcrime.org/wp-content/uploads/2019/05/US-CentAm-Corruption-List.pdf.

76. Sarah Chayes, *When Corruption Is the Operating System: The Case of Honduras* (Washington DC: Carnegie International Endowment for Peace, 2017).

77. US Department of State, *Country Reports on Human Rights Practices for 2015: Honduras*, https://2009-2017.state.gov/j/drl/rls/hrrpt/humanrightsreport/index.htm#wrapper; United Nations Human Rights Office of the High Commissioner, "Preliminary Observations on the Official Visit to Honduras by the Special Rapporteur on Extrajudicial, Summary or Arbitrary Executions, 23 to May 27, 2016," United Nations Human Rights Office of the High Commissioner, www.ohchr.org/EN/NewsEvents/Pages/DisplayNews.aspx?NewsID=20030&LangID=E.

78. Stephen Dudley, "Elites and Organized Crime," *InsightCrime* (no date), www.justice.gov/eoir/file/861076/download.

79. Hannah Stone, "Honduras' New Top Cop Comes with Dark Past," *InSight Crime*, May 29, 2012, www.insightcrime.org/news/analysis/honduras-new-top-cop-comes-with-dark-past/

80. Elisabeth Malkin and Alberto Arce, "Files Suggest Honduran Police Leaders Ordered Killing of Antidrug Officials," *The New York Times*, April 15, 2016,

www.nytimes.com/2016/04/16/world/americas/files-suggest-honduras-police-leaders-ordered-killing-of-antidrug-officials.html.

81. United Nations Human Rights Council, "Annual Report of the United Nations High Commissioner for Human Rights on the Human Rights Situation in Honduras," February 9, 2017.

82. Christopher Sherman, Martha Mendoza, and Garance Burke, "Secret Report: Honduras' New Top Cop Helped Move Cocaine," *Associated Press*, January 26, 2018, www.apnews.com/0cc4031c058545fb9247ce5095c644c0.

83. Department of Justice, US Attorney's Office, Southern District of New York, "Former Honduran Cabinet Official Pleads Guilty In Manhattan Federal Court To Money Laundering Charge," August 29, 2017, www.justice.gov/usao-sdny/pr/former-honduran-cabinet-official-pleads-guilty-manhattan-federal-court-money-laundering.

84. United States Drug Enforcement Agency, "DEA Announces Arrest of Former Honduran Congressman and Brother of Current President of Honduras for Drug Trafficking and Weapons Charges," November 26, 2018, www.dea.gov/press-releases/2018/11/26/dea-announces-arrest-former-honduran-congressman-and-brother-current.

85. Ryan Dube, "Honduran President Is Accused of Drug Conspiracy," *Wall Street Journal*, August 3, 2019, www.wsj.com/articles/honduran-president-is-accused-of-drug-conspiracy-11564876238.

86. Cecilia Menjavír and Shannon Drysdale Walsh, "The Architecture of Feminicide: The State, Inequalities, and Everyday Gender Violence in Honduras," *Latin American Research Review*, 52 (2) (2017), pp. 221–240.

87. Sonia Nazario, "Someone Is Always Trying to Kill You," *New York Times*, April 5, 2019, www.nytimes.com/interactive/2019/04/05/opinion/honduras-women-murders.html.

88. Inter-American Commission on Human Rights, "IACHR Has Concluded Its Visit to Honduras and Presents Its Preliminary Observations" August 3, 2018, www.oas.org/en/iachr/media_center/PReleases/2018/171.asp.

89. TransGender Europe, "Trans Murder Monitoring 2015," May 8, 2015, https://tgeu.org/tmm-idahot-update-2015/.

90. Global Witness, "Honduras: The Deadliest Country in the World for Environmental Activism," January 2017, www.globalwitness.org/fr/campaigns/environmental-activists/honduras-deadliest-country-world-environmental-activism/.

91. Nina Lakhani, "Berta Cáceres Murder Trial Plagues by Allegations of Cover-ups Asset to End," *The Guardian*, November 29, 2018, www.theguardian.com/global-development/2018/nov/29/berta-caceres-trial-plagued-by-allegations-of-cover-ups-set-to-end.

92. Eva Thorne, "Land Rights and Garífuna Identity," *NACLA*, September 25, 2007, https://nacla.org/article/land-rights-and-gar%C3%ADfuna-identity.

93. OHCHR, *Human Rights Violations in the Context of the 2017 Elections in Honduras*, www.ohchr.org/Documents/Countries/HN/2017ReportElectionsHR Violations_Honduras_EN.pdf.

94. Miguel Salazar, "The Honduran Government Is Trying to Steal an Election," *The Nation*, December 6, 2017, www.thenation.com/article/the-honduran-government-is-trying-to-steal-an-election/.

95. Organization of American States, *Organization of American States Electoral Observation Mission, General Elections, Honduras*, November 26, 2017, www.oas.org/documents/eng/press/preliminary-report-eom-honduras-2017-4dec-.pdf.

96. Jack Guy, "Why Hondurans are Taking to the Streets or Leaving the Country", *CNN*, July 6, 2019, www.cnn.com/2019/07/06/americas/honduras-protests-explainer-intl/index.html.

97. "US Border Patrol Southwest Apprehensions by Sector Sector Fiscal Year 2019," www.cbp.gov/newsroom/stats/sw-border-migration/usbp-sw-border-apprehensions.

98. The Editors, *World Politics Review*, "Why Honduras Remains the Most Unequal Country in the World," January 6, 2017. www.worldpoliticsreview.com/insights/20856/why-honduras-remains-latin-america-s-most-unequal-country.

RECOMMENDED READINGS AND RESOURCES

Acker, Alison. 1989. *Honduras: The Making of a Banana Republic*. Boston, MA: South End Press.

Anderson, Thomas P. 1982. *Politics in Central America: Guatemala, El Salvador, Honduras, and Nicaragua*. New York: Praeger.

Argueta, Jose R. 2008. *The Dynamics of Electoral Accountability in Two-Party Systems: The Case of Honduras*. Verlag/Jahr: VDM Verlag Dr. Müller.

Benjamin, Medea. 1989. *Don't Be Afraid, Gringo: A Honduran Woman Speaks from the Heart: The Story of Elvia Alvarado*. New York: Harper Perennial.

Brondo, Keri Vacanti. 2013. *Land Grab: Green Neoliberalism, Gender, and Garífuna Resistance in Honduras*. Tuscon, AZ: University of Arizona Press.

Euraque, Darío. 1996. *Reinterpreting the Banana Republic: Region and State in Honduras, 1870–1972*. Chapel Hill, NC: University of North Carolina Press.

Frank, Dana. 2018. *The Long Honduran Night: Resistance, Terror, and the United States in the Aftermath of the Coup*. Chicago, IL: Haymarket Books.

Lakhani, Nina. 2020. *Who Killed Berta Caceres?: The Murder of an Indigenous Defender and the Race to Save the Planet*. London: Verso.

Morris, James A. 1984. *Honduras: Caudillo Politics and Military Rulers*. Boulder, CO: Westview Press.

Morris, James A. 1984. "Honduras: The Burden of Survival in Central America." In Steve C. Ropp and James A. Morris, eds. *Central America: Crisis and Adaptation*. Albuquerque, NM: University of New Mexico Press, pp. 189–226.

Nazario, Sonia. 2007. *Enrique's Journey*. New York: Random House.

Reichman, Daniel. 2011. *The Broken Village: Coffee, Migration, and Globalization in Honduras*. Ithaca, NY: Cornell University Press.

Rosenberg, Mark and Phillip Shephard. 1986. *Honduras Confronts Its Future*. Boulder, CO: Lynne Rienner Publishers.

Rudolph, James D. 1984. *Honduras: A Country Study*. American University Foreign Area Studies Series. Washington, DC: US Government Printing Office.

Ruhl, J. Mark. 2004. "Curbing Central America's Militaries." *Journal of Democracy* 15 (3): 137–151.

Schulz, Donald E. and Deborah Sundloff Schulz. 1994. *The United States, Honduras, and the Crisis in Central America*. Boulder, CO: Westview Press.

Tucker, Catherine. 2008. *Changing Forests: Collective Action, Common Property, and Coffee in Honduras*. New York: Springer.

9

POLITICAL PARTICIPATION, ATTITUDES, AND DEMOCRACY

CLASSICAL DEMOCRATIC THEORY DEFINES *DEMOCRACY* AS CITIZEN participation in governing a society. Political participation includes voting, partisan activity, contacting public officials, community activism, civil-society engagement, and protest. Such participation conveys citizens' preferences to government, and thus partly constrains the expectations and actions of officials and elites. A society is more democratic when more citizens take part in politics in varied activities that affect more arenas of civic life.[1] This chapter employs data from recent public-opinion surveys to explore political engagement among Central Americans.

Participation, however, only tells part of the story about Central Americans and democracy. We need to know to what extent the five nations have begun to consolidate their democratic regimes. *Democratic consolidation*, the institutionalization of democratic expectations and rules within a polity, rests partly on citizens' attitudes and norms.[2] In more consolidated democracies, citizens share more democratic attitudes, reject authoritarian norms and military rule, and believe their governments are legitimate. We will examine these attitudes among Central Americans.

273

Domestic and external political contexts shape citizens' beliefs and behaviors. All five countries in Central America had become civilian-democratic regimes by the late 1990s. But many factors other than formal regime type also influence citizen political engagement and attitudes. Despite common elements, Central American political histories, political and social violence, crime, corruption, and economic environments vary widely. In some undemocratic countries citizens embraced democratic norms through contact with more democratic societies as their citizens traveled and worked abroad, through media exposure, or because such norms helped them resist repression.[3] The behavior of regimes and of their international sponsors also affects citizen participation and attitudes and thus influences consolidation.[4] Individuals' education and economic resources diverge, as do their experiences with official corruption and crime, and these too shape their political behavior and support for government. This chapter explores how such factors may be affecting Central America's democratic consolidation.

CITIZEN PARTICIPATION

We begin with a comparative examination of political participation in 2012–2014 (Table 9.1).[5] To explore the stability of political behavior and attitudes in Central America, we also compare some of these findings with those from previous editions of *Understanding Central America.*

Of voting-age Central Americans, 91 percent reported being registered to vote in 2014 (Table 9.1), comparing favorably to the United States, where only 65 percent of eligible adult citizens were registered in 2014.[6] Most Central American nations use a national identity card (*cédula*) as qualification for voting, effectively registering all age-eligible citizens. Under this system, 98 percent of Costa Ricans and 97 percent of Salvadorans reported being registered that year, effectively unchanged from 2004. El Salvador implemented election reforms in the early 2000s, including a universal identification/voter registration card, so that registration rose from 80 percent in 1990 to 97 percent in 2012. Guatemalans were the least likely to be registered (78 percent) in 2014. Unlike other isthmian countries, Guatemala requires voter registration separate from the national identity registry. Lower reported registration rates occurred where other governments made less conscientious efforts at registering all eligible citizens, or changed rules and procedures (Nicaragua).

Table 9.1 presents voting (survey respondents reported voting in the most recent presidential election) as of 2014. The region-wide self-reported average turnout of 73 percent was unchanged from 2004. Nicaraguans reported

TABLE 9.1 Political Participation, Central American Nations, 2012–2014

Type of Participation	Costa Rica	El Salvador	Guatemala	Honduras	Nicaragua	Regional Mean
VOTING BEHAVIOR						
Registered to vote, 2014 (%)	98	97	78	94	88	91
Voted in last presidential election, 2014 (%)	72	75	72	75	70	73
CAMPAIGNING AND PARTISAN ACTIVISM						
Attended political party meetings, 2014 (%)[a]	5	6	5	7	17	8
Attempted to persuade someone how to vote, 2012 (%)	29	22	35	28	20	27
Worked for a political campaign or candidate, 2012 (%)	11	8	8	6	11	9
COMMUNAL ACTIVISM[a]						
Attended community improvement group, 2014 (%)	9	13	25	16	24	18
Worked with others to solve community problem, 2014 (%)	12	16	16	17	19	16
CIVIL SOCIETY ACTIVISM[a]						
Church-related group, 2014 (%)	47	72	75	65	54	63
School-related group, 2014 (%)	14	30	38	39	44	33
Business-professional group, 2012 (%)	4	4	8	8	8	7
Mean group activism (%)[b]	22	36	40	37	35	34
CONTACTING PUBLIC OFFICIALS						
Local official, 2014 (%)	8	22	23	10	18	16
Legislative deputy, 2012 (%)	4	7	5	7	7	6

(continues)

TABLE 9.1 (*continued*)

Type of Participation	Costa Rica	El Salvador	Guatemala	Honduras	Nicaragua	Regional Mean
PROTEST PARTICIPATION						
Protested or demonstrated within last year, 2014 (%)	7	4	2	5	7	5

[a] Percentages are for reporting attendance at meetings of each group "once or twice a month" or more frequently, at least an intermediate or higher level of involvement.
[b] Average of church, school, and business-professional group attendance at an intermediate level of involvement ("from time to time" or more often).
Source: 2012 and 2014 Surveys by the Latin American Public Opinion Project, Vanderbilt University, www.vanderbilt.edu/lapop/

voting least (70 percent). These survey-reported turnout rates exceed actual turnout rates reported by national election officials by a regional average of 10 percent[7] because some voters reported to interviewers having voted when they had not. (Over-reporting of having voted is common in survey research, usually attributed to a desire to comply with desirable social norms.)

Central Americans are active voters (a regional average greater than 60 percent of voting-age population) when compared to US citizens (52 percent turnout in 2012).[8] We surmise that so many Central Americans vote because of the region's past experience with dictatorship, political violence, and election fraud. Free elections may provide a refreshing opportunity after decades of violence. Compared to the United States, Central America's intimate political arenas may also encourage voting. Finally, presidential elections in the isthmus are direct, and thus free of the confounding intervening indirect-election mechanism of the US Electoral College. With other influences held constant, in the 2012 survey older citizens voted more than younger ones, although turnout declined somewhat among those over 65. Better-educated and better-off citizens voted more, as did respondents expressing support for the political system and approval of government economic management.[9]

We analyzed official national presidential election turnout rates in Central America from the 1970s through the most recent election, a period since before democratization in four countries (Costa Rica had already democratized). Four long-term trends appear. First, as one might expect, the turnout percentage among voting-age populations (VAP) rose after democratization in El Salvador, Guatemala, and Honduras. El Salvador and Guatemala experienced large turnout gains after their civil wars ended. El Salvador's turnout increased 29 percent from 1994 to 2009, and Guatemala's 37 percent between 1995 and 2011. Both countries also improved their election administration systems during these periods, making it easier to register and vote.

Second, differently from the other cases, VAP turnout rates in Nicaragua were roughly stable in the mid 70 percent range across four decades from 1974 to 2011, pre- and post-democratization. We believe the Somoza dictatorship pressured citizens to vote to create evidence of its popular support, and as a means for citizens to curry favor with the regime. In contrast, the other non-democracies such as Guatemala and El Salvador did not encourage voting. Indeed, Guatemala discouraged voting by indigenous citizens. Nicaraguan voting turnout declined markedly for a second time in 2016 (see below). This followed the breakdown of the opposition Liberal movement in the 2011 and 2016 elections, and the FSLN's dominance of the courts and electoral apparatus. Electoral rule changes, the collapse of opposition, and various anti-democratic practices meant that Nicaragua had effectively become an autocratic regime.

Third, all countries other than Honduras experienced a turnout decline in their last one or two presidential elections. In Honduras VAP turnout in the late 2009 national election fell to 53 percent after the coup ousting President Zelaya earlier that year. Turnout recovered in the 2013 election, then declined slightly in 2017. (Official results of this election were highly questionable. We reclassified Honduras as a semi-democracy in 2009 and as a civilian autocracy in 2017 based on problems related to that election.) Guatemala's VAP turnout fell the most in the region—from 61 percent in 2011, to 49 percent in 2015, to 33 percent in the 2019 presidential runoff. In Nicaragua (also a civilian autocracy), VAP turnout declined second most, from 81 percent in 2006 to 72 percent in 2011 to 58 percent in 2016. El Salvador experienced a slight turnout decline in 2019.[10]

Fourth, and strangely, over the long term Costa Rica—the only fully fledged democracy in the region for over six decades—experienced a 32 percent voter turnout decline between its 1990 (85 percent) and 2014 national elections (53 percent).[11] Turnout there then recovered to 65 percent in 2018 in a hotly contested presidential runoff. Clearly Costa Rican democracy does not survive on voter turnout alone (nor does any nation's). Nevertheless, the decline of citizen engagement in electoral politics has troubled observers.

Partisan activity, another way of participating in the national arena, requires more time and effort than voting. The surveys asked how often respondents attended meetings of political parties; Table 9.1 reveals a 2014 regional mean of 8 percent who attended at least once a month. The lowest party attendance at that level reported was in Costa Rica, at 5 percent. Costa Rica's two major parties adopted primary elections in the late 1980s, which curtailed local party meetings and "retail" party politics. The National Liberation Party (PLN) and Social Christian Unity Party (PUSC) also experienced major corruption scandals in the late 1990s and 2000s, with sharp electoral reversals for each.[12] Both factors likely depressed turnout. Elsewhere, at the high end of party activism for the region, 17 percent of Nicaraguans reported attending party meetings in 2014. This, however, was sharply lower than in previous surveys, and came following the effective collapse of Nicaragua's Liberal movement in the prior elections.

In Honduras, compared to 2008 and following the 2009 coup, attending political party meetings in 2014 had declined from 19 percent to 7 percent. Elsewhere party meeting participation at least monthly ranged from 5 to 6 percent. Surveys from the 1990s through 2014 consistently reveal Central Americans' very low confidence in parties—typically the least trusted of all national institutions.

Other factors held constant, men and older citizens (tapering off after 65), reported more political party participation in 2012. Evaluative attitudes also shaped party activism: those expressing greater of satisfaction with government economic management, national economic performance, and the political system attended political party meetings more.[13]

Campaign involvement is the third type of political participation linked to elections. The 2012 survey asked people whether they had ever attempted to persuade someone how to vote or worked for a political campaign or candidate (Table 9.1) and we can compare those to 2008 data.[14] The regional average for campaign participation declined from 12 percent in 2008 to 9 percent in 2012, with the only observed increase in Nicaragua (from 6 to 11 percent). For attempting to persuade others how to vote, the regional average dropped 10 percent from 2008 to 2012. Hondurans had previously reported the most such efforts, but their efforts plunged from 59 to 28 percent between 2008 and 2012 (after the 2009 coup). For the same period Costa Ricans reported a 15-point decline (to 29 percent) in vote-persuasion efforts. Guatemala was the only country with an increase, rising eight points to 35 percent in 2012.

When considered together, the observed regional decreases in attendance at party functions, electioneering, and vote-persuading since 2008 suggest that by 2014 partisan and election activism had lost vibrancy compared to the early 2000s. This may have happened because the novelty of such activity being safer than under dictatorships either wore off in some countries, or political repression crept back up. Other contributing factors in partisan and campaign activity were that so many citizens held parties in low esteem that political cor-ruption became endemic, and that in Costa Rica, El Salvador, and Honduras trust in elections had declined.[15] Other factors held constant, in 2012 males, the better educated, and older citizens (albeit eroding among the elderly) were more likely to be party- and campaign-active. Citizens with higher evaluations of national economic performance, government economic management, and institutions in general reported higher party and campaign activism.[16]

Outside the electoral arena, communal activism—collective self-help or community-improvement work—has a rich history in Central America. Cit-izens work together to address local problems that government often ignores. Communal activism persisted throughout the conflict and repression of the 1980s and early 1990s, possibly because such cooperative activity among neighbors did not appear to challenge authoritarian regimes.[17] Respondents to the 2004 survey reported a region-wide average of 20 percent at least occa-sionally attending a community-improvement group meeting. A decade later in 2014 the share was little different at 18 percent (Table 9.1). Region-wide, working with others to solve a community problem (16 percent) was only half of the level it had been in 2004. We suspect that resolution of the civil wars, government infrastructure spending, and gradual economic improvement may have reduced some of the felt need for such cooperation.

A review of data reveals that attending meetings of communal improve-ment groups had decreased slightly by 2014 compared to 2004 for the region. Modest decreases occurred in Costa Rica, El Salvador, and Guatemala. Two big changes stood out in Honduras, where intermediate levels of activity had fallen from 29 percent in 2004 to 16 percent in 2014. One possible expla-nation for the large decline of communal activism in Honduras was a crime wave that one survey reported had frightened people into staying home for safety.[18] Growing crime and crime victimization over the last decade in El Sal-vador have reportedly driven people to stay home for their safety, which likely suppresses community problem-solving efforts—to say nothing of motivating emigration to safer countries. Another notable change was a large increase in attending communal organizations in Nicaragua between 2004 and 2014—up from 18 to 24 percent. Both the Liberal and Sandinista governments in power over this era promoted community problem-solving organizations.

Another aspect of citizens' collaboration is participation in civil society (for-mal organizations), which provides collective ways to promote their interests. Table 9.1 presents the percentage of citizens attending meetings at least monthly in church-related, school-related, and business and professional organizations. In 2014, 72 percent of Salvadorans, 75 percent of Guatemalans, and 65 percent of Hondurans reported such involvement in church-related groups. At least 47 percent of respondents elsewhere took part in church-related organizations. We compared these 2014 data to those from a similar Central American survey from the early 1990s and discovered that Central Americans everywhere but Nicaragua reported big increases (dozens of percentage points) in involvement in church-related groups. The likely cause is the rapid growth of evangelical Protestantism and congregations across this period. From just 2004 to 2014, the region-wide increase in such attendance was 7 percent.

In Costa Rica in 2014, with its well-established education system, participation in school-related groups was below half the participation rates of other countries. Between 29 and 45 percent of other Central Americans, however, reported intermediate attendance at school-related groups. Across most of the region school-related group involvement declined from 40 to 33 percent from 2004 to 2014. The exception to this trend was Nicaragua, where rapid urbanization was involving more children in education beyond the primary level. Finally, fewer than 1 in 15 respondents region-wide reported business or professional group activity (Table 9.1), unchanged from the prior decade.

Over time, our regional summary measure of mean group involvement remained stable (34 percent participation at intermediate levels) between 2004 and 2014 (Table 9.1). Closer inspection reveals that civil-society activism remained unchanged in Guatemala and Nicaragua but slightly lower in Honduras. Two large changes occurred over this decade, however. Salvadorans increased their civil society activity considerably, mainly owing to a near doubling of religious-related group engagement. In contrast, Costa Ricans' civil society activism declined mainly due to reduced school- and church-related participation.

Other factors held constant, Central Americans in 2012 who were more active in organizations tended to be women, older, wealthier, and residents of smaller communities. People with confidence in the political system also took part more in groups.[19]

Citizens typically contact public officials to demand services, benefits, or government attention to problems; 16 percent of Central Americans reported having contacted a local public official (Table 9.1) during the year prior to the 2012 survey, a three-point increase above 2008. Guatemalans, Salvadorans, and Nicaraguans contacted local officials more, Costa Ricans and Hondurans considerably less. Only 6 percent reported having contacted a national legislative deputy in the year prior to the 2012 survey, with little variation region-wide.[20] Overall and holding other factors constant, the most important individual traits contributing to contacting public officials were being older (except for the most elderly) and a small-town or rural resident. Citizens approving of national economic performance and the government's economic management also contacted officials more.[21]

Protest provides an important tool for communicating to government. An average of 5 percent of Central Americans reported protesting or demonstrating in the year before the 2014 survey (down from 8 percent in 2004). Protest participation, while low in general, is context-sensitive, depending on how much local authorities are likely to repress it and on events or conditions worthy of publicly complaining. In 2014 Costa Ricans and Nicaraguans (7 percent each) were most likely to have protested, followed by Hondurans at 5 percent. Guatemalans at 2 percent remained the least protest-engaged (Table 9.1), as they were in 2008 and 2004 (see also Figure 9.1). Protest across the whole region generally declined from 2004 to 2014 from 8 to 5 percent. The most abrupt and largest changes in protest over this period levels occurred in Honduras. There self-reported protest participation went from 7 to 18 percent between 2004 and 2008 in the increasingly turbulent years before the 2009 coup. Protest levels then subsided to 5 percent by 2014 after President Zelaya's exile, subsequent elections, and crackdowns on protest behavior by post-coup governments. Protests broke out again in 2015, 2017, and 2019 in reaction to corruption scandals and election irregularities—indicating mobilizing contextual issues—so more recent surveys might indicate higher protest activity.

FIGURE 9.1 **Protest Participation (Self-Reported)**
over Time, 2004–2014

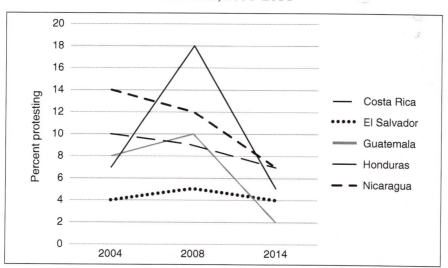

Source: The AmericasBarometer by the Latin American Public Opinion Project (LAPOP), www.LapopSurveys.org

Nicaragua experienced high levels of protest activity in the post-revolutionary 1990s and 2000s as working-class groups, unions, and organizations linked to the FSLN challenged many of the austerity and privatization plans of non-Sandinista governments. Nicaragua's 14 percent protest rate for 2004 (Figure 9.1) declined to 7 percent by 2014, likely because the Sandinistas had recaptured power in the 2006 election and their supporters and organizations felt less called to protest than when they were in opposition. Data on protest participation for Nicaragua in 2018 unfortunately remained unavailable at this writing. All indications are that demonstrations and violent regime responses to them were much greater during that year's confrontations between critics and supporters of the Sandinista regime's policies.

Costa Rica's 4 percent protest rate was stable for the decade. Although protest squares poorly with Costa Rica's placid image, the country nevertheless has a lively record of citizens protesting.[22] Other factors held constant, across the region protesters came from across the age spectrum, but were more educated, urban, and male.[23]

To sum up, in 2014 surveys many Central Americans engaged their political systems through voter registration, voting, and communal and group activity. Some campaigned, tried to persuade others how to vote, attended party meetings, contacted officials, and protested. There were distinctive national patterns. Despite their record of declining voter turnout, Costa Ricans actively persuaded other voters and worked for political campaigns but otherwise reported very low attendance at party meetings once primary elections undercut citizens' direct engagement with parties. Costa Ricans were the least active Central Americans in community improvement and organizations. We surmise that Costa Ricans' do less organizational and communal self-help activity because, compared to their neighbors, their higher living standards and better developed service infrastructure motivate less collective problem solving.

Comparing which country ranked first in each type of participation in Table 9.1 allows us to make rough overall comparisons of citizen engagement across the region. Overall, Guatemalans were the most engaged, leading at civil society, community self-help, contacting officials, and persuading others how to vote. However, they registered to vote least in 2014 (due to a poorly designed inscription system) and they protested the least. In contrast, Costa Ricans protested the most (tied with Nicaraguans) but were otherwise the region's least-engaged citizens, especially in civil society and community activity and contacting officials. But these contrasts make some sense considering that Costa Ricans, residing in the region's oldest and most prosperous democracy, are probably more complacent about their social and economic situations. In contrast, residents of the younger democracies and poorer countries like Guatemala are still flexing their muscles as citizens and working together to advance their interests. Huge and sustained protests took place in Guatemala and Honduras in 2015, and again in Honduras in 2017 and 2019. In Guatemala, this public protest contributed to the resignation of the president and vice president. In Honduras protests led to the establishment of an anti-corruption agency but failed to deter Honduran officials from further dismantling democracy there. The intensity and modalities of citizen engagement kept evolving even as elites changed the rules of the political game in some countries.

Among the individual traits affecting participation across the region, our regression analyses found that age, education, and residence in smaller communities predicted higher participation. Men were more active in protesting, campaigning, and party activity, women more active in organizations. Household wealth had little effect on most forms of participation other than modestly elevating voting and group activism.

Evaluations moved several types of participation. Positive views of government economic management increased voting, party and campaign activity, contacting, and (curiously) protest behaviors. General system support encouraged voting, party/campaign work, and civil-society activism. Positive views of the national economy elevated campaign and party activism, but reduced contacting. In a separate analysis of 2008 data from Central America, positive evaluations of local government, the president, and national economic performance encouraged greater participation.[24] Intriguingly, that study found the most-satisfied and the least-satisfied citizens were the most politically active in various participation modes, while those in the middle on these attitudes took part less. Democracy in Central America was thus allowing those at both ends of the legitimacy spectrums to engage the system at high levels. This could be good news for democratic consolidation because frustrated citizens in these democracies were not dropping out or rebelling. Rather, just as those who approved of the system engaged with it at higher levels, those who were most critical also engaged more.

CITIZEN ATTITUDES

Latin American political culture once had strong authoritarian components: deference to authority, preference for strong leaders, intolerance of regime critics, and anti-democratic norms.[25] Reinforced by the protracted authoritarian rule, Central American countries shared these cultural traits. Recently these old patterns have changed across Latin America. Researchers reported higher democratic norms than anticipated among Nicaraguans—equal in fact to those of Costa Ricans—during the late 1980s despite Nicaragua's limited prior experience with democracy.[26] The emergence of formal democracy in four of five countries and questions about Central Americans' commitment to democracy calls us to evaluate authoritarian and democratic norms and their evolution.

We begin with a question from the 2004 and 2014 AmericasBarometer asking whether respondents believed that in some circumstances authoritarian rule might be preferable to democracy, democracy would be preferable always, or they felt indifference, scored as an index of 0 to 100, with the authoritarian value the high score. As Table 9.2 reveals, in 2014, Central Americans overall registered low authoritarianism (an index score of 18 out of 100, down 3 points from 2004). Hondurans expressed the highest authoritarianism in 2014 (24 out of 100), followed by Nicaraguans (21), and Salvadorans (18)—each essentially unchanged from 2004. The lowest authoritarianism in 2014 appeared in Costa Rica and in Guatemala. Both revealed declining citizen authoritarianism from 2004 to 2014, down 5 index points in Costa Rica and 13 points in Guatemala. A related 2014 item sought agreement/disagreement that "democracy is the best form of government," with replies ranging from 0 (strongly disagree) to 100 (strongly agree). Costa Ricans led the region on this democratic norm with a mean of 74, while the other countries averaged in the high 60s.

TABLE 9.2 Political Attitudes, Central American
Nations, 2004–2014

Attitudes	Costa Rica	El Salvador	Guatemala	Honduras	Nicaragua	Regional Mean
Authoritarianism, based on agreement that "in certain circumstances an authoritarian government might be preferable to democracy" (range 100 = strongest agreement, 50 = indifference, 0 = least agreement).						
2004	18	19	26	24	19	21
2014	13	18	13	24	21	18
Support for a Military Coup d'état Index of **support for a military coup** under certain circumstances—high or excessive crime or corruption (range 0 = low support … 100 = high support)						
2004	47	51	40	50	32	44
2014	29	39	38	36	45	38

Democratic Norms

Support for general political participation rights[a] (range 0 = low support ... 100 = high support)

2004	71	50	59	67	72	64
2014	61	48	38	35	59	56

Tolerance for political participation rights for regime critics[b] (range 0 = low support ... 100 = high support)

2004	58	51	46	56	55	53
2014	47	42	29	43	47	41

Support for civil disobedience[c] (range 0 = low support ... 100 = high support)

2004	25	23	22	38	30	27
2014	31	30	23	28	31	26

Support for violent rebellion against an elected government[d] (range 0 = low support ... 100 = high support)

2004	8	16	21	24	17	17
2014	16	15	17	17	19	17

System Support

Index of **general or diffuse support for the political system**[e] (range 0 = low support ... 100 = high support)

2004	68	60	49	52	49	56
2014	62	55	49	52	62	56

Index of **evaluation of national economic performance**[f] (range 0 = lowest evaluation ... 100 = highest evaluation)

2014	30	36	23	28	44	32

[a] This item registers approval of taking part in a legal demonstration.
[b] This index incorporates support for possible behaviors by critics of the political system: voting, carrying out peaceful demonstrations, running for public office, and giving a speech on television.
[c] This item registers approval of taking part in street blockages.
[d] This item registers approval of "taking part in group that wishes to overthrow an elected government by violent means."
[e] This index incorporates general or diffuse support for the national political system, its protection of basic rights, pride in the system, and a sense of obligation to support the political system.
[f] This index incorporates citizen evaluation of the performance of the national economic system and their own personal economic situations: "How is the country's economy (and your personal economic situation) compared to a year ago?" Comparable data for 2004 not available.
Source: 2004 and 2014 Surveys by the Latin American Public Opinion Project, Vanderbilt University, www.vanderbilt.edu/lapop/

Latin American Public Opinion Project (LAPOP) surveys asked whether a military coup might be justified if crime or corruption were very high: 38 percent of the respondents region-wide agreed, down 6 percent from 2004. Costa Ricans were the least coup-supportive in 2014 at 29 percent, Nicaraguans the most at 45 percent. Region-wide, support for a hypothetical military coup under conditions of high crime or corruption declined 6 percent from 2004. Costa Ricans reported the largest decrease from 2004 (-18 percent), followed by post-coup Hondurans (-14 percent), and Salvadorans (-12 percent). Support for a hypothetical coup rose only in Nicaragua (up 13 percent to 45 percent in 2014). The fact that Liberal faction supporters registered much higher coup support suggests that between 2004 and 2014 anti-Sandinista elements came to view the armed forces as the only way to remove President Ortega from power.

Coup justifiers tended to be females, younger, and less educated. They also had negative evaluations of economic performance, felt insecure in their neighborhoods, and were more often victimized by acts of official corruption (i.e., being solicited for a bribe).[27] In sum, perceived insecurity from crime, corruption, and disappointment with the economy's performance generated potential popular support for anti-democratic adventurism by elites.

When asked what hypothetical problems might justify a military takeover of their governments, Central Americans in 2014 cited "high levels of crime" (36 percent) and "a lot of corruption" (55 percent). These findings reveal that, region-wide, Central Americans' commitment to civilian rule remains partly contingent on their regimes' performance. Public corruption and threats to personal security deeply trouble many. Should they become sufficiently severe, we believe, armed forces or other plotters against the constitutional order might find citizen forbearance for a coup d'état justified by such problems.[28]

Table 9.2 reports the national means of a measure of agreement with the right to demonstrate legally, a fundamental participation right in democracy. On a scale of 0 to 100 (from least supportive to most), the citizens of all five countries averaged in the positive end of the scale in 2004 (regional mean of 64), but by 2014 the regional mean had declined 12 points, a large negative shift. Salvadorans, Guatemalans, and Hondurans in 2014 moved to the disapproving end of the scale, while Costa Ricans and Nicaraguans remained positive, despite erosion in both. We view with interest this ebbing of support for peaceful demonstration rights across the region, but note that massive demonstrations have taken place in several countries since 2015, such average opinions notwithstanding. A third of AmericasBarometer survey respondents in 2014 who reported having protested also disapproved of legal protests. Thus Central Americans' distaste for demonstrations may not stop them from protesting. Another measure of democratic values, also a 0 to 100 scale, shows less tolerance among Central Americans for participation rights for regime critics (those "who speak badly of our form of government") than for participation rights in general. This index measures citizens' belief in one of democracy's more challenging but important precepts, that of allowing regime critics to engage in politics and try to convince others of their positions. Table 9.2 shows that regionally political tolerance declined 12 scale points between 2004 and 2012, declining well into the intolerant range. Costa Ricans and Nicaraguans were the more tolerant of system critics' participation rights in 2014, each averaging 47. Tolerance of political system critics among Guatemalans was the region's lowest in 2004 and 2014; their mean declined 17 points to 29 out of 100 across the decade. Other factors held constant, men and the more educated were more likely to support participation rights for dissenters. Those with higher support for the system, who voted, contacted officials, protested, had not experienced bribe solicitations, and who engaged more in organizations were more politically tolerant.[29]

Another aspect of citizens' attitudes is their receptiveness to civil disobedience and political violence. Evaluating citizen reaction to these methods is tricky. On the one hand, protest and even political confrontation may be necessary to create, nurture, or maintain democracy.[30] On the other hand, within formal democracies confrontational tactics tend to be unpopular, and if used to extremes may threaten democracy itself. Bearing in mind these complexities, we see in Table 9.2 that on a 0 to 100 scale the region-wide average support for civil disobedience was 27 in 2004 and 26 in 2014, an effectively unchanged shared bias against such techniques. Hondurans most favored civil disobedience (at 38 points in 2004), but this subsided to 28 points in 2014. Salvadorans' and Costa Ricans' support for such tactics rose several points each across this decade.

We also compared support for confrontational political methods (also including invading public and private property) between the 1990s survey and the 2004 survey (urban samples only) and noted an increase in support everywhere but Honduras.[31] As repression diminished with the end of two civil wars and the establishment of formal democracy more broadly, Central Americans became more supportive of confrontational tactics. Interestingly, the trend also applied for Costa Ricans, who had enjoyed stable democracy for several decades. We surmise that some of the increase there arose from reaction to unpopular neoliberal economic reforms imposed during that era.

Other factors held equal, Central Americans favoring confrontational tactics tended to be younger and less educated than those who opposed them. Supporters of confrontation were politically active; they protested more but also contacted public officials and engaged in party/campaign work. They were less active in organizations than other citizens. These patterns confirm previous evidence that protest provides a preferred political tool for people with modest resources.[32] Lacking the resources availed by age, education, and organization that could provide influence over policymakers, disadvantaged citizens may view protest as useful for promoting their interests. Other factors contributing to greater support for confrontational political tactics included experiencing insecurity in one's own neighborhood and political corruption.

In sum, in 2004 and 2014 about three quarters of Central Americans disapproved of confrontational political tactics, but over half approved of demonstrating legally, and 1 in 20 reported taking part in a protest. Central Americans supported less-confrontational legal demonstrations much more than illegal street blockages or property invasions that disrupt the lives or livelihoods of others.

Going beyond demonstrations and confrontational tactics, we also asked respondents how much they would approve of someone taking part in a "group wishing to violently overthrow an elected government," an act inimical to democracy itself. Approval of armed rebellion was lower than for civil disobedience, with a mean for the region of one in six expressing approval in both 2004 and 2014 surveys (Table 9.2). Support for hypothetical rebellion varied between countries in 2014. The biggest change noted across the decade was a doubling of Costa Ricans' approval of rebellion (rising from 8 to 16 percent). Meanwhile Hondurans' approval or rebellion declined 7 out of 100 points.

We interpret the willingness to support armed rebellion as openness to resisting even an elected government that abuses rights or fails its fundamental obligations to the citizenry. Thus despite the horrors of insurrection and war that widely afflicted the isthmus from the 1970s into the 1990s, some Central Americans still reserve the right to challenge and rebel against a bad regime. Other factors held constant, younger and less-educated citizens were more likely to support rebellion. Voters were less likely to endorse rebellion, while protesters, communal self-help activists, and those who felt unsafe in their neighborhoods expressed greater approval.[33]

These findings raise the important issue of how much Central Americans supported their governments. Table 9.2 provides a measure of each regime's political legitimacy—general confidence the national system. There we see that the regional mean on the system-support index remained unchanged at

56 out of 100 from 2004 to 2014—that is, somewhat in the positive end of the scale. Costa Ricans' and Nicaraguans' general system support rose 11 points to a regional high (62).

Our last edition explored Central Americans' support in 2012 for nine specific institutions, which was mostly lower than for their systems in general. A similar gap existed 2004. The regional mean on specific institutional support was only 46, below the scale's midpoint. Institutional approval scores for Salvadorans and Nicaraguans were just above the scale midpoint and citizens elsewhere expressed net dissatisfaction. Regionally, the most trusted institutions were the armed forces and municipal governments, each scoring above the approval scale midpoint.[34] Trust for the police, however, ranked very low in 2012, and was worst in Guatemala and Honduras. Continuing revelations about police involvement in drug smuggling and rising crime levels likely caused such poor evaluations. Political parties and legislatures also earned low popular confidence in most countries. We surmise this is because they generate noisy issue conflict. Honduras's and Costa Rica's legislatures were the region's least liked in 2012, the former tainted by scandal and the latter by Honduran 2009 coup. The relatively high evaluations of militaries regionwide surprises somewhat, given these institutions' nasty track records during past authoritarian episodes. The militaries, however, returned to their barracks and accepted reforms and downsizing after the civil wars. Moreover, in several countries they provided relief following natural disasters, earning good will. The region's militaries may have also earned popular respect for staying out of politics and attending to national security. Of course, the glaring exception to this is the Honduran military, which participated in the 2009 coup. The 2014 surveys omitted several of these institutions, but those evaluated revealed similar patterns.

Overall, these low and eroding evaluations reveal widespread disappointment with their governmental institutions Central Americans. Perhaps the most troubling evaluations appear in Costa Rica, the region's oldest democracy. Years of scandal involving major parties and successive governments have seemingly disappointed Costa Ricans with many of their institutions (the courts and elections remained exceptions). But this problem extends well beyond Costa Rica, and raises doubts for anyone worried about democratic consolidation in the region. We do not expect Central Americans to rebel because of these attitude trends, but we do fear that anti-democratic elites might take such views as justifications to undermine democracy.

The final legitimacy norm is citizens' evaluations of the economy, shown to be the type of legitimacy that most shapes political participation. Table

9.2 demonstrates that Central Americans in 2014 evaluated their economies poorly (41 out of 100 scale points). The two highest economic-performance evaluations were 46 in the richest nation, Costa Rica, and 49 in much poorer Nicaragua. The economic growth data in earlier chapters reveal clearly that in economic performance over time all the other countries have lagged far behind Costa Rica, both in current GDP per capita and in long-term growth. We are not at all surprised that Costa Ricans (while still not even quite at the scale midpoint) were the second-most satisfied given the country's overall position and recent high growth rates (Chapter 4). In contrast, however low their national output per capita, Nicaraguans reacted favorably to its recent improvement (Chapter 5).

FACTORS SHAPING ATTITUDES AND PARTICIPATION

In 2014 Central Americans were active in their political systems—behaving democratically—but their attitudes over time showed increased ambivalence about key political participation rights. Most people still held democratic norms and repudiated authoritarian rule. However, over a third believed a military coup could be justified given sufficient corruption or crime. Support for authoritarian rule and for coups had decreased since 2004, but so had support for basic political participation rights and tolerance of dissent. General support for the region's political systems in 2014 registered slightly above the scale midpoint, masking losses in El Salvador and Costa Rica and a large increase in Nicaragua. Evaluations of specific national institutions averaged in the negative end of confidence scales and had eroded since 2004. And finally, one person in six reported willingness to approve others seeking to overthrow elected regimes.

We now explore what might account for such indifferent and declining support. We suspect that several factors shape regime support, including differing national histories, records of repression, and economic activity as explored in previous chapters. We have seen how, at the political system level, civil wars ended and repression declined. Four countries entered a formally democratic track (see Figures 2.1 and 2.2) by the 1990s. But since then two have backslid out of full democracy since 2009. Since 2000, repression has risen, some democracy scores have eroded, and sharp national differences in economic performance have persisted. At the individual level, we expect that citizens' resources, experiences, and beliefs affect regime support.

Table 9.3 summarizes some possible macro and micro influences on regime evaluations in 2014. We assumed that the better a country's citizens evaluated its performance, the higher would be their support for its institutions. Relevant contextual measures of performance vary widely (Table 9.3). Real GDP per capita in 2014 ranged from $8,993 for Costa Rica down to $1,775 for Nicaragua, giving the former a 300 to 500 percent economic advantage over its neighbors. Following in Table 9.3 are 2014 national democracy scores, a measure of state political terror and violence, and another of general societal violence by nonstate actors. Last is the Economist Intelligence Unit's ten-point scale of government competence. Costa Rica outperformed the other four nations in the isthmus on three of these four measures and tied them only for societal violence. Guatemala and Honduras stood out for higher societal violence, confirming widespread accounts of one motivation for the emigration of many of their citizens.[35]

Personal experiences that might lower political support include experiencing crime and political corruption. If the state cannot protect citizens, victims may withdraw support from their regime. Table 9.3 shows that from 11 to 25 percent of Central Americans reported being solicited for a bribe in the year before the 2014 survey. When asked in 2012 how widespread perceived corruption in government might be (not bad=0 to 100=extremely bad), their responses averaged between 62 and 77. Between 13 and 19 percent of respondents reported being a crime victim in the year before the survey, and from 16 to 25 percent had family members who were crime victims. Hondurans and Salvadorans reported the most crime victimization. When asked how *in*secure they felt (on a 0 to 100 scale), respondents' answers ranged only from the scale midpoint of 50 to 56 (Honduras and Nicaragua shared the high score). When asked to evaluate how well their governments protected citizens' security, Costa Ricans and Guatemalans gave disapproving replies (43 and 44 out of 100, respectively). Nicaraguans felt best protected at 67 and gave their police the region's highest confidence rating in the region, at 58 of 100.

Presidents in many countries symbolize the government to the people. Presidential approval is volatile, especially compared to general system support. We expected opinions of presidential performance to affect other evaluations of the political system. The 2014 AmericasBarometer surveys asked: "How would you rate the job performance of President (incumbent)?" Table 9.3 reveals wide regional variation. Nicaraguans were the most approving in 2014, rating President Daniel Ortega at a mean score of 67, one of the highest in the whole hemisphere in 2014. Indeed, Nicaraguans' evaluation of President Ortega rose 24 points over 2008, despite the nation's poverty and eroding democratic and governmental performance. In stark comparison, the scandal-plagued presidency of Costa Rica's Laura Chinchilla as her term ended earned an approval score of only 37 out of 100. This disjuncture between Nicaraguan and Costa Rican presidential performance evaluations reveals that Central Americans do not evaluate their political systems by comparison with their neighbors, but only by how things are going within their own national contexts. Proof of this point came following the intense repression of 2018 protests in Nicaragua by police and FSLN supporters. President Ortega's approval among Nicaraguans in June 2019 had plunged by half to 29 percent.[36]

TABLE 9.3 Possible Sources of Low Legitimacy Norms
Among Central Americans

	Costa Rica	El Salvador	Guatemala	Honduras	Nicaragua
Political-Economic Context					
GDP per Capita 2014 (in constant 2010 US$)[a]	8,993	3,235	3,008	2,012	1,775
Combined democracy score 2014[b]	9.2	8.3	7.4	6.8	7.7
Political Terror Scale[c] (range 1 = low ... 5 = high) 2014	2	3	3	3	3
Political Terror Scale[c] (range 1 = low ... 5 = high) 2018	1	3	3	3	3
Societal Violence Scale[c] 2014 (range 1 = low ... 5 = high)	3	3	4	4	3
Functioning of Government Index[d] 2014	7.9	6.1	6.1	5.7	3.3
Personal Experience 2014[e]					
Percentage Experiencing Corruption (solicited for bribe by an official within past year)	21	11	24	25	11
Percent Victimized by Crime (in past year)	13	19	17	18	17
Perceptions of the Political System 2014[e]					
Perceived Level of Personal Insecurity (scale 0 = none ... 100 = extremely high)	51	51	50	56	56

		Costa Rica	El Salvador	Guatemala	Honduras	Nicaragua
Evaluation of Presidential Performance: "How would you rate the job performance of ___ (current president)?" (scale 0 = very low ... 100 = very high)		37	67	54	66	67
Perceived Protection of Citizens' Security by Government (scale 0 = very poor ... 100 = very high)		43	50	44	53	67
Percentage of	Triply Dissatisfied Citizens[f]	7	12	27	12	7
	Triply Satisfied Citizens[f]	18	18	6	13	28

[a] World Bank Indicators, https://data.worldbank.org/indicator/NY.GDP.PCAP.KD?locations=, accessed July 27, 2019.

[b] Authors' combined democracy index, mean for 2014 scale 0 = no democracy ... 10 = high democracy, based on Polity IV Regime Trends, www.systemicpeace.org/polity/nic2.htm, and Freedom House 2015 Report, https://usa2mom.wordpress.com/2015/02/03/freedom-house-2015-report/, accessed July 27, 2019.

[c] Political Terror Scale and Societal Violence Scale, www.politicalterrorscale.org/Data/Download.html, accessed July 27, 2019.

[d] Functioning of Government scale evaluates political system for freely elected policymakers; legislative supremacy; checks and balances; freedom from undue military influence; free from undue foreign control; freedom from undue influence by special economic or religious groups; accountability mechanisms between elections; authority over national territory; governmental transparency; corruption prevalence, civil service competency; and several attitudes if available from recent World Values Surveys. (Source: Economist Intelligence Unit (EIU), *The Economist Intelligence Unit's Index of Democracy 2015*, www.sudestada.com.uy/Content/Articles/421a313a-d58f-462e-9b24-2504a37f6b56/Democracy-index-2014.pdf, accessed July 27, 2019)

[e] Source: LAPOP 2014 surveys.

[f] Triple dissatisfaction measures the share of the population simultaneously below the scale midpoints on support for general democratic rights, general institutional support, and evaluation of economic performance. Triple satisfaction is the opposite—those simultaneously above the scale midpoints on all three attitudes.

Turning to evaluations of economic performance, we anticipated that system performance and a person's own economic wellbeing and resources would considerably affect this attitude. Other things held equal, a multiple regression analysis of 2014 data revealed that economic performance evaluation was higher among those with more household income, but that national GDP per capita did not matter. By far the strongest predictor of national economic evaluation in 2014 was a political factor—approval of presidential performance—followed by the respondent's age, male sex, education, feeling safe in one's neighborhood, general system support, and a lower political violence level.

We also explored factors affecting Central Americans' broad general support for one's political system in 2014. Positive presidential approval contributed most strongly to system support, followed by lower levels of political system violence, positive economic evaluation, political tolerance, not experiencing crime or corruption, perceiving oneself to live in a safe neighborhood, and household income. These factors make sense on their face. Approving of the government in power and the economy, having personal resources, being and feeling safe, and experiencing less political violence should of course increase governmental legitimacy. However, some of these perceptions among Central Americans and the conditions that shape them are volatile and worsening. At the time of these 2014 data, crime and repression were increasing as government performance eroded. Citizens' evaluations of these changes could eventually undermine legitimacy.

Analysis of specific support for nine national institutions (e.g., political parties, the legislature, the Supreme Court) using 2012 data revealed higher confidence among those most satisfied with presidential performance with the national economy. Being poor, a victim of corruption or crime, fearing for one's personal safety, and living in a large community all lowered support for specific national institutions. Again, it is commonsensical that Central Americans would vest little confidence in public institutions that cannot control crime or corruption. Sex, age, and education made no difference in specific institutional support.

In summary, legitimacy—the evaluation of government performance by citizens—varied in Central America in 2012–2014 in predictable and rational ways based on perceptions of whether people's lives were safe and free, how the government behaved and what it delivered, and on measurable system-level economic and political performance characteristics. Demographic factors exerted little influence on either diffuse or specific institutional support, while crime and corruption experiences and beliefs, and one's evaluation of political actors and the economy influenced both.

Given the collapse of Honduran democracy, it is important to review that case. In 2008 Hondurans expressed the region's greatest support for an unelected, strong-man leader (39 percent), the greatest support for a hypothetical military coup, the lowest general system support, lowest support for specific institutions, and as the lowest evaluation of national economic performance.

These patterns suggested unconsolidated and deteriorating support for democracy. To the extent that Honduran political elites were aware of these attitudes, they likely felt little popular pressure to comply with democratic norms and constitutionality. Hondurans' views three years after the coup suggest that they had learned some lessons. However, by 2014 they had retreated on support for a military coup and expressed the region's highest authoritarianism and the lowest support for citizen participation rights. Thus, the coup appears to have lowered support for coups, but also weakened other democratic norms owing to the anti-democratic performance of Honduran political elites.

DEMOGRAPHIC SUBPOPULATIONS

Women

We now examine more closely demographic subgroups mentioned in passing, beginning with women and then racial/ethnic groups. Detailed analysis of these subpopulations would go far beyond the scope of this volume.[37] (For those seeking such detail we recommend Booth and Richard's analysis of political culture in Latin America—including these nations—by gender, age, race, and ethnicity.[38]) Booth and Richard noted one important difference between these subpopulations—men and women share each other's social spaces consistently, something not necessarily true of varied racial/ethnic/linguistic subpopulations, often to some extent separated from one another for historic, linguistic, or political reasons. Booth and Richard found more similarity than differences between the political attitudes of women and men across Latin America than among self-identified racial/ethnic groups. Women were, however, less interested in politics, perceived themselves to be less familiar with national issues, and held slightly weaker democratic norms than men. They expressed more support for gay rights and agreed more than men that women would make better political leaders and better national economic managers.

In 2014 Central American women reported having about a half year less education and modestly lower household living standards than men. These differences were widest in Guatemala and El Salvador, narrowest in Costa Rica. Somewhat more women reported being widowed, living unmarried in a free union, or single than men. Honduras and Nicaragua had the most free unions (heterosexual couples cohabiting) and fewest married adults; Guatemala and Costa Rica had the most married adults and fewest free unions. Costa Rica had the most divorced adults. Central American women reported feeling significantly less safe in their neighborhoods than men (although men reported being crime victims slightly more).

Women evaluated their economic situations more poorly than did men on multiple measures, especially in Nicaragua and El Salvador. This undoubtedly arose from females' comparative employment status, household responsibilities, and obligations to care for children. Some 68 percent of men reported working outside the home, compared to 29 percent of women. Meanwhile, 58 percent of women reported attending to household duties (only 2.5 percent among men). Women in 2014 reported having significantly more children under 13 years old living at home than did men, whether single, married, in free unions, or widowed.

We have noted along the way certain gendered attitude and participation patterns in Central America. For example, women engaged significantly less in community improvement, political party meetings, and school-related groups than men, but much more in church-related groups. In contrast both sexes registered and voted at the same rate, engaged in government-encouraged activities in 2014, and protested at the same frequency. On balance, women were a few scale or percentage points less active. Though not legal barriers, familial obligation, resource disadvantages, and gender posed obstacles to women participating as much as men and thus likely curtailed their political influence.

Other gendered differences were sharper in the isthmus than elsewhere in Latin America. Women expressed significantly lower trust in their neighbors than men, less interest in politics, and less agreement that men make better political leaders. They supported democratic liberties including tolerance of opposition less than men but supported a hypothetical military coup under high crime or corruption conditions more. Females believed themselves less well versed in national problems than males believed themselves to be. Women were significantly more tolerant than men of rights for homosexuals, but the means were low (males = 24 out of 100, females = 27). Guatemalans overall tolerated rights for homosexuals to marry or seek office the least (males = 14, females = 15). Costa Ricans indicated the most tolerance of these rights for homosexual (females = 40 out of 100, males = 38). Women approved less than men of rebellion, civil disobedience, and vigilantism (taking the law into one's own hands). Women region-wide indicated less intention to emigrate (19 percent) than men (26 percent).

Attitudes on which Central American men and women reported little difference included approving authoritarian rule (low at 18 out of 100), and support for democracy as the best political system (high at 68). Women averaged fractionally more support for political institutions than men (2 points out of 100), not a substantively important difference. Central American countries tightly restrict abortions; Nicaragua, El Salvador, and Honduras bar it out-right.[39] Surprisingly to us, mean support for the right to an abortion to save the life of the mother (allowed only in Costa Rica and Guatemala) was 47 out of 100 region-wide. The lowest mean was 26 of 100 among Honduran women.

Ethnic/Racial Subpopulations

We have shown previously that Central American governments, dominated by Spanish-descended elites and later Hispanicized mixed-race (mestizos), strove violently and effectively to exclude indigenous and African-origin peoples from participation. We anticipated that the lingering effects of these old and ongoing racist practices may shape how different groups participate and their attitudes, which could have implications for political stability. We determined the ethnic groups by employing the AmericasBarometer item asking survey respondents to classify themselves by race or ethnicity using categories employed locally. "Do you consider yourself a white, mestizo, indigenous, African-origin, mulatto, or other person?" (Because of small numbers, we grouped African-origin and mulattos together, and we excluded "others," to leave four categories. Fewer than five Guatemalans self-identified as either "white" or black/mulatto, so those cases were dropped.)

Political participation by self-described ethnicity across the region revealed significant differences that defy summary. Many behaviors and attitudes previously discussed reveal significant differences by ethnic groups in particular countries. Because the national contexts are so important, we focus only on within-country variations. Personal resources distribute differently across ethnic/racial lines. One consistent pattern in Central America is that on average indigenous and black/mulatto citizens live in poorer households and have about two years less education than others. The education gap looms widest in Guatemala, where indigenous citizens averaged 4.9 years of schooling compared to mestizo citizens' 7.7 years. Nicaraguan inequality across ethnic/racial lines is also large; African-origin citizens there averaged 2.5 fewer years of schooling than mestizos. These differences indicate that these subpopulations address the political system with fewer personal resources. Moreover, Caribbean coast populations of Honduras, Nicaragua, and Costa Rica and Guatemala's indigenous areas are isolated from national centers and have historically been underserved by the state or repressed.

Strikingly, in 2014 we found Guatemala's indigenous population to be slightly more engaged in almost all types of participation than the country's mestizos. Guatemalans were particularly active in civil society with indigenous

Guatemalans leading the way. Compared to white and mestizo Nicaraguans, the indigenous there reported high levels of civil society, community improvement, and political party activism. The party organizations promoted by the FSLN government (CDCs), as well as the special administrative zones on the Caribbean coast and local community groups have engaged many people there. Black/mulatto Nicaraguans also registered, voted, and took part in civil society more than whites and mestizos, likely for similar reasons. In contrast, indigenous Costa Ricans (several groups live in reserves in the southeast of the country in isolated mountainous terrain) reported exceedingly low voting and party activism. They appear poorly integrated into the formal political system when compared to whites and mestizos, who both voted and did party activities at much higher rates.

Turning to attitudes, we focus on just a few, looking for signs of distinctiveness across racial/ethnic lines within countries. We expected system support to be low among indigenous people given their abysmal treatment in some places. We did find lower region-wide average system support among the indigenous than other subpopulations. In Guatemala, however, where the indigenous population had been subjected to genocide, 52 percent of the population reported modestly higher system support than others. They expressed less support for a hypothetical coup, and a higher intention to emigrate, but otherwise had views like mestizo Guatemalans.[40]

Self-described whites in El Salvador believed less than their compatriots that democracy was the best form of government. While indigenous and black/mulatto Salvadorans manifested low tolerance for coups and weak support for democracy as the best type of government, they were far less sympathetic to coups.[41] Honduras' whites (23 percent of the population) expressed two anti-democratic norms, low tolerance for regime critics and a high willingness to justify coups compared to other racial/ethnic groups. Mestizos (65 percent of Hondurans) registered the opposite pattern, expressing greater tolerance and lower coup-justifying. The indigenous (7 percent of Hondurans) were strongly more system supportive than any other subgroup and expressed the lowest intention to emigrate within the next three years. Some 48 percent of Honduran blacks/mulattos expressed an intention to emigrate, by far the most of any group.

Costa Rica's tiny (2 percent) indigenous population stood out from other groups for their low system support, low tolerance of system critics, high justification of coups, and high mean desire to emigrate (25 percent). Blacks/mulattos (16 percent of Costa Ricans) expressed lower than average system support, political tolerance, preference for democracy, and preference for democracy, and 15 percent intended to emigrate.

Compared to other groups, blacks/mulattos (8 percent of Nicaraguans) expressed significantly below average political tolerance, preference for democracy, and system support but well above average coup justification and desire to emigrate (27 percent). In contrast, the indigenous (7 percent of the population) manifested greater tolerance of system critics and less coup justifying and emigration orientation than other Nicaraguans.

In short, these findings identify significant differences within countries, but few generalizable patterns for the region. Three important results stand out. First, Guatemala's indigenous people, despite their awful treatment for centuries and until recently, do not appear alienated from the political system or to diverge from the mestizo population in attitudes or actions. Second, despite lower democratic norms and system support among some indigenous and blacks/mulattos in certain countries, their numbers are relatively small. Third, and more concerning, the self-described whites and mestizos of Honduras and El Salvador manifest lower democratic norms and more receptivity to coups than their fellow citizens. They are also the most active in political parties and elections, and together constitute large majorities in each country.

IMPLICATIONS FOR STABILITY AND EMIGRATION

Political Satisfaction and Stability

What might legitimacy levels mean for potential political stability? A 2004 study isolated Central Americans who expressed (1) low levels of institutional support (i.e., below the scales' midpoints), (2) low evaluations of economic performance, and (3) low commitment to basic democratic principles. The authors reasoned that "triply dissatisfied" citizens—those who combined all three traits—could not be relied upon to support democracy and its institutions, that they might be vulnerable to appeals by anti-democratic elites, and that populations with many of them might encourage anti-democratic demagogues.[42] They reported that in 2004 Hondurans (12 percent) and Guatemalans (15 percent) were much more likely to be low on all three attitudes than other Central Americans. They inferred that, given an observed association of triple dissatisfaction with higher political participation levels, Guatemala and Honduras were more prone to experience higher political participation at that time, including protest. In Honduras, there later occurred a big increase in triple dissatisfaction (to 30 percent of citizens) the year before the 2009 coup. By 2014, however, the percentage of triply dissatisfied Hondurans had receded to 12 percent, equal to the fraction who were triply satisfied (above the scale midpoint on basic democratic norms, political system support, and evaluation of the economy). The potential for turmoil appeared lower in Honduras in 2014, but massive protests soon broke out after the problematic 2017 election and again in 2019.

We have repeated this analysis of triple dissatisfaction among Central Americans using 2014 data. We found 27 percent of Guatemalans *triply dissatisfied*, while the triply satisfied portion was only 6 percent, thus leaving nearly five times more very disgruntled Guatemalans than very satisfied ones. To the extent that the triply dissatisfied might protest and organize more, Guatemala appeared to have an increased potential for political effervescence and possibly instability.

Two other cases registered far more triple satisfaction than dissatisfaction. Costa Rica had 18 percent triply satisfied citizens in 2014 versus only 7 percent of triply dissatisfied citizens. Triple dissatisfaction there had risen a bit since 2004, but the dissatisfied-to-satisfied proportions and ratios suggested no destabilizing implications. Nicaragua's share of the triply dissatisfied (at 7 percent) in 2014 had not changed since 2004. Those who were triply satisfied rose from 13 percent in 2004 to 28 percent in 2014. Thus despite Nicaragua's poverty, the Sandinista government was in 2014 somehow doing the region's best job of pleasing its citizens on economic and institutional performance. It did so while the main opposition Liberal family of political parties had effectively collapsed after losing to the FSLN in successive national elections.

These patterns could matter in Central America because political satisfaction (legitimacy) may affect how citizens participate. Compared to other more satisfied citizens, the triply dissatisfied in 2004 protested more than others and expressed more support for confrontational political tactics.[43] They also expressed less support for democracy, basic participation rights, and tolerance of dissenters' rights. Such public traits, we fear, could encourage anti-democratic elites to undermine democracy in anticipation of public acceptance. However, in 2004 those who were the most satisfied also tended to be more engaged in politics than the average citizen. In our data, citizens who were triply dissatisfied *and* triply satisfied engaged more in protesting and civil society activity than citizens of mixed orientations on this scale. So, the bigger the portion of the populace at either end of the legitimacy and evaluation scales, the more group activism and protest could be expected. If the triply disgruntled were both very numerous and very engaged, it could raise the possibility of destabilizing political conflict that could invite recourse to repression by anti-democratic security elements.

We believe that these patterns suggested more risk of instability or public disloyalty to democracy in Guatemala as of 2014 than in the other countries. Guatemala's party system had changed dramatically in previous decades, and voter turnout slumped several points in 2015, though protests succeeded in driving the president and vice president from power. In 2015 Guatemala elected a politically inexperienced actor-comedian, Jimmy Morales, president on a conservative-populist anti-corruption campaign platform. His disruptive term in office was marked by widespread corruption scandals, including himself and his own family members, and a successful effort to dismantle an international anti-corruption agency, CICIG (Chapter 7).

Elsewhere, Costa Ricans have not turned openly against their government or abandoned democratic values, although the latter have eroded somewhat. Both diffuse and specific institutional support have declined there. Meanwhile in Nicaragua, outside and domestic critics of the Ortega administration had harshly evaluated the government, but citizens as of 2014 on balance appeared rather contented. Something obviously changed by 2018 in Nicaragua when anti- and pro-regime demonstrations and violent protests and counter-protests erupted over altered social security policies and evolved into demands for greater democracy. We look forward to examining the legitimacy data on Nicaraguans in 2016 and 2018 when they become available.

Potential Emigrants

What might these attitudes matter for emigration, the movement of people out of Central America? The 2014 LAPOP survey asked: "Do you have intentions to go to live or work in another country within the next three years?" Only 10 percent of Costa Ricans answered yes, but the rest of the region differed greatly. Guatemalans (18 percent), Nicaraguans (23 percent), El Salvadorans (28 percent), and Hondurans (32 percent) affirmed an intent to move abroad within the next three years. These intentions speak volumes to the migration crisis currently afflicting Central America, Mexico, and the United States, as more and more families seek asylum at the US border.

An analysis of which Central Americans intended to emigrate, whether south to Costa Rica (many Nicaraguans' destination) or north toward the United States (Hondurans, Salvadorans, and Guatemalans), deeply underscores the extent and gravity of the migration situation and helps explain how it has become a crisis. We disaggregated the triple satisfaction/dissatisfaction variable into its three components and found none of them to have much influence on emigration intent in 2014. Other characteristics of intended migrants, in descending order of importance, included youth, being Honduran, or Salvadoran, males, persons from less democratic countries, crime victims, those strongly politically tolerant and democratically inclined but low on system support, and group activists. Interestingly, self-reported intended migrants came from across the economic, educational, and community-size spectrums. Contrary to the image of immigrants promoted by some, then, those who intended to emigrate were victims rather than perpetrators of crimes, and as likely as not to be well-educated and prosperous.

CONCLUSIONS

Early in the twenty-first century, most Central Americans were behaving in ways necessary to and consistent with democracy by participating in politics in diverse arenas. However, certain values supportive of democracy had eroded since previous editions of this book. Although a strong majority of Central Americans supported basic democratic participation rights and repudiated coups and authoritarian rule in 2014, in contrast system support, support for participation rights, and tolerance of regime critics had declined significantly from the previous decade. Support for confrontational political tactics rose, but support for rebellion remained stable across the region in the period covered by our surveys. The citizenries' part of consolidation—stably embracing democratic norms—remains incomplete in the region and invites further mischief by political elites who should be strengthening rather than undermining democratic practice. This leaves us unsure about whether democracy will consolidate in the isthmus, or whether more democracies will fail. Central Americans, no strangers to previous bad regimes and economic turmoil, appeared willing to extend their rulers only so much rope.

The most dangerous challenges to poorly consolidated democratic regimes arise among the elites who hold political, institutional, or economic power. They are the wild card in democratic consolidation, and one cannot easily predict whether increased public disaffection or protest would encourage anti-democratic elite actors should they decide to undermine democratic practices in particular countries. Given this partly discouraging panorama of public opinion, what might these countries' rulers or even outsiders do to strengthen the prospects for democratic stability in Central America, especially in the most vulnerable cases like Guatemala and El Salvador?

Willing power holders could redouble efforts to promote true elite settlements—inclusive, widely based agreements to abide by democratic rules of the political game and accept the institutionalized uncertainty that necessarily entails. At this writing, elite behavior in El Salvador and Guatemala—especially predatory corruption—appears to be corroding the institutions and their legitimacy, as well as democratic norms. Governments could, if they would, enact legal reforms and prosecute bribe takers. They could further reduce political repression by improving police training and curtailing official violence and repression. Building or maintaining high-quality election systems and rules would also likely increase support for political institutions. Indeed, real progress in this arena has occurred in El Salvador and Guatemala. But ground has been lost in both countries in the matter of corruption.

One thing that might encourage Central American elites to improve rather than weaken their fragile democracies is steadfast, credible encouragement from the United States. This should be offered on many fronts—support for the rule of law, transparency, clean elections, increased economic development assistance to ameliorate poverty, and greater flexibility in economic development models than rigid neoliberalism allows. Such policies and programs could contribute to the legitimacy of the political and economic systems by making them more liveable for Central Americans. In the foreseeable short term, however, the United States appears unlikely to move consistently in this direction.

NOTES

1. Aristotle, *Politics (Aristotle's Politics)*, Richard Robinson, trans. (Oxford: Clarendon Press, 1962); Carl Cohen, *Democracy* (New York: Free Press, 1971); Robert A. Dahl, *On Democracy* (New Haven, CT: Yale University Press, 1998); John Stuart Mill, *Considerations on Representative Government* (Indianapolis, IN: Bobbs-Merrill, 1958); Carole Pateman, *Participation and Democratic Theory* (Cambridge: Cambridge University Press, 1970); and David Held, *Models of Democracy*, 3rd ed. (Stanford, CA: Stanford University Press, 2006). Works emphasizing democracy and democratization in Latin America include Larry Diamond, et al., eds., *Democracy in Developing Countries: Latin America* (Boulder, CO: Lynne Rienner Publishers, 1999); Paul Drake, *Between Tyranny and Anarchy: A History of Democracy in Latin America, 1800–2006* (Stanford, CA: Stanford University Press, 2009); John A. Peeler, *Building Democracy in Latin America* (Boulder, CO: Lynne Rienner Publishers, 2004); Peter H. Smith, *Democracy in Latin America: Political Change in Comparative Perspective* (Oxford: Oxford University Press, 2016).

2. Elites and influential foreign actors may also influence democratic consolidation. When elites share a broad consensus on democratic rules of the political game it

strengthens democracy by reducing disruptive challenges to the system. Hegemonic powers, neighboring countries, significant donors of foreign aid, and international organizations who prefer democratic rules of the game can impose costs that make it harder for local actors to abandon democratic institutions. They may also pressure local actors so as to imperil democracy. See Samuel Huntington, *The Third Wave: Democratization in the Late Twentieth Century* (Norman, OK: University of Oklahoma Press, 1991); and Larry Jay Diamond, *Developing Democracy: Toward Consolidation* (Baltimore, MD: Johns Hopkins University Press, 1999). Peter Smith's *Democracy in Latin America* provides a cautionary note concerning the consolidation and quality of Latin American democracy.

3. Mitchell A. Seligson and John A. Booth, "Political Culture and Regime Type: Evidence from Nicaragua and Costa Rica," *Journal of Politics* 55 (August 1993), pp. 777–792.

4. John A. Booth and Patricia Bayer Richard, *Latin American Political Culture, Public Opinion, and Democracy* (Washington, DC: Congressional Quarterly Press, 2014); John A. Booth and Patricia Bayer Richard, "Civil Society, Political Capital, and Democratization in Central America," *Journal of Politics* 60 (August 1998), pp. 780–800; John A. Booth and Patricia Bayer Richard, "Civil Society and Political Context in Central America," *American Behavioral Scientist* 42 (September 1998), pp. 33–46; and John A. Booth and Patricia Bayer Richard, "Repression, Participation, and Democratic Norms in Urban Central America," *American Journal of Political Science* 40:4 (November 1996), pp. 1205–1232; Seligson and Booth, "Political Culture and Regime Type."

5. The 2014 and previous years' survey data were collected by research teams from Latin American countries under the auspices of the Americas Barometer of the Latin American Public Opinion Project (LAPOP). Each nation was surveyed, using a large core of identical survey items. National probability samples of approximately 1,500 respondents were interviewed from each nation. Respondents were selected using stratified national sampling frames, with respondent clusters within sampling units chosen with their probability of selection proportionate to size. In the results reported here, each national sample size is weighted to 1,500 respondents, for a regional sample of 7,500. Respondents were voting-age citizens of each country. The authors thank LAPOP and its major supporters for the data.

6. US Census Bureau, "Reported Voting and Registration, by Sex and Single Years of Age: November 2014," Table 1, www.census.gov/data/tables/time-series/demo/voting-and-registration/p20-577, accessed July 8, 2019.

7. The unweighted average voter turnout rate in the most recent presidential elections through 2014 for these Central American countries was 63 percent (International Institute for Democracy and Electoral Assistance (IDEA), "Voter Turnout by Country," presidential elections, www.idea.int/data-tools/region-view/21/, accessed July 9, 2019.

8. Ibid.

9. Results of a multiple regression analysis of 2012 LAPOP surveys reported voter registration using as predictor variables sex, age, age squared, educational attainment, standard of living, size of one's community of residence, evaluations of government economic management, overall national economic performance, and institutional support. Country dummies were included to control for specific national effects with Costa Rica as the reference case. For details see the sixth edition of John A. Booth, Christine J. Wade, and Thomas W. Walker, *Understanding Central America; Global Forces, Rebellion and Change* (Boulder, CO: Westview Press, 2015), Chapter 9, note 23 for further detail.

10. See International Institute for Democracy and Electoral Assistance (IDEA), Voter Turnout Database for all official results; accessed July 13, 2019.

11. Ibid.

12. John A. Booth, "Political Parties in Costa Rica: Sustaining Democratic Stability in a Latin American Context," in Paul Webb and Stephen White, eds., *Party Politics in New Democracies* (Oxford: Oxford University Press, 2007), pp. 305–344.

13. See Booth, Wade, and Walker, *Understanding Central America*, 6th edition, Chapter 9, note 12 for details on this a multiple regression analysis using frequency of attendance at political party meetings as the dependent variable.

14. Ibid, Table 9.1.

15. Regional average citizen confidence in parties (on a 0 to 100 scale) remained low at 34 in 2014, statistically unchanged from 2004. Confidence in parties by country was volatile over this decade (not uncommon because events such as a corruption scandal may easily alter such views may in the short term). For example, confidence in parties declined in Costa Rica from 35 in 2004 to 31 out of 100 in 2012, but then recovered to 38 in 2014. Confidence in parties reached 36 in Guatemala (up 7 points from 2004), then plunged to 25 in 2014. In Nicaragua it rose 8 points to 37 in 2014. Confidence in elections trended downward several points out of 100 from 2004 to 2014 except in Nicaragua. Trust in elections rose considerably there, as it did with support for the Ortega administration despite growing problems with election administration and quality.

16. See Booth, Wade, and Walker, *Understanding Central America*, 6th edition, Chapter 9, note 19 for details on this a multiple regression analysis of party and campaign activism (the average of persuading others how to vote, party meeting attendance, and campaign activity).

17. John A. Booth and Patricia Bayer Richard, "Untangling Social and Political Capital in Latin American Democracies," *Latin American Politics and Society* 54:3 (September 2012), pp. 33–64; Booth and Richard, "Civil Society and Political Context in Central America"; and Booth and Richard, "Repression, Participation, and Democratic Norms in Urban Central America."

18. The Honduran National Human Rights Commission in 2007 surveyed Hondurans' experiences with crime. It reported that 65 percent of Hondurans said they had quit going out at night for fear of violence, 44 percent curtailed their use of public transportation, and 43 percent had stopped visiting family and friends. See Borge y Asociados, *Encuesta Nacional de Opinión Pública: Seguridad Ciudadana* (Tegucigalpa: Comisionado Nacional de los Derechos Humanos, August 2007), www.conadeh.hn/documentos.htm, accessed June 10, 2009.

19. See Booth, Wade, and Walker, *Understanding Central America*, 6th edition, Chapter 9, note 23 for details.

20. These results are not comparable to those reported in the fourth edition of *Understanding Central America* because the question wording in 2004 was different so as to elicit higher reported contacting rates.

21. See Booth, Wade, and Walker, *Understanding Central America*, 6th edition, Chapter 9, note 25 for details.

22. Costa Rican governments typically respond to protests with study and policy change; see John A. Booth, *Costa Rica: Quest for Democracy* (Boulder, CO: Westview Press, 1998).

23. See Booth, Wade, and Walker, *Understanding Central America*, 6th edition, Chapter 9, note 27 for details.

24. This pattern of U-shaped legitimacy–participation relationships confirms the findings of Booth and Seligson in *The Legitimacy Puzzle in Central America* (Chapter 5).

25. John A. Booth and Patricia Bayer Richard, *Latin American Political Culture, Public Opinion, and Democracy* (Washington, DC: Public Opinion Quarterly Press, 2014).

26. Seligson and Booth, "Political Culture and Regime Type."

27. See Booth, Wade, and Walker, *Understanding Central America*, 6th edition, Chapter 9, note 32 for details.

28. Kaitlin J. Cassell, John A. Booth, and Mitchell A. Seligson, "Support for Coups in the Americas: Mass Norms and Democratization," *Journal of Latin American Politics and Society* 60:4, November 2018, pp. 1–25.

29. See Booth, Wade, and Walker, *Understanding Central America*, 6th edition, Chapter 9, note 36 for details.

30. Michael W. Foley, "Laying the Groundwork: The Struggle for Civil Society in El Salvador," *Journal of Interamerican Studies and World Affairs* 38 (1996), pp. 67–104.

31. Again, the data compared between the early 1990s and 2004 are for urban samples only.

32. See Booth, Wade, and Walker, *Understanding Central America*, 6th edition, Chapter 9, note 39 for details. See also Booth and Richard, *Latin American Political Culture, Public Opinion, and Democracy.*

33. See Booth, Wade, and Walker, *Understanding Central America*, 6th edition, Chapter 9, note 40 for details.

34. Because it has no national armed forces, Costa Rica was excluded from this calculation for the military only.

35. Sonia Nazario, "Pay or Die," *New York Times* Sunday Review, July 28, 2019, pp. 1, 6–7; Azam Ahmed, "Either They Kill Us or We Kill Them," *New York Times*, May 5, 2019, pp. 1, 12–13.

36. Planeta Político, "Los presidentes con mayor aprobación en América Latina," June 2019, https://planetapolitico.com/los-presidentes-con-mayor-aprobacion-en-america-latina/.

37. The authors could not find survey data on gay, bisexual, or transsexual populations in Central America.

38. Booth and Richard, *Latin American Political Culture*, Ch. 7, using 2010 and 2012 AmericasBarometer surveys.

39. Guttmacher Institute, "Abortion in Latin America and the Caribbean," March 2018, www.guttmacher.org/fact-sheet/abortion-latin-america-and-caribbean.

40. This pattern has been reported previously in Booth and Richard, *Latin American Political Culture*, pp. 159–162.

41. El Salvador's self-identified ethnic division as indigenous or black/mulatto (4.6 and 6.6 percent respectively seemed high for 2014 to the authors. However, a four-survey analysis of AmericasBarometer El Salvador results with a total N of 6,000 produced an average of 5.3 percent for both indigenous and black/mulatto. Consistently more Salvadorans seem to self-identify as such than most scholars would expect.

42. John A. Booth and Mitchell A. Seligson, *The Legitimacy Puzzle in Latin America: Political Support and Democracy in Eight Nations* (Cambridge: Cambridge University Press, 2009).

43. Ibid.

RECOMMENDED READINGS AND RESOURCES

Booth, John A. 1998. *Costa Rica: Quest for Democracy*. Boulder, CO: Westview Press.

Booth, John A. 2007. "Political Parties in Costa Rica: Sustaining Democratic Stability in a Latin American Context." In Paul Webb and Stephen White, eds. *Party Politics in New Democracies*. Oxford: Oxford University Press, pp. 305–344.

Booth, John A. and Patricia Bayer Richard. 1996. "Repression, Participation, and Democratic Norms in Urban Central America." *American Journal of Political Science* 40 (4): 1205–1232.

Booth, John A. and Patricia Bayer Richard. 1998. "Civil Society, Political Capital, and Democratization in Central America." *Journal of Politics* 60 (August): 780–800.

Booth, John A. and Patricia Bayer Richard. 2014. *Latin American Political Culture, Public Opinion and Democracy*. Washington, DC: Congressional Quarterly Press.

Booth, John A. and Mitchell A. Seligson. 1995. *Elections and Democracy in Central America Revisited*. Chapel Hill, NC: University of North Carolina Press.

Booth, John A. and Mitchell A. Seligson. 2009. *The Legitimacy Puzzle in Latin America: Political Support and Democracy in Eight Nations*. Cambridge: Cambridge University Press.

Cassell, Kaitlin J., John A. Booth, and Mitchell A. Seligson. 2018. "Support for Coups in the Americas: Mass Norms and Democratization." *Journal of Latin American Politics and Society* 60 (4): November, 1–25.

Dahl, Robert A. 1998. *On Democracy*. New Haven, CT: Yale University Press.

Diamond, Larry, Juan J. Linz, and Seymour Martin Lipset. 1989. *Democracy in Developing Countries, Volume 4: Latin America*. Boulder, CO: Lynne Rienner Publishers.

Drake, Paul. 2009. *Between Tyranny and Anarchy: A History of Democracy in Latin America, 1800–2006*. Stanford, CA: Stanford University Press.

Hume, Mo. 2013. "El Salvador." In Diego Sánchez-Ancochea and Salvador Martí i Puig, eds. *Handbook of Central American Governance*. London: Routledge, pp. 385–399.

Huntington, Samuel. 1991. *The Third Wave: Democratization in the Late Twentieth Century*. Norman, OK: University of Oklahoma Press.

Latin American Public Opinion Project (LAPOP). 2004–2009. Nashville, TN: Vanderbilt University Press. www.vanderbilt.edu/lapop/.

Pateman, Carole. 1970. *Participation and Democratic Theory*. Cambridge: Cambridge University Press.

Peeler, John A. 2004. *Building Democracy in Latin America*. Boulder, CO: Lynne Rienner Publishers.

Seligson, Mitchell A. and John A. Booth. 1993. "Political Culture and Regime Type: Evidence from Nicaragua and Costa Rica." *Journal of Politics* 55 (August): 777–792.

Smith, Peter H. 2016. *Democracy in Latin America: Political Change in Comparative Perspective*. Oxford: Oxford University Press.

Webb, Paul and Stephen White, eds. 2007. *Political Parties in New Democracies*. Oxford: Oxford University Press.

10

POWER, DEMOCRACY, AND US POLICY IN CENTRAL AMERICA

THE UNITED STATES EXERTS GREAT INFLUENCE ON CENTRAL American politics. US proximity and the disparities in population and wealth between the region's major hegemon and its tiny neighbors have allowed US policy to shape the region, sometimes detrimentally. Washington's Cold War–era definition of its interests in Central America and its strategies for achieving them were short-termed, reactive, and preoccupied with political stability. The US effort to contain leftist influence and insurgency from the 1960s through the 1990s intensified national conflicts. By the mid-1990s civil wars had killed over 300,000 people (mainly civilians), battered regional economies, displaced millions of people, and left countless others jobless, orphaned, or physically or psychologically maimed. While by no means the only cause of this tragedy, US policy contributed importantly to it.

The Cold War between the United States and the Soviets ended in 1990, and Central America's revolutionary–counterrevolutionary conflicts ended by 1996. US fears of Communist-inspired uprisings and subversion accordingly waned and the United States briefly scaled back its intervention in the region and for a few years stepped up its promotion of democracy. Yet, Washington resumed political intervention in the region in the late 1990s and after 2001, still promoting security and neoliberal economics but increasingly considering narcotics trafficking and migration from the region as aspects of security. So although the tactics and emphases of US policy toward the isthmus have evolved, overall US objectives have remained consistent. US governments have always sought to protect US economic and security interests.

THE PROBLEM OF POWER

Power is the basic currency of politics. Simply put, groups within a given polity generally benefit from the prevailing political regime in rough proportion to the amount of power they can bring to bear on that regime. The powerful receive the most; the powerless, little or nothing. Charles W. Anderson argued that the traditional "power contenders" in Latin American society—the Church, the military, the rural and urban economic elites—allowed new groups to enter and receive benefits from the political system only when these groups demonstrated their own "power capabilities."[1] We argued in Chapter 2 that regime changes in Central America—especially struggles for democratization—have involved conflict and the reconfiguration of relationships among traditional power contenders and newer groups from the working, middle, and even upper classes.

Power capabilities vary from group to group. The Catholic Church exercises authority through its belief systems and moral suasion. The military and police hold much of the means of violent coercion. Economic elites use their wealth to influence policy and institutions. In contrast, lower-class groups have scant resources but can sometimes wield influence by organizing, striking, protesting, and voting. But normally, most Central American peasants, urban and rural workers, and slum dwellers lack enough organization and resources to give them much effective power. During the Cold War, when such groups attempted to amplify their power by organizing, existing power holders called them subversives and "Communists" and violently repressed them. Because Central America's poor majorities held little power, policymakers usually ignored their plight. Previous chapters have shown how this situation generated popular grievances, and how some regimes suppressed them and thus made violence the people's last recourse.

Great disparities of power between the small privileged upper class versus the emerging middle-class and underprivileged, impoverished majority generated the Central American crises of the late twentieth century. As noted in earlier chapters, power relationships in the five countries had deep historical roots. It is no accident that Costa Rica, with the most egalitarian society, and

Honduras—an economic backwater that was late to develop a cohesive and exploitative national elite—had less turmoil. It is also no surprise that Guatemala, El Salvador, and Nicaragua, the countries with the greatest historically rooted power disparities, experienced the region's highest levels of violence. Their elites, long accustomed to their lopsided power advantage, resisted sharing power and making policies to promote the genuine development of all sectors of society.

DEMOCRACY

Democracy can provide a base of legitimacy for contemporary governments, and most regimes today claim to be democratic. The meaning of the term *democracy*, however, is contested. Socialist theorists usually stress distributive economic and social criteria, whereas those from the industrially developed West tend to emphasize procedural rules. In the United States, one definition with which few would quarrel is that democracy is "government of, by, and for the people." However simple this definition may sound, it sets forth two principles fundamental to effective democracy: first, that the system should be as participatory as possible, and, second, that it should facilitate general well-being.[2]

In the 1980s the United States promoted civilian rule and elections in Central America. When these developed Washington hailed the birth of "democracy" in its client states, Guatemala, El Salvador, and Honduras, but condemned its alleged absence in revolutionary Nicaragua. Only in 1990, when Nicaraguans elected US-backed Violeta Barrios de Chamorro president, did Washington finally recognize Nicaragua as democratic. Closer inspection, however, reveals the US interpretation of democratization to have been skewed in service to other foreign policy objectives.[3] All four countries held nationwide, internationally observed elections. Observers pronounced elections in three countries—except El Salvador's in the 1980s—to be procedurally clean. But democracy requires more than simply holding procedurally correct elections or establishing formal civilian rule. A critical issue is popular participation in elections and in other political affairs.

The elections in Guatemala in 1985 and 1990 as well as those in El Salvador in 1982, 1984, 1988, 1989, and 1991 occurred while state-sponsored terror was taking tens of thousands of lives, disarticulating civic and political organizations, and suppressing independent media. Repression limited citizens' participation only to voting. Tiny minorities of center and right-wing parties nominated candidates and campaigned, while repression kept turnout low.

In Nicaragua in 1984 and 1990, in contrast, there was no program of state-sponsored terror. Organizations representing the poor majority had been encouraged to develop and make demands on government. Opposition parties and elite interest groups openly participated in politics. International human rights organizations concurred that the torture and elimination of political opponents, widespread and institutionalized in Guatemala and El Salvador, were absent in Nicaragua. Though important rightists boycotted the 1984 Nicaraguan election, three parties on the Sandinista National Liberation Front's (Frente Sandinista de Liberación Nacional, FSLN) right and three on their left challenged the Sandinistas. Nicaragua's anti-regime media (including *La Prensa* and Radio Católica), though partly censored, carried an anti-Sandinista message to the voters. The six participating opposition parties enjoyed extensive, uncensored free access to state-sponsored radio and television. Participation by citizens and organizations was freer there than in Guatemala and El Salvador.

One may also question the US application of the term *democracy* in Central America during the Cold War by asking: were there governments "for the people"? In whose interest did they rule? The Sandinista revolution established programs to promote literacy, disease prevention, agrarian reform, housing, social security, and improve the status of women. By 1984, even its critics credited the government with "significant gains against illiteracy and disease."[4] Eventually the US-backed Contra war and economic embargo diverted public spending away from social welfare into the military budget. Nicaragua's disastrous economic and political situation in 1990 led its citizens to use the democratic election system established by the revolutionary regime to vote the FSLN out of office and end the revolution. This Sandinista handover of power to the opposition in 1990 flowed from democratic rules of the game already in place and confirmed Nicaragua's transition to a civilian-democratic regime in 1987.

In contrast, regime change toward democracy during the last decade of the Cold War proceeded differently in El Salvador and Guatemala. In each, the reformist military regime that overthrew the previous military-authoritarian rulers acted with so much violent repression that many observers detected no meaningful political transformation. And when each country's reformist military regime ceded power to a transitional civilian government, skepticism abounded about whether civilians ruled or the militaries still held veto power. Civilian politicians, however, did gradually gain independence from the armed forces. Formerly excluded power contenders were eventually allowed to take part. Honduras followed a similar path of gradual transition to democracy, albeit without a civil war or such intense repression.

Eventually all four countries established elected civilian regimes under pressure from the United States, but the quality of their democracies remained in flux. Some argue that not only must formal rules of democracy and repression-free popular participation exist but, more importantly, socioeconomic foundations must also prevail. To truly participate and thus influence decisions in a formally democratic country, the poor majority needs economic well-being and the fundamental human and political resources it provides. By the late 1990s Nicaragua, El Salvador, Guatemala, and Honduras all had formal civilian democracies, but poverty and maldistributed income and wealth left poor citizens largely without the socioeconomic requisites of an effective democracy. Elite behavior has since undermined democratic performance, as confirmed by the country narratives in earlier chapters and by independent evaluations (see Table 9.3 and Figure 2.1). Critics have accordingly tagged the new regimes in Central America as "low-intensity democracies" or "polyarchies" to distinguish them from more egalitarian regimes that provide rule "by the people and for the people."[5] Thus elites—albeit including a broader circle of power contenders than in the 1970s—continue to dominate these systems and poorly meet democracy's basic electoral or distributive norms.

MOBILIZATION

Following World War II, awareness grew that something was seriously wrong in Latin America. Those who viewed mass poverty as rooted in an extremely unequal distribution of power began advocating its broader diffusion. In the 1940s and 1950s, social democratic and Christian democratic parties talked of "penetrating" the masses, of promoting party-oriented labor, peasant, and neighborhood organizations to express mass interests. Catholic educators such as Brazil's Paulo Freire argued that mass empowerment required the emergence of a socially, politically, and linguistically literate citizenry. Followers of these teachings began promoting adult-education consciousness-raising programs in which poor people examined and questioned their social conditions.[6]

Jolted by the Cuban revolution in 1959, the United States at first supported reform in Latin America with programs like the Alliance for Progress (to promote economic growth) and the Peace Corps (to promote community development by mobilizing, educating, and empowering poor people to solve their own problems). For a while, thousands of idealistic US citizens worked with Latin America's poor and promoted collective self-help programs. The US Agency for International Development (USAID) encouraged Central American governments to develop hundreds of community-action and -improvement programs and cooperatives. Such efforts eventually brought a surge of democratic participation by ordinary Central Americans. Soon, however, some Central American elites viewed this mobilization by the poor as a threat and accused the Peace Corps of associating with "Communists." Eventually, central governments complained to US diplomats, and the Nixon administration terminated Peace Corps community-action programs. Keeping good relations with pro-US regimes mattered more to Washington than promoting democratization.

The Latin American Catholic Church extensively promoted mobilization in the 1960s. Beginning in the 1950s, Church figures such as Dom Helder Câmara of Brazil promoted "liberation theology," which advocated social justice and uplifting the oppressed majority. By the beginning of the next decade, they found a powerful ally in the Vatican as Pope John XXIII undertook his *aggiornamento*, or updating, of the Catholic Church. Part of this process, as expressed by the Second Vatican Council, was to focus on the problems of Latin America, by then the largest segment of world Catholicism. This, in turn, stimulated Latin American Catholics to examine more deeply the problems of their region.

The Second General Conference of Latin American Bishops, held at Medellín, Colombia, in 1968 examined poverty and exploitation in Latin America. The bishops used a form of structural analysis resembling dependency theory (see Chapter 2). They argued that Catholic clergy should make a "preferential option for the poor" by promoting Christian base communities (*comunidades eclesiales de base*, CEBs).[7] In these grassroots organizations people of all classes would discuss community or national problems in light of the social gospel. In addition, natural community leaders (lay "delegates of the word") would be trained to preach the social gospel and act as community organizers.[8]

The Medellín bishops' conference deeply affected Central America. Thousands of priests and nuns—and even some bishops—began implementing these ideas almost immediately. By the 1970s, newly created CEBs were promoting grassroots mobilization in the region's four northern countries. Tens of thousands of poor people were learning that they had rights to fair treatment, dignity, and justice from their governments and employers. Though the CEBs were nonviolent, elite-dominated governments viewed them as subversive. Again the label "Communist" was applied. Tens of thousands of Catholics, including dozens of priests and nuns and even one archbishop, died in the resulting official repression.

By the mid- to late 1970s, social mobilization became widespread throughout northern Central America among peasant unions, cooperatives, urban labor unions, organizations of teachers, medical personnel, students, and women. As noted in Chapter 8, the Honduran regime accommodated or only mildly repressed mobilization, thus avoiding open insurrection. In Somoza's Nicaragua, and in Guatemala and El Salvador, however, the more entrenched elites instead violently suppressed new popular demands. Repression begat violence as increasing numbers opted for insurrection. In Nicaragua, mobilization, responding repression, and insurrection ultimately led to a revolutionary coalition victory in 1979. In Guatemala and El Salvador, state-sponsored terrorism (with especially heavy US material support—see Table A.3) curtailed or reversed civilian mobilization and stalemated rebels.

The mobilization that had brought the rebel victory in Nicaragua continued under the revolutionary government thereafter. Prior to the victory, Catholics from the CEB movement had joined with nationalist Marxists from the FSLN and others to organize a variety of grassroots organizations (see Chapter 5). After 1979 the CEBs continued and other grassroots organizations emerged among farmers and ranchers. A 1984 estimate put between 700,000 and 800,000 Nicaraguan citizens—around half of all adults—in such organizations.[9] Grassroots organizations defended the revolution, promoted political socialization, mobilized volunteers for social programs, and provided venues where many Nicaraguans experienced their first meaningful political participation. The revolutionary government also conducted a basic literacy crusade in its first year in power. This greatly reduced adult illiteracy, built workforce skills, and empowered citizens (and also earned Nicaragua a United Nations prize).[10]

THE ROOTS OF US POLICY IN CENTRAL AMERICA

At least until the end of the Cold War, the United States had certain legitimate and consensual security interests in Central America. Most agreed that it was in the interest of the United States that no Soviet military alliances, bases, troops, advanced weapons, or nuclear arms be present in the isthmus. It was and remains in the interest of the United States that Central American societies enjoy sufficient prosperity, democracy, and political stability that their citizens would not emigrate massively. Similarly, Central American nations needed peace among themselves, and appropriately sized military forces to avoid regional war or threats to the vital Panama Canal or trade routes. However, many critics of US policy in Central America believe that US actions during the Cold War actually harmed rather than advanced these interests. In order to understand how this came about, we must review the roots of US policy.

US interests in Central America have evolved over time and have sometimes been subject to intense debate within the United States. During the nineteenth century, encouraging trade, coping with massive British naval power, and transit across the isthmus dominated US concerns. US sea power supplanted British dominance in the late nineteenth century and as the United States rapidly industrialized. Desire for a trans-isthmian canal led to US intervention in Panama in 1903. Once built and operating, the United States used troops in Panama and Nicaragua to assure its continuing canal monopoly and protect the waterway. American diplomats (sometimes assisted by the US marines) aggressively promoted US business and geopolitical interests throughout Central America in the early twentieth century. During World War II, the United States protected the Panama Canal from Axis interference through cooperative security arrangements with regional governments.

During the Cold War, US interests in Central America remained focused on economic and security concerns—especially containing Soviet-inspired Communism. Despite the boom brought about by the Central American Common Market (CACM) in the 1960s, US investments in Central America remained modest compared to those in most other parts of the world. Nevertheless, promotion of a "healthy business climate" in Central America also heavily influenced US policy choices.

From the late 1940s on, Washington increasingly viewed popular mobilization in Central America as problematic. Mobilization especially worried some of Central America's entrenched elites, who responded with state terror to discourage participation. Hearkening to their cries of "Communist subversion," Washington joined the fray. A first example came with the 1944–1954 Guatemalan "revolution," in which a working- and middle-class movement re-established democracy after decades of military rule (Chapter 7). Ten years later, a US Central Intelligence Agency (CIA)-backed rightist movement overthrew the elected, reform-oriented government; it implemented a wave of repression and helped re-establish three decades military rule. Thus the US government allied with the privileged minority in Central America in its campaign against participatory mobilization. US policy in the region perhaps responded more to domestic political fears, misperceptions, and rhetoric in the United States and the fears of local elites than to the reality of the situation in the isthmus.

As a capitalist country, the United States promoted capitalism and protected US business interests abroad. US policymakers usually formulated national security—especially in Central America and the Caribbean—as much in business and trade terms as along military and geostrategic lines. From the early twentieth century on, the impulse to contain this "threat of Communism" motivated conservative politicians and cowed their critics. Accelerating after the Cuban revolution began in 1959, the fear of Soviet-inspired Communism in our "backyard" shaped US policy in Central America. Local reformers were usually viewed as incompatible with US interests because American politicians feared being accused of "losing ground" to Communism. Thus even US leaders sympathetic to socioeconomic reform and democracy supported demobilization of "subversive" Central Americans. (During the Cold War, the only Central American country where some popular mobilization and socioeconomic reform succeeded with US support was Costa Rica. There social-democratic reformers of the National Liberation movement allied with conservatives to oust Communists from power in 1948.)

Much of the US preoccupation with Communism in Central America, however, was unfounded (see below).[11] Correctly or not, most administrations from the 1940s through the 1980s strongly believed that Communism threatened. They transmitted this concern to Latin American military establishments as part of a doctrine of national security that justified a widespread demobilization campaign in Central America.

As taught in war colleges and military training centers around the hemisphere, the doctrine of national security was a product of both US anti-Communism and Latin American elaboration. It originated in the US CIA and National Security Council in the late 1940s. In 1950, National Security Council document NSC-68 described an expanding Communist menace and urged huge increases in military expenditures. This framework guided US behavior in the early Cold War and spread to Latin America through US training programs for most military establishments of the hemisphere.

Latin America in the 1950s and 1960s provided fertile ground for these Cold War security concepts. Though local Communist parties were weak and there were almost no external threats, political elites and their military allies found it convenient to portray popular mobilization and protest as subversive and Moscow-controlled. National security ideas from the United States were quickly adapted and refined into a guiding doctrine, complete with training centers, military philosophers, literature, and annual meetings of the Latin American Anti-Communist Confederation. The geopolitical ideology viewed national and international politics as a zero-sum game between Communism and the "free world." Internal politics became a battlefield, while social and political justice concerns became irrelevant or threatening.

The national security doctrine, inherently elitist, held the military uniquely capable of understanding the national good, having the right to run the state and make decisions for society as a whole if military leaders disliked civilian politicians' performance. The doctrine equated democracy with a visceral anti-Communism. Accordingly, strange as it may seem, the harshly authoritarian anti-Communist "national security states" created under this ideology were often labelled "democratic" by their apologists.

All opposition to national security states—and most civilian organizations except those of the right—was viewed as subversive, "Communist," or "Communist-inspired." Brutal demobilization of civil society was accepted as appropriate. US personnel sometimes encouraged their Latin American colleagues to employ "counterterror" (extra-legal arrest, torture, and murder) to quiet so-called subversive groups.[12] Most Latin American militaries and police received technical and material assistance and training, including counterterror techniques. The tactics of torture, murder, and disappearance employed by security forces and government-sponsored death squads were similar from country to country.[13]

By the late 1960s and early 1970s, the USAID's Office of Public Safety had close links to the security forces of Brazil, Uruguay, and Guatemala, countries whose radical demobilization programs practiced death squads, torture, murder, and disappearance.[14] In the early 1970s these links became a scandal in the United States and throughout the world. The US Congress investigated US program links to state-sponsored terror in Latin America. In 1974, Congress terminated US police and internal security aid programs and ordered the Department of State to submit yearly reports on the human rights performance of all countries receiving US aid. But these measures did not solve the problem. In practice, State Department human rights reports seemed to be influenced more by the status quo-oriented policy goals of Washington than by the objective reality of the countries in question.[15] Some objectionable US links were discreetly terminated, yet state-sponsored terror and US assistance continued to rights-violating regimes and forces. Starting in 1982, the Reagan administration successfully petitioned Congress to waive the prohibition against US assistance to the security forces of El Salvador, Guatemala, and Honduras.

COMMUNISM IN CENTRAL AMERICA

Because so much US policy turned on the question of Communism in Central America, we must explore its meaning and influence. Most Central American insurgents and many intellectuals found Marxist and, in some cases, Leninist analysis useful in understanding the reality around them. Nevertheless, it is misleading to equate the intellectual acceptance of those analytical tools with subservience to a Communist agenda of a Soviet-oriented international Communist movement. Most Central Americans were too pragmatic and nationalistic to accept such control. Indeed, Soviet-oriented Communist parties fared poorly in Central America. Communists, socialists, and anarchists—many of them European exiles—influenced Central American intellectual life and labor movements in the early twentieth century. The Communists, followers of Karl Marx, received a boost over their leftist competitors because of the Soviet revolution in Russia. Although always targets of repression, Communists gained leadership roles in Central American labor movements in the 1930s. The Soviet alliance with the West during World War II gave the region's tiny Communist parties and their unions a political opening in the early 1940s. Although repression of the left resumed in most countries after 1945, brief exceptions occurred in Costa Rica in the 1940s and Guatemala in the early 1950s, where Communist elements became junior partners with more conservative parties in government coalitions. Communist parties generally fared poorly because the Soviets tightly limited local affiliates' flexibility to pursue national solutions. The Stalin–Hitler pact of 1939 discredited Communists in Central America and elsewhere. Soviet insistence later on that Latin American Communists accommodate local dictators further tarnished their already poor image. Moscow's strictures on local Communist parties caused many impatient advocates of sociopolitical reform in the 1960s to resign and emulate Castro's successful Cuban insurgency.

Throughout most of their histories, therefore, local nationalists—including many Marxists—mistrusted the small, Moscow-oriented Central American Communist parties. Most knew that the Cuban Communist Party, faithful to Soviet orders to peacefully coexist with Fulgencio Batista, opposed Fidel Castro until just before the rebel victory. In Costa Rica, the local Communist Party, the region's largest, backed presidents Rafael Calderón Guardia (1940 to 1944) and Teodoro Picado Michalski (1944 to 1948). When Calderón Guardia and his allies won the 1948 election, the anti-Communist opposition claimed fraud and successfully rebelled. Thereafter Costa Rica's Communists never won more than 5 of 57 seats in the Legislative Assembly. By the mid-1980s their influence faded to nil.

In Nicaragua the Communist-led labor movement collaborated with the Somoza dictatorship in the 1940s. The FSLN's founders broke away from the pro-Soviet Nicaraguan Socialist Party because it offered no solutions to Nicaragua's problems. Only just before the FSLN victory did the local Communists join the rebel cause. After the rebel victory, no Moscow-oriented Communist party played more than a peripheral role in the new government.

In the 1984 election, Nicaragua's three Communist parties, which had lambasted the FSLN for allegedly selling out the revolution, garnered only 3.8 percent of the total vote.[16] After 1984, Nicaragua's traditional Communists remained opposed to the FSLN. In El Salvador, local Communists joined the insurrectionary effort just shortly before the would-be "final offensive" of late 1980 and early 1981.

In summary, during the Cold War traditional Central American Communist parties influenced labor movements and participated in government in Costa Rica and Guatemala in the 1940s and early 1950s. Otherwise, at their strongest they remained weak, unpopular, opposed to revolution, and subservient to Moscow.

Central America's Marxist revolutionary movements were more complex than the Communist parties. Most of the principal leaders of Nicaragua's FSLN, El Salvador's Farabundo Martí National Liberation Front (Frente Farabundo Martí de Liberación Nacional, FMLN), and Guatemala's National Revolutionary Union (Unidad Revolucionaria Nacional Guatemalteca, URNG) were Marxist-Leninists. They shared socialism's predilection for distributive justice as an answer for unjust societies. Their revolutionary strategy followed Castro's in Cuba—guerrilla warfare against the regime and its armed forces, supplemented by tactical alliances with other social and political forces. Marxist-Leninist rebels, as we have shown, gained support largely because of the repressiveness of the regimes they challenged. Nicaragua's Sandinistas built their support base and broad coalition as the most viable alternative for those brutally repressed by the Somoza regime. In El Salvador and Guatemala, intense governmental repression blocked moderate, centrist options for redress of grievances and drove many into Marxist-led guerrilla movements.

Marxist-Leninist rebels regarded Cuba as an ally and received some Cuban aid in their struggles. Soviet and Eastern bloc assistance to insurgents was limited, in keeping with Moscow's skepticism about their prospects. Once the Sandinistas won, however, their links to the Soviet bloc became overtly friendly and Moscow more cooperative. After the West refused to provide Nicaragua military assistance in 1980, and correctly anticipating increased American hostility, the Sandinistas turned to Cuban and Soviet arms and advice for reorganizing their security forces.[17] As US antagonism mounted in the early and mid-1980s, Nicaragua rapidly strengthened its Eastern bloc links to counter an expected invasion, fend off the Contras, and replace embargoed Western aid, trade, and credit.[18]

Despite such links, the Sandinistas remained pragmatic on policy. Instead of imposing Soviet-style Stalinist economic centralism and one-party monopoly of the revolution (as Castro had in Cuba), they promoted a mixed economy and retained political pluralism. Although the Sandinistas never hid that they found parts of Marxist and Leninist analysis useful, their social, economic, and political policies revealed them to be pragmatic and nationalists, not orthodox Communists.

Nicaragua's critics highlighted the Sandinista government's friendly relationship with the socialist bloc, but that link should be put in perspective. Nicaragua increased its ties not only to the Eastern bloc but also to many non-Communist regimes. Trade, aid, and diplomatic relations multiplied with governments as disparate as those of Brazil, Canada, Chile, France, Libya, the People's Republic of China, the Scandinavian countries, and Spain. Although Nicaragua frequently voted with the USSR in the United Nations, it sometimes abstained or voted against the USSR on important UN issues. Nicaragua's UN voting record from 1979 through 1985 revealed that, although Nicaragua often voted against US positions and with the USSR, it agreed almost as often with most Latin American countries, especially Mexico.[19] Although Nicaragua eventually relied almost exclusively on the socialist bloc for military supplies, the Sandinistas had first asked the United States to help standardize its military equipment. Despite the Pentagon's endorsement of that proposal, the Carter administration—facing a conservative, Cold War-embracing Ronald Reagan in the 1980 election campaign—rejected that request.[20]

Like the Sandinistas, other Central American insurgents appeared to be Marxist-Leninists with respect to revolutionary strategy, but pragmatic nationalists in concrete policy matters. They recognized that US influence in the isthmus would probably doom any purely Communist regime or government, especially one that allowed Soviet troops or missiles within its borders. Moreover, by the 1980s evidence of the failure of Stalinist political and economic centralism abounded, so that for these revolutionaries to ape failed systems would have been unrealistic.

Although the United States had been intensely worried about Communism in Central America for decades, in retrospect its concerns appear overblown. Communist parties were weak. Marxist-Leninist guerrillas had not prospered in Honduras and Costa Rica, where regimes were not excessively repressive. America's worries about Communism produced counterproductive policies—the ugliest of which was to assist repressive regimes in their campaigns of demobilization.

DEMOBILIZATION IN CENTRAL AMERICA

Conservative regimes in Central America used varying demobilization tactics to undermine their actual or potential political opponents. On the less repressive end these regimes used economic and legal barriers, election systems, and the police and military to exclude critics, opposition parties, unions, and others from the political arena, policy-making, and public goods. When economic downturns generated protest and reform demands, tactics became more repressive, especially during the Cold War. Security forces spied upon, arrested, and violently repressed popular organizations and protests and the military seized control of the state apparatus. When armed insurgent groups challenged these regimes, state terror escalated into overt and covert war on their own citizens, justified by the national security doctrine and encouraged and financed by the United States. Whatever the form, the objectives remained constant—to render the ordinary citizenry of Central America passive and to deny power and benefits to outside-the-regime actors. For the United States, demobilization facilitated continued rule by pro-US elites, allies in the presumed containment of Communism.

It is easy to veer too far into dry details of budgets, aid, and foreign policy shifts. However, it is useful to note that the United States spent $436 million nominal dollars on military aid to Central America between 1946 and 1992, and another $2.3 billion on economic aid which propped up and allowed some governments to shift their domestic resources to their armed forces (see Table A.3). We could detail army and police killings of the 350,000 people who died in demobilization campaigns, only a tiny fraction of them actual rebels, or the flow of US arms, advisers, intelligence, and CIA-contracted supply flights and C5A strafing in El Salvador that shredded towns and their residents. We could detail the murders of national and foreign priests and nuns, of peasant and union activists, college and high school students, teachers, and doctors. Previous editions have shared photos of government body dumps. The details could so overwhelm that it would obscure the bigger picture.

Despite some death squad activity in Honduras in the early 1980s, systematic mass demobilization programs occurred largely where traditional elites were the most entrenched—Guatemala, El Salvador, and Nicaragua under the Somozas. In Guatemala and El Salvador, demobilization took the form of state-sponsored terror. Nicaragua experienced state-sponsored terror prior to the Sandinista victory of 1979, followed by US-sponsored Contra terror against the Sandinista revolution (1981–1990).

Demobilization—or at least the US link to it—lasted longest and was most brutal in Guatemala.[21] It commenced with the US-sponsored overthrow of elected reformist president Jacobo Arbenz in 1954. Uprising leader Carlos Castillo Armas took over as president, and CIA personnel assisted in blacklisting an estimated 70,000 alleged Communists among supporters of the ousted government. First banning those listed from public employment and subjecting them to imprisonment without trial, this register ultimately became a death list that guided assassinations. Previously nonviolent politicians without options under the new dictatorship fled or joined incipient rebel groups in the early 1960s. By the late 1960s, the insurgents and the political opposition in general were alike labeled "terrorists." Washington became increasingly involved in Guatemalan affairs; it blocked a return to democracy in the early 1960s and provided escalating security assistance, advice, and military training.

Guatemala's military practiced "counterterror" featuring the torture, murder, and disappearance of thousands of alleged subversives. Uniformed soldiers and government-sanctioned death squads carried out the demobilization. By the early 1970s, rural areas had been "pacified" of guerrillas. State terror then moved to the cities as President Carlos Arana Osorio eliminated alleged subversives (e.g., party leaders, intellectuals, media persons, and labor organizers). After a mid-1970s lull in violence, military officers' appropriations of traditional indigenous lands brought renewed protests and indigenous support for new guerrilla forces. Several insurgent groups merged into the URNG in 1981 (see Table A.4). The regime responded by renewing rural demobilization in the early 1980s. This included coercing peasants into military-led militias that massacred numerous indigenous villages.

Guatemala's egregious human rights abuses—committed with US assistance—became so embarrassing that from the mid-1970s through 1984, the US Congress and Carter administration reduced military aid to Guatemala (see Table A.3). Fiscal sleight-of-hand mitigated this aid "cutoff." Under the Reagan and first Bush administrations, economic assistance dipped fractionally, then escalated rapidly. US military training continued throughout, material military aid was disguised and resumed, and US ally Israel filled in for the United States as Guatemala's arms supplier.[22] A coup in 1982 installed General Efraín Ríos Montt in the presidency; he further increased demobilization in indigenous areas. Military leaders then ousted Ríos Montt in 1983. They decided to return nominal control of the executive and legislative branches to civilians. Washington encouraged this change because it would facilitate increased military and economic assistance to Guatemala.

Civilian Vinicio Cerezo Arévalo won the 1985 election. The civilian transitional regime thereafter erratically moved toward controlling the armed forces and ending the civil war, at first with little avail. In 1993 President Jorge Serrano Elías attempted a disastrous self-coup. Guatemala's Congress and the judiciary (with US backing) removed him, which boosted the peace process. With the Cold War over by 1990, El Salvador's civil war settled in 1992, and with increasing US encouragement, Guatemala's military finally allowed five decades of demobilization to end. President Alvaro Arzú, elected in 1995, completed peace negotiations with the URNG in 1966, began curbing the military and reforming the police, and instituted a more inclusive, formal civilian-democratic regime.

What were the human costs of the lengthy war against Guatemala's center, left, and civil society? In 1999 the Historical Clarification Commission estimated the death toll at more than 200,000 Guatemalans (2.5 percent of the population), and the displaced at 1.5 million internal or foreign refugees (19 percent of the population).[23] (For perspective, a similar percentage of today's US population would be 8,250,000 dead and 62 million displaced.) The carnage was labelled genocidal, having most afflicted the indigenous peoples (83 percent of the victims and over 600 Mayan communities massacred). The report judged US military aid to have contributed importantly to the human rights violations.[24] One can hardly imagine the lingering corrosive effects on Guatemala's political culture of five decades of state terror and internal war.

El Salvador, too, undertook demobilization in the 1970s and 1980s in which the United States played an even larger role than in Guatemala. Demobilization there was nothing new. The military, on behalf of the agrarian elite, systematically killed around 30,000 poor people in the early 1930s, known today as la matanza (the slaughter), when the world depression set off mass-based reform pressures.

El Salvador's US-sponsored demobilization campaign of the late twentieth century resorted again to carnage, killing at least 70,000 by 1988 (1.5 percent of the population) and leaving more than one million displaced. A burst of popular mobilization responding to the economic problems of the early to mid-1970s was not contained by presidents Arturo Molina and Humberto Romero. International criticism of their governments' escalating rights abuses, however, led the US Carter administration to reduce US military assistance (see Table A.3). But when revolutionaries overthrew Anastasio Somoza in neighboring Nicaragua in July 1979, an alarmed Carter quickly restored military aid to El Salvador to help forestall yet another revolution (Iran's shah had also fallen to Islamic revolutionaries that year). Reformist elements in the Salvadoran military, private sector, and opposition parties overthrew Romero on October 15, 1979. Conservatives on the junta soon blocked civilian reformists as the military increased human rights abuses. Military hard-liners and conservative Christian Democrats took over the junta by early 1980. Marxist guerrilla groups unified into the FMLN in 1980.

American economic aid to El Salvador rose 900 percent and military aid 6,000 percent after the coup. Despite touting moderation and reform, the new government used this flood of resources to deploy torture, murder, and disappearances against parties, unions, and other popular organizations demanding change. Violence soared above previous levels.[25] In March 1980 the junta imposed a state of siege that gave the military draconian powers over civilians. For the next several years, security forces systematically dismantled grassroots party and interest organizations and trampled human rights. US officials dissembled, publicly blaming the tens of thousands of killings on "violence of the right and the left" and falsely depicting the regime as moderates trying to control violence.

The US Congress eventually demanded that El Salvador reduce the shocking human rights abuses. In 1982 and 1983, with congressional approval for further military aid at stake, the Reagan administration pressured the junta and military to curtail the killings.[26] Death-squad killings declined, but aerial bombardment of civilian populations in rebel-controlled areas escalated. But by then the demobilization had largely succeeded. The leaders and many members of most grassroots party and interest organizations to the left of the Christian Democrats had been killed, driven underground, or exiled. The two opposition newspapers had been terrorized into extinction. The assassination of regime critic Archbishop Oscar Arnulfo Romero and numerous clergy and lay activists by the government and its sympathizers had cowed the once-critical Catholic Church.

News of the Salvadoran military's bloody record in the early 1980s reduced the certainty of continued aid from the US Congress. President Reagan consequently changed strategies and pressed El Salvador to adopt an elected, constitutional government. The junta accordingly held a constituent assembly election to draft a new constitution. Extreme rightist parties dominated the assembly. Violence slackened somewhat pending the 1984 election of center-right Christian Democrat, José Napoleón Duarte, as president. The civilian-transitional regime, shored up by redoubled US assistance, had limited power over public policy (US advisers were running much of the government) and effectively none over the armed forces.

The regionally sponsored Esquipulas peace accord was signed in August 1987, but death-squad terror again escalated in El Salvador as the right and military attempted to sabotage peace negotiations and instead pursue victory. When the government rebuffed an FMLN offer in 1989 to participate in the upcoming presidential election, the rebels responded with a major urban offensive in San Salvador to demonstrate their strength and thus press their case for settling the conflict. World and regional geopolitical change (the end of the Cold War, Nicaragua's revolution, and the Contra war) brought a George H. W. Bush administration policy shift to endorsing peace. Under this US pressure, President Alfredo Cristiani signed a peace agreement with the FMLN in 1992. It provided for major security force reduction and reforms, demobilization of the rebels, and their admission to the legal political arena.

Nicaragua suffered demobilization before and after the revolutionary victory of 1979. The Somoza regime conducted one wave from 1975 through July 1979. US-backed Contras carried out the second wave from 1981 through mid-1990. Together, these campaigns took nearly 81,000 lives, around 50,000 in the earlier period and almost 31,000 in the latter. Though some of the dead were combatants, most were civilians.

The barbarity of the Somoza regime's efforts to pacify Nicaragua and perpetuate itself in power is well documented.[27] Worth reiterating, however, is the longstanding close relationship between the US government and National Guard (GN). US marines occupied Nicaragua for most of the period from 1912 to 1933, from 1927 on seeking to demobilize rebel forces led by Augusto Sandino (Chapter 5). This involved creating, training, and leading the GN, which Anastasio Somoza García took over in 1932 upon the US marines' withdrawal. Thereafter, Somoza father and sons utilized the GN to build and protect their dynastic dictatorship. By 1979 the Guard had absolutely and proportionally more American-trained personnel than any other military in Latin America.[28]

Various tiny Nicaraguan rebel groups emerged in 1959–1961, imitating Castro's Cuban model, among them the FSLN—the lone survivor after 1962. The Marxist-Leninist FSLN labored in obscurity during the 1960s CACM economic boom and burgeoning inequality. When the triple catastrophes of the 1972 Managua earthquake, CACM decline, and OPEC (Organization of Petroleum Exporting Countries) embargo generated mobilization for reform in the early 1970s, the FLSN built new links to opposition civil society. It staged a hostage-taking incident that badly embarrassed the regime. President Anastasio Somoza Debayle responded with a three-year rural state of siege in which the GN tried to demobilize the FSLN and suspected supporters by killing several thousand rural Nicaraguans.

The US Carter administration pressed Somoza to lift the state of siege in 1977, but surging protests brought on redoubled repression that killed hundreds of youths and drove many others into the growing FSLN. The assassination of the opposition newspaper *La Prensa*'s editor spawned spontaneous uprisings across urban Nicaragua in 1978, while political parties, unions, Catholic Church, and business groups demanded an end to the regime. The FLSN scrambled to gain the initiative in resistance to the dynasty. The GN unleashed war on nodes of resistance, subjecting several towns to artillery barrages and firebombing that slaughtered civilians and demolished infrastructure. By July 1979 Somoza's allies in government began deserting the country. The encircled GN, fighting Sandinistas and popular volunteers on several fronts, soon collapsed and fled the country. The Carter administration helped Somoza escape, but futilely sought to prevent the FLSN from taking power. The economy was demolished, the treasury looted, and 50,000 Nicaraguans had died—the cost of a failed joint effort by the Somoza regime and United States to keep a friendly anti-Communist government in power.

The Sandinista revolution began, saddled with debt and destruction. Presciently fearing that the United States would try to overthrow them, the new government set up a pluralistic government and tried to build a mixed, rather than socialist, economy. The Carter administration made gestures of accommodation and provided some aid, but when Ronald Reagan replaced Carter in 1981, aggressive harassment of the Nicaraguan revolution ensued. There were CIA attacks on infrastructure, a US military buildup in Honduras, a crippling economic embargo, and—most damaging—the creation of a counterrevolutionary force made up mainly of ex-GN forces. Based in neighboring Honduras, the Contras were organized, funded, trained, supplied, and advised by Washington. Many who never served in the GN joined the lower ranks, but Contra officers were mostly ex-GN.[29]

The demobilization tactics employed by the counterrevolutionaries and their US backers evolved. When the Contras in their first two years employed crude terrorist tactics, the CIA commissioned a manual for Contra officers, *Psychological Operations in Guerrilla Warfare*.[30] Some Contra units apparently followed the tactically sound CIA advice. Pockets of civilian support developed in remote, lightly populated central departments of Boaco and Chontales and in the north. But the Contras mostly failed to achieve such discipline and behaved brutally.[31]

Although the Contras grew in numbers in the mid-1980s, their military accomplishments remained limited. The government's military buildup in response, however, eventually disrupted the Nicaraguan economy and undermined its support. Contra tactics changed to terrorize and sabotage rural economic infrastructure, social service infrastructure, and their personnel (130 teachers, 40 medical personnel, and 152 technicians).[32] The Contras mined rural roads, killing and mutilating hundreds. By forcing heavy defense spending, the Contras eroded social services, caused scarcity and inflation, and seeded popular discontent. Agricultural output declined and the national economy soured. Opposition protests and union resistance to austerity programs grew in 1986–1987, and the Sandinista government began repressing its critics and opponents and curtailing civil liberties.

By the February 1990 national elections, the US-sponsored program of demobilization had so undercut the Sandinistas' legitimacy and intimidated the populace that the victory of the US-endorsed candidate, Violeta Barrios de Chamorro, was all but inevitable.

US POLICY IN THE POST-COLD WAR PERIOD

The Cold War's end in 1989–1990 dramatically altered parts of US foreign policy. Because the Soviet Union and the socialist bloc no longer appeared to threaten to US interests, Washington re-evaluated Central America and reversed policy on the civil wars in El Salvador and Guatemala and endorsed UN-backed efforts to negotiate peace settlements. This facilitated peace deals first in El Salvador (1992) and then Guatemala (1996), and various intra-elite accords modifying the rules of the political game in Nicaragua in the mid-1990s. Washington helped broker and bolster civilian-democratic regimes in all three war-ravaged countries. The Clinton administration (1993–2001) embraced engagement rather than interference and apologized for the US role in the Guatemalan civil war.

But this new approach to the region proved short-lived, and US policy toward Central America began fluctuating dramatically. The September 11, 2001 terrorist attack on the United States distracted Washington's focus on Latin America. Additionally, President Bush appointed several Reagan-era Cold War ideologues to key Latin American policy positions. The more cooperative Clinton approach to Central America soon evaporated.[33] Rather than promoting democracy in the region, the new Bush administration interfered with and manipulated elections in Nicaragua (2001, 2006) and El Salvador (2004). Washington in the early 2000s again pushed neoliberalism in the form of a Central American Free Trade Agreement (CAFTA) to lower trade barriers to regional markets (see below). American pressure on Central American nations to embrace CAFTA soon generated popular protest in the region and some official resistance.

The election of Barack Obama brought another swerve in US policies. An early crisis, the June 2009 coup in Honduras against President Manuel Zelaya, challenged the new Obama administration's policy in the region. Zelaya's populism and economic support from Venezuela's leftist Chávez government had smacked of danger to containment-oriented elements in Washington, but Obama called the coup illegal and a "terrible precedent."[34] Secretary of State Hillary Clinton, however, was more reluctant to condemn the coup and pushed new elections that would "render the question of Zelaya moot."[35] The United States eventually withheld $16.5 million in military aid and supported Honduras's suspension from the Organization of American States (OAS). President Obama visited Central America twice. His 2011 visit to El Salvador focused largely on security, but the 2013 visit emphasized the need for investment in infrastructure, energy, and human capital, particularly to benefit women, girls, and indigenous persons.[36] He made no mention of immigration reform, which the region's leaders encouraged him to do in anticipation of growing regional migratory trends.

Other aspects of US policy, however, changed little with the end of the Cold War. Principal among them was the continued promotion of a strongly capitalist economic model. Washington insisted on harsh structural adjustment policies that emphasized smaller government and opening markets to foreign investment. Such policies favored overall growth but also concentrated income and hurt the poor majority. By the 2000s, dynamic contradictions had emerged between this income-concentrating neoliberalism, the consolidation of civilian democracy, both promoted by the United States, and an unexpected surge in emigration northward from Central America. The administration of Donald Trump in 2017 soon revealed these tensions within US foreign policy and their impact on Central Americans.

Candidate Trump in 2016 brought the idea of an "invasion" of Latin Americans of the United States squarely into his presidential campaign, election, and subsequent administration. US Latin American policy under Trump became unsettled and unpredictable. The Trump administration recognized the re-election of Juan Orlando Hernández in Honduras, despite serious irregularities and calls from the OAS and opposition for new elections. As of December 2019 no US ambassador had been appointed or confirmed in Honduras for more than two years. The Trump administration made no protest when Guatemalan president Jimmy Morales shuttered the anti-corruption agency, the International Commission Against Impunity in Guatemala (Comisión Internacional Contra la Impunidad en Guatemala, CICIG), despite evidence it had been integral to exposing corruption and reducing violence. Both Guatemala and Honduras joined the US in recognizing Jerusalem as the capital of Israel. The Trump administration targeted Nicaragua following the regime's response to protests in 2018. The United States sanctioned Daniel Ortega, Rosario Murillo, Laureano Ortega, and others individually, and called for "free, fair, and early elections in Nicaragua to give the Nicaraguan people a true voice and vote in their future."[37]

Trump contended that most US trade deals, including the North American Free Trade Agreement (NAFTA), were deeply flawed, and forced NAFTA's renegotiation. This seeded doubt about the stability of other previously negotiated arrangements and institutions. Trump sought the removal of Venezuela's Maduro regime and imposed severe economic sanctions on Venezuela and many of its officials. Under President Obama, strict immigration enforcement had reversed the immigration flow of Mexicans, as more left than arrived in the United States. However, Central Americans replaced Mexicans as the principal undocumented population seeking entry near the end of the Obama administration. Central American families with children seeking asylum thus became targets of Trump's rhetorical and policy ire. Washington in 2017–2019 variously and confusingly tightened barriers to entry to the United States along the southern border, mobilized the US National Guard to assist with immigration management, and pressured Mexico and Central American nations to deny migrants access to the US border. The Trump administration ordered cuts in foreign aid to countries that failed to deter migration, which elicited some cooperation from the region and much more from Mexico.[38]

CAFTA and the Economy

One key goal of the US economic agenda in Latin America after the Cold War was promoting free trade. In 1989 the first Bush administration proposed a hemispheric free-trade area. In early 2002 the second Bush administration announced negotiations for CAFTA.[39] CAFTA sought increased access to the Central American market for American firms by reducing tariff and investment barriers.[40] Lowered investment barriers would allow US companies to compete for the provision of public services, one neoliberal prescription for reforming the public sector.[41] Costa Rica's government-owned telecommunications and insurance sectors became a major sticking point in the negotiations with the United States. Other Central American countries had already privatized many such industries, but Costa Rica, responding to domestic pressure, had retained them. After protests and a strike by public employees, Costa Rica temporarily withdrew from CAFTA talks but ultimately agreed to reconsider such policies. Like NAFTA, the CAFTA agreement also would further reduce state autonomy by allowing US corporations to sue their host countries over "unfair" regulations.[42] There was also disagreement over protection for key commodities, subsidies, and intellectual property rights for generic drugs.[43] The initial CAFTA agreement was signed by the five Central American countries and the United States in May 2004, but ratification hit snags.

The US Congress narrowly passed CAFTA in 2005. Central Americans had little enthusiasm for the agreement. Farmers, workers, small business, civil society, and center-left political parties vocally opposed the trade agreement over issues of sovereignty, constitutionality, the inability of local agricultural products to compete against subsidized US products, labor exploitation, and environmental degradation.[44] Opposition in the region attracted intense US criticism. In May 2005 US commerce secretary Carlos Gutierrez referred to CAFTA's opponents as "the same opponents of democracy and freedom of 20 years ago," a sentiment widely echoed in the region's conservative press.[45] Eventually, under heavy US pressure, four legislatures ratified the treaty, and in 2007 Costa Ricans approved it by referendum.

CAFTA's middle-run effects of have been mixed. Trade overall has risen, and the US exports of industrial products and agricultural commodities to the region have grown. Costa Rica's and Honduras's foreign direct investment (FDI) has increased. Nicaragua has expanded maquiladora (assembly plant) industries and jobs. Since 2010 Costa Rica and Nicaragua have had real GDP per capita gains (see Table A.1). Most post-2010 growth in Honduras has been driven by increasing remittances from abroad. Meanwhile Guatemala's and El Salvador's FDI have remained essentially flat since 2010. The northern triangle countries have seen agricultural production undercut by US products, increased rural unemployment, urbanization, and the growth of gangs and narcotics trafficking. These, combined with population growth, lower mortality rates, and drought, have become powerful motors of emigration.[46]

The US introduced other economic initiatives into the region. The Millennium Challenge Corporation (MCC), a US aid agency established in 2004, operated in El Salvador, Honduras, and Nicaragua. Typical programs focused on infrastructure, education, and good governance. Good governance was also a funding criterion, though some expressed concern it was selectively applied. For example, the US terminated funds to Nicaragua (about $62 million) following allegation of 2008 municipal election fraud. In contrast, only about $10 million was temporarily withheld following the 2009 coup in Honduras.[47] El Salvador was one of four countries worldwide to participate in the 2010 US Partnership for Growth initiative, which focused on generating growth by engaging local constituencies in planning and transparency exercises. But the program also gave the US a significant role in determining Salvadoran policy. The US required El Salvador to enact a public–private partnerships law, co-written by the US, the International Monetary Fund (IMF), and the Funes administration, before agreeing to a second distribution of MCC funds.[48] Results of the Partnership appeared meager in growth terms. El Salvador's foreign investment for the period was essentially flat, and its annual average growth of GDP per capita for 2011 to 2018 was just 2 percent per year, far less than the 21 percent of GDP annually provided by remittances from Salvadorans abroad.[49]

Immigration Policy

Immigration of one's ancestors to the United States is the source of most of its current populace. From 1860 to 1930 from 12 to 15 percent of US residents were consistently foreign born. This share declined by around half until 2010, when the foreign born (documented and undocumented) again reached nearly 13 percent.[50] Foreign-born US residents arrive in myriad ways—on visas for tourism, business, and study, as temporary workers, by stealthy and dangerous crossing or legal entry, as refugees of wars, disasters, and economic and other hardships, seeking asylum from political or other kinds of persecution, and as the minor children of all of the above. Those in the country without authorization reached 12 million individuals around 2008, and under vigorous Obama administration enforcement declined to ten million by 2017.[51] The main laws regulating immigration are the 1986 Immigration Reform and Control Act, passed during the Reagan administration, and the Refugee Act of 1980. These were enacted when cultural conservatives (opposed to much immigration for racist reasons) were outweighed by political conservatives (supportive of anti-Communist Cuban and Vietnamese refugees) and business conservatives (who valued a low-cost labor supply). Since then, cultural conservatives in the US Republican Party have become ascendant. They blocked a proposed immigration reform law in Congress in 2007, and their views eventually aligned with President Donald Trump, whose election and strategy to retain his political base for re-election involve a barrage of efforts to exclude and/or deport the undocumented foreign born.

Unable to pass comprehensive immigration reform, President Obama continued his predecessor's aggressive enforcement and removal policies. The Bush and Obama administrations respectively deported approximately 2 million and 2.5 million immigrants.[52] Approximately 18 percent of those deported in 2011 were Central Americans.[53] Yet hundreds of thousands of Central Americans continued making the perilous, expensive journey. Most sought work in the earlier years, but recently more and more sought refuge from crime, asylum from persecution by criminal gangs, or family unification.

According to the 2010 US Census there were approximately 4 million Central Americans living in the United States, an increase of 137 percent over 2000 (7.9 percent of US Hispanics). From 2000 to 2010 the US-resident Guatemalan population grew by 180 percent), that of Honduras 191 percent, and El Salvador's by an almost 152 percent increase.[54] Salvadorans remained the largest Central American immigrant group; between 1.8 and 2 million Salvadorans were living in the US by the end of 2013.

President Trump has taken numerous steps to dissuade Central Americans and others from immigrating, whether legally or illegally, to the United States. Also unable to get desired legislation through Congress, his administration has relied heavily on executive orders, administrative rule changes, and deployment of federal resources. These have included promoting more and improved barriers along the US–Mexican border, reprogramming revenue appropriated by Congress for other purposes to fund border wall construction, mobilizing National Guard troops to assist the Homeland Security Department agencies, implementing practices by Customs and Border Patrol (CBP) and Immigration and Customs Enforcement (ICE) to apprehend undocumented persons, process those apprehended, and to discourage, delay, and deny asylum applicants. Among the most controversial practices have been separation of immigrant children from their families, deporting parents without their minor children, failing to track family members so they become lost from each other in the system, detaining children and families (in often inhumane conditions) and for periods longer than applicable court orders allow, violating the rights of asylum petitioners under US law, denial of medical attention to detainees in US custody, numerous other human rights violations, and forcing asylum applicants to return to Mexico to await hearings. The Trump administration in 2019 alone threatened to cancel a just-signed trade deal to force Mexico to deploy troops to help curtail immigration flows from Central America and restrict migrants' access to the US border. Washington also brow beat first Mexico and then Guatemala, El Salvador, and Honduras to accept so-called "safe third country agreements" that would require migrants in transit to apply for asylum there upon first entry and thus forfeit the right to apply in the United States. The United States also announced the suspension of $500 million in aid (for anti-poverty and violence reduction programs) to El Salvador, Guatemala, and Honduras.[55] Most of these actions by the Trump administration have been challenged in court, some successfully. It appears that these policies, intended to dissuade immigration, have worsened the social conditions driving it or encouraged an emigration surge toward the United States in case entry should become even harder.

Remittances

Migration and remittances directed home by workers abroad have provided important safety valves for Central American governments long incapable of generating sufficient economic growth or employment for their citizens. As 2020 approached, remittances by Central Americans abroad, especially from the United States, had become the region's new monocrop. These funds (often called *migradólares*) had become a vital part of the Central American economies. In 2000 Central Americans sent home $3.3 billion in remittances, more than FDI or official external development assistance.[56] By 2018 remittances grew sixfold to $20.3 billion. Growth was dramatic in Guatemala (16 times greater than in 2000) and Honduras (ten times greater); Nicaragua's remittances quintupled and El Salvador's tripled. Even Costa Rica's remittances almost quadrupled, but over a smaller base and so had less impact.[57] In El Salvador and Honduras in 2018, remittances averaged over 20 percent of GDP, and in Nicaragua and Guatemala about 12 percent of GDP.

These citizen-to-citizen transfers mitigated much of the costs associated with neoliberal policies by providing income to both the urban and rural poor. The growing reliance on remittances resulted in the growing number of Central America-linked hometown associations (HTAs), long popular among other migrant communities.[58] Salvadorans used their role as remitters to underscore their demands for voting rights for nationals living abroad, a fight they won for the 2014 elections.[59]

These remittances were made possible, of course, by the steady migration flow from Central America to the United States. Hundreds of thousands of Central Americans (mostly Salvadoran) were in the United States on temporary protected status (TPS), having fled civil wars (El Salvador, Nicaragua) or natural disasters (Honduras and Nicaragua after Hurricane Mitch, El Salvador after the 2001 earthquakes). In late 2017 the Trump administration ended TPS for Salvadorans, Hondurans, and Nicaraguans. Challenged in court, this policy change for these countries was enjoined in 2019 and remained so as this went to press.[60] Should TPS end migrants would be forced to return to their home countries, and the economic impact would be devastating. Not surprisingly, regional presidents have lobbied for the extension of TPS for their populations.

Security

In the Latin American context, the US "war on drugs" became intertwined with the "war on terror." That was easy because the Revolutionary Armed Force of Colombia (Fuerza Armada Revolucionaria de Colombia, FARC) taxed production of all goods produced within its area of control. But FARC's narcotics involvement, though less than Colombia's rightist paramilitary forces', allowed the United States to label it and other guerrillas "narcoterrorists."

Central America became an important transshipment route for cocaine, and the United States enlisted regional governments in its counter-narcotics efforts. This brought a partial remilitarization of the isthmus through increased US military aid.[61] In 2000 the United States established its own anti-narcotics military base in El Salvador.[62] United States Drug Enforcement Agency (USDEA) operations in the region included intelligence, training, and interdiction. Operation Central Skies provided army helicopters, police and security training, logistics support, and personnel to Costa Rica, El Salvador, Guatemala, and Honduras. Political and economic pressures urged cooperation in the American "war on drugs." The United States "decertified" Guatemala (declaring its non-cooperation and withholding certain assistance) following a dramatic decline in narcotics seizures there.

Growing instability in Mexico and the encroachment of the drug war into the southwestern United States had become a major security issue for the United States by 2006. In 2007 the US announced the Mérida Initiative, a three-year, $1.6 billion program targeting drug trafficking, organized crime, and gangs in Mexico and Central America. In 2008 Congress approved $65 million for programs in Central America that included drug interdiction, public security, capacity building, and promoting the rule of law.[63] The earlier crackdown on Mexican cartels had displaced their operations southward into Guatemala and Honduras. Accordingly, the Mérida Initiative sought to offset potential bad effects of free trade in Central America that might turn people to narcotrafficking to replace income lost to rising unemployment.[64]

The plan ultimately evolved into the Central America Regional Security Initiative (CARSI), which focused on counter-narcotics and law enforcement, strengthening institutions and prevention strategies. CARSI did not reduce violence or narcotrafficking in the region. It focused on removing cartel leaders (kingpins) and may have spread trafficking routes to new areas such as Belize. Cartels' staggering resource accumulation has furthered corruption of police and local officials. Critics argued that too much of CARSI's budget went to anti-narcotics efforts and law enforcement rather than poverty reduction, and that disbursement of funds lagged.[65] Furthermore, the American push to militarize policing and security policy in the region seemed increasingly at odds with the evolving regional policy preferences, as presidents increasingly called on the United States to reduce its own demand for narcotics.[66]

Gangs

Central America's growing gang problem was another transnational phenomenon. During the 1970s and 1980s tens of thousands of Central Americans fled bloody civil wars and disasters to the United States, often settling in urban areas such as Los Angeles, California. Out of place and threatened by pre-existing Latino gangs, Central American youths formed gangs of their own such as Calle 18 and the now notorious Mara Salvatrucha (MS-13). By the 1980s, US gangs began trafficking cocaine and numerous criminal activities including extortion, prostitution, and human trafficking.[67] In the early 1990s, American immigration authorities began "repatriating" Central Americans convicted of crimes to their homelands (although many had never lived there), including over 1,000 Salvadorans deported following the Los Angeles riots.[68] In 1992 the US Immigration and Naturalization Service (INS) created the Violent Gang Task Force, the same year in which MS-13 established itself in El Salvador and mixed with existing youth gangs in the country. The Illegal Immigration Reform and Immigrant Responsibility Act of 1995 (IIRIRA) targeted immigrants, regardless of legal status, with criminal records. Between 1994 and 1997 11,235 Salvadorans, Guatemalans, and Hondurans with criminal records were deported.[69] The deportations raised the region's crime rates and promoted the growth of gangs.

This new gang activity greatly aggravated Central America's crime wave, particularly in El Salvador, Guatemala, and Honduras (Chapters 6–8). Gangs committed countless murders (many quite brutal), kidnappings, and robberies and trafficked narcotics and human beings. El Salvador, Guatemala, and Honduras passed controversial anti-gang laws, and in 2004 all but Costa Rica signed an agreement to coordinate anti-gang measures and share arrest warrants. The US "war on terror" coincided nicely with the Central American "war on gangs." El Salvador, Guatemala, and Honduras sent military forces into the street to battle gangs, endangering the recently developed balance between new civilian police forces and the old style of military-dominated internal security. The policies were ineffective and merely forced the gangs underground. By 2010 gang violence, increasingly intertwined with drug trafficking, organized crime, and homicides, had escalated dramatically. The population-weighted regional homicide rate was 52 per 100,000, though it was higher in El Salvador and approached 80 per 100,000 in Honduras. By 2016 the homicide rate in El Salvador was 80 and in Honduras nearly 60 per 100,000.[70] The violence dislocated citizens, many emigrating to the United States. US asylum requests based on regional violence increased correspondingly.[71] In 2012, the US added MS-13 to its list of Transnational Criminal Organizations, which would allow the government to target its financial assets.[72]

CONCLUSIONS

US policy in Central America during the Cold War was destructive, ill-advised, and counterproductive to the interests of the United States and the peoples of the isthmus. American policy responded more to US domestic political pressures and outmoded conceptions of security and economic interests than to the concrete reality of Central America. It jousted with a vastly overblown perceived Communist threat for over 40 years. The United States sided with a tiny, exploitative elite on demobilization strategies that killed over 300,000 people and uprooted millions; the economic damage was incalculable. Furthermore, American policy undermined the concept and the practice of democracy in the region. Power and democracy go hand in hand. Using counterterror to exclude a wide swath of civil society from the political arena blocked democratization.

The end of the Cold War at first facilitated peace and democratization in the region. The US imperative shifted from fighting Communism to promoting the so-called Washington Consensus (neoliberalism) and democratization. Neoliberal economics, however, blinded Washington to the need for an economically active state to promote welfare policies to advance equitable growth and human welfare and thus enhance regime legitimacy—essentially the Costa Rican model. But a swerve away from nurturing democracy and economic development, especially after the 2001 al Qaeda attack on the United States, turned attention back to US national security and to other foreign policy arenas. De-emphasizing democratization and prioritizing the terrorism–drug–gang nexus created a climate of insecurity that further endangered Central American democracies. Dumping Central American gang members back in the region aggravated a growing crime wave, undermined citizen security, and enhanced pressures to emigrate.

The Obama administration struck a new tone in the region on some key issues, but underperformed in certain respects. Its profession of neutrality in the region's elections, the easing of sanctions on Cuba, and opposition to the June 2009 Honduran coup suggested a commitment to a democratic path forward with the region. Meanwhile, the US failure to pass immigration reform, Obama's increased deportations, and his continued emphasis on a neoliberal economic development strategy disappointed many. Since then, the Trump administration has shocked Central America in ways that continue to unfold as we write this. The president's overtly racist denigration of Latin Americans, his administration's erratic policy pronouncements and enforcement on trade, foreign aid, and especially refugees, immigration, and asylum continue to develop. Renewed US interventionist behavior reminiscent of the Big Stick era may well leave lingering setbacks to US–Central American relations, with no promise to improve economic development or democracy, and considerable potential for damage.

NOTES

1. Charles W. Anderson, "The Latin American Political System," in his *Politics and Economic Change in Latin America: The Governing of Restless Nations* (New York: Van Nostrand Reinhold, 1967), pp. 87–114.

2. See Robert A. Dahl, *A Preface to Democratic Theory* (Chicago, IL: University of Chicago Press, 1956); E.E. Schattschneider, *The Semisovereign People: A Realist's View of Democracy in America* (New York: Holt, Rinehart, and Winston, 1960).

3. See, for instance, John A. Booth and Mitchell A. Seligson, eds., *Elections and Democracy in Central America* (Chapel Hill, NC: University of North Carolina Press, 1989), *passim*.

4. National Bipartisan Commission on Central America, *Report of the National Bipartisan Commission on Central America* (Washington, DC: National Bipartisan Commission on Central America, 1984), p. 30.

5. William I. Robinson, *Promoting Polyarchy: Globalization, US Intervention, and Hegemony* (Cambridge: Cambridge University Press, 1996); and William I. Robinson, *Transnational Conflicts: Central America, Social Change, and Globalization* (London: Verso, 2003).

6. Paulo Freire, *The Pedagogy of the Oppressed* (New York: Herder and Herder, 1968).

7. Second General Conference of Latin American Bishops, *The Church and the Present-Day Transformation of Latin America in the Light of the Council* (Washington, DC: United States Catholic Conference, 1973).

8. Edward L. Cleary, *Crisis and Change: The Church in Latin America Today* (Maryknoll, NY: Orbis Books, 1985).

9. Estimate of US Embassy, Managua, June 25, 1985, to coauthor Thomas Walker.

10. See Deborah Barndt, "Popular Education," in Walker, ed., *Nicaragua: The First Five Years*, pp. 317–345.

11. Lars Schoultz, "Communism," in his *National Security and United States Policy toward Latin America* (Princeton, NJ: Princeton University Press, 1987), pp. 106–139.

12. Tayacán, *Psychological Operations in Guerrilla Warfare: The CIA's Nicaragua Manual*, prepared by the Central Intelligence Agency (New York: Vintage Books, 1985); US Department of Defense (DOD), "Fact Sheet Concerning Training Manuals Containing Materials Inconsistent with US Policy" (Washington, DC: DOD, September 1996).

13. Michael McClintock, *The American Connection, Volume 1, State Terror and Popular Resistance in El Salvador* (London: Zed Books, 1985), p. 47.

14. Michael Klare, *War without End* (New York: Alfred A. Knopf, 1972), Ch. 9.

15. Americas Watch, *Review of the Department of State's Country Reports on Human Rights Practices for 1982: An Assessment* (New York: Americas Watch, February 1983), pp. 1–9, 37–46, 55–61, 63–70. The report stated "a special effort appears to have been made to exculpate current leaders considered friends of the United States—such as President Ríos Montt of Guatemala" (p. 5).

16. Latin American Studies Association, *The Electoral Process in Nicaragua: Domestic and International Influences* (Austin, TX: LASA, 1984), p. 17.

17. Thomas W. Walker, "The Armed Forces," in Walker, ed., *Revolution and Counterrevolution in Nicaragua* (Boulder, CO: Westview Press, 1991).

18. John A. Booth and Thomas W. Walker, *Understanding Central America*, 3rd ed. (Boulder, CO: Westview Press, 1999), Appendix, Table A.9.

19. Mary B. Vanderlaan, *Revolution and Foreign Policy in Nicaragua* (Boulder, CO: Westview Press, 1986), p. 322.

20. Excerpts from State Department and Pentagon, Congressional Presentation Document, Security Assistance Programs, FY 1981, in Robert Matthews, "The Limits of Friendship: Nicaragua and the West," *NACLA Report on the Americas* 19, No. 3 (May–June 1985), p. 24.

21. Michael McClintock, *The American Connection, Volume 2, State Terror and Popular Resistance in Guatemala* (London: Zed Books, 1985), pp. 32–33. For additional information about demobilization in Guatemala see Tom Barry and Deb Preusch, *The Soft War: The Uses and Abuses of U.S. Economic Aid in Central America* (New York: Grove Press, 1988).

22. Andrew and Leslie Cockburn, *Dangerous Liaisons: The inside Story of the U.S. Israeli Covert Relationship* (New York: HarperCollins, 1991), p. 218; Leslie H. Gelb, "Israelis Said to Step up Role as Arms Suppliers to Latins," *New York Times*, December 17, 1982, p. A.11; George Black, "Israeli Connection: Not Just Guns for Guatemala," *NACLA Report on the Americas* 17, No. 3 (May–June 1983), pp. 43–44; Benjamin Beit-Hallahmi, *The Israeli Connection: Who Israel Arms and Why* (New York: Pantheon Books, 1987), p. 78; Philip Taubman, "Israel Said to Aid Latin Aims of U.S.," *New York Times*, July 21, 1983, p. A4. The authors thank Richard E. Clinton Jr. for his research in this matter.

23. Estimates based on 1984 population, midway through the conflict.

24. Historical Clarification Commission, *Guatemala: Memory of Silence*, Guatemala City, 1999, http://shr.aaas.org/guatemala/ceh/report/english/toc.html.

25. See McClintock, *The American Connection*, Volume 1.

26. On US pressuring El Salvador to improve its human rights performance: "El Salvador," *Mesoamérica*, November 1982, p. 6; "El Salvador," *Mesoamérica*,

October 1983, p. 6; "El Salvador," *Mesoamérica*, November 1983, p. 6; "El Salvador," *Mesoamérica*, December 1983, pp. 5–6; and "Reagan Says Death Squads Hinder Fight," *Miami Herald*, December 21, 1983, p. 18A.

27. Organization of American States, *Report on the Situation of Human Rights in Nicaragua: Findings of the "On-site" Observation in the Republic of Nicaragua, October 3–12, 1978* (Washington, DC: General Secretariat of the OAS, 1978).

28. Richard L. Millett, *Guardians of the Dynasty: A History of the U.S.-Created Guardia Nacional De Nicaragua and the Somoza Family* (Maryknoll, NY: Orbis Press, 1977), p. 252.

29. Arms Control and Foreign Policy Caucus, the United States House of Representatives, "Who are the Contras?" *Congressional Record* 131, 48 (Daily Edition, April 23, 1985, H2335). The head of the Contras was a former guard officer, Enrique Bermúdez.

30. Tayacán [the CIA], *Operaciones sicológicas en guerra de guerrillas* [1983] (later translated and published commercially as *Psychological Operations in Guerrilla Warfare: The CIA's Nicaragua Manual*.

31. The documentation of Contra brutality is massive, including Americas Watch's numerous reports; Reed Brody, *Contra Terror in Nicaragua, Report of a Fact-Finding Mission: September 1984–January 1985* (Boston, MA: South End Press, 1985); and Christopher Dickey, *With the Contras: A Reporter in the Wilds of Nicaragua* (New York: Simon and Schuster, 1985).

32. Data from the Nicaraguan Ministry of the Presidency, January 1990.

33. Among key Reagan-era Central America policy team players rehabilitated by George W. Bush was John D. Negroponte, former ambassador to Honduras (1981 to 1985); Elliott Abrams was a Reagan-era assistant secretary of state for Inter-American Affairs who pleaded guilty to two counts of Iran-Contra offenses and was pardoned in 1992 by president George H.W. Bush, and Otto Reich headed the Reagan-era State Department's Office of Public Diplomacy. See *Central America and Mexico Report*, "Elliott Abrams Appointed to NSC," 2001, Vol. 3, rtfcam.org/report/volume_21/No_3/article_3.htm, accessed January 5, 2005; and CNN.com, *Inside Politics*, January 11, 2002, http://archives.cnn.com/2002/ALLPOLITICS/01/11/recess.appointments/, accessed January 5, 2005.

34. Arshad Mohammed and David Alexander, "Obama Says Coup in Honduras Is Illegal," Reuters, June 29, 2009, www.reuters.com/article/topNews/idUKTRE55S5J220090629?sp=true.

35. Stephen Zunes, "The US Role in the Honduras Coup and Subsequent Violence," *National Catholic Reporter*, March 14, 2016, www.ncronline.org/blogs/ncr-today/us-role-honduras-coup-and-subsequent-violence.

36. Remarks by the President at a Working Dinner with SICA Leaders, May 3, 2013, www.whitehouse.gov/the-press-office/2013/05/04/remarks-president-working-dinner-sica-leaders.

37. The White House, "President Donald J. Trump Is Pressuring the Nicaraguan Regime to Restore Democracy and the Rule of Law," November 27, 2018, www.whitehouse.gov/briefings-statements/president-donald-j-trump-pressuring-nicaraguan-regime-restore-democracy-rule-law/.

38. Jason DeParle, "Shift against Immigration Lifted a Young Firebrand," *New York Times*, August 18, 2019, pp. 1, 22–23; Kim Chipman and Ros Krasny, "Trump Renews Threat to Close Border, Cuts Aid to Central America," *Bloomberg*, March 29, 2019, www.bloomberg.com/news/articles/2019-03-29/trump-says-he-ll-close-border-if-mexico-doesn-t-stop-migration.

39. The Caribbean Basin Initiative, to liberalize trade, began in 1983 to admit Caribbean goods duty-free to US markets. It also promoted economic development and, consistent with neoliberalism, export diversification.

40. Full text of the agreement available at ustr.gov/Trade_Agreements/Bilateral/DR-CAFTA/DR-CAFTA_Final_Texts/Section_Index.html, accessed January 5, 2005.

41. Beatrice Edwards, "IDB Plan to Sell the Public Sector: The Cure or the Ill?" *NACLA Report on the Americas*, January/February 2003, pp. 13–19.

42. Ibid. See Article 20 and relevant subsections.

43. On generic drugs, see Latin American Database, "Congress, Kerry, Could Kill CAFTA," *NotiCen* 9, No. 21 (June 3, 2004); Latin American Database, "El Salvador First to Ratify CAFTA, But Followers May be Few," *NotiCen* 10, No. 1 (January 6, 2004).

44. See Mark B. Rosenberg and Luis G. Solis, *The United States and Central America: Geopolitical Realities and Regional Fragility* (New York: Routledge, 2007), Ch. 4.

45. "US Employs Cold War Rhetoric to Discredit CAFTA Opponents," *Central America Report* 3230 (August 2, 2005).

46. Hector Perla, "The Impact of CAFTA: Drugs, Gangs, and Immigration," *Telesur*, March 1, 2016, www.telesurenglish.net/opinion/The-Impact-of-CAFTA-Drugs-Gangs-and-Immigration-20160301-0008.html; Kimberly Amadeo, "CAFTA Explained, with Its Pros and Cons," *The Balance*, May 5, 2019, www.thebalance.com/what-is-cafta-3305580; World Bank Group, Indicators, accessed August 21, 2019, https://data.worldbank.org/indicator/BX.KLT.DINV.WD.GD.ZS?locations=HN-GT-SV; Charles Lane, "People are Leaving Guatemala because Life Is Getting Better," *Washington Post*, August 19, 2019, www.washingtonpost.com/opinions/global-opinions/people-are-leaving-guatemala-because-life-is-getting-better-we-cant-respond-unless-we-understand-that/2019/08/19/5bc2eef6-bde4-11e9-a5c6-1e74f7ec4a93_story.html?noredirect=on.

47. Tim Rogers, "Honduras Becomes Poster Child for the U.S. Millennium Challenge Corporation," *The Tico Times*, September 30, 2010, www.ticotimes.net/Region/Nicaragua/Honduras-Becomes-Poster-Child-for-the-U.S.-Millennium-Challenge-Corporation-Friday-October-01–2010.

48. Lily Moodey, "P3 Legislation in El Salvador: An Aggressive Reassertion of Neoliberal Economics?" Council on Hemispheric Affairs, August 7, 2013, www.coha.org/p3-legislation-in-el-salvador-an-aggressive-reassertion-of-neoliberal-economics/.

49. World Bank Group, Indicators, accessed August 21, 2019, at https://data.worldbank.org/indicator/NY.GDP.PCAP.KD?locations=NI-SV, and https://data.worldbank.org/indicator/BX.TRF.PWKR.DT.GD.ZS?locations=NI-HN.

50. Fred Dews, "What Percentage of the U.S. Population Is Foreign Born?" *Brookings Now*, October 3, 2013, www.brookings.edu/blog/brookings-now/2013/10/03/what-percentage-of-u-s-population-is-foreign-born/.

51. Jens Manuel Krogstad, Jeffrey S. Passel and D'Vera Cohn, "5 Facts about Illegal Immigration in the U.S." Pew Research Center, FactTank, June 12, 2019, www.pewresearch.org/fact-tank/2019/06/12/5-facts-about-illegal-immigration-in-the-u-s/.

52. Suzy Khimm, "Obama Is Deporting Immigrants Faster Than Bush. Republicans Don't Think That's Enough," *Washington Post*, August 27, 2012, www.washingtonpost.com/blogs/wonkblog/wp/2012/08/27/obama-is-deporting-more-immigrants-than-bush-republicans-dont-think-thats-enough/.

53. United States Department of Homeland Security. *Yearbook of Immigration Statistics: 2011*, Washington, DC: US Department of Homeland Security, Office of Immigration Statistics, 2012, www.dhs.gov/sites/default/files/publications/immigration-statistics/yearbook/2011/ois_yb_2011.pdf.

54. Sharon R. Ennis, Merarys Rios-Vargas, and Nora G. Albert, "The Hispanic Population: 2010," *US Census Briefs*, May 2011, www.census.gov/prod/cen2010/briefs/c2010br-04.pdf.

55. Marcos Aleman, "US Aid Cuts Will Spur Central America Migration, Experts Say," www.census.gov/prod/cen2010/briefs/c2010br-04.pdf; Associated Press, April 2, 2019, https://apnews.com/0d61a99f032c49f89828c6c140ad2ab3; DeParle, "Shift Against Immigration."

56. Inter-American Dialogue, *All in the Family: Latin America's Most Important International Flow, Report of the Inter-American Dialogue Task Force on Remittances* Washington, DC: January 2004, pp. 3–4.

57. World Bank Group, Indicators, Personal Remittances Received (current US$), https://data.worldbank.org/indicator/BX.TRF.PWKR.CD.DT?locations.

58. Manuel Orozco and Eugenia Garcia-Zanello, "Hometown Associations, Transnationalism, Philanthropy and Development," *Brown Journal of World Affairs* XV, No. II (Spring–Summer 2009), pp. 1–17.

59. Organizations such as Salvadoreños en el Mundo (Salvadorans in the World, SEEM) pressed for the right to vote via absentee ballot for three million Salvadorans living abroad.

60. Miriam Jordan, "Trump Administration Ends Temporary Protection for Haitians," *New York Times*, November 20, 2017, www.nytimes.com/2017/11/20/us/haitians-temporary-status.html.

61. See Adam Isacson, Joy Olson, and Lisa Haugaard, *Blurring the Lines: Trends in U.S. Military Programs with Latin America*. Latin American Working Group Education Fund-Center for International Policy, and the Washington Office on Latin America, Washington, DC, 2004, http://wola.org/military/blurringthelinesfinal.pdf.

62. Dean Brackley, "Yanquis Return to El Salvador," *NACLA Report on the Americas* 34, No. 3 (November–December 2000), pp. 20–21.

63. Colleen W. Cook, Rebecca G. Rush, and Claire Ribando Seelke, "Merida Initiative: Proposed U.S. Anti-Crime and Counterdrug Assistance for Mexico and Central America," CRS Report for Congress, June 3, 2008, www.wilsoncenter.org/news/docs/06.03.08%20CRS%20Report.pdf.

64. Susan Fitzpatrick Behrens, "Plan Mexico and Central American Migration," *NACLA Report on the Americas*, January 12, 2009, https://nacla.org/node/5406; Laura Carlsen, "A Primer on *Plan Mexico*," Americas Policy Program Special Report Washington, DC: Center for International Policy, May 5, 2008, americas.irc-online. org/am/5204.

65. US Department of State, "The Central America Regional Security Initiative: A Shared Partnership," April 25, 2013, www.state.gov/p/wha/rls/fs/2013/208592. htm; David Rosnick, Alexander Main, and Laura Jung, "Have US-Funded CARSI Programs Reduced Crime and Violence in Central America?" Washington, DC: Center for Economic and Policy Research, September 2016, http://cepr.net/images/stories/reports/carsi-2016-09.pdf; Steven Dudley, "How Drug Trafficking Operates, Corrupts in Central America," *Insight Crime*, July 6, 2016, www.insightcrime.org/news/analysis/how-drug-trafficking-operates-corrupts-in-central-america/; Michael Shifter, statement before the Committee on Foreign Affairs, Subcommittee on the Western Hemisphere, "Regional Security Cooperation: An Examination of the Central America Regional Security Initiative (CARSI) and the Caribbean Basin Security Initiative (CBSI)," June 19, 2013, http://thedialogue.org/PublicationFiles/ShifterCARSICBSICongressionaltestimonyFINAL.pdf.

66. United Nations Office on Drugs and Crime, "Transnational Organized Crime in Central America and the Caribbean: A Threat Assessment," UNODC, September 2012, www.unodc.org/documents/data-and_analysis/Studies/TOC_Central_America_and_the_Caribbean_english.pdf.

67. On Central American gangs see Washington Office on Latin America (WOLA), *Youth Gangs in Central America: Issues in Human Rights, Effective Policing, and Prevention* (Washington, DC: WOLA, 2006); Ana Arana, "How the Street Gangs Took Central America," *Foreign Affairs*, May/June, 2005, pp. 98–110; Donna DeCesare, "Deporting America's Gang Culture", *Mother Jones*, July–August, 1999, pp. 44–51.

68. Margaret H. Taylor and T. Alexander Aleinikoff, *Deportation of Criminal Aliens: A Global Perspective* (Washington, DC: Inter-American Dialogue, 1998).

69. Jerry Seper, "Al Qaeda Seek Ties to Local Gangs," *Washington Times*, September 28, 2004.

70. President Barack Obama, press conference, June 23, 2009; Rocio Cara Labrador and Danielle Renwick, "Central America's Violent Northern Triangle", Council on Foreign Relations, June 26, 2018, www.cfr.org/backgrounder/central-americas-violent-northern-triangle.

71. Fox News Latino, "Central Americans Seeking Asylum Quadrupled in Last Five Years," *Fox News*, July 17, 2013.

72. Hannah Stone, "US Defends Blacklisting of Salvador Street Gang," *Insight Crime*, November 29, 2012, www.insightcrime.org/news-analysis/us-defends-blacklisting-of-salvador-street-gang-ms13.

RECOMMENDED READINGS AND RESOURCES

Aravena, Rojas and Francisco Pedro Caldenty del Pozo. 2013. "Central America's Relations with Latin America." In Diego Sánchez-Ancochea and Salvador Martí I Puig, eds. *Handbook of Central American Governance*. London: Routledge, pp. 322–334.

Coatsworth, John. 1994. *Central America and the United States: The Clients and the Colossus.* New York: Twayne.

Dominguez, Jorge. 1998. *International Security and Democracy: Latin America and the Caribbean in the Post–Cold War Era.* Pittsburgh, PA: University of Pittsburgh Press.

García, María Cristina. 2006. *Seeking Refuge: Central American Migration to Mexico, the United States, and Canada.* Berkeley, CA: University of California Press.

Hamilton, Nora. 2001. *Seeking Community in Global City: Guatemalans and Salvadorans in Los Angeles.* Philadelphia, PA: University of Pennsylvania Press.

Hunt, Sarah. 2013. "The Role of International Financial Institutions in Central America." In Diego Sánchez-Ancochea and Salvador Martí I Puig, eds. *Handbook of Central American Governance*. London: Routledge, pp. 350–364.

Menjívar, Cecilia. 2000. *Fragmented Ties: Salvadoran Immigrant Networks in America.* Berkeley, CA: University of California Press.

Nazario, Sonia. 2007. *Enrique's Journey.* New York: Random House.

Palmer, David Scott. 2006. *US Relations with Latin America during the Clinton Years: Opportunities Lost or Opportunities Squandered?* Gainesville, FL: University of Florida Press.

Pastor, Robert. 2001. *Exiting the Whirlpool: US Foreign Policy toward Latin America and the Caribbean.* Boulder, CO: Westview Press.

Perla, Héctor, Salvador Martí I Puig, and Danny Burridge. 2013. "Central America's Relations with the United States of America." In Diego Sánchez-Ancochea and Salvador Martí I Puig, eds. *Handbook of Central American Governance.* London: Routledge, pp. 309–321.

Robinson, William I. 2003. *Central America, Social Change, and Globalization.* London: Verso.

Rosenberg, Mark B. and Luis G. Solís. 2007. *The United States and Central America: Geopolitical Realities and Regional Fragility.* New York: Routledge.

11

REFLECTIONS AND PROJECTIONS

WE NOW REFLECT ON PATTERNS EMERGING FROM OUR EXAMINATION of Central America over the last several decades and consider the region's possible future. Years of studying Central American politics, however, have taught us that it is easier to sum up than to predict. We recognize that our individual and joint writings—like those of most other observers over the years—contain faulty predictions.

REFLECTIONS: REPRESSION, MOBILIZATION, AND DEMOCRATIC TRANSITION

The Crises

Central America's crises over the latter half of the twentieth century arose from several factors: (1) centuries of socioeconomic formation; (2) rapid economic growth in the 1960s followed by a sharp downturn in the mid-1970s; (3) elite and government intransigence in the face of mobilization driven by the economic crisis; and (4) Cold War politics and the behavior of the United States. We disagreed with Washington's interpretation that the violent upheavals of the 1970s and 1980s occurred mainly because of Soviet and Cuban meddling.

The early social and economic formation of the five major Central American countries powerfully shaped the crises and process we have examined. Colonial Guatemala, El Salvador, and Nicaragua developed strong, largely Hispanic ruling classes, which exploited the indigenous majority and enslaved Africans to produce primary export products. This foundation on inequality and repression favored the development of violent, military-dominated polities. In the other two countries, less exploitative systems developed, but for different reasons. Costa Rica's native peoples were either killed or driven out of the central highlands, leaving almost no racially distinct underclass to exploit. Divisions among elites remained minor, so civilian rather than military government became the Costa Rican norm. Honduras, the poorest country with ample land, never really developed the powerful, self-confident, and exploitative elite minority of its three closest neighbors. Elites from Liberal and Conservative factions, often military officers, seized ruling power from each other repeatedly from 1839 to 1972.

By the twentieth century these differing social formations had conditioned governing elites to respond divergently to local sociopolitical crises. In Costa Rica they acted with relative moderation and accommodation. Honduran elites plotted against one another and seldom faced much resistance from peasants. Where accommodation or even mere cooptation prevailed, as often true in Honduras and especially Costa Rica, social peace survived. In contrast, Guatemalan, Salvadoran, and Nicaraguan elites tended toward intransigence and violent repression when challenged. When in the 1970s broad opposition demanded reform, regime intransigence gave insurgents legitimacy, and they eventually toppled the government (Nicaragua) or waged protracted civil wars (Guatemala and El Salvador).

At this juncture, US interference exacerbated a problem it sought to solve. Seized by inflated Cold War fears of Soviet-Cuban penetration into Central America, the United States misinterpreted mobilizing popular demands for social justice and democracy. Listening almost exclusively to the voices of intransigent elites and its own foreign policy establishment deeply suspicious of the left, Washington rallied to the trumpets of anti-Communism. Thus, in the 1950s—at the height of McCarthyism at home—the Central Intelligence Agency (CIA) helped overthrow Guatemala's first socially progressive democracy. US aid strengthened the military and police of all four local dictatorships and trained local militaries to implement repression and counterinsurgency. This began in Guatemala and Nicaragua in the 1960s, El Salvador in the 1970s, and Honduras in the 1980s. Facing increasingly violent intransigence and no democratic avenues for redress, guerrilla movements formed and expanded—first in Guatemala and Nicaragua, then El Salvador, and still later in Honduras. We believe that, had local dictatorships been less protected by US arms, less encouraged by American support, and more responsive to the needs and mobilized demands of the suffering majority, such accommodation might have kept the opposition and reformers from becoming insurrectionary movements.

CENTRAL AMERICA'S UNIQUE PATTERNS OF TRANSITION

Central America offers useful examples of several types of regime change transition both toward and away from democracy. Costa Rica's democratic transition during the first half of the twentieth century came a half century before its neighbors in the isthmus. Several historic factors contributed: inauguration of extensive public education in the late nineteenth century; expansion of working-class organizations and other civil society during the 1930s; a tradition of civilian rule and elections—albeit elitist and often fraudulent; and a split in the ruling cafetalero elite in the 1940s. An unstable alliance between the organized working class and one elite faction culminated in the brief civil war of 1948 led by middle-class insurgents. Though the rebels prevailed, they lacked the strength to govern without cooperation from some cafetalero elites and the forbearance of the working class. The resolution of this stalemate involved the constitutional revision of 1949 that abolished the armed forces, retained the social reforms of the ousted government, and gave the presidency to the bourgeois faction allied with the rebels in 1949. A working inter-elite accord thus emerged in the early 1950s that ensured a continuing civilian-democratic regime that would not have to endure military intervention.

Although later buffeted by the turmoil that convulsed the region in the 1970s and 1980s, Costa Rica maintained its stability and democratic practices with accommodation of opposition, good human rights performance, and public policy that improved middle- and working-class living standards. More recently intermittent economic problems, the imposition of neoliberalism, and party modernization upended the party system, splitting the National Liberation Party, elevating and nearly destroying the Social Christian Unity Party, and introducing several new parties. Realignments among the political elite and serial corruption scandals have probably not undermined elites' consensus on democratic rules of the game. Despite their growing prosperity, Costa Rican citizens express growing dissatisfaction with their institutions and leaders and their democratic norms have eroded somewhat. The system remains a consolidated civilian-democratic regime, but warrants careful observation.

Of the five countries, Honduras—with a fragile state and divided elite—historically oscillated between military and civilian rule. The Carter administration pressed Honduras to become more democratic. Honduras' top military officers grew keenly aware of the Nicaraguan revolution next door and the potential institutional cost to the military of remaining in power. It thus moved quickly from military-authoritarian through reformist-military to transitional-civilian democratic regimes in the early 1980s. This coincided with the Reagan administration's choice of Honduras as its staging ground for attacks on the Nicaraguan revolution and Salvadoran insurgency.

Honduras became a democracy in 1996 when civilians reformed the military and exerted greater control over it. Political elites, however, soon demonstrated their lack of commitment to democratic norms. A Liberal intra-party feud contributed to a coup d'état in mid-2009. After assisting Congress and the Supreme Court in deposing and exiling President Manuel Zelaya, the armed forces stood down. Strong international pressure on the de facto interim regime sought Zelaya's return to office to finish his term, but Honduras's Congress balked. The regularly scheduled 2009 election took place, and Porfirio Lobo became president in January 2010. Subsequent actions by Congress, the courts, the Electoral Tribunal, and political elites confirmed democracy's complete failure in Honduras. President Hernández packed the Supreme Court, secured a language and logic-defying interpretation reversing the ban on presidential re-election, contested and won a deeply flawed election in 2017, and violently repressed protests of these anti-democratic acts.[1] Honduras thus became a civilian autocracy.

In the other three countries transitions from dictatorship to democracy occurred at gunpoint. In each, economic strains in the 1970s led to opposition and popular mobilization for change, to which each government responded with violent intransigence. In Nicaragua, the Sandinista National Liberation Front (FSLN) overthrew the Somoza dictatorship in 1979 and attempted revolution. Moderate in comparison to other Marxist-led regimes, the Sandinistas moved from de facto rule with wide grassroots democratic participation under FSLN leadership (1979–1984) to an elected civilian-led revolutionary transitional government (1984–1987). Between 1979 and 1987 the multiclass coalition that had toppled the old regime fragmented. Ideological factions and class forces struggled to establish political space for themselves either within the unusually inclusive framework of the revolutionary coalition or outside it entirely. Those who broke away and joined the Contra war received extensive US backing. The Sandinistas and others who remained within the revolutionary framework struggled to design institutions that would accommodate working- and middle-class interests without provoking a pro-Contra US invasion. The 1987 constitution provided an institutional framework for civilian-democratic rule. By 1990, however, damage from the Contra war, US-orchestrated economic strangulation, and aspects of revolutionary policy had deeply polarized and beggared the country. Nicaraguans of all classes availed themselves of the election to end the Sandinista revolution and Contra war by electing Violeta Barrios de Chamorro president.

The FSLN remained out of power for three presidential terms, during which Daniel Ortega consolidated his power in the party and ejected its moderates. Liberals under Arnoldo Alemán won the 1997 election, and again in 2002 under Enrique Bolaños. Ortega and Alemán, meanwhile, forged a pact that gave them control over the Supreme Court and Supreme Electoral Council. Electoral competition deteriorated badly after 2006 while small parties were squeezed out of competition. In 2006 and 2011 the fractious Liberals failed to produce a consensus candidate against the FSLN's Daniel Ortega and effectively collapsed, leaving a one-party system in which Ortega has been re-elected three times. Voter turnout slumped in 2016. Protests of policy decisions broke out in 2018 and the regime violently repressed them, killing 300 people and arresting thousands. We reclassified Nicaragua as a semi-democracy effective in 2006 and as a civilian autocracy as of 2016. Nicaragua has come full circle, back to autocratic rule as under the Somozas.

Guatemala and El Salvador passed from military-authoritarian regimes through military-reformist regimes and civilian-transitional regimes and ultimately to civilian democracy by way of civil war and negotiated peace settlements. Although they began with hopes of defeating their respective dictatorships and establishing revolutionary regimes, both the Farabundo Martí National Liberation Front (FMLN) of El Salvador (by 1982) and the Guatemalan National Revolutionary Union (URNG) (by 1986) had abandoned that objective as unrealistic. They had witnessed US policy toward the Nicaraguan revolution and became convinced, in the words of Rubén Zamora (the leader of the Salvadoran Revolutionary Democratic Front, an alliance of civilian opposition), that outright "victory would be ashes in our mouths." The United States and its two client governments resisted negotiated settlements until after the end of the Cold War. Meanwhile, Washington and key elites in each country, including the military, pursued a gradualist strategy of using elections and transition to nominally civilian government to enhance governmental legitimacy and thus deny rebels a broader coalition. With the Cold War and the Nicaraguan revolution over, Washington and local actors eventually accepted peace agreements. Thus civilian-democratic regimes emerged from decades of violent conflict, with former rebels included in the political arena and newly restrained militaries.

The legacy of transition at gunpoint, as seen in Nicaragua, El Salvador, and Guatemala, appears mixed. All three countries forged at least formally democratic political institutions. Civic life and political conditions improved over those existing prior to their insurrections. Further, because grassroots participation contributed to all three transitions, subsequent democratic regimes featured increased political participation by ordinary citizens and their organizations. These benefits remain where democracy persists in Central America.

Central America's transitions to democracy also had negative aspects. To begin, civilian democratic regimes' collapses into autocracy in Honduras and Nicaragua revealed how frail new democracies can be, especially when external incentives to maintain these systems had declined. Political elites had not fully embraced democratic rules, while the payoffs for betraying them became ever greater. Violence against underrepresented groups, including LGBT persons and indigenous and Afro-descendant communities, was also a serious problem in the region, signaling the failure to address structural inequalities or deeply entrenched social norms.

As in all civil wars, the fratricides of the 1970–1990s and accompanying personal loss and black propaganda left polarization and partisan hatreds that lingered for years. New political-economic elites in the new regimes manipulated these divisions and fears to distract citizens from their class interests and thus to undermine the influence of the political left in elections. The Nationalist Republican Alliance Party (ARENA) in El Salvador and the Liberals in Nicaragua stoked fears of possible punishments by the United States to help them win elections. The tactic eventually lost its power, however, as the FMLN (in 2009 and 2014) and FSLN (in 2006, 2011, and 2016) captured and recaptured power through elections. In El Salvador, after two successive presidential wins, the FMLN finished third and ARENA had its worst showing in three decades.

Crime became a grievous and growing problem in three of the new democracies. Aggravating conditions included the rapid demobilization of tens of thousands of government and insurgent fighters, arms remaining from the conflicts, and police reforms that cashiered large numbers of officers in Guatemala and El Salvador. These drove high levels of armed criminal delinquency—and sporadic renewed insurgency in Nicaragua—that threatened individual and public security. In Guatemala and El Salvador, the reformed police could not cope with surging violent crime, much of it originating from fired former police officers. Honduras and El Salvador also developed serious gang problems as the United States deported immigrants to their native countries. Finally, the narcotics-trafficking cartels of Latin America infiltrated and corrupted the police and armed forces, particularly in Guatemala and Honduras. Gangs, carjackings, armed assaults, murders and especially femicides (murders of women), resource theft, police corruption, and drug trafficking became and remain grave problems in several countries. El Salvador and Honduras had some of the highest homicide and femicide rates in the world. Weak security forces and justice institutions, often suborned by criminals, lacked the capacity and will to address major organized crime. Mano dura policies proved ineffectual against gangs and generated a surge of human rights abuses. Nicaragua's police were sufficiently disciplined to escape these problems and crime there was lower.

Finally, the legacy of US intervention against the three revolutionary movements during the 1970s and 1980s played a role in post-Cold War politics in Central America. The US State Department and members of the US Congress repeatedly sought to sway elections in Nicaragua and El Salvador in the 2000s. They warned against presidential candidates of the leftist parties FSLN and FMLN, and in El Salvador threatened the immigration status of US resident Salvadorans and their remittances to their families. Venezuelan aid and Nicaragua's lower remittance flows somewhat insulated it from these pressures. Such external manipulation of elections is anti-democratic on its face.

Our current assessment of these three cases divides. The Liberal-Sandinista pact (circa 2000) between Arnoldo Alemán and Daniel Ortega began undermining civilian democracy by excluding small parties from elections, putting the FSLN and Liberals alone in control of elections and eroding their quality, and by the judiciary's constitution-contradicting ruling allowing presidential self-succession. The effective collapse of the Liberals and the FSLN's landslide re-election in 2011 set legislative conditions for extended FSLN dominance of the system. Nicaragua became a civilian autocracy.

El Salvador persists as a civilian-democratic regime, but a close reading of its evolution raises red flags. Its elections have been judged transparent despite evidence some parties have criminal gang links and resulting voter intimidation. Corruption is endemic. Former president Saca was sentenced in 2018 in a massive embezzlement case, while former president Funes continued to evade arrest while living in Nicaragua. Legislative and executive branch interference in the courts has marred the justice system. Citizens' security is poor given nearly omnipresent gangs nationwide that extort and intimidate businesses and individuals. Women's reproductive rights are extremely curtailed and femicide is a major problem.[2]

Guatemala also warrants observers' concerns. Voters failed to enact constitutional reforms to bring the badly under-represented indigenous population more fully into the governance. As noted in Chapter 7, the party system has deteriorated into a panoply of transitory parties led by celebrities and the wealthy. Public officials dismantled the country's successful anti-corruption institution. Freedom House's 2019 report stated that although "elections ... are generally free, organized crime and corruption severely impact the functioning of government. Violence and criminal extortion schemes are serious problems ... Journalists, activists, and public officials who confront crime, corruption, and other sensitive issues risk attack."[3] Guatemala, too, shows serious signs that democracy remains unconsolidated and is eroding.

PROJECTIONS: PROSPECTS FOR DEMOCRATIC CONSOLIDATION

The External Setting

Most theories on democratic consolidation focus on facilitating or impeding domestic considerations. In Central America, however, we must examine Central America's international environment, particularly US behavior, which has long affected local regime types. This should not surprise anyone. The United States emerged from World War II as the world's most powerful nation and by the end of the twentieth century had at least temporarily become the world's only superpower. Washington exercised tremendous influence over the tiny nearby Central American republics through its diplomacy, assistance, willingness to project military power into the region, regional military ties, and its influence over critical international lenders like the International Monetary Fund, World Bank, and Inter-American Development Bank.

Although many twentieth-century US policymakers might have preferred democracy in the isthmus, economic and security interests often eclipsed such views. The impulse to contain perceived Communist threats overwhelmed US scruples about Central American dictators and motivated US support for demobilization. Even when the Reagan and first Bush administrations pushed for civilian governments in El Salvador and Guatemala, they simultaneously supported counterterrorism campaigns that made resulting elections far from democratic. Washington also delayed negotiated settlements that would have enhanced democracy and human rights. With the Cold War over in the 1990s, US policy largely reversed field although American officials continued trying to discourage the election of leftists well into the 2000s. Cold War habits lingered in American policy in the region.

New centers of international influence within Latin America have developed in recent decades. Mexico and Brazil emerged as important economic and political actors. The Organization of American States (OAS), once dependably subservient to US preferences, adopted policies reflecting Latin American countries' interests. One dramatic example of this was the vote of the OAS in 2009 to invite Cuba to rejoin the organization, a position long opposed by the United States. (Cuba has declined.) Another important new hemispheric player was Venezuela under presidents Chávez and Maduro. Venezuela used its oil and wealth to counter to US influence in the region. It provided energy and economic assistance to oil-poor Nicaragua, Guatemala, Honduras, and some municipalities in El Salvador. All three countries became members of the Venezuela-promoted organization Bolivarian Alternative for Latin America and the Caribbean (ALBA), though Honduras withdrew in 2010 following the 2009 coup. When the Obama administration announced a $62 million cut in aid to Nicaragua in June 2009, Venezuela pledged $50 million to replace the lost American funds. Venezuela provided foreign assistance, in some cases greater than aid from the United States, to states and municipalities governed by parties of the left to counterbalance US influence in the region. Venezuela's and ALBA's aid to El Salvador, Honduras, and Nicaragua, however, has essentially evaporated since 2010 as its economy contracted sharply with oil price decreases, US sanctions, and economic management problems.[4]

The Obama administration's policies on immigration, aid, and narcotics interdiction essentially continued those of his predecessor. When Venezuela and other Latin American countries differed with US policies and backed those differences with foreign aid, we believe some Central American leaders felt less constrained by US preferences than when no countervailing policies existed. Nicaragua, Guatemala, and Honduras have all undertaken actions the US opposed.

At this writing, almost three years into the Trump administration, US policy still looms large in Central America but its disruptive style and erratic direction leave its effects unclear. US efforts to dissuade Central American immigration to the United States have multiplied rapidly in terms of presidential rhetoric, border enforcement, economic assistance policy, and diplomacy. They have at times, however, seemed contradictory or self-defeating—for example, cutting economic assistance designed to improve local conditions that would reduce pressures to emigrate. US threats to further tighten immigration and asylum rules and "close the border" have reportedly increased Central Americans' sense of urgency to emigrate sooner rather than later. Intimidation of Mexico and Guatemala to tighten their policies toward migrants passing through have roiled relations, but also elicited enforcement cooperation. Immigration enforcement raids within the United States and family separation policies at the border have traumatized immigrant communities and caused untold suffering without greatly discouraging immigration.[5]

Internal Factors

At the end of the twentieth century, all Central American nations had elected, civilian, constitutional regimes, a circumstance practically inconceivable as recently as 1980. In each newly democratized nation, power had changed hands through peaceful elections among civilian candidates several times. As we have so frequently argued in the preceding pages, Central America's old (Costa Rica) and new (all the rest) civilian-democratic regimes faced difficult challenges. In the newer democracies their political actors had to work to preserve their fledgling democratic regimes from powerful and often unpredictable forces. As we have seen, some have failed this effort and others may follow.

Practically speaking the consolidation of democracy in Central America would have required the four newer democratic regimes to devise political structures and processes more like those that have existed in Costa Rica since the 1950s. They would have needed to sustain political and civil-society participation, and to protect individual political rights.[6]

Students of democratic consolidation identify several important consolidation factors. Among the most important is (1) an elite settlement, a consensus among a broad array of elites to accept and accommodate each other's participation in the political game, to accept democratic procedures, and to allow the mass public and civil society to take part in politics. Such accords, typically shaped by what Larry Diamond and Juan Linz call "founding democratic leadership,"[7] must allow for some evolution so the regime can accommodate new power contenders.[8]

Another element is (2) an autonomous civil society (political participation and organized interest activity). Especially in matters of economic policymaking, civil-society engagement helps communicate citizens' needs to government and restrain state power. Other factors include: (3) a mass culture of support for democratic norms; (4) strong but moderate political parties; (5) a strong legislature; (6) a strong and effective government; (7) a small military that is allegiant to civilian leadership; (8) some de-concentration of wealth or amelioration of poverty; (9) moderate economic growth; and (10) as noted above, the support of important external actors.[9]

To evaluate all ten points for all five Central American countries would exceed this chapter's scope. Nevertheless, a review of some issues will illuminate the dimming prospects for democratic consolidation in Central America.

Prospects

When US foreign policy both values and reinforces democracy in Central America, it exerts pressure for (but does not assure) local elites to play by democratic rules. Unfortunately, current trends are not positive. As noted, several administrations in Washington have interfered in elections in El Salvador and Nicaragua to discourage voting for parties of the once-revolutionary left. US endorsement of, and suspected involvement in, the abortive coup d'état against Venezuela's constitutionally elected late populist Hugo Chávez in 2002 and its active role in the removal of popularly elected Haitian president Jean-Bertrand Aristide in 2004 stood at odds with America's stated commitment to democratic and constitutional order in Latin America. While the Obama administration reversed the second Bush administration's policy of manipulating elections, some question whether it overcorrected in this regard. US condemnation of the coup was tepid, and recognition of the Lobo government signaled greater US interest in ending the issue than supporting democracy. Support for the questionable re-election of Hernández in 2017 also undermined US support for democratic norms. Continued flows of military aid to governments for fighting crime also had potential to undermine democratic institutions. The Trump administration's announced suspension of foreign assistance to Central America in 2019 undercut potentially legitimacy-building programs aimed at ameliorating poverty and violence.

During the 1980s other key outside actors, of lesser (but growing) influence than the United States, also encouraged democracy in Central America, especially European countries and the Catholic Church. Since the early 2000s, however, Europe has somewhat withdrawn from this effort, its countries' and organizations' definitions of democracy have remained contested and imprecise.[10] Central America's Latin American neighbors—many new democracies themselves—used diplomacy to promote Central American peace and democracy during the 1980s when US direct armed intervention in the isthmus seemed possible. Latin American governments on balance appeared likely to prefer civilian democracy. However, since then several (Venezuela, Bolivia, Ecuador, and Brazil) strengthened their presidencies, weakened checks and balances, or moved toward a populist leadership style that carries risks for democracy. Multiple democratic breakdowns in Latin America could further weaken regional support for electoral democracy in the isthmus and might encourage anti-democratic actors. Indeed, we classify Nicaragua and Honduras as civilian autocracies, and believe Guatemala and El Salvador are at risk.[11]

Elite Settlement. Did national elites reach broadly inclusive agreements to abide by democratic rules of the game? Costa Rica's elite settlement had been in place for decades, a cornerstone of that nation's political stability. Progress toward elite settlement elsewhere was somewhat less certain. Several specific accords and pacts have been signed among formerly warring elites in Nicaragua (ending the Contra war in 1990), El Salvador (the 1992 peace accord), and Guatemala (the 1996 peace accord). Governments and their armed opponents agreed to nominally democratic political rules, formerly excluded players were allowed into the legal political arena, clean elections were held, and power has subsequently transferred peaceably from incumbents to victorious opponents several times in every country.

However, in Nicaragua an accord between the FSLN and Liberal caudillos directly narrowed political space, undermined democratic rules of the game, and allowed repression of growing opposition. In El Salvador, Guatemala and Honduras periodic assassinations of human rights activists, journalists, candidates for office and gang members revealed some political actors' wishes to intimidate others, ignore civil liberties, or even destabilize the democratic regimes. Indeed, various illegal and unconstitutional behaviors of diverse elites in the 2009 Honduran constitutional crisis and coup and since reveal beyond any doubt the lack of a broad elite consensus on democratic rules of the game.

In Guatemala, courts blocked the efforts of former military dictator Efraín Ríos Montt to return to Guatemala's presidency in 1999, but he later won a congressional seat and became majority leader of the Congress for a term. In 2009 a raft of sensational charges were made as part of an attempt to cut short Alvaro Colom's presidency. These incidents demonstrated a lack of commitment to democracy and the rule of law within Guatemala's political elite. Since then presidential efforts to dismantle the anti-corruption agency International Commission Against Impunity in Guatemala (CICIG) and disrupt corruption investigations bespeak disregard for the rule of law. Similar efforts to undermine anti-corruption programs by court-packing and intimidation of witnesses and journalists have also occurred in El Salvador, Honduras, and Nicaragua. Political elites across the isthmus appear more set on maintaining kleptocratic access to state resources than to keeping democracy or the rule of law.

Repression and political terror in the four newer Central American democracies remained middling or higher into the 2010s and have been rising, contrasting with Costa Rica's minimal repression (see Figure 2.2). Compared to Costa Rica, democracy and civil liberties performance in the other four countries also remained problematically low (and eroding) by standards for electoral democracies (see Figure 2.1).

In summary, while some Central American elites played by democratic rules seemed in the early 2000s, pockets of resistance have become clearer ever since. Elites have not controlled rights violations—indeed, they have increased in response to soaring crime rates. Some elites had never demonstrated clear commitment to democratic rules and others appeared to be moving away from them, while in two countries rulers have rejected democracy outright. We consider the outlook poor for elite accords on democracy.

Participation and Civil Society. Turning to political participation, surveys from as far back as the early 1990s and several in the 2000s from all Central American nations (Chapter 9) reported active engagement in registration, voting electioneering, contacting officials, organizational activism, and communal self-help in all five nations. The range and breadth of citizen political activity was remarkable, especially given the history of turbulence in some countries. What most limited participation in the early 1990s was political repression. Because repression declined following peace accords, we expected citizen participation to increase after democratization. Indeed, from 2004 to 2008 we found that citizen participation increased in Guatemala and El Salvador, suggesting a payoff from reduced repression and increased democracy there. By 2012 and 2014 Guatemalans were the most engaged Central Americans, especially excelling in group and community improvement activism. Nicaraguans' participation also rose notably over prior surveys. In contrast, participation has declined steadily in Costa Rica. The oldest and best-established democracy in the region has the least active citizens in the region. Focusing on civil society, there was consistent evidence over time that activism within organizations increased Central Americans' support for democracy and political activity.

Our findings on participation and civil society offer a mixed result regarding democratic consolidation in Central America. Central Americans in 2014 were active in diverse organizations, with considerable variation by group type among the nations. Church- and school-related groups engaged the most citizens, followed by community-improvement activity. Church-group activity increased from 2004 to 2014, except in Costa Rica, where it declined. Involvement in school groups and professional-business groups declined in most of the region from 2004 to 2014. We suspect this rather broad demobilization trend across Central America indicated that civil-society activism cooled as political conflict subsided. Costa Ricans, blessed with a better-performing system, engaged less in interest groups than other Central Americans.

Public Attitudes and Culture. Did the citizens of Central America support democratic rules of the game? In the early 1990s, high levels of repression reduced popular support for democratic liberties. Thus the subsequent waning of state repression might lead one to expect that, other things equal, citizen support for democratic liberties would increase. Our analysis showed that large majorities of Central Americans rejected authoritarian government and supported democratic liberties in the early 1990s and in 2004. Democratic norms had declined by 2014, however, especially tolerance of regime critics. However, support for coups declined markedly over this eight-year span.

Guatemalans and Hondurans had the region's lowest levels of general democratic norms and tolerance for critics in 2014. Support for confrontational political methods remained stable across the 2004–2014 decade. One Central American in six supported the violent overthrow of an elected government in 2014, and one in four supported civil disobedience.

Central Americans' evaluations of governmental legitimacy were essentially stable from 2004 to 2014. Costa Ricans and Nicaraguans reported the highest levels of general system support in 2014, while support for several specific institutions (e.g., courts, legislature, and parties) fell below the scale midpoint and was essentially unchanged from 2008. Evaluation of national economic performance was low across the entire region.

The Honduran case warrants special emphasis in light of the events of 2009. In 2012, Hondurans expressed the weakest support for democracy and for their institutions (as in 2008). Their support for rebellion and coups, however, had declined sharply from 2008 after experiencing the coup. The Honduran mass public, of course, did not overthrow President Zelaya in June 2009. However, the public's comparative ambivalence about democracy likely placed little restraint on the actions of the anti-democratic elites who unconstitutionally ousted an elected president. Hondurans' support for civil disobedience and rebellion declined sharply after the 2009 coup. These opinions may have changed because of hard lessons learned from increased repression following the overthrow and evolving democratic breakdown.

Based on these patterns, only Costa Rica and Nicaragua manifested consolidating popular support for its political institutions. The broad pattern for the region is one of gradually weakening democratic norms and lower system support. System support in Nicaragua had moved in the other direction as of 2014, likely responding to public sector spending on anti-poverty programs. Surveys from mid-2019, however, appear to tell a different presidential approval story in the wake of Nicaragua's 2018 turmoil and crackdown.

President Ortega in 2019 had fallen from one of the best-evaluated to one of the worst-evaluated presidents of the hemisphere—an approval rating of 24 percent.[12]

Party Systems. Do Central American nations approach the model of other stable democracies in having two strong but moderate (ideologically centrist) political parties? The short answer is no, but the complex picture has changed considerably in the last three decades. Nicaragua is an outlier—the field of competitors there has narrowed to a single effective party, the FSLN. In the other four nations parties have multiplied in number, especially in Guatemala. Formerly powerful parties have divided or declined (Honduras' PLH, Costa Rica's PUSC and PLN, Nicaragua' Liberals). Revolutionary parties that emerged from civil wars have had very different trajectories: Nicaragua's FSLN became dominant after a period out of power. El Salvador's FMLN won two successive presidencies but lost badly in 2019. Guatemala's URNG failed to ever gain traction with voters. No regional ideological pattern had emerged as of 2019: the leftist FSLN prevailed in Nicaragua and the center-left Citizen Action Party (PAC) held the Costa Rican presidency, while rightist parties (two of them new) occupied the Northern Triangle countries' presidencies. Finally, after the last round of elections, except in Nicaragua no party occupying the presidency also held a majority of legislative seats. Most of these tendencies do not offer—and may be moving away from—the near-term prospect of a stabilizing two-party centrist system. Governing elites acting under party banners in Nicaragua and Honduras have imposed themselves upon their people in violation of their own democratic constitutions' plain language.

Armed Forces. To what extent were the region's militaries small and loyal to civilian rule? In the Central American isthmus as recently as 1990 this question was risible, but by the late 1990s there had been significant progress. In 1990, only one government approached the criterion of having a small and allegiant military—Costa Rica had dismantled its army in 1949. All the other countries had large armies swollen by war (or in Honduras by US aid). After 1990 change came rapidly. After settling the Contra war in 1990, the new Nicaraguan government reduced the size of its military by 80 percent, civilianized the police, passed a new military code, and professionalized and renamed the army. Nicaraguan military behavior after 1990 suggested a willingness to accept civilian control, but Daniel Ortega's return to power has again concentrated authority over the military in the presidency. In the protests and turmoil of 2018, the police repressed opposition protesters, ignored armed pro-FSLN thugs who attacked them, and detained thousands. Human rights monitors estimated 300 protesters died in these incidents.[13] Evidence suggests a decline of security force neutrality and re-emergence of a Nicaraguan historical pattern of subservience to the president.

After the Salvadoran and Guatemalan civil wars ended the armies of both countries shrank and came under increased civilian influence. Top officers were retired and reassigned. But rising crime threatened this demilitarization. El Salvador established an anti-gang unit of the armed forces to assist the police in 2006. Honduras also increasingly relied on new militarized police forces in public security. In a troubling trend, Guatemala's military became somewhat resurgent in national politics during the early 2000s. Several presidents ordered the military to assist the police in controlling crime. Judicial authorities tried and convicted numerous members of the military in a variety of cases related to the civil war. In 2013 former coup leader, president, and conservative politician Efraín Ríos Montt was prosecuted and convicted of genocide and crimes against humanity. The conviction was overturned days later and a retrial ordered, but Ríos Montt's death in 2018 truncated the process.

In the mid-1990s the Honduran military also submitted to reforms that included abolition of the draft, reassignment of officers, and civilianization of the police. For a while it seemed the old joke about Honduras had become passé—that the capital city Tegucigalpa should be named "Tegucigolpe" because of the frequency of military coups (*golpe* is Spanish for coup.) In their distaste for president Manuel Zelaya, the military revived the old joke. As part of the coup engineered by the Congress and Supreme Court and in violation of the constitution, the army arrested and exiled Zelaya. Human rights violations following the coup have involved the military as mano dura anti-gang policies have put the army back to work assisting the police.

Experts on the regions' armed forces expressed approval that Central American militaries in the early 2000s had become smaller, less human-rights abusive, and more cooperative with civilian officials. Mark Ruhl called the reduced political power of the area's armies "a great achievement for the region" and characterized the status quo in all four as falling between "democratic control" and "conditional subordination" to civilian authorities.[14] No one familiar with the history of Central America's militaries could be too sanguine about their prospects for obeying civilian governments, especially considering events in Honduras. Indeed, increased presidential control under Daniel Ortega recalls aspects of the era when the Nicaraguan National Guard served as an instrument of political control.

GLOBALIZED ECONOMIES AND DEMOCRACY

We have focused mostly on Central America's transformed political regimes but must also emphasize how the region's economies have changed and how that will shape Central America's future for decades to come. From the 1970s forward, civil war, energy-price increases, deteriorating terms of trade, excessive external borrowing, and the collapse of the Central American Common Market bedeviled the region's economies. In varying degrees, each at some time experienced severe economic crisis and required international help. In exchange for the credit required to prevent economic ruin, the United States, the World Bank, and the International Monetary Fund exacted fundamental economic concessions. Under this intense outside pressure, and with the collaboration of modernizing local capitalists, all Central American countries eventually altered their economic models to embrace neoliberalism.

Regarding neoliberalism's effects, Kaufman and Segura-Ubiergo reported that trade openness and integration into global markets, canons of the neoliberal economic model, "had a consistently negative effect on the aggregate social spending," and that democracies with such neoliberal policies tended to protect social security programs but spend less on health and education.[15] Portes and Hoffman reported increased income inequality, greater concentration of wealth, and a decline in public-sector employment. These forced new survival strategies among middle and lower classes, including micro-entrepreneurship, violent crime, and migration abroad for work.[16] Weyland found that neoliberalism's openness to global pressures discouraged elites from rejecting democracy but simultaneously undermined unions and leftist parties who speak for workers, depressed political participation, and weakened government accountability.[17]

We have shown that the neoliberal economic reforms pressed upon Central America reduced government spending on social welfare, education, and infrastructure, at least in the short term (although some recovery has occurred more recently). Governments streamlined payrolls, reduced budget deficits, privatized publicly owned corporations and services, curtailed regulatory efforts, and generally reduced the state's role in their economies. They slashed tariffs and import quotas to open Central American economies to foreign goods and investment, aggressively promoted nontraditional exports, and sought national advantage in the international economy in tourism and as suppliers of cheap labor for light manufacturing. These nearly revolutionary reforms attracted some new domestic and international investment and contributed to economic recovery in some countries. Neoliberalism advanced the economic fortunes of the local capitalists who took advantage of the new openings to the world capitalist economy and the reforms their lending allies demanded. With this support, these economic actors gained new political power in the emerging civilian-democratic regimes of the region. The new openness of the region's economies to the world undermined local manufacturing. New assembly plants had to compete in a global economy, which exerted relentless downward pressure on wages in those industries and left them vulnerable to relocation to the next cheaper labor market to develop. The prospect for continued foreign investment in assembly plants remained very uncertain as Africa and Haiti could offer even lower-wage environments. The deterioration of the welfare of the poor majority of Central Americans seemed increasingly likely. In the last decade there has been some reduction of poverty, but this comes from broad economic recovery and especially from escalating remittances rather than redistribution of system benefits toward the poor.

Neoliberalism's effects on social and political systems were mixed. Positive political effects include the external pressure that dissuaded Guatemalan institutions from succumbing to the self-coup by President Serrano in 1993, thus preserving constitutional rule. And international actors facilitated peace settlements in Nicaragua, El Salvador, and Guatemala, and contributed to the democratization of the latter two. Negative effects were numerous. Neoliberalism shrank the capacity of Central American governments to improve the general welfare of their citizens, promote economic growth, and invest in human capital (see Table A.5). Governments with international financial monitors and structural adjustment agreements found themselves with more unemployed citizens, lower average wages, and fewer government resources to redistribute income or ameliorate poverty. Governments thus lacked tools with which to promote their citizens' welfare. Social pathologies such as urban gangs, narcotics use and trafficking, prostitution and sex tourism, violent crime, and public corruption increased across the region in the 1990s and 2000s. Trimmed-down states and underfunded and ill-trained police found themselves ineffective against and sometimes complicit in these growing problems.[18]

These pernicious political and economic trends, derived from Central America's traditional economic weaknesses, its elites' scant enthusiasm for reform, and the effects of neoliberal economic policies, appeared unlikely to sustain democracy in the region. Our data have shown some demobilization of civil society engagement and election participation in the region, though we cannot link them directly to the effects of the neoliberal model. Flawed by their poor human rights performances, the democracies that emerged from regime transformation in Central America were widely and rightly criticized, and their citizens evaluated their institutions poorly. In one sense, neoliberalism's economic effects appeared certain to continue to limit some Central Americans' capacity to participate effectively in politics because so many lacked the resources or human capital required to influence public decisions. Central American nations, operating leanly and meanly under the rules of the global economy, would lack both the resources and elites with the will to improve their citizens' life chances. Recent evidence shows improved education spending, health, and life-expectancy statistics, so not all trends are negative. As we write this, neoliberalism is well entrenched, but some politicians have worked against its premises as recovering economies allow. Deeper democracy has failed in two countries and trends in others are worrying. We do not yet know whether the low-intensity democracy encouraged by neoliberalism might remain the best that Central Americans outside of Costa Rica can expect for many decades to come.

CONCLUSIONS

On balance we see both negative and positive signs for the consolidation of formal civilian democracies in Central America during the twenty-first century's second decade. In political terms, collectively the citizens of the isthmus still enjoyed more human rights and greater political freedom than before 1990. Central Americans' preference for democracy over dictatorship and democratic norms have eroded in recent years, but not vanished. Some political elites have followed formal democratic rules, but others have weakened or abandoned them. External actors' support for democratic regimes has fluctuated and sometimes flagged. The great experiment of the Nicaraguan revolution—a regime that pushed for much more participatory democracy and greater social justice than the polities that survived it—had failed under a combination of fierce US pressure and its own errors. Nicaragua has returned to its traditions of caudillo-style leadership, repression, and electoral impropriety.

Critics derided the new democracies of Central America as "low-intensity" or "light" democracies, and this criticism has gained weight. Formal democratic rules and procedures in a socioeconomic context of inequality and widespread poverty provide poor and unorganized Central Americans little influence over public policy. In the middle run, the great neoliberal economic experiment imposed upon the region by international actors has exacerbated inequality and poverty. Thus the only long-run hope for increased resources for the poor majority under neoliberal development models—and thus for increased popular political power and the deepening of democracy—appeared to be for the economies of the region to produce sustained and rapid growth. Fortunately, the recession that braked the world economy sharply in 2009 had limited effects in Central America, and growth resumed. But in four of five countries much of the apparent economic growth has come from remittances from their citizens living abroad. Some economic progress has occurred, but much of it would evaporate were these person-to-person foreign assistance programs suddenly to shrink. Realistic prospects for systemic growth appear to range from modest in more robust economies (Costa Rica) to grim in the nearly prostrate Honduras and Nicaragua.

Legitimacy of specific political institutions across Central America was low and, given poor performance, eroding as we wrote this. Yet such poor performance evaluations of the governments do not constitute a legitimacy crisis as such. Formal democracy with low repression provides intensely dissatisfied citizens opportunities to work for change within their systems. Indeed, evidence exists that those with low legitimacy norms increased their participation within the system but protested less. Except for Guatemala, the numbers of the most dissatisfied and least democratic citizens—a potential reservoir of support for anti-democratic elites, or of protest and rebellion—remained small in 2014. The multi-disgruntled were not much more active in politics than the region's more satisfied citizens. In Guatemala, however, the multi-disgruntled were sufficiently numerous——27 percent in 2014—to arouse concern. Guatemalans' commitment to democracy and system support were also weaker than elsewhere. The Honduran coup of 2009 and subsequent violent mass protests on both sides demonstrate the risks of a multi-dissatisfied and polarized citizenry.

We do not expect mass publics to overthrow democracy anywhere in the region. That is certainly not what happened in Honduras in 2009 and 2017. Instead, large groups of multi-disgruntled populations could provide a reservoir of support for anti-democratic elites who might work to undermine democracy. In 2014 nearly one Central American in five agreed that "in certain circumstances an authoritarian government might be preferable to democracy" (see Table 9.2). Well over a third of Guatemalans could support a coup under certain hypothetical circumstances. These data suggest very little in Guatemalan public opinion that might restrain anti-democratic elites.

There was also a prospect of more protest, which could either sustain or undermine democracy. Only one in 20 Central Americans reported taking part in protests in the year before our 2014, but one in four approved of civil disobedience and one in six approved of armed rebellion against an elected government. Protest or political turmoil can offer a pretext for anti-democratic elites to disrupt the democratic order. Since the Honduran coup and in Nicaragua in 2018 protests have intensified political conflict and justified the suppression of civil liberties by autocratic regimes.

Thus, aside from Costa Rica, what Central America had achieved as we wrote this was low-intensity democracy in two countries, with an even chance that even that will deteriorate, and two failures of democracy. Central Americans still marginally embraced the idea of democracy, but most evaluated their systems' performances harshly.

Alternatively, low-intensity democracy or illiberal democracy were, we believe, better than no democracy at all, especially in one regard well known to all Central Americans. At least 300,000 lost their lives to authoritarian repression during the decades-long struggle for formal democracy. Whether democratic or semi-democratic, elected civilian governments—especially with curtailed militaries—intimidate, imprison, maim, and kill much less than do unelected or military regimes. Inequalities and economic limitations notwithstanding, citizens who may organize, contact officials, vote, and protest can defend and pursue their interests more effectively than those who cannot. In the traumatic 1970s, 1980s, and 1990s, millions of ordinary Central Americans won the right to become protagonists in their own political reality. This right remains in several countries, but its survival everywhere appears much less certain than upon our last evaluation.

NOTES

1. President Lobo had previously moved the military back into internal security activity. The Supreme Court blocked prosecution of the generals involved in the 2009 coup. Congress in 2012 replaced four of the five Supreme Court justices because they overruled a police-reform law. Congress also passed new laws undermining due process for public employees and denying citizens' rights to challenge the constitutionality of laws. In the 2013 election, PN candidate Hernández won the presidency with only 37 percent of the vote. A Supreme Electoral Tribunal decision in 2016 allowed Hernández to seek a second term.

2. Freedom House, https://freedomhouse.org/report/freedom-world/2019/el-salvador.

3. Freedom House, https://freedomhouse.org/report/freedom-world/2019/guatemala.

4. World Bank Group, Indicators, https://data.worldbank.org/indicator/NY.GDP. PCAP.KD?locations=VE; https://data.worldbank.org/indicator/BX.KLT.DINV.WD. GD.ZS?locations=HN-NI-SV.

5. Jie Zong, Jeanne Batalova, and Micayla Burrow, "Frequently Requested Statistics on Immigrants and Immigration in the United States," Migration Policy Institute, March 14, 2019, www.migrationpolicy.org/article/frequently-requested-statistics-immigrants-and-immigration-united-states.

6. Michael Burton, Richard Gunther, and John Higley, "Introduction: Elite Transformations and Democratic Regimes," in John Higley and Richard Gunther, eds., *Elites and Democratic Consolidation in Latin America and Southern Europe* (Cambridge: Cambridge University Press, 1992); John Peeler, *Building Democracy in Latin America* (Boulder, CO: Lynne Rienner Publishers, 2004).

7. Larry Diamond and Juan J. Linz, "Introduction: Politics, Society and Democracy in Latin America," in Larry Diamond, Juan J. Linz, and Seymour Martin Lipset, *Democracy in Developing Countries, Volume 4: Latin America* (Boulder, CO: Lynne Rienner Publishers, 1989), p. 15.

8. Ibid., pp. 10–17.

9. Diamond and Linz, "Introduction"; Samuel Huntington, *The Third Wave: Democratization in the Late Twentieth Century* (Norman, OK: University of Oklahoma Press, 1991), pp. 208–316; John A. Booth, "Elections and Democracy in Central America; A Framework for Analysis," in John A. Booth and Mitchell A. Seligson, eds., *Elections and Democracy in Central America* (Chapel Hill, NC: University of North Carolina Press, 1989), pp. 16–21.

10. Stefano Palestini, "Defending Democracy in Latin America ... But which Democracy?" Open Democracy, February 15, 2017, www.opendemocracy.net/en/democraciaabierta/defending-democracy-in-latin-america-but-which-democracy/.

11. Freedom House, Freedom in the World 2019, https://freedomhouse.org/report/freedom-world/2019/; Economist Intelligence Unit, *Democracy Index 2018: Me Too? Political Participation, Protest and Democracy* (London: 2019), file:///C:/uca7/eiu%20democracy%20scores%202017.pdf; Wikipedia, Polity Data Series, https://en.wikipedia.org/wiki/Polity_data_series.

12. Consulta Mitofsky, "Ranking mandatarios América y el mundo 2019," *El Mundo*, September 2019, www.consulta.mx/index.php/estudios-e-investigaciones/el-mundo/item/1120-ranking-mandatarios.

13. Freedom House, Freedom in the World 2019, Nicaragua Report, https://freedomhouse.org/report/freedom-world/2019/nicaragua.

14. Mark Ruhl, "Curbing Central America's Militaries," *Journal of Democracy* 15 (July 2004), p. 148.

15. Robert R. Kaufman and Alex Segura-Ubiergo, "Globalization, Domestic Politics, and Social Spending in Latin America: A Time-Series Cross-Section Analysis, 1973–97," *World Politics* 53, No. 4 (2001), p. 553.

16. Alejandro Portes and Kelly Hoffman, "Latin American Class Structures: Their Composition and Change during the Neoliberal Era," *Latin American Research Review* 38, No. 1 (2003), pp. 41–82.

17. Kurt Weyland, "Neoliberalism and Democracy in Latin America: A Mixed Record," *Latin American Politics and Society* 46, No. 1 (2004), pp. 135–157.

18. Barbra Dozier, "The Political and Economic Effects of Neoliberalism on Modern Society," Barbra Dozier's Web Log, Wordpress.com, December 16, 2015, https://barbradozier.wordpress.com/2015/12/16/the-political-and-economic-effects-of-neoliberalism-on-modern-society/.

RECOMMENDED READINGS AND RESOURCES

Booth, John A. and Mitchell A. Seligson. 1998. *The Legitimacy Puzzle in Latin America: Political Support and Democracy in Eight Nations*. Cambridge: Cambridge University Press.

Hoffman, Kelly and Miguel Angel Centeno. 2003. "The Lopsided Continent: Inequality in Latin America." *Annual Review of Sociology* 29 (2003): 363–390.

Mahoney, James. 2001. *The Legacies of Liberalism: Path Dependence and Political Regimes in Central America*. Baltimore, MD: Johns Hopkins University Press.

Paris, Roland. 2002. *At War's End: Building Peace After Civil Conflict*. Cambridge: Cambridge University Press.

Peeler, John. 2004. *Building Democracy in Latin America*. Boulder, CO: Lynne Rienner Publishers.

Portes, Alejandro and Kelly Hoffman. 2003. "Latin American Class Structures: Their Composition and Change during the Neoliberal Era." *Latin American Research Review* 38 (1): 41–82.

Sánchez-Ancochea, Diego and Salvador Martí Puig, eds. 2013. *Handbook of Central American Governance*. London: Routledge.

Smith, William C. and Roberto Patricio Korzeniewicz, eds. 1997. *Politics, Social Change and Economic Restructuring in Latin America*. Miami, FL: North-South Center Press.

Wade, Christine J. 2016. *Captured Peace: Elites and Peacebuilding in El Salvador*. Athens, OH: Ohio University Press.

Walker, Thomas W. and Christine J. Wade. 2016. *Nicaragua: Emerging from the Shadow of the Eagle*. London: Routledge.

Weyland, Kurt. 2004. "Neoliberalism and Democracy in Latin America: A Mixed Record." *Latin American Politics and Society* 46 (1): 135–157.

APPENDIX

TABLE A.1 Selected Economic Data for Central America,
by Country, 1950–2018

	Costa Rica	El Salvador	Guatemala	Honduras	Nicaragua	Region[a]
GDP[b]						
1960	3,874	2,670	6,155	2,234	2,670	17,603
1970	6,936	9,422	10,517	3,558	5,135	35,568
1980	12,007	11,791	18,229	5,848	5,389	53,264
1990	15,237	11,343	19,886	7,736	4,701	58,903
2000	24,457	15,763	29,765	10,570	6,561	87,116
2010	37,269	18,448	41,339	15,839	8,759	121,654
2017	48,120	22,090	52,841	20,481	12,537	156,069
GDP per capita[c]						
1960	2,906	1,910	1,462	1096	1,504	1,620.44
1970	3,752	2,568	1,871	1,310	2,170	2,109.93
1980	5,025	2,574	2,503	1,590	1,658	2,490.41
1990	4,922	2,158	2,147	1561	1,134	2,201.45
2000	6,230	2,686	2,555	1,620	1,305	2,622.57
2010	8,199	2,993	2,826	1,933	1,526	3,097.12
2017	9,809	3,464	3,124	2,211	2,016	3,594.34
Percent change in GDP/capita						
1960–1970	29	34	28	20	44	30
1970–1980	34	0	34	21	-24	18
1980–1990	-2	-16	-14	-2	-32	-12
1990–2000	27	24	19	4	15	19
2000–2010	32	11	11	19	17	18

(continues)

TABLE A.1 Selected Economic Data for Central America,
by Country, 1950–2018 *(continued)*

Percent change in GDP/capita						
2010–2017	20	16	11	14	32	16
1990–2017	99	61	46	42	78	63
1960–2017	238	81	114	102	34	122
Percent[d] employed in agriculture						
1960	51	62	67	70	62	63[h]
1980	29	50	55	63	39	47[h]
2017	14	21	31	39	31	27[h]
Percent[d] employed in manufacturing						
c. 1950	11	11	12	6	11	10[h]
1983	16	14	15	13	15	15[h]
2017	22	20	12.8	20.9	18	19[h]
Percent of GDP from manufacturing						
1960	14	15	13	12	16	14[h]
1980	22	18	17	16	25	18[h]
2017	21	28	23	29	24	25[h]
Remittances as a percent of GDP						
1990	0.0	7.4	1.4	4.4	0.0	2.6
2018 (est.)	0.9	22.0	12.7	20.6	10.8	11.2
US foreign assistance[e]						
2013 total	1.6	27.6	80.8	52.0	8.6	170.60
2013 military and domestic security	1.6	2.8	1.9	4.0	2.8	13.10
2018 total	5.7	57.7	120.1	79.8	10.0	273.30
2018 military and domestic security	0.4	2.7	2.8	4.8	2.7	13.40
2018 US aid total as percent of GDP	0.0	0.2	0.2	0.3	0.1	0.2
External debt[f]						
1980	2.7	0.9	1.2	1.5	1.2	7.7[g]
1990	3.8	2.1	2.8	3.5	10.7	22.8[g]
2000	2.4	2.3	2.2	3.7	4.3	14.9[g]
2017	26.8	15.5	22.9	8.6	11.3	85.2[g]

(continues)

TABLE A.1 *(continued)*

Foreign debt as a percent of GDP						
1970	11.5	5.2	3.6	9.5	10.9	8.2[h]
1982	110.3	42.0	17.6	69.4	121.5	77.2[h]
1991	73.0	36.7	29.8	118.9	649.1	181.5[h]
2000	15.6	17.5	12.5	52.0	87.1	36.9[h]
2017	46.0	62.5	30.3	37.5	81.9	51.7[h]

[a] Weighted averages or totals unless otherwise specified.
[b] In millions of constant 2010 US dollars; regional value is sum for all nations.
[c] In 2010 constant US dollars.
[d] Of economically active population.
[e] In millions of current US dollars.
[f] Disbursed total external debt, in billions of current US dollars.
[g] Sum of country totals.
[h] Unweighted mean.
Sources: World Bank Group, Indicators, https://data.worldbank.org/indicator/NY.GDP.
MKTP.KD?locations=CR-SV-GT-HN-NI, accessed May 2, 2019; John A. Booth and Thomas
W. Walker, *Understanding Central America* (Boulder, CO: Westview Press, 1993), Table 2; US
Central Intelligence Agency, *The World Factbook* (Washington, DC, 1993), country reports, US
Central Intelligence Agency, *The World Factbook* (Washington, DC, 2004), accessed January
6, 2005, and US Central Intelligence Agency, *The World Factbook* (Washington, DC, 2013),
accessed November 17, 2013, www.cia.gov/cia/publications/factbook/, country reports, and US
Central Intelligence Agency, *The World Factbook* (Washington, DC, 2013), www.cia.gov/library/
publications/the-world-factbook, accessed April 11, 2019; World Bank, Migrant Remittance
Inflows (US$ millions), www.worldbank.org/en/topic/migrationremittancesdiasporaissues/
brief/migration-remittances-data, accessed May 3, 2019; US State Department, Map of Foreign
Assistance, www.foreignassistance.gov/explore#, accessed May 3, 2019.

TABLE A.2 Selected Social Data for Central America, by Country, 1960–2019

	Costa Rica	El Salvador	Guatemala	Honduras	Nicaragua	Region[a]
Population (in millions)						
1960	1.2	2.6	4.0	1.9	1.5	11.2[b]
1980	2.3	4.5	6.9	3.7	2.8	20.2[b]
2000	3.9	5.9	11.7	6.5	5.0	33.0[b]
2019	5.0	6.2	16.9	9.3	6.14	43.6[b]
Population density (persons per km²)						
1998	72	294	106	55	39	81
2019	98	306	161	85	49	103

(continues)

374   *Appendix*

TABLE A.2 Selected Social Data for Central America, by Country, 1960–2019 *(continued)*

Annual population growth rate for selected years (percentage)					
1960	3.6	2.8	3.0	2.8	3.2	3.1
1970	2.8	2.6	2.8	3.0	3.0	2.8
1980	2.7	1.7	2.5	3.1	2.9	2.6
2000	1.9	0.7	2.3	2.6	1.5	1.8
2018	1.0	1.0	1.0	1.0	1.0	1.0
Percentage indigenous population					
1978	1	2	60	2	2	14
2012[c]	1	4	41	4	4	11
Percentage Afro-origin population					
2012[c]	7	5	0	4	8	5
Percentage urban population					
1960	34	38	31	23	40	34
1990	50	49	42	40	53	50
2017	79	71	50	56	58	64
Percentage literate					
1960	86	42	40	30	32	42
c. 2000	96	80	70	76	67	78[c]
2017	98	88	82	89	83	88
Primary school enrollment ratio					
1980	107	75	73	98	94	89
1990	101	81	78	108	94	92
c. 2016	97	86	88	81	92	89
University enrollment as percentage of university-age population					
c. 2001	20	17	8	14	12	14
c. 2011	43	25	[d]	21	[d]	[d]
Life expectancy at birth					
1980–1985	73	57	59	60	60	60
c. 2003	78	70	66	66	69	70

[a] Unweighted averages for region unless otherwise specified.
[b] Sum for region.
[c] Self-identified as belonging to this group; AmericasBarometer surveys, www.LapopSurveys.org.
[d] Not available.
Source: John A. Booth and Thomas W. Walker, *Understanding Central America* (Boulder, CO: Westview Press, 1993), Appendix Table 2; Inter-American Development Bank, *Economic and Social Progress in Latin America: Science and Technology. 1988 Report* (Washington, DC, 1988), pp. 384, 408, 416, 440, 464; Inter-American Development Bank, *Economic and Social Progress in Latin America, 1992 Report* (Washington, DC: Johns Hopkins University Press, 1992), country tables; World Bank Group, World Bank Indicators, https://data.worldbank.org/indicator, accessed May 18, 2019; U.S. Central Intelligence Agency, *CIA World Factbook*, www.cia.gov/library/publications/the-world-factbook/, accessed May 18, 2019.

TABLE A.3 Mean Annual US Military and Economic Assistance to Central America, 1946–1992

	Costa Rica	El Salvador	Guatemala	Honduras	Nicaragua	Region[a]
Military Assistance[b]						
1946–1952	–	–	–	–	–	–
1953–1961	0.01	0.03	0.19	0.14	0.24	0.61
1962–1972	0.16	0.72	3.31	0.9	2.36	7.45
1973–1976	0.03	2.08	0.83	2.23	0.28	5.45
1977–1980	1.25	1.60	1.25	3.13	0.85	8.08
1981–1984	3.95	98.85	.00	41.48	.00	144.28
1985–1988	3.93	112.78	5.20	57.73	.00	179.64
1989–1992	0.10	63.10	2.35[c]	25.6	.00	91.15
Total	9.43	279.16	13.13	131.21	3.73	436.66
Mean per year	0.24	7.16	0.34	3.36	0.10	11.20
Economic Assistance[b]						
1946–1952	1	0.4	1.65	0.42	1.03	4.5
1953–1961	5.8	1.23	13.48	3.9	3.73	28.14
1962–1972	9.41	11.95	14.52	8.42	12.95	57.25
1973–1976	14.1	6.1	19.6	24.43	26.9	91.13
1977–1980	13.65	21.85	17.28	27.88	18.63	99.29
1981–1984	112.75	189.43	21.13	79.53	16.55	419.39
1985–1988	171.13	383.38	135.9	179.33	0.1	869.84
1989–1992	5.83	287.68	116.73	150.18	206.8	767.22
Total	333.67	902.02	340.29	474.09	286.69	2,336.76
Mean per year	7.25	19.61	7.40	10.31	6.23	50.80

[a] Includes only Costa Rica, El Salvador, Guatemala, Honduras, and Nicaragua.
[b] Millions of US dollars.
[c] The George H.W. Bush administration canceled Guatemala's 1990 military assistance of $3.3 million for human rights reasons, leaving the aid delivered less than originally appropriated.
Sources: G. Pope Atkins, *Latin America in the International Political System* (New York: The Free Press, 1977), Tables D, E, and G. Pope Atkins, *Latin America in the International Political System* (Boulder, CO: Westview Press, 1989), Tables 10.2 and 10.4; and Office for Planning and Budgeting, US Agency for International Development, *U.S. Overseas Loans and Grants and Assistance from International Organizations: Obligations and Loan Authorizations*, July 1, 1945–September 30, 1992 (Washington, DC: Congressional Information Service, microfiche, 1993).

TABLE A.4 Central American Rebel Groups, 1959–1989

	Costa Rica	El Salvador	Guatemala	Honduras	Nicaragua
1959–1960				FMLH[a]	Various groups[b] (1959–1961)
1961					FSLN
1962			MR-13, FAR FGEI[c]		
1963–1969					
1970	FPL				
1971			ORPA		
1972	ERP		EGP		
1973–1974					
1975		FARN			
1976		PRTCS			
1977				PRTCH	FSLN splits[d]
1978			PGT-DN	MPL	
1979	La Familia	FAL			Reunification of FSLN, MPU-FPN[e]
1980	PRTC	FMLN[f], FMLN-FDR[g]	MRP-Ixim		
1981			URNG[h]	FPR	
1982					
1983				DNU[i]	
1984–1988					
1989				ERP-27	

[a] Only sporadically active through late 1979, when it resumed armed struggle.
[b] Of some 20 groups formed, only the FSLN survived beyond 1963.
[c] MR-13 disappeared after late 1960s counterinsurgency campaign; core of FAR survived to renew guerrilla activity in 1978; core of FGEI survived counterinsurgency and helped form EGP.
[d] Under heavy counterinsurgency pressure, FSLN split into three factions with tactical differences.
[e] MPU-FPN coalitions linked broad-front political opposition with FSLN.
[f] FMLN included all five Salvadoran guerrilla organizations.
[g] FMLN-FDR linked FMLN guerrillas with broad-front political opposition coalition.
[h] URNG linked the guerrilla groups EGP, FAR, ORPA, and the PGT-DN; MRP-Ixim not a member.
[i] DNU linked the MPL, FPR, and FMLH guerrilla organizations.

TABLE A.5 Comparative Data on Central Government Expenditures

	Costa Rica	El Salvador	Guatemala	Honduras	Nicaragua
Percent of national budget expenditures, by program area, c. 1978					
1. Defense	2.7	24.6	11.0	10.5	12.8
2. Education	24.5	15.5	13.0	20.7	16.9
3. Health	3.6	8.1	7.1	14.7	4.1
4. Social security/welfare	28.3	3.7	4.1	4.7	19.9
5. Total human services (2+3+4)	56.3	27.3	24.2	40.1	40.9
Ratio of human services to defense (5:1)	21.1	1.1	2.1	4.1	3.1
Government expenditures by program area as percent of GDP, 2016					
6. Health	5.4	4.4	1.8	3.6	4.4
7. Education	7.4	3.9	2.0	6.0	4.1
8. Health and education (6+7)	12.8	8.3	3.8	9.6	8.5
Government consumption as percent of GDP, 2017					
	17.3	15.8	9.7	13.8	15.3

Sources: John A. Booth, Christine J. Wade, and Thomas W. Walker: *Understanding Central America: Global Forces, Rebellion, and Change* (Bolder, CO: Westview Press, 2015) Appendix, Table A.5; World Bank Group, Indicators, https://data.worldbank.org/indicator, accessed March 15, 2019; Economic Commission for Latin America and the Caribbean, Statistics and Indicators, http://interwp.cepal.org/sisgen/ConsultaIntegradaFlashProc_HTML.asp, accessed February 11, 2019.

TABLE A.6 Selected Presidential Election Results by Percentage of Valid Vote, Central America*

Costa Rica, 1994–2018[a]

	1994	1998	2002[b]	2002[c]	2006	2010	2014[b]	2014[c,d]	2018[b]	2018[c]
PLN	49.6	44.4	31.0	58.0	40.5	46.8	29.7	22.2	18.6	
PUSC	47.5	46.9	38.5	42.0	3.4	3.9	6.0		16.0	
PAC			26.2		40.3	25.2	30.6	77.8	21.6	60.6
PML		0.4	1.7		8.5	20.8	11.3		1.0	
Frente Amplio							17.3		0.8	

(continues)

TABLE A.6 Selected Presidential Election Results by Percentage of Valid Vote, Central America* *(continued)*

Costa Rica, 1994–2018[a]

	1994	1998	2002[b]	2002[c]	2006	2010	2014[b]	2014[c,d]	2018[b]	2018[c]
PRN									25.0	39.4
Integración Nacional										
Total parties/ alliances competing	7	12	12		7	9	13		15	

[a] Constitution requires a minimum of 40 percent of the vote to avoid a runoff election.
[b] General election, first round (absolute majority required for victory).
[c] Runoff election.
[d] In 2014 PLN candidate Johnny Araya withdrew from the runoff several weeks before the final vote, effectively assuring victory for PAC candidate Luis Guillermo Solís.

El Salvador, 1994–2019

	1994[a]	1994[b]	1999	2004	2009	2014[a]	2014[b]	2019
ARENA	49.1	68.3	52.0	57.7	48.7	39.0	49.9	31.7
FMLN	25	31.7	39.0	35.6	51.3	48.9	50.1	14.4
PCN			3.8	2.7				
PDC[c]	16.3		5.7					
CDU[c]			7.5					
Movimiento Unidad[d]						11.4		
GANA								53.1
Others				3.9		0.7		0.8
Total parties/ alliances competing	9		7	4	2	5		4

[a] General election, first round (absolute majority required for victory).
[b] Runoff election.
[c] Total vote for the CDU and PDC coalition in 2004 was 3.9 percent.
[d] The PDC, GANA, and PCN ran in coalition in 2014.

(continues)

TABLE A.6* *(continued)*

Guatemala, 1999–2019

	1999[a]	1999[b]	2003[a]	2003[b]	2007[a]	2007[b]	2011[a]	2011[b]	2015[a]	2015[b]	2019[a]	2019[b]
FRG	47.7	68.2	19.2		7.3							
GANA				54.1	17.2							
PP			34.5		23.5	47.2	36.0	53.7	4.5			
UNE			26.5	45.9	28.2	52.8			19.8	32.6	25.6	42.1
PAN	30.3	31.8			2.6		2.8		3.1		2.7	
UCN					3.2		8.6		3.4			
LIDER							23.2	46.3	19.4			
CREO							16.4		3.5		3.8	
URNG									2.1		2.2	
VIVA									6.0		5.9	
FCN									24.0	67.4	4.1	
Fuerza									6.5			
Vamos											14.0	57.9
Winaq											5.2	
MLP											10.4	
PH											11.2	
PAN-P											6.1	
Others[c]											8.8	
Total parties/alliances	11		11		14		10		14		19	

[a] General election, first round (absolute majority required for victory).
[b] Runoff election.
[c] Less than 1 percent each.

(continues)

TABLE A.6 Selected Presidential Election Results by
Percentage of Valid Vote, Central America* *(continued)*

Honduras, 1993–2017[a]							
	1993	1997	2001	2005	2009	2013	2017
PLH	52.3	52.6	42.2	49.9	38.1	20.3	14.7
PN	40.7	42.8	52.2	46.2	56.6	36.8	43.0
LIBRE						28.8	
LIBRE-PINU-SD							41.4
PAC						13.6	0.2
APH						0.2	0.2
PDC						0.2	0.2
PINU						0.1	
FAPER-UD						0.1	
UD							0.1
Frente Amplio							0.1
Mov. Solidario							0.1
Total parties/ alliances competing	4	5	5	5	5	8	9

[a] The Honduran constitution provides for the election of the president by a "simple majority" (i.e., the largest number of votes).

Nicaragua, 1990–2016[a]						
	1990	1996	2001	2006	2011	2016
FSLN	40.3	37.8	43.0	38.1	62.5	72.4
UNO	54.7					
PLC		51.1	55.5	26.2	5.9	15.0
PLI					31.0	4.5
ALN					0.4	4.3
PCN			1.4	29.0		2.3
MRS				6.4		
AR					0.2	1.4
Total parties/alliances competing	10	22	3	5	5	6

[a] The Nicaraguan constitution provided for the election of the president by a "relative majority" of 40 percent. The Electoral Law (Law No. 331) further provided that a candidate can win with 35 percent if that candidate receives 5 percent more than the second place candidate. A constitutional amendment effective in 2016 provides for election of the president by simple majority (most votes).

* Note on sources: These tables were compiled from data acquired from the respective countries' electoral tribunals, where available, from the Political Database of the Americas website, and Wikipedia.

TABLE A.7 Distribution of Legislative Seats Held Following Selected Elections, Central America*

Costa Rica. Distribution of Legislative Assembly Seats by Party, 1994–2018 (57 seats)							
Party/year	1994	1998	2002	2006	2010	2014	2018
PLN	28	23	17	25	23	23	17
PUSC	25	27	19	5	6	6	9
PAC			14	17	11	11	10
PML			6	6	9	4	
PRN				1	1	1	14
Fte. Amplio						9	1
Others	4	7	1	3	7	5	4

El Salvador. Distribution of National Assembly Seats by Party, 1994–2018 (84 seats)ᵃ									
Party/year	1994	1997	2000	2003	2006	2009	2012	2015	2018
ARENA	39	28	29	27	34	32ᵇ	33	32	35
FMLN	21	27	31	31	32	35	31	31	18
PDC	18	10	5	5	6	5		1	2
PCN	4	11	14	16	10	11	7	4	8
CDU	1	2	3	5					
CD					2	1	1		1
GANA						ᵇ	11	11	10
ARENA-PCN								3	3
PCN-PDC								1	1
PCN-PSD								1	
FMLN-CD									3
Independentsᶜ									1
Others	1	6	2			1			2

ᵃ Note: El Salvador holds legislative elections every three years.
ᵇ GANA was created by 12 ARENA defectors in the Assembly in early 2010.
ᶜ Independent candidates, not party affiliated.

(continues)

TABLE A.7 Distribution of Legislative Seats Held Following
Selected Elections, Central America* *(continued)*

Guatemala. Distribution of Seats in Congress by Party, 1995–2019 (158 seats since 2003)							
Party/year	1995	1999	2003	2007	2011	2015	2019
UNE			30	52		32	54
Vamos							16
Valor							9
Bienestar							8
Semilla							7
Humanista							6
Prosperidad							3
Ciudadano							3
Victoria							3
Podemos						12	1
GANA			49[a]	37			
GANA-UNE					48		
PP			[a]	29	56	18	
FRG	21	63	41	14	1		
EG				4		7	
PU			7	6	1	1	3
FDNG	6						
PAN	43	36	17	3	2	3	2
ANN		10	7				
UCN					14	7	12
LIDER					14	45	
CREO					12		6
Todos						18	7
FCN						11	8
CREO-PU						5	
VIVA						5	7
Convergencia						3	
Fuerza						1	0
Winaq-URNG-MAIZ						1	

TABLE A.7* *(continued)*

Guatemala *(continued)*							
Party/year	**1995**	**1999**	**2003**	**2007**	**2011**	**2015**	**2019**
Winaq							4
MLP							1
URNG-MAIZ						1	
URNG							3
Others	10	4	7	13	10	0	
Total seats	80	113	158	158	158	158	160[b]

[a] In 2003 GANA and PP ran in coalition, along with two other parties. In 2011 GANA ran in coalition with UNE.
[b] Provisional assignment of seats, subject to revision.

Honduras. Distribution of Seats in Congress by Party, 1993–2017 (128 seats)							
Party/year	**1993**	**1997**	**2001**	**2005**	**2009**	**2013**	**2017**
PLH	71	56	55	62	45	27	26
PN	55	60	61	55	71	48	61
PINU	2	3	4	2	3	1	4
UD		5	5	5	4	1	1
PDCH		4	3	4	5	1	1
LIBRE						37	30
Anticorrupción						13	1
APH							4
Others[a]						0	

[a] Five other parties and independent candidates competed but won no seats in 2013.

(continues)

TABLE A.7 Distribution of Legislative Seats Held Following
Selected Elections, Central America* *(continued)*

Nicaragua. Distribution of National Assembly Seats by Party, 1990–2016 (90+ seats)[a]						
Party/year	1990	1996	2001	2006	2011	2016
UNO	51					
FSLN	39	36	52	38	63	70
PLC			38	25	2	13
ALN-PCN				22		
ALN		42				2
PLI					27	2
MRS		1		5		
PCN		3	1			
Others		11				3

[a] Losing presidential candidates who win a certain percentage of the vote also receive legislative seats, accounting for the deviation from the base number of 90 regular seats.

* Note on sources: These tables were compiled from data acquired from the respective countries' electoral tribunals, where available, from the Political Database of the Americas website, and Wikipedia. Some variations in reporting of results were found. In evaluating these data consider that seats won in elections may shift after the vote due to party defections, and bloc voting and alliance changes. Also, Guatemala expanded its Congress twice in the period covered.

ABOUT THE AUTHORS

John A. Booth is Regents Professor Emeritus of Political Science at the University of North Texas. He is author of *The End and The Beginning: The Nicaraguan Revolution* and *Costa Rica: Quest for Democracy*, and coauthor of *Latin American Political Culture: Public Opinion and Democracy*, and *The Legitimacy Puzzle in Latin America: Political Support and Democracy in Eight Nations*.

Christine J. Wade is Professor of Political Science and International Studies at Washington College. Her most recent books include *Latin American Politics and Development* (9e), *Captured Peace: Elites and Peacebuilding in El Salvador*, and *Nicaragua: Emerging from the Shadow of the Eagle* (6e).

Thomas W. Walker is Professor Emeritus of Political Science and Director Emeritus of the Latin American Studies Program at Ohio University. He is the author, coauthor, or editor of 11 books, most on Central America. The sixth edition of his *Nicaragua: Emerging from the Shadow of the Eagle* with Christine Wade as coauthor, appeared in 2016.

INDEX

90; satisfaction/dissatisfaction 91, 300, 301, 349; *see also individual political parties*
Costa Rican-based Contra forces 110
Council of Popular and Indigenous Organizations of Honduras (COPIHN) 259
Council of State (Nicaragua) 111, 112
counterrevolution 1, 237; *see also* repression
counterterrorism 45, 318, 323, 337, 354
coups: El Salvador 157, 158; Guatemala (1982) 199; Honduras (2009) 251–255, 261; and regime change 44; support for military **284**, 286, 294, 296, 298, 360; *see also* self-coup; slow motion coup
Court of Constitutionality (Guatemala) (CC) 203, 207
crime 65, 364; aggravating conditions 352; El Salvador 164, 168, 170, 177, 336, 352; failure to manage 48; Guatemala 204, 208, 209, 210, 336, 352; Honduras 247, 248–249, 251, 261, 279, 336; Nicaragua 118, 128, 353; and political attitudes and participation 286, 291, **292**, 294; and potential emigration 302; *see also* murders; organized crime
crime control/prevention: Costa Rica 90; El Salvador 175; Guatemala 214; Nicaragua 128; US assistance 357
crimes against humanity 134, 176, 211, 213, 217, 218, 362
criminal prosecutions/convictions: Costa Rica 89; El Salvador 171, 172, 173, 174, 176; Guatemala 203, 205, 209, 210, 211, 216, 217–218, 219, 362; Honduras 253, 256, 257, 258, 259; Nicaragua 122, 123
criminalization: of abortions 171; of gang membership 166, 170; of protests 135, 168; of violence against women 210
criollos 61

Cristiani, Alfredo 161, 162, 169, 326
Cuba 23, 32, 45, 104, 108, 109, 320, 355; *see also* Batista, Fulgencio; Castro, Fidel
Cuban Communist Party 319
Cuban Revolution (1959) 67, 313, 317
cultural conservatives (US) 332
cultural diversity 58
culture: and democratic consolidation 360–361; *see also* political culture; social culture
currency devaluation 28, 116, 246

Danielistas 45, 119
D'Aubuisson, Roberto 160, 161
Dávila, Aldo 219
de-democratization *see* democracy, failure/breakdowns
de Léon Carpio, Ramiro 203
death squads: El Salvador 156, 164, 325, 326; Guatemala 194, 198, 205, 208, 323; Honduras 239, 248, 322; Latin America 318
death tolls: due to authoritarian repression 367; Guatemalan war 205, 219, 324; Hurricane Mitch (1998) 247; Nicaraguan revolution 109, 111, 326; Salvadoran civil war 324
debt cancellation/relief 247, 249, 250
debt crisis: Costa Rica 87
debt forgiveness 29, 121
decentralization 250
Decree 743 (El Salvador, 2011) 172
defense spending **377**
DeFronzo, James 35
delegates of the word 314
demobilization 322–328, 337, 359, 364; US support for 317, 318, 354; *see also individual countries*
democracy 311–313; in 2019 72; classical theory definition 273; commitment to 299, 366; equated with anti-Communism 318; ethnicity and 298, 299; evolving Central American views